HEALTH & NUTRITION

God's Word
for the
Biblically-Inept™ SERIES

Kathleen O'Bannon
Baldinger

CARTOONS BY
Reverend Fun
(Dennis "Max" Hengeveld)
Dennis is a graphic designer
for Gospel Films and the
author of *Has Anybody Seen
My Locust?* His cartoons can
be seen worldwide at
www.gospelcom.net/rev-fun/
and monthly in *Charisma*
magazine.

STARBURST PUBLISHERS®
P. O. Box 4123, Lancaster, Pennsylvania 17604

To schedule Author appearances, write Author Appearances, Starburst Publishers, P.O. Box 4123, Lancaster, Pennsylvania 17604 or call (717) 293-0939.

www.starburstpublishers.com

CREDITS:
Cover design by Dave Marty Design
Text design and composition by John Reinhardt Book Design
Illustrations by Melissa A. Burkhart
Cartoons by Dennis "Max" Hengeveld

Unless otherwise noted, or paraphrased by the author, all Scripture quotations are from the New International Version of The Holy Bible.

"Scripture taken from the HOLY BIBLE: NEW INTERNATIONAL VERSION®. NIV®. Copyright © 1973, 1978, 1984 by International Bible Society."

Reverend Fun cartoons ©Copyright Gospel Films Incorporated.

This book is intended for educational purposes only. Neither the publisher nor the author intends this book to be used for diagnosing or prescribing in any way. If you have any medical or health problems, see your doctor or the appropriate health-care practitioner. If you have spiritual concerns, consult with your pastor or a counselor specializing in this area.

To the best of its ability, Starburst Publishers® has strived to find the source of all material. If there has been an oversight, please contact us, and we will make any correction deemed necessary in future printings. We also declare that to the best of our knowledge all material (quoted or not) contained herein is accurate, and we shall not be held liable for the same.

First Printing, April 1999

ISBN: 0-914984-05-5
Library of Congress Number 98-83164
Printed in the United States of America

READ THESE PAGES BEFORE YOU READ THIS BOOK . . .

Welcome to the *God's Word for the Biblically-Inept*™ series. If you find reading the Bible overwhelming, baffling, and frustrating, then this Revolutionary Commentary™ is for you!

Each page of the series is organized for easy reading with icons, sidebars and bullets to make the Bible's message easy to understand. *God's Word for the Biblically-Inept*™ series includes opinions and insights from Bible experts of all kinds, so you get various opinions on Bible teachings—not just one!

There are more *God's Word for the Biblically-Inept*™ titles on the way. The following is a partial list of upcoming books. We have assigned each title an abbreviated **title code**. This code along with page numbers is incorporated in the text **throughout the series**, allowing easy reference from one title to another.

Health & Nutrition—God's Word for the Biblically-Inept™
Kathleen O'Bannon Baldinger   **TITLE CODE: GWHN**

Health & Nutrition—God's Word for the Biblically-Inept™ gives scientific evidence that proves that the diet and health principles outlined in the Bible are the best diet for total health. Experts include Pamela Smith, Julian Whitaker, Kenneth Cooper, and T. D. Jakes.

(trade paper) ISBN 0914984055 $16.95   **AVAILABLE NOW**

Revelation—God's Word for the Biblically-Inept™   **TITLE CODE: GWRV**
Daymond R. Duck

Revelation—God's Word for the Biblically-Inept™ is the first in this new series designed to make understanding and learning the Bible as easy and fun as learning your ABC's. Reading the Bible is one thing, understanding it is another! Includes every verse of the Book of Revelation, icons, sidebars, and bullets along with comments from leading experts.

(trade paper) ISBN 0914984985 $16.95   **AVAILABLE NOW**

Daniel—God's Word for the Biblically-Inept™   **TITLE CODE: GWDN**
Daymond R. Duck

Daniel—God's Word for the Biblically-Inept™ is a Revolutionary Commentary™ designed to make understanding and learning the Bible easy and fun. Includes every verse of the Book of Daniel, icons, sidebars, and bullets along with comments from leading experts.

(trade paper) ISBN 0914984489 $16.95   **AVAILABLE NOW**

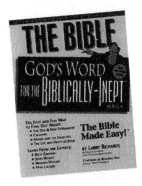

The Bible—God's Word for the Biblically-Inept™   TITLE CODE: GWBI
Larry Richards

The Bible—God's Word for the Biblically-Inept™ is an overview of the Bible written by Larry Richards, one of today's leading Bible writers. Each chapter contains select verses from books of the Bible along with illustrations, definitions, and references to related Bible passages.

(trade paper) ISBN 0914984551 $16.95   AVAILABLE NOW

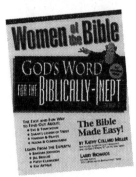

Women of the Bible—God's Word for the Biblically-Inept™
Kathy Collard Miller   TITLE CODE: GWWB

Women of the Bible—God's Word for the Biblically-Inept™ shows that although the Bible was written many years ago, it is still relevant for today. Gain valuable insight from the successes and struggles of women such as Eve, Esther, Mary, Sarah, and Rebekah. Comments from leading experts will make learning about God's Word easy to understand and incorporate into your daily life.

(trade paper) ISBN 0914984063 $16.95   AVAILABLE NOW

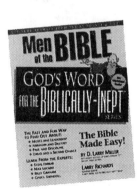

Men of the Bible—God's Word for the Biblically-Inept™
D. Larry Miller   TITLE CODE: GWMB

Men of the Bible—God's Word for the Biblically-Inept™ presents the good, bad, and the ugly about the life experiences of the men of the Bible. Learn how the inspirational struggles of men such as Moses, Daniel, Paul, and David parallel the struggles of today's man. It will inspire and build Christian character for any reader.

(trade paper) ISBN 1892016079 $16.95   AVAILABLE JULY '99

New Titles Are Coming!

Starburst Publishers plans to continue adding to the *God's Word for the Biblically-Inept™* series. Look for future titles about the following topics and Biblical books:

- **Genesis**
- **Prophecies of the Bible**
- **The Life of Christ**
- **Romans**
- **Book of John**

What's in the Bible for . . .™

What's in the Bible for™ . . . Teens   **TITLE CODE: WBFT**

Mark Littleton

From the creators of the *God's Word for the Biblically-Inept*™ series comes a brand new series called *What's in the Bible for . . .*™. The first release is a book that teens will love! *What's in the Bible for . . .*™ *Teens* contains topical Bible themes that parallel the challenges and pressures of today's adolescents. Learn about Bible Prophecy, God and Relationships, and Peer Pressure in a conversational and fun tone. Helpful and eye-catching "WWJD?" icons, illustrations, and sidebars included.

(trade paper) ISBN 1892016052 **$16.95**   AVAILABLE JUNE '99

Also Look For:

What's in the Bible for™ . . . Women

Coming This September!!!

Purchasing Information

Books are available from your favorite bookstore, either from current stock or special order. To assist your bookstore in locating your selection, be sure to give title, author, and ISBN. If unable to purchase from a bookstore, you may order direct from **STARBURST PUBLISHERS®** by mail, phone, fax, or through our secure website at:

www.starburstpublishers.com

When ordering enclose full payment plus $3.00 for shipping and handling ($4.00 if Canada or Overseas). Payment in U.S. Funds only. Please allow two to three weeks minimum (longer overseas) for delivery.

Make checks payable to and mail to:

Starburst Publishers®
P.O. Box 4123
Lancaster, PA 17604

Credit card orders may also be placed by calling 1-800-441-1456 (credit card orders only), Mon–Fri, 8:30 A.M.–5:30 P.M. (Eastern Time). Prices subject to change without notice. Catalog available for a 9 x 12 self-addressed envelope with 4 first-class stamps.

What Readers Tell Us . . .

"Congratulations on an outstanding piece of work! I look forward to seeing the entire *Biblically-Inept™* series. I absolutely love it!"

—Ken Abraham, *best-selling author*

"Fantastic! What a fascinating approach to presenting the book of Revelation. It makes studying Bible prophecy easy, exciting, and interesting for everybody. Good content, great quotes, dynamic graphics. This book has more 'bells and whistles' than anything I've ever seen. It's user-friendly to the max!"

—Dr. Ed Hindson, *Assistant Pastor,*
Rehoboth Baptist Church, and best-selling author

"I am currently involved in studying the book of Revelation and find your study guide very informative, concise, and helpful. It makes reading and understanding the book of Revelation easier . . ."

—Jeffrey, *Bloomington, Indiana*

"The Revelation book arrived this morning. I spent a few minutes glancing through it and am confident that you have a winner. The layout—the artwork—the interaction are marvelous. . . . I AM IMPRESSED!"

—Dan Penwell, *Manager, Trade Products,*
Hendrickson Publishers

"I am writing to voice my approval of Starburst Publishers' *God's Word for the Biblically-Inept™* series. I have three books in the series: THE BIBLE, DANIEL, and REVELATION. . . . I hope Starburst Publishers continues to add to the *God's Word for the Biblically-Inept™* series. Ideally, I would like the series to include 67 books—one for each book of the Bible, plus your already published [books] . . . May I compliment you for this new, interesting, and easy-to-understand series."

—Wayne, *Burr Oak, Kansas*

INTRODUCTION

Welcome to *Health & Nutrition—God's Word for the Biblically-Inept*™. This is the fifth book of an extraordinary series that takes the Bible and makes it fun and educational. This is not the traditional, humdrum, boring Bible study or commentary that you are used to seeing. It is a REVOLUTIONARY COMMENTARY™ designed to uncomplicate the Bible. It makes discovering what's in this amazing book easy and fun. You *will* learn The Word™.

To Gain Your Confidence

Health & Nutrition—God's Word for the Biblically-Inept™ is a unique book. In it, I have compared modern scientific research with what the Bible has to say about topics like food, exercise, and eating disorders. Scientists and theologians can make things so complicated, it's very difficult to make any sense of what they're saying. You can be sure that I have tried to make this material as simple as possible without sacrificing accuracy. I believe using the Bible to learn about health and nutrition should be useful and exciting!

Why Use The Bible To Learn About Health and Nutrition?

One New Testament writer put it this way: *All Scripture is God-breathed and is useful for teaching, rebuking, correcting and training in righteousness, so that the man of God may be thoroughly equipped for every good work* (II Timothy 3:16–17). From this and other passages we learn that the Bible should be used as a "guide for life." No matter what area of your life needs help, the Bible can guide you. I have found this to be especially true in the area of health and nutrition, and as you read this book, I think you will find the same.

Let's Get Started
(Let's Get Started)

> **Genesis 1:1** In the beginning God created the heavens . . .

(Verse of Scripture)

☞ **GO TO:**

Matthew 9:14-15 (fasting)

(Go To)

Church: the followers of Jesus Christ, as opposed to the building where people meet to worship

The Languages Of the Bible And When It Was Written

The first books of the Bible, written about 1400 B.C., and most of the Old Testament, which was completed about 400 B.C., were written in Hebrew. However, parts of the books of Daniel and Ezra were written in Aramaic, a related language spoken by most Near Eastern peoples from about 600 B.C. onward. The people of Jesus' day also spoke Aramaic in everyday situations but studied the Bible in their ancient tongue, Hebrew. About 100 years before Christ, the Old Testament was translated in Greek, because most people throughout the Roman Empire spoke Greek.

The New Testament was written in the Greek spoken by ordinary people. This meant that the New Testament was easy for all people throughout the Roman Empire to understand, so the message of Jesus spread quickly. All of the New Testament books were written between about 40 and 95 A.D.

Because the Old and New Testament books were recognized as holy, first by Jews and then by Christians, they were copied accurately and carefully preserved. Much later, chapters and verse divisions were added to the Bible to make it easier to find and remember the location of specific teachings. The many Bible translations we now have all try to express the original words of God in ways that people today can understand his message.

What's Amazing About The Bible?

1 The Bible is like no other book. It was written over a span of some 1,500 years. It is a collection of 66 different books by a number of different authors. Yet the Bible is one book, with a single story to tell!

2 The first book of the Bible was written in Hebrew some 3,400 years ago, and the last book was written in Greek about 1,900 years ago. Yet the Bible we read in English today is essentially the same as when its words were first written. Uncertainties about Greek words take up no more than a half page in the Greek New Testament—and not one uncertainty affects any basic Bible teaching.

Our English Bibles give a reliable and trustworthy account of what was originally written in Hebrew and Greek thousands of years ago!

3 The Bible contains predictions about the future *which have come true!* Hundreds of predictions have been fulfilled—centuries after they were written. There is only one way this was possible. God knew what would happen ahead of time, and he guided the Bible writers when they wrote their predictions down!

(Warning!)

Why Use The New International Version (NIV)?

I have tried to look at the Bible as the experts would, but I have also tried to write for the *Biblically-Inept.* I want this book to be easy to read and understand. That's why the *God's Word for the Biblically-Inept* series uses the New International Version (NIV) of the Bible. It is a scholarly translation that accurately expresses the original Bible in clear and contemporary English while remaining faithful to the thoughts of Biblical writers.

(From the Kitchen)

A Word About Words

There are several interchangeable terms: Scripture, Scriptures, Word, Word of God, God's Word, etc. All of these mean the same thing and come under the broad heading "the Bible." I will use each at various points throughout the book.

How Is This Book Organized?

As you study *Health & Nutrition—God's Word for the Biblically-Inept*™ keep in mind its two main divisions: "God's Word on Nutrition" and "God's Word on Good Health." "God's Word on Nutrition" is about what foods to eat and how they will help you. "God's Word on Good Health" is about healthy living—things like exercise, weight loss, eating disorders, feasting, and fasting.

ON Target:
Reading the Scriptures and resting while fasting

OFF Target:
Being under stress while fasting

(On Target / Off Target)

How To Use *Health & Nutrition— God's Word for the Biblically-Inept*™

There are basically two ways to read this book. You can either start on page 1 and read straight through to the end or you can use the Table of Contents (what we call "Chapters at a Glance") to go immediately to a chapter that you find particularly interesting.

This book is divided by topic with a verse or passage of Scripture beginning each new section of information. Following each verse or passage you will find my thoughts and a variety of special features that will help you learn. These features are illus-

OLIVES
Eat olives or use olive oil daily.

(Daily Bread)

NUTRITIONAL FACT

Fasting one day a week, when properly done, can improve your health.

(Nutritional Fact)

Study Questions

(Study Questions)

CHAPTER WRAP-UP

(Chapter Summary)

trated in the sidebar of this Introduction, but here is a list of them with a brief explanation of each:

Sections and Icons	What's it for?
CHAPTER HIGHLIGHTS	the most prominent points of the chapter
Let's Get Started	a chapter warm-up
Scripture	biblical verse or passage
Commentary	my thoughts on what the Scripture means
GO TO:	other Bible verses to help you better understand (underlined in text)
What?	the meaning of a word (bold in text)
KEY POINT	a major point in the chapter
What Others are Saying:	if you don't believe me, listen to the experts
Illustrations	a picture is worth a thousand words
Something to Ponder	interesting points to get you thinking
Remember This . . .	don't forget this
WARNING	watch out for this!
From the Kitchen	practical cooking advice (only in Part 1)
ON Target/OFF Target	what to do and what not to do
DAILY BREAD	instructions for everyday use
NUTRITIONAL FACT	fact about health and/or nutrition
Study Questions	questions to get you discussing, studying, and digging deeper
CHAPTER WRAP-UP	the most prominent points revisited

One Final Tip

God gave us the Bible so that by reading it we would enjoy fuller, more healthy lives. Before jumping into the Bible, ask God to help you learn whatever he wants to teach you. With prayerful study of the Scriptures, your life is bound to change for the better! Along with the psalmist, let me urge you to *Taste and see that the Lord is good. . . .* (Psalm 34:8).

CHAPTERS AT A GLANCE

PART ONE: God's Word on Nutrition

1: THE BIBLE DIET   **3**

God Creates 3
Lots and Lots of Water 5
The Mediterranean Diet/The Bible Diet 7

2: THE FOUNDATION OF THE BIBLE DIET   **19**

A Grainy Dream 19
Eat 'Em Every Day 21
Wheat—Grain #1 23
Barley in the Bible 25
Millet, Not Mullet 27
The Case of the Missing Rice 28
Fed on Bread 29
Can't Stand the White Stuff 31

3: EZEKIEL'S PUNISHMENT: OUR HEALTH FOOD   **35**

Ezekiel's Punishment 35
Beans—Our Health Food 38
Lentils: The Bible's First Vegetable 44
Soybeans: They Didn't Have 'Em, But We Do! 45
Ezekiel's Punishment Really Is Our Health Food 47

4: DANIEL AND HIS DIET FOR STRENGTH   **49**

Daniel Put Vegetables to the Test 49
How Much Should I Eat? 50
What Is a "High-Fiber Diet"? 54
Solomon Said! 55
Powerhouses of Phytochemicals 55
Repeating Vegetables 58
Bobbing for ~~Apples~~ Vegetables 61
You Decide 62

5: SOLOMON'S GARDEN   **65**

Whadduh You, Nuts! 65

Fruit in the Mediterranean Diet 71

Olives: the Green and Black Fruits 75

6: MILK AND CURDS   **81**

Moooooooooooo! 81

Milk: To Drink or Not to Drink 84

Breast Milk 88

Fermenting Helps 91

Cheese: Can You Stomach This? 93

Milk in the New Testament 95

7: FISH FOR 5,000   **97**

Catch Any? 98

Fish in the Mediterranean Diet 100

Eating Fish 105

**8: THE PASSOVER FEAST—BITTER HERBS
AND UNLEAVENED BREAD**   **109**

Passover Feast and Bitter Herbs 109

Parsley, the King of Herbs 112

Dandelion, the Not-So-Lowly Weed 113

Greens and Herbs: Not Just for Cows 116

9: ALL THE FAT IS THE LORD'S   **121**

No Fat Allowed! 122

Fat Gets a Bad Wrap 123

Fat Can Make You Fat 125

How Much Protein Do You Need? 126

What to Do? 127

Which Came First: the Chicken or the Egg? 129

Keep It Clean 132

10: SWEETS, SALT, WATER, AND WINE   **135**

Land of Milk and Honey 135

Sweets and the Mediterranean Diet 137

If You Knew What's Good for You 138

Salt in the Bible Diet 141

Water: Liquid of Life 145

Wine Is a Mocker! 146

PART TWO: God's Word on Good Health

11: ALL FOOD IS CLEAN   151

Are You Eating Unclean Foods? 152
Peter's Vision 154
Wash Those Hands and Feet 157
Dig a Hole 160
Regulations about Mildew 160
Let's Wrap It Up! 163

12: ELIJAH AND AHAB   165

Elijah's Story: Does This Sound Familiar? 165
Angelic Help 169
Ahab: Eat, Eat, Eat! 171
The Most Incredible Diet! 171
Music Lifts and Depresses the Soul 174
Just Get Over It 175
Herbs and Other Things that Can Help 176

13: FOOD CRAVINGS, WEIGHT LOSS, AND EATING DISORDERS   179

Is This All We Get? 180
Don't Fall for It 180
How Your Body Works 181
Yeah, Yeah, but I Want to Know about Weight Loss 183
Eating Disorders in the Bible 188
Bitter? Who's Bitter? 190
Who Is Rebellious? 191

14: CURSES AND WASTING DISEASE   195

Whew! 196
Not Enough Love 198
The Cure! 199
A Grimm Lesson 202
Pray for Each Other 203

15: GOD'S SACRED TEMPLE   207

Your Body Is God's Temple 207
A Poultice of Figs 209
Forgiveness 210
Turn to God 211
The Rainbow of Hope 213

16: AND JESUS WENT A'WALKIN'   215

   Jesus the Walker 215

   Not Your Everyday Stroll 217

   Make It Really Count 218

   Walking the Straight and Narrow 220

17: FEASTING, FEASTING, FEASTING   223

   Seven Feasts 223

   They Ate on a Couch 226

   Why Can't I Eat That Anymore? 227

18: FASTING, FASTING, FASTING   233

   Fasting from What? 233

   Why Fast? 235

GLOSSARY OF NUTRITIONAL AND MEDICAL TERMS   243

APPENDIX A—MAP OF MEDITERRANEAN REGION   253

APPENDIX B—THE ANSWERS   255

APPENDIX C—THE EXPERTS   259

APPENDIX D—RECIPES   261

APPENDIX E—SOURCES OF NUTRIENTS   291

ENDNOTES   303

INDEX   311

Part One

GOD'S WORD ON NUTRITION

Reverend Fun

As the plague of frogs tormented the land, the Pharaoh once again hardened his heart.

1 THE BIBLE DIET

CHAPTER HIGHLIGHTS

- God Creates
- After the Flood
- The Mediterranean Diet / The Bible Diet

Let's Get Started

Are you trying to find the "perfect diet" that will bring you extreme health, great energy, and freedom from many common **diseases**? Perhaps you have read books, articles in newspapers, and entire magazines devoted to health and are still no closer to a healthy diet than before you began your search. Is your head swirling with facts that don't mean anything to you? Well, you can just relax. The Bible has the answer. Yep! God has outlined the perfect diet for you and your family in the Bible. Chapter 1 is an overview of the foods found in the "Bible Diet." Each chapter that follows in Part I, The Bible Diet, will open up to you a simple, easy-to-follow lifestyle plan that will show you the way to be as healthy as you can be. This lifestyle plan comes from the diet outlined in the Bible; that's why we call it the "Bible Diet!"

> **Genesis 1:1** In the beginning God created the heavens and the earth.

God Creates

In Old Testament times the Hebrew verb for **created** was used only when referring to divine activity, not human activity. Only God could create. It is fitting that the very first chapter in the Bible, Genesis 1, gives the account of Creation (see GWBI, pages 3–5) and outlines the foods that God created for us to eat.

diseases: abnormal conditions of the body that impair normal functioning

☞ **GO TO:**

Genesis 1:21; Genesis 1:27; John 1:3; I Timothy 4:4 (created)

created: to cause to exist

And Heeeeeeeeere's Man And Woman!

After God had created the earth and sky, light and darkness, water, dry ground, vegetation of seed-bearing plants and trees, birds, sea creatures, livestock, creatures that move along the ground, and wild animals, God created the first <u>man and woman</u>—Adam and Eve. God created a garden in the east—in Eden—for them to live and be together in (see Illustration #1, page 5). Adam and Eve were allowed to eat of all of the plants and trees except for the **Tree of the Knowledge of Good and Evil** (see GWBI, page 7). In other words, the first humans had a wide variety of foods to choose from.

There are many people who look at this passage from Genesis and think we were created to eat only fruits, nuts, and vegetables. Make sure you read the "entire" Bible before deciding what foods God created for us to eat.

☞ **GO TO:**

Genesis 1:27 (man and woman)

Genesis 2:9 (Tree)

Remember This . . .

What Others are Saying:

Tree of the Knowledge of Good and Evil: a tree in Eden that signified the ability to know good and evil by personal experience

Billy Graham: Human history began at Eden where God planted a garden and made man for his eternal fellowship.[1]

> **Genesis 2:15, 16** The Lord God took the man and put him in the Garden of Eden to work it and take care of it. And the Lord God commanded the man, "You are free to eat from any tree in the garden; but you must not eat from the Tree of the Knowledge of Good and Evil for when you eat of it you will surely die."

Forbidden Fruit?

All of the food in the Garden of Eden was available for Adam and Eve, except the fruit of one tree. God forbade them from eating of the Tree of the Knowledge of Good and Evil. We do not know what the tree was or what the "fruit" of it was, but we do know that the fruit of disobeying God was a curse on Adam and Eve that can still be felt today.

What Others are Saying:

T. D. Jakes: When you understand that vitamin-rich fruits and vegetables will build your energy so you will enjoy your family more, you can see that the right food becomes inviting and pleasing to the eye.[2]

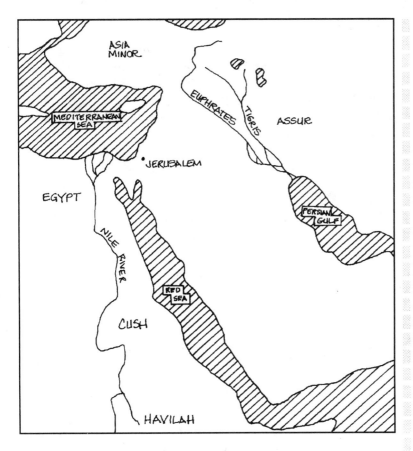

Illustration #1

Map of Eden—Genesis places Eden in this area, probably at the head of the Persian Gulf. Four streams are named, but only two of them are known today, the <u>Tigris and Euphrates</u> (see GWRV, page 133).

☞ **GO TO:**

Genesis 2:14 (Tigris and Euphrates)

Lots And Lots Of Water

Many generations after Adam and Eve, <u>Noah</u> (see GWBI, pages 9–11) was born. God told Noah to save a male and female of each kind of living creature and to put them into an **Ark**, which he was to build according to God's instructions. He was to include his wife, his sons, and his sons' wives. He was also to include all the food they would need for the voyage. After the Flood, when the water started to recede, God talked to Noah again and gave him some new instructions on what to eat.

☞ **GO TO:**

Genesis 6:9–22 (Noah)

Ark: a large, floating vessel

> **Genesis 9:2, 3** The fear and dread of you will fall upon all the beasts of the earth and all the birds of the air, upon every creature that moves along the ground, and upon all the fish of the sea; they are given into your hands. Everything that lives and moves will be food for you. Just as I gave you the green plants, I now give you everything.

☞ **GO TO:**

Genesis 27:9, 10;
  Deuteronomy 12:15
  (meat)

grains: *small hard seeds produced by grasses*

husbandists: *people who raise animals*

**Something
to Ponder**

proteins: *the basic element of all plant and animal tissues*

Key Point

The first food a baby should eat is mother's milk, then fruits and vegetables, which can include beans, followed later by grains, and lastly meat is added.

Gotta Have My Meat!

Since Genesis 9, man has been allowed to eat the <u>meat</u> of all animals. For many years before the Flood, man ate only plant foods such as vegetables, fruits, **grains**, beans, and nuts and seeds. But in Genesis 9 God added meat and all other animal products to man's diet. This changed man from just a gatherer to a hunter/farmer/fisherman. This is good news for hunters, animal **husbandists**, and people who need animal protein for growth and health.

When you think about it, there are some similarities between the development of man's diet (in Genesis) and the development of a baby's diet. The first food a baby should eat is mother's milk, then fruits and vegetables, which can include beans, followed later by grains, and lastly meat is added.

Only The Right Foods

A wide variety of foods is essential for a healthy body and mind. A healthy diet contains fresh fruits (this includes olives and avocados as they are considered fruits), fresh vegetables and dried beans, whole grains, nuts and seeds, and animal **proteins**. They are the foods that are now proven by science and medicine to be the most healthy, the most healing, the most nourishing, and essential for a vital, fulfilled, and healthy life.

> **Psalm 104:14** He makes grass grow for the cattle, and plants for man to cultivate—bringing forth food from the earth . . .

Work The Fields

God taught man to cultivate the plants he made for them to eat, and man became a farmer. Before the Flood, food was found by foraging and digging. But with the advent of farming, after the Flood, man was able to grow the plants he preferred in the quantities necessary to feed himself, his family, and perhaps his neighbors. Man was becoming civilized; he was fending for himself.

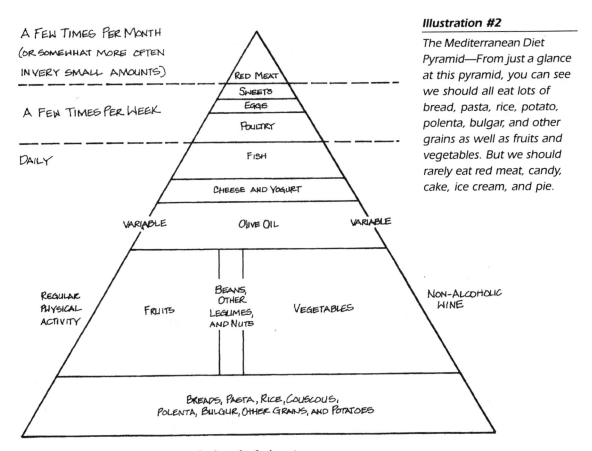

A FEW TIMES PER MONTH
(OR SOMEWHAT MORE OFTEN
IN VERY SMALL AMOUNTS)

A FEW TIMES PER WEEK

DAILY

RED MEAT
SWEETS
EGGS
POULTRY
FISH
CHEESE AND YOGURT
VARIABLE   OLIVE OIL   VARIABLE
REGULAR PHYSICAL ACTIVITY
FRUITS
BEANS, OTHER LEGUMES, AND NUTS
VEGETABLES
NON-ALCOHOLIC WINE
BREADS, PASTA, RICE, COUSCOUS, POLENTA, BULGUR, OTHER GRAINS, AND POTATOES

SOURCE: USDA Nutrient Data Laboratory, www.nal.usda.gov/fnic/foodcomp/

Illustration #2

The Mediterranean Diet Pyramid—From just a glance at this pyramid, you can see we should all eat lots of bread, pasta, rice, potato, polenta, bulgar, and other grains as well as fruits and vegetables. But we should rarely eat red meat, candy, cake, ice cream, and pie.

The Mediterranean Diet / The Bible Diet

The **diet** people followed in **Bible times** is still being eaten to-day in the **Mediterranean region** of the world (see Appendix A). It has been touted as the healthiest diet and is called either the "Mediterranean Diet" or the "Bible Diet," which is under-standable because the Mediterranean area is where most of the events in the Bible took place. The Bible Diet is derived from two biblical sources: specific instructions of what to eat, and general information about the foods available in Bible times. It is simple to follow, and the rewards are great. The Mediterra-nean Diet Pyramid (see Illustration #2, this page) is a visual picture of which foods should be in your diet and how much you should eat of each. The more space a particular group of foods takes up, the more you should eat from that group. By

diet: *the usual food and drink of a person or animal*

Bible times: *from approximately 1500 B.C. to 50 A.D.*

Mediterranean region: *area bordering the Mediterranean Sea*

just looking at this graph, you can plan a diet every day that will be healthy and complete. It will enable you to follow all the dietary guidelines of the Bible.

What Others are Saying:

Reginald Cherry, M.D.: A great interest has arisen in medical and health circles today about the foods that have been eaten for centuries in the lands of the Bible. The diet of Middle Eastern people is of particular interest. One name given to this group of foods that prevent disease and help to cure diseases is the "Mediterranean Diet." This is very similar to the one described in Genesis.[3]

Grains, Grains, Grains

The foundation, or base, of the Mediterranean Diet is grains. It is the widest section of the pyramid but not necessarily the largest (see Illustration #2, page 7). This means that grains should be the base or foundation of a daily diet. The grains available today are wheat, rye, barley, oats, **spelt**, rice, **millet, triticale, kamut, quinoa**, and sometimes corn. The suggested amount to eat daily is two to eleven servings. One serving is considered to be one piece of bread, so a sandwich would be two servings of grains. If you also ate another serving of grain for lunch or dinner, like rice or barley, you would meet the minimum daily requirement. Many people decide to eat the grains as snacks. Things like whole-grain pretzels, crackers, and toast are great sources of grains.

spelt: an ancient form of grain from the wheat family

millet: a high protein grain of small yellow or brown seeds

triticale: a blended grain of rye and wheat

kamut: an ancient grain found in the pyramids

quinoa: a grain native to Central and South America

DAILY BREAD

GRAINS
Each of us should eat 2–11 servings of potato, bread, pasta, couscous, polenta, bulgar, or other grains each day.

> **Proverbs 30:8** . . . give me neither poverty nor riches, but give me only my daily bread.

☞ **GO TO:**

Matthew 6:11; Luke 11:3 (daily bread)

Matthew 6:9–13 (Lord's Prayer)

GIVE US THIS DAY OUR DAILY BREAD . . .

In Bible times the basic grain was barley. It was made into a round, heavy, full-bodied loaf that was baked fresh every day. This was the "daily bread" that Jesus mentioned in what we call the Lord's Prayer. Much of the bread eaten in Bible times was made of barley and emmer wheat. Emmer wheat is similar to the spelt we have available today.

Daily bread was very important to all people living in the Middle East. Jesus <u>encouraged</u> all people to pray for their daily bread and trust God for it rather than rely on the government of Rome to provide it.

Daily bread was so important for the Israelites that they preferred it over riches. Daily bread was distributed in Roman times to Roman citizens. A recently excavated pyramid showed that workers were paid in "daily bread" while building the pyramids around 2575 B.C. in the Giza Plateau, Egypt (see Appendix A).[4]

WHOLE GRAINS—THE GOOD GRAINS

Because only whole grains were available in Bible times, it is obvious that we are supposed to eat whole grains, not **refined** ones. Whole grains contain protein (differing amounts for each type of grain), **fiber**, **nutrients**, and **carbohydrates** or **starch**. Whole grains have the nutrients that God intended people to eat when he made food. When grains like rice, wheat, barley, and spelt are refined, much of the fiber is lost as well as most of the **B complex vitamins**. Fiber and B complex vitamins play important roles in the digestion of the starch in these grains.

Julian Whitaker, M.D.: Whole grains are highly desirable, because they help supply B complex vitamins.[5]

The Largest Food Group Of The Pyramid

The next section up from the base of the pyramid is the group comprised of fruits, beans and other **legumes**, and vegetables (see Illustration #2, page 7). This is the largest section of the Mediterranean Pyramid because it is the group of foods that you should eat the most of each and every day.

Dried beans such as navy, kidney, turtle, lima, pinto, and others are really the seeds of the same kinds of plants that produce the green and yellow beans we eat as fresh vegetables. Yellow beans produce a black seed that is used in black bean soup. When the green or yellow beans are left to grow until the green or yellow part is dried out, the seed inside is harvested as a dried bean. It can be used as the seed to plant and grow more beans the following year, or it can be soaked, cooked, and eaten as food.

Something to Ponder

☞ **GO TO:**

Luke 18:1–8 (encouraged)

refined: *coarse ingredients have been removed*

fiber: *the indigestible part of plants*

nutrients: *a substance needed by plants and animals for life and health*

What Others are Saying:

carbohydrates: *a substance in plant-based foods that contains carbon, hydrogen, and oxygen*

starch: *a carbohydrate found in plants*

B complex vitamins: *needed for health of hair, nails, nerves, skin, liver, mouth, and eyes; found in plant and animal sources*

legumes: *seeds of plant, also called beans*

> **Genesis 1:12** The land produced vegetation: plants bearing seed according to their kinds and trees bearing fruit with seed in it according to their kinds. And God saw that it was good.

POWERHOUSES OF NUTRIENTS

The foods in this largest section of the pyramid, the ones that should be eaten most during the day, are also the same foods God created for the first people on earth. Grains, fruits, beans, nuts and seeds, and vegetables contain **vitamins**, **minerals**, proteins, carbohydrates, fiber, essential fatty acids, and amino acids. These are the powerhouses of health, vitality, and well-being. The concentrated vital nutrients in these foods should be eaten in abundance every day. This group of foods is comprised of all the foods mentioned in Genesis 1:29: *Then God said, "I give you every seed-bearing plant on the face of the whole earth and every tree that has fruit with seed in it. They will be yours for food."*

What Others are Saying:

Kenneth Cooper, M.D.: The Mediterranean Diet is characterized by an abundance of plant foods such as fruits, vegetables, breads, cereals, potatoes, beans, nuts, and seeds. Fresh fruit is the typical daily dessert and olive oil is the principal source of fat.[6]

Key Point

Your daily diet should be made up mostly of fruits, legumes, and vegetables.

Julian Whitaker, M.D.: . . . you should eat plenty of citrus fruits, because they supply you with lots of vitamin C. . . . And green leafy vegetables provide the important vitamin E.[7]

DAILY BREAD

NUTRITIONAL FACT

Vegetables and fruits contain vitamins, minerals, fiber, and other nutrients.

VEGETABLES AND FRUITS
Eat vegetables at every meal and as snacks; always eat at least one serving of raw vegetables and one serving of fruit each day.

Remember This . . .

The United States Department of Agriculture has recommended that all people need to eat at least five half-cup servings of vegetables and fruit a day and one serving must be raw. This is the least amount of these foods that you need to stay alive, think properly, be alert, heal wounds, grow, maintain proper body weight, and have enough energy to live healthily and be able to exercise daily.[8]

> **Leviticus 24:2** Command the Israelites to bring you clear oil of pressed olives for the light so that the lamps may be kept burning continually.

Olive Oil

In Bible times the <u>oil</u> in olives was used for heating, as lamp fuel, in cooking and baking, for **anointing**, and for healing. Olive oil is part of the Mediterranean Diet (see Illustration #2, page 7) because olives grow in abundance in the **Middle East**, Italy, Greece, and Spain. Olive oil is high in **monounsaturated fatty acids**. This "good fat" has been shown to help reduce the "bad **fat**" or **cholesterol** that sticks to the arteries and may cause many different diseases. The olive oil section of the pyramid shows that it is to be used as the main fat or oil in the diet. This should replace the saturated fats that come mainly from animal sources and the **polyunsaturated fats** that are found in a highly processed form in manufactured bakery products such as crackers and sweet rolls, and some other processed and packaged foods.

Oil In The Grain Offering

Oil was so important that God commanded it be used for the consecration of priests—the ceremony included anointing with oil and was part of the **grain offerings**. The grain offerings were made with grain or bread and olive oil to symbolize devotion to God (see GWBI, page 35). Offerings were important because without an offering, an Israelite was not allowed to approach God.

DAILY BREAD

OLIVE OIL
In Biblical times, the people used olive oil every day for preparing their meals, and we should do the same today.

☞ **GO TO:**

Leviticus 2:4 (oil)

Exodus 30:26 (anoint)

anointing: *putting oil on*

Middle East: *the area from Libya east to Afghanistan (see GWRV, page 211)*

monounsaturated fatty acids: *acids that come from olive and canola oil*

fat: *an oily solid or semisolid that is the main part of many animal tissues*

cholesterol: *a necessary component of cells manufactured by all creatures with backbones*

polyunsaturated fats: *come from vegetable sources*

☞ **GO TO:**

Leviticus 2:1 (offerings)

grain offerings: *grains mixed with oil and presented to God*

 **NUTRITIONAL FACT**

Olive oil contains monounsaturated fatty acids, which are helpful in reducing cholesterol levels.

What Others are Saying:

antioxidants: any substance that inhibits or blocks harmful reactions with oxygen

oxidation: combining with oxygen

LDL cholesterol: Low Density Lipoprotein or "bad" cholesterol

atherosclerosis: when fatty substances cling to arteries

yeast: a fungus that produces fermentation in grains that acts as leavening

Kenneth Cooper, M.D.: It is possible that natural **antioxidants** in olive oil help prevent **oxidation** of "bad" **LDL cholesterol**, the major, underlying cause of **atherosclerosis**, or clogging of the arteries.[9]

> **Exodus 29:2, 3** And from fine wheat flour, without **yeast**, make bread, and cakes mixed with oil, and wafers spread with oil. Put them in a basket and present them in it—along with the bull and the two rams.

A BULL AND TWO RAMS?

Fine flour and oil were presented to those men who were chosen to become priests, along with a bull and two rams. Imagine the importance of olive oil, if cakes mixed with oil, and wafers (or crackers) spread with oil, held the same importance as a bull and two rams.

> **Jeremiah 41:8** But ten of them said to Ishmael, "Don't kill us! We have wheat and barley, oil and honey hidden in a field." So he let them alone and did not kill them with the others.

I'LL GIVE YOU MY OIL FOR YOUR . . .

Oil was so important that it was a major export product of the time. Ancient Greece (see Appendix A) was one of the largest producers of olive oil. One of the reasons it was important to their economy was olive trees could grow and thrive in rocky soil, which could produce very few other crops. They were also known to live for a long time. Olive production began when a tree was about five years old and was at the height of production between forty and fifty years old. Oil was essential for life because it was used for cooking, lighting, cosmetics, and medicine. Because of its value, the men in Jeremiah 41:8 were able to convince Ishmael to spare their lives when he was thinking about killing them. And why? They knew of a valuable supply of oil hidden in a field. So valuable was this oil, as well as the other foods they mention, that their lives were spared for the sake of obtaining them.

Dairy In The Diet

The next section of foods is even smaller: cheese and yogurt (see Illustration #2, page 7). Cheese and yogurt are already partially broken down, which makes them easier to digest than milk. In Bible times people did not drink milk, and neither do most people living in the Mediterranean region today. Small quantities of cheese and yogurt can be consumed daily. Of all the available proteins, cheese and yogurt are the best choice for small amounts of daily protein.

> **Genesis 18:8** He then brought some curds and milk and the calf that had been prepared, and set these before them.

Whey? Never Heard Of It

In most translations of the Bible, "curds" is taken to mean either yogurt or butter, but sometimes it means cheese. Curds can also mean something similar to cottage cheese or **yogurt cheese**. It is easy to understand why there are so many variations in Biblical translation when you take into account how each of these foods is made.

Milk is generally curdled with some form of acid. This separates the curd from the **whey**. The same process is used to make any kind of cheese, including cottage cheese. The curds are then pressed to form the more solid cheeses like cheddar or feta cheese, which is popular in the Mediterranean. The whey is the liquid that drains off, which in many places is either made into some form of cheese, fed to animals, or drunk by children. Butter is made by allowing the milk to sour and separate slightly or by causing it to sour and form curds with the addition of some form of souring agent. It is then shaken or stirred until the butter fat separates from the milk, leaving buttermilk, which still contains the curds and the whey and the actual butter.

Pamela Smith: Keep power snacks available wherever you are—in your car, your desk drawer, your briefcase, a purse, or a diaper bag. They can be as simple as fresh fruit or a box of raisins with low-fat cheese or yogurt.[10]

KEY POINT

Cheese and yogurt are the best choice for small amounts of daily protein.

yogurt cheese: a semi-soft cheese made of the solids left after draining the liquid out of yogurt

whey: liquid part of milk containing most of the B vitamins and very little protein

 **NUTRITIONAL FACT**

Yogurt and cheese contain protein, carbohydrates, *calcium, potassium*, and other nutrients.

calcium: mineral essential for bone, teeth, and organ health

What Others are Saying:

potassium: mineral essential for muscle function

Something to Ponder

fermented: *made to sour using acid, bacteria, or enzymes*

kefir: *a fermented milk product*

☞ **GO TO:**

Genesis 3 (Fall)

Genesis 1:26, 28 (fish)

Fall of man: *sin is introduced*

omega-3 essential fatty acids (EFAs): *found in raw nuts and seeds, legumes, grape seeds, soybeans, and other vegetable oils*

What Others are Saying:

vegetarian: *a person who eats only vegetable foods*

DAILY BREAD

CHEESE AND YOGURT
Eating cheese and/or yogurt provides nutrients for health.

Generally when "milk" is mentioned in the Bible it means yogurt or a thickened and **fermented** form of something similar to yogurt called **kefir**. Fresh milk could not be stored or carried around, but cheese and fermented milk products could be. "Curds" can also mean butter, cheese, or something similar to yogurt.

> **Matthew 7:9, 10** Which of you, if his son asks for bread, will give him a stone? Or if he asks for a fish, will give him a snake?

Fish, Not A Snake

Jesus considered bread and fish good gifts for children. In the Bible snakes are often used as symbols for evil. For example, in Genesis 3 Eve was tempted by a snake (or serpent), which triggered the **Fall of man**. Obviously a decent father would not want to give his son a snake. However, he would want to give his son bread and <u>fish</u>, the very foods that Jesus multiplied for feeding the multitudes.

Fish is a staple protein food in the Mediterranean Diet (see Illustration #2, page 7) just as it was in Jesus' time. This is why it has its own section in the Mediterranean Diet Pyramid. <u>Fish</u> is high in protein, relatively low in saturated fats, and contains **omega-3 essential fatty acids** or EFAs.

Jack and Judy Hartman: Jesus wasn't a **vegetarian**, he ate fish. It is interesting to note that he ate broiled fish instead of the fried fish so many people eat today.[11]

DAILY BREAD

FISH
Fish can be eaten daily in small amounts.

What's A Vegetarian?

There are many kinds of vegetarians. All vegetarians eat vegetables, fruits, grains, and nuts and seeds. Lacto-ovo vegetarians eat dairy products and eggs, lacto vegetarians eat dairy products but not eggs, ovo vegetarians eat eggs but not dairy products. Vegans have nothing to do with any animal products, which is to say they do not eat meat, dairy products, eggs, or honey, nor do they use any animal products that require an animal to be killed (for example: leather shoes or belts). Some vegans do not even wear wool, even though obtaining wool does not require killing sheep.

> **Isaiah 10:14** As one reaches into a nest, so my hand reached for the wealth of the nations; as men gather abandoned eggs, so I gathered all the countries; not one flapped a wing, or opened its mouth to chirp.

Which Came First: Chickens Or Eggs?

In this passage, God is quoting an Assyrian king, who boastfully claims full credit for Assyria's victories when they were actually all God's doing. God seems to be using egg gathering as a **metaphor** for political triumph. It would have been an effective metaphor because the Israelites and Romans kept chickens for their eggs and their meat, and they gathered the eggs of chickens that were allowed to wander around.

Poultry and eggs are in the section of foods that are recommended to be eaten a few times per week (see Illustration #2, on page 7). This would mean that once a week you might have eggs for breakfast, an egg sandwich for lunch, and chicken once for lunch and once for dinner.

Maureen Salaman: Eggs are mentioned in various parts of the Scriptures, and it is common knowledge that they were eaten in Old and New Testament times when available.[12]

> **Nehemiah 8:10** Nehemiah said, "Go and enjoy choice food and sweet drinks, and send some to those who have nothing prepared. This day is sacred to our Lord. Do not grieve, for the joy of the Lord is your strength."

Something to Ponder

NUTRITIONAL FACT

Fish is a good source of omega-3 essential fatty acids.

ON Target:

Broiled, poached, baked, stewed fish

OFF Target:

Breaded or deep fried fish, composition fish sticks

metaphor: a word or phrase that symbolizes something else, as in "a mighty fortress is our God"

What Others are Saying:

☞ **GO TO:**

Nehemiah 8:18 (Law)

Exodus 24:7 (read)

Nehemiah 8:10
(Nehemiah)

Nehemiah 8:14
(Trumpets)

Law: *the Law of Moses; the Ten Commandments and other Old Testament laws*

Feast of Trumpets: *an assembly on a day of rest commemorated with trumpet blasts and sacrifices; later called Rosh Hashanahs*

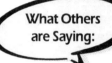

What Others are Saying:

sweet: *containing or derived from sugar or honey*

NUTRITIONAL FACT

Sugar contains no nutrients.

KEY POINT

The average American eats more than 42 teaspoons of sugar a day.

A Sweet And Joyful Feast

Ezra (see GWBI, pages 135–139), the priest commissioned to teach the **Law**, had been in Babylon for years; he returned to Judah to read the Law. This was such an important occasion that women and children were allowed to be there. Ezra praised God and <u>read</u> the Law, which took from daybreak to noon, and afterwards <u>Nehemiah</u> the governor declared the beginning of the **Feast of Trumpets**. He also instructed the Israelites to share the feast with those who had nothing prepared so that they too would be able to share the food and *joy of the Lord* that came from reading the Law.

Sweets For The Sweet

Sweets are to be eaten on special occasions only, like the Feast of Trumpets Nehemiah opened. We are not supposed to eat sweets every day (see Illustration #2, page 7), whether it is **sweet** foods or sweet drinks. By "sweets" I mean those foods that have been sweetened with honey, sugar, or artificial sweeteners. Naturally sweet fruits and vegetables (like carrots) are to be eaten daily.

Dr. Mary Ruth Swope: When we eat large amounts of concentrated sweet foods (the sugars and starches in the form of candies, baked desserts, ice cream, pancakes with syrup, biscuits with honey) the body is put under great stress.[13]

DAILY BREAD

DAILY SWEETS
Many of us have over-developed our sweet tooth, but we need to remember that sweets must not be eaten daily, because sweets can harm our bodies. Sweets are to be eaten on special occasions only.

> **Genesis 27:9** Go out to the flock and bring me two choice young goats, so I can prepare some tasty food for your father, just the way he likes it.

That Meat Again

Eventually God allowed people to eat meat, so it became part of many special occasions like feasts, celebrations, weddings, and other important gatherings. Isaac (see GWBI, pages 19–20) was fond of roasted goat and other meat, so his wife, Rebekah, sent their son Jacob out to get a couple of goats for his father. The meal came just before Isaac, who was dying, gave his blessing to Jacob—a very special occasion.

The Few-Times-Per-Month Food

Of all the foods found in the Mediterranean Diet, red meat is the only one listed as a food that should be eaten in small amounts, like a few times per month (see Illustration #2, page 7). Beef, lamb, mutton, goat, and venison are the main red meats we eat today that were also eaten in Bible times. Many people eat pork as well, which the Israelites did not eat because Old Testament Law declared it unclean. Most people in Bible times ate meat during special feasts or **Passover**. It's reasonable to estimate they ate red meat a few times per month, which is exactly what the Mediterranean Diet recommends. The main red meats eaten today in North America are beef, lamb, mutton, goat, and venison, the same meats as in Bible times. The main difference is that North Americans also eat pork in the form of roasts, ham, bacon, and hot dogs, and in Bible times Israelites did not eat any pork or pork products.

Anne and David Frähm: All animal products contain cholesterol. The typical American diet, with meat at its core, burdens our bodies with unwanted and unusable cholesterol.[14] Beef, mutton, and pork all have the "double whammy" of cholesterol accompanied by high levels of saturated fat.[15]

Dr. Mary Ruth Swope: The dietary lifestyle you choose will affect your body performance, body size, resistance to disease, and your life expectancy. If you're sick and tired of feeling sick and tired, only YOU can effect the remedy. There is no magic solution.[16]

DAILY BREAD

MEAT
Eat small amounts of meat and large amounts of vegetables.

ON Target:
Eating naturally sweetened fruits and vegetables

OFF Target:
Eating artificially sweetened foods on a daily basis

Something to Ponder

☞ **GO TO:**

Exodus 12:11 (Passover)

What Others are Saying:

Passover: *a Jewish festival commemorating the Exodus of the Israelites (see GWBI, pages 23–32)*

KEY POINT

Many cultures of the world do not eat red meat.

 **NUTRITIONAL FACT**

Your liver uses saturated fats to make cholesterol.

WARNING

A diet high in saturated fats can lead to many diseases of the arteries, heart, intestines, stomach, and gallbladder that can be avoided with a lower fat, higher vegetable diet.

ON Target:
Meat as a **condiment**

OFF Target:
Meat as the main component of a meal

condiment: *a seasoning for food like mustard or catsup*

Study Questions

1. Which foods did God give us to eat in the Garden of Eden? Are they still available today and where?
2. Which foods did God allow man to eat after the Flood? Name some occasions when they were eaten in Bible times. When do you eat them?
3. How can we know which foods to eat? Do you ever eat foods more often than recommended? Which ones and why?
4. What is the Mediterranean Diet Pyramid? What are its eight food groups?
5. Of all the foods God gave us to eat, which do you eat daily and which do you never eat? Why? According to the Mediterranean Pyramid, what foods should you be eating the most of?
6. Of all the foods God gave us, which should we eat sparingly? Why?

CHAPTER WRAP-UP

- God created two kinds of foods for man to eat: plant foods and animal foods.
- Before the Flood man was to be a vegetarian, after the Flood he could eat animal products. (Genesis 1–6)
- The Mediterranean Diet is the same as the Bible Diet. (Genesis 1)
- Medical doctors, scientists, nutritionists, and many health care practitioners agree that the healthiest diet consists of a foundation of whole grains, lots of fruits and vegetables, smaller amounts of dairy products and fish, and minute amounts of fats, sweets, and red meats.
- The foods that the Bible tells us to eat in large quantities are the healthiest for us. The foods that the Bible tells us to eat on special occasions or with discernment are less healthy for us but still useful if eaten in moderation.

2 THE FOUNDATION OF THE BIBLE DIET

CHAPTER HIGHLIGHTS

- Grains
- Whole Grains
- Grains in the Bible
- Jesus and Grains

Let's Get Started

Grains have always been the foundation of a healthy diet, in Bible times and in our times. This means every day you should eat something made with grains, just as the Israelites did. It does not mean grains are the largest part of a healthy diet; they are actually the second largest part (see Illustration #3, this page).

In this chapter you will see how and why it is essential to eat grains every day, which kinds are best for you and why, and how to prepare them so they can be added to your diet with grace and ease.

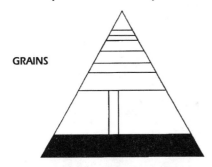

GRAINS

Illustration #3

The Grains Section—The darkened section of this pyramid represents how much of your diet should be devoted to grains.

> **Genesis 41:22** In my dreams I also saw seven heads of grain, full and good, growing on a single stalk.

A Grainy Dream

Pharaoh dreamed of seven good heads of grain and asked Joseph, the young Hebrew, what this meant. Joseph, who was gifted with dream interpretation, answered that it meant there would be seven years of great abundance in the land of Egypt. Because grains were a very important part of the lives of all people in the Mediterranean region, it is not surprising that the Pharaoh would have grains in his dream, and that Joseph would be able to understand the significance of grains in a dream. Grains held an important part in the everyday life of the people, which is why we call grains, and bread made from grains, the **staff of life**—the very foundation of a healthy diet.

This Grain, That Grain, Every Kind Of Grain!

There is a large variety of grains, each with a distinct flavor and use. The most basic and universally available grain in the West is wheat. Hard wheat is used for making bread and thickening. Soft wheat or spring wheat is used for pastries, cakes, pies, muffins, and quick breads. Other common grains are rice, barley, rye, millet, corn, triticale, **durum wheat**, oats, spelt (a kind of wheat), **buckwheat**, and corn. Many ancient grains are becoming popular because they have a heartier taste and are higher in nutrients than the **hybridized** grains used in North America. The most popular are **kamut**, **quinoa**, and **amaranth**.

God provided us with bread for our health and healing, but today we must be careful to choose the correct bread. Look for barley bread, whole-wheat bread, and breads containing spelt and millet. Breads containing millet and spelt can help ease premenstrual cramps and heal wounds. Barley bread can help our bodies to lower cholesterol, improve digestion, and reduce cancer risk. Whole-wheat bread provides us with B complex vitamins, phosphorous, iron, and vitamin E that protect against heart disease and cancer. Also, the fiber in whole-wheat bread can help protect against colon cancer.

Modern and Ancient Grains

Modern Grains		Ancient Grains
Hard Wheat	Rye	Kamut
Soft Wheat	Millet	Quinoa
Durum Wheat	Corn	Amaranth
Buckwheat	Triticale	
Rice	Oats	
Barley	Spelt (a kind of wheat)	

> **Luke 6:1, 2** One **Sabbath** Jesus was going through the grainfields, and his disciples began to pick some heads of grain, rub them in their hands and eat the **kernels**. Some of the Pharisees asked, "Why are you doing what is unlawful on the Sabbath?"

Can't Do That!

In Jesus' day, many people ate grain right out of the field, while it was still **green**. Just like you can have fresh or green lima beans and dried lima beans, you can also have fresh or green grains and dried grains. Usually we eat them dried. In fact, grain is always dried before it is ground into flour. Jesus and his disciples got in trouble for eating the grains, not because they were in somebody else's field (they were allowed to **glean** in those days) but because they were picking grains on the Sabbath which was considered work and that was not allowed on the Sabbath. The grains had nothing to do with it.

Eat 'Em Every Day

Grains are good sources of protein, carbohydrates, and fiber only if they are whole grains. Whole grains have not been polished or "refined" to remove any of the nutritional part of the grain. The outer layer of most grains—wheat, rice, and barley especially—contains the B vitamins essential for digesting the starch or carbohydrates in the grain. The fiber is roughage that is essential for healthy intestines and good digestion. God made grains to contain a high amount of nutrients so that they could be the foundation of a healthy diet.

Something to Ponder

Research published as recently as 1998 has shown that people who eat whole grains are at less risk of dying from many diseases that were previously thought to be incurable. Whole-grain intake has been shown to reduce the risk of **ischemic heart disease** in postmenopausal women.[1] According to medical studies, eating whole grains also reduces the risk of getting many kinds of cancers including cancer of the oral cavity and pharynx, esophagus, stomach, colon, rectum, liver, gallbladder, pancreas, larynx, breast, ovary, prostate, bladder, kidney, and thyroid, as well as Hodgkin's disease and non-Hodgkin's lymphomas.[2] In short, eating whole grains protects you against many kinds of cancers.[3]

Pamela Smith: Whole grain is a must for fiber and nutrition. The word "whole" should be the first word on the ingredient list, such as "whole wheat," "whole oats."[4]

Will The Real Whole Grain Please Stand Up?

White flour and white flour products are not whole grains. White rice is not a whole grain. They are refined, or stripped of most nutrients, and processed to remove all the fiber. Oftentimes wheat flour is even bleached to make it look whiter.

bran: outer fiber covering grains

Cheryl Townsley: White flour has been robbed of its color, taste, smell, and nutrition. Not even cockroaches will eat white-flour based products. Twenty-six essential nutrients, plus the **bran**, have been removed from wheat to produce white flour. Four of the removed nutrients are returned (in a chemical form) to produce "enriched" flour. What an enriching process![5]

DAILY BREAD

GRAINS

Eat at least 6–11 servings of grain products a day.

NUTRITIONAL FACT

God's whole grains contain fiber.

Whole Grains To Protect You

What is there about whole grains that make them such power-houses of health and nutrition? They contain antioxidants and **phytoestrogens** that are known to protect you against many chronic diseases including cancer and **cardiovascular** disease.[6] Whole grains help to protect you against cancer by binding to **carcinogens** and removing them from your body.[7]

phytoestrogens: plant-based hormonal substances

cardiovascular: having to do with the heart and circulatory systems

carcinogens: substances that are capable of causing cancerous changes in your body

ephah: 3/5 bushel, a Biblical unit of measurement

roasted grain: grain roasted whole over an open fire to toast it, or dry roasted in a heavy pan over fire

> **I Samuel 17:17** Now Jesse said to his son David, "Take this **ephah** of **roasted grain** and these ten loaves of bread for your brothers and hurry to their camp."

Roasting On An Open Fire . . .

Many grains will cook faster and have a nutty taste if they are roasted first. This might be why Jesse sent roasted grains to the soldiers; they would take less time to cook and they could even eat them roasted as soon as they got them. During the Vietnam War many Vietnamese soldiers were found with roasted rice in their pockets. Often, this was all the food they had. Rice, wheat, barley, and buckwheat are often roasted or toasted in a heavy pan over a medium-low heat before water is added to cook them. If whole-wheat bread flour is roasted this way before it is used as a thickening agent or in gravy, it will take less time to thicken and taste fully cooked.

During Bible times, the only grains people had were whole grains. Grain refinement had not been invented yet. They often roasted grain whole before eating it as a snack. When grains were ripe, they either roasted them or cooked them in a liquid just as you do when you eat whole oats, wheat **groats**, or whole barley. People of the Bible also made them into flour to make flour products such as bread and flat breads, just the same as we do today.

Remember This . . .

groats: *unmilled, unpolished whole grains*

I often dry roast barley and/or brown rice before I cook them for a sweeter, nuttier taste. This can make a dish of barley or rice, which might be bland by itself, taste rich. If you cook the roasted grains in a flavored broth such as vegetable or chicken broth, instead of water, it will turn these grains into a dish fit for a king.

From The Kitchen

Wheat—Grain #1

Wheat is the most common grain used in the West, so we will start with it. There are many kinds of wheat: winter wheat, spring wheat, hard wheat, soft wheat, and emmer wheat, just to name a few. There are also several ancient grains that are in the wheat family but are not the same as the wheat we use today. These are spelt and kamut.

wheat: *an edible grass*

Reginald Cherry, M.D.: Wheat and spelt lower your risk for heart disease.[8]

What Others are Saying:

Fiber Sweeps You Clean

Wheat, barley, and rice fiber are all also called "bran." When you eat whole grains you are eating the natural bran or fiber that God created to be part of a healthy diet. Fiber has at least two roles in your health:

1. It binds undesirable **toxins** and chemicals to itself and removes them from your body.
2. It acts like a broom and sweeps out unwanted materials from your intestines or bowels.

toxins: *poisons that harm your body*

NUTRITIONAL FACT

Whole wheat contains protein, carbohydrates, fiber, calcium, phosphorus, iron, potassium, magnesium, zinc, copper, selenium, folate, phytic acid, saturated fat, monounsaturated fat, polyunsaturated fat, and the vitamins B_1, B_2, B_3, B_6, C, E. (See Glossary for definitions of these terms.)

spelt: *an edible grass*

husk or hull: *the outer layer of fiber*

Something to Ponder

What Others are Saying:

abbess: *female head of a convent*

Your body needs fiber, bran, and B complex vitamins to digest the starch or carbohydrates in wheat. While these nutrients are already a part of whole wheat, they are refined out of white flour, which makes white flour products very difficult to digest. For example, your body needs B complex vitamins to digest the starch in wheat. If you were to eat, say, a whole-grain piece of bread, within the bread are all the B complex vitamins you need to digest it. On the other hand, if you were to choose a piece of bread made from white flour, your body is forced to rob B vitamins from somewhere else in your body, causing a stress. The result may be that you become deficient in B vitamins, which could cause health problems either directly related to this lack of B vitamins or to the stress your body goes through when robbing B vitamins from elsewhere.

Spelt

Spelt is an ancient grain that was known to the Romans as "farrum" and has been traced as far back as 5000 B.C. in the area we now call Iran. It is also called "farro" and "dinkle." Spelt has a nutty taste that gives it a stronger presence in baked goods. Many people who are sensitive to wheat can often eat whole-grain spelt products with no reaction. Because spelt retains its **husk or hull,** it is also more resistant to disease and pollution than wheat which has been bred to lose its husks. This also means that it requires fewer pesticides and other chemicals. Purity Foods reintroduced spelt to the West in 1987, and it has become very popular since.

Spelt was used extensively as medicine by Hildegard von Bingen, or St. Hildegard as she is often called. Hildegard was an **abbess** who lived from 1098 to 1179.

Hildegard von Bingen: The spelt is the best of grains. It is rich and nourishing and milder than other grain. It produces a strong body and healthy blood to those who eat it and it makes the spirit of man light and cheerful.[9]

Barley in the Bible

Barley in the Field

Exodus 9:31; Deuteronomy 8:8; Ruth 1:22; 2:23; 3:2; II Samuel 21:9; I Chronicles 11:13; Job 31:40; Isaiah 28:25; Joel 1:11

Barley in Measures

Leviticus 27:16; Numbers 5:15; Ruth 2:17, 23; 3:2, 15, 17; II Samuel 17:28; I Kings 2:28; II Kings 7:1, 16, 18; II Chronicles 2:10, 15; Jeremiah 41:8; Ezekiel 45:13; Hosea 3:2; Revelation 6:6

Barley Products

Judges 7:13; II Kings 4:42; II Chronicles 27:5; Ezekiel 4:9, 12; 13:19; John 6:9, 13

> **Revelation 6:6** Then I heard what sounded like a voice among the four living creatures, saying, "A quart of wheat for a day's wages, and three quarts of <u>barley</u> for a day's wages, and do not damage the oil and the wine."

☞ **GO TO:**

II Kings 7:1, 16; II Chronicles 2:10, 15 (barley)

barley: a cereal grass

KEY POINT

The less grains are changed from their original form, the better they are for health, and the closer they are to the food God created for us to eat.

What Others are Saying:

Barley In The Bible

Barley is one of the most mentioned whole grains in the Bible. It was considered a "lowly" grain and fit for nonroyalty. This is why it was used by Elisha and Jesus; they dealt with the common man. Wheat was worth a lot more money than barley, about three times as much.

While barley was not valued as highly as whole wheat, we know barely's great value today. It helps to lower our risk of heart disease and cancer. Barley stops heart disease in these two ways: it prevents the dangerous LDL cholesterol from sticking to our artery walls, and it prevents tiny blood clots from forming. Barley fights cancers, because barley contains cancer-fighting selenium and vitamin E.

Dr. Mary Ruth Swope: Since barley was very possibly the first cereal grain known to man, it should come as no surprise that God built it so nutritionally perfect. The nutrient profile of barley is just about perfect. Nearly everything the human system needs is present in ideal proportions.[10]

Reginald Cherry, M.D.: Barley also helps to lower your risk of heart disease.[11]

> **John 6:9–11** "Here is a boy with five small barley loaves and two small fish, but how far will they go among so many?" Jesus said, "Have the people sit down." There was plenty of grass in that place, and the men sat down, about five thousand of them. Jesus then took the loaves, gave thanks, and distributed to those who were seated as much as they wanted. . . .

☞ **GO TO:**

II Kings 4:42–44 (Elisha)

Matthew 14:15–20;
  Mark 6:35–44;
  Luke 9:12–17;
  John 6:9–13 (loaves)

Barley Bread Multiplies

Elisha and Jesus both multiply a few loaves of barley bread to feed large numbers of people (see Illustration #4, page 27). There are four times listed in the Bible when Jesus multiplies loaves of bread to feed the crowds, but only one of them, John 6:9–13, mentions that the loaves of bread are made of barley. The people who followed Jesus were common people, not royalty. Their bread would have been the kind that took the least expense to make and was, therefore, the least processed. The less grains are changed from their original form, the better they are for health, and the closer they are to the food God created for us to eat.

Barley Water

Barley water is an old-fashioned remedy for diarrhea, constipation, and an upset stomach. Generally it is called "lemon barley water" or "ginger barley water" and often is called "barley gripe water."

KEY POINT

Barley protects against heart disease and cancer. In addition, it tastes great.

Four Healthy Ways to Eat Barley

Barley as:	Health Benefits:
Loaves or cakes	• Great for people who can't eat wheat
Crackers	• Do not usually contain wheat
	• Often used as teething biscuits for babies
Soup	• Full meal
	• Whole grains in a form kids like
Water	• Great cure for gas and diarrhea in babies

Illustration #4

Jesus Multiplies Bread—Jesus took the loaves of barley, gave thanks, and distributed them to the people.

Barley is often in baby-teething crackers and is almost always in vegetarian soup. Mushroom and barley soup is a real comfort food (see recipe on page 265). Made in 20 minutes, the barley will be firm and still in the form of the grain itself. If barley is left to simmer on low for an hour or more (make sure there is enough water for this before you try it), the barley will begin to absorb the water or other liquid and swell. Some of the creamy goodness of the barley will become a great base for the soup. Cooked overnight or throughout the day in a slow cooker of some type, barley soup will be an easy and hearty meal. Barley and mushroom or barley and vegetable soup is a great way to introduce whole-grain barley into your diet.

From The Kitchen

Millet, Not Mullet

Millet is mentioned in the Bible only once. Small and round, this grain is often used to feed songbirds. For a grain, millet is low in starch and high in protein. It contains no **gluten,** so it is very difficult to be made into a loaf of bread on its own. Millet is very good cooked into a porridge and eaten for breakfast. It can also be eaten as a cooked grain at meals in place of rice. I often use it in soups because it opens up or explodes in the pot when it is boiled, and this makes for nice thickening.

☞ **GO TO:**

Ezekiel 4:9 (millet)

millet: an edible grass

gluten: a protein found in wheat, rye, barley, and oats; the elastic substance in flour

NUTRITIONAL FACT

If you eat refined white-flour products, replace the B vitamins with 1/8 teaspoon nutritional yeast and replace the fiber with 1/2 teaspoon wheat or rice bran to avoid nutritional deficiencies.

pilaf: rice cooked with beans, or meat, or shellfish

risotto: rice cooked in broth and flavored with vegetables or cheese

KEY POINT

To ease premenstrual discomfort and to speed healing in wounds, consume millet and spelt in the form of bread.

Reginald Cherry, M.D.: Millet and spelt can help to ease premenstrual discomfort and to speed healing in wounds.[12]

The Case Of The Missing Rice

Grasses and cereals are mentioned in the Bible, but rice is not mentioned by name. We know that people in Bible times had rice, however, because there are recipes using rice that were published around the time of Jesus.

Rice Is A Grain

Brown rice or unpolished rice is a whole grain. White rice of any kind—polished, enriched, fortified, or instant—is still not a whole grain. Whole-rice or brown-rice flour is whole-grain flour. White-rice flour is not. This means that most ethnic restaurants that serve rice (for example: Chinese, Japanese, Greek, Italian, Mexican, East and West Indian, Spanish, Portuguese, and African restaurants) are not serving whole-grain rice.

In restaurants, read the menu and ask questions if you want whole-grain rice. Ask the server if the restaurant offers brown, unpolished rice. Look for brown, unpolished rice on your grocery shelves. Don't neglect rice, since rice plays a prominent role in the Mediterranean Diet and in your health. Besides, rice can be enjoyed in many wonderful ways, from rice **pilafs**, **risottos**, and cold rice salads, to thick soups and stews.

Rice Pasta

Rice pasta is very popular in oriental cooking. Alas, it is not whole-grain or brown rice. However, health food stores and health food sections of large supermarkets often have brown-rice pasta available. It is generally considered an "allergy" product because people who are allergic to wheat or gluten can often eat rice products, as they do not contain gluten.

The White And Brown Of It

White rice of all kinds takes less time to cook than brown or whole-grain rice. This makes it almost impossible to gradually introduce brown rice in with white rice, unless you plan ahead. By precooking brown rice and adding it to the final stage of cooking white rice, you can introduce brown rice to your family slowly. Once you develop a taste for whole grains and their rich, nutty flavors, you won't have to be concerned with this; you will be able to serve brown rice on its own!

> **Joshua 5:11** The day after the Passover, that very day, they ate some of the produce of the land: unleavened bread and roasted grain.

Roasted Grain—Brown Rice

Roasted grain was very popular in Bible times because it was partially cooked by the roasting, and people could eat it without any further cooking. It also had more taste than nonroasted grains.

Roasting grains before cooking is done in many different recipes using brown rice, barley, or wheat. Brown rice is excellent when it is roasted before adding water or liquid to cook it. Try roasting it over medium heat in a heavy pan until it begins to give off a nutty smell. Stir it frequently. It can also be roasted in a small amount of olive oil or clarified butter until it browns or roasts. Then add the required amount of liquid for cooking. Popped corn might be considered the modern version of roasted grains.

A baked brown-rice pudding, with roasted rice, dried fruit, and roasted nuts, is a wonderful dessert, whether it is made with dairy, soy, or rice milk. Often, roasting the rice first shortens the cooking time.

> **Acts 2:42** They devoted themselves to the apostles' teaching and to the fellowship, to the breaking of bread and to prayer.

Fed On Bread

Breaking bread together was almost a necessity of hospitality in Bible times, and still is in the Middle East. Whole-grain flour products, like breads and crackers, are an easy way to eat whole grains. Bread is the most popular way to eat wheat, the grain of choice for North Americans. As long as the bread is made of whole grains, it is nutritious. Whole-grain bagels, muffins, pita bread, pasta, biscuits, cookies, crackers, and even pretzels are available in most grocery stores and health food stores. Look for whole-grain mixes to make cakes, quick breads, pancakes, and waffles. Whole-grain bread can also be made in bread machines, and there are many natural whole-grain bread mixes available.

KEY POINT

In the Bible, the word "bread" and the word "food" are practically interchangeable. That's how important bread was, in these ancient times.

 *From The Kitchen*

Illustration #5

The Last Supper—Jesus and his disciples most likely ate whole-grain, unleavened bread on the evening before the crucifixion.

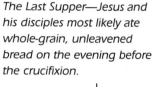

What Others are Saying:

Remember This . . .

☞ **GO TO:**

Matthew 6:11 (daily bread)

Leviticus 2:1–7 (fine flour)

Acts 2:42 (breaking of bread)

Maureen Salaman: When we talk about "our daily bread," that is the correct name for it. In biblical times, people ate bread at every meal, mainly barley bread for the poor and wheat bread for the wealthy.[13]

In Bible times bread was the main part of every meal. This bread was much coarser than the bread we have today. The grains were ground with stone-grinding wheels and very fine flour was reserved for wealthy people. The common man ate a heavy bread made of coarsely ground grains. Every day was bread-breaking day in Bible times. The barley or wheat flour was mixed with water and salt, shaped into loaves, and then baked. At the Last Supper, Jesus described the breaking of the unleavened bread of Passover as a symbol of himself, and early Christians remembered Jesus' words in a ceremony called "breaking of bread" (see Illustration #5, this page).

The breads that contain cooked whole grains or coarsely ground grains are much healthier than breads made of just flour. Bread made from branless flour is generally not considered a whole-grain product.

"Whole grain," "whole wheat," and "made with only whole grains" are the phrases to look for on the label of bakery products. If the label says "wheat flour," "unbleached wheat flour," or anything other than "whole grain" or "whole wheat," chances are the product is not entirely made of whole grains.

Something to Ponder

Many food companies would like you to think that their breads, rolls, and crackers are entirely made of whole grains, or that their products are made from the entire grain. This is not always the case. Many products advertise that they contain whole grains, and they do. But they are made from refined wheat flour with very few whole grains added. This is not a whole-grain product! Please read the labels before you buy a product.

WARNING

> **Acts 20:11** Then he went upstairs again and broke bread, and ate. After talking until daylight, he left.

Jesus Told Me To Do It, So I'm Gonna Do It

The disciples were always breaking bread as Jesus had shown them to do (see Illustration #5, page 30); it is called the Lord's Supper now. Even Paul performed this remembrance act in Troas. While he was talking, or giving the sermon, one of the people listening, Eutychus, sank into a deep sleep, fell out of the third-story window, and died. Paul came out and hugged him, and he was raised from the dead. Then Paul went upstairs again, performed the Lord's Supper, and talked until daylight. Presumably nobody else fell out of the window.

☞ **GO TO:**

I Corinthians 11:20 (Lord's Supper)

Acts 20:5–7 (Troas)

Acts 20:9 (Eutychus)

Can't Stand The White Stuff

Whole-grain pasta is the easiest way to introduce whole-grain products to your family. Whole wheat, spelt, durum wheat, buckwheat, rice, and mixed-grain pastas are available in health food stores and many grocery stores. I especially like the spelt pastas that are made by Purity Foods and sold under the name VitaSpelt. Many companies make whole-grain pastas; just read the label. Even a pasta product that is only partially made up of whole grain is better than one that has no whole grains in it at all. Once you and your family get used to the taste of whole grains and whole-grain pastas, you will not be able to eat the white stuff again. Now that you have read this information on how important whole grains are, please consider changing to a whole-grain diet.

ON Target:
Brown rice and brown-rice pasta

OFF Target:
White rice and white-rice pasta

From The Kitchen

If you or your family have trouble wanting to eat the very heavy, natural, whole-grain bread that is the most healthful, which is also the most similar to the bread eaten in Bible times, start slow. Start by eating bread that contains some whole grains. When you have become accustomed to this, switch to a product that contains 100 percent of the grain and no refined flours.

Pasta In The Bible

Nope, there is no mention of pasta in the Bible. But there are recipes published during the time of Jesus that refer to "paste" in various dishes. This paste is made of flour and water, and sometimes eggs, which is rolled flat. That sounds suspiciously like pasta!

What Others are Saying:

Cheryl Townsley: Many people have moved to pasta as a way to eliminate fat from their diet. They select pasta made from white enriched flour. What a waste! That type of food sticks to the intestinal tract like glue while containing almost no nutrition.[14]

Something to Ponder

Although it is very important for your health to eat whole grains, it is also important to keep your sanity about it. If you are out to eat at a friend's house or a potluck, don't make a big scene. Just eat what is provided. It is better to eat refined grains once in a while than to offend your friends and neighbors by refusing them. Worrying about your health is not recommended either.

☞ **GO TO:**

Luke 12:22, 23
(worrying)

Study Questions

1. When is the best time to eat grains? How many different times do you think you should eat grains?
2. Name at least five health benefits of eating whole grains.
3. Which grains were eaten in Bible times? Which ones should you eat and why?
4. What kind of bread did Elisha and Jesus multiply and why? What made bread in Bible times different than bread today?

- God made grains to contain carbohydrates, proteins, amino acids, B vitamins, vitamin E, minerals, fiber, and every good thing essential for health. (Genesis 1:11,12)

- God made whole grains, and people in Bible times, like Elisha and Jesus, ate whole-grain barley bread. (I Kings 4:42–44 and John 6:9–13)

- Wheat, spelt, barley, millet, and rice were eaten in Bible times and are still considered to be the most healthful grains today.

- Jesus told us to eat bread daily, as was the custom in those days. (Matthew 6:11)

3 EZEKIEL'S PUNISHMENT: OUR HEALTH FOOD

CHAPTER HIGHLIGHTS

- Ezekiel Bread
- Amino Acids
- Beans
- Fiber for Health
- Soybeans

Let's Get Started

The second level of the Mediterranean Food Pyramid has three categories. In this chapter we will start with the second-level's smallest section: beans and other **legumes** (see Illustration #6, page 35). Beans and legumes played a very important role in the food supply of people in Bible times and still do today for all people the world over.

legumes: plants that have edible seeds within a pod

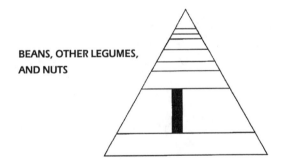

BEANS, OTHER LEGUMES, AND NUTS

Illustration #6

Beans, Other Legumes, and Nuts Section—The darkened section of this pyramid represents how much of your diet should be devoted to beans, other legumes, and nuts.

> **Ezekiel 4:9** "Take wheat and barley, beans and lentils, millet and spelt; put them in a storage jar and use them to make bread for yourself."

Ezekiel's Punishment

Ezekiel was of a priestly family, and he was called upon to be a prophet among the Jews who were exiled in Babylon. God told him to put the sins of the house of Israel upon himself and lie on his left side for 390 days and then to lie on his right side for 40 days. During this time he was to eat only this special food at set times with water to go with it.

Ezekiel Bread

Flour or bread made with a combination of wheat, barley, millet, spelt, beans, and lentils is generally called "Ezekiel bread" or "Ezekiel 4:9 Bread." Many of the specialty breads use **sprouted** grains and sprouted beans to make the flour for this bread. Most often the ingredients are ground into flour and then made into bread. Some recipes call for a combination of whole-grain flours and precooked beans that are simply mixed together and then baked.

Often grains and **pulses** are sprouted and then ground, or the beans are cooked and added to the grain flours. Any combination of these ingredients is called Ezekiel bread.

From The Kitchen

What Others are Saying:

Rex Russell, M.D.: Ezekiel bread has been analyzed and eaten by many people through the years. It has the complete package of essentials for health. It can be bought either as flour or bread at some whole food stores (see chart below). Many people have used it during times of sickness and have given good reports.[1]

pulses: another name for beans

Two Kinds of Stores

What kind of store?	What do they sell?
Health Food Store	supplements, herbs, teas, remedies, beauty products, and sometimes books and snack foods
Whole Food Store	vegetables (often organically grown), grains, canned and frozen goods, packaged foods, teas, herbs, remedies, books, beauty products, paper products, cleaning and laundry supplies; often has a butcher shop, bakery, and deli

amino acids: the building blocks of protein

essential amino acids: tryptophan, leucine, isoleucine, lysine, valine, threonine, methionine, phenylalanine

complete protein: containing all the essential amino acids in a nearly equal complement

It's Essential!

All animals and plants need protein, which is made of **amino acids**. There are twenty-two known amino acids, and of these eight are considered to be essential for humans. The **essential amino acids** cannot be made in your body as the other amino acids can; that is why it is "essential" to get them from your food. Foods that contain all the essential amino acids are sources of **complete protein**. Dairy products, all animal meats, eggs, and soybeans are the only foods that contain complete protein. Grain, beans, nuts, and seeds contain incomplete proteins.

COMPLEMENTARY PROTEINS

Since the 1970s, there has been much controversy about the nutritional value of eating foods that do not contain all the amino acids. For example, wheat and other grains are low in an amino acid called lysine. Beans, however, are high in lysine. So it was thought that the solution was simply to eat grains, like wheat or rice, at the same meal with beans. These were called complementary proteins, since they complemented each other to make a complete protein. It was done with several combinations—beans with rice or wheat, beans with nuts or seeds, or dairy products with grains and/or beans. Ezekiel bread contains grains and beans combined to make complementary proteins.

A BALANCING ACT: AMINO ACIDS

When Frances Moore Lappé published *Diet For A Small Planet* in 1971, her theory was that the amount of available amino acids was determined by whatever was the lowest level of any of the amino acids in all the food eaten at one meal. So a lot of people actually kept track of which foods they ate and whether they had complete protein at each meal. Nutritionists now know that the amount of amino acids in each meal does not determine the amount of amino acids for the entire day. It is possible to have a high-lysine food at one meal and wheat at another and still have a balance of amino acids.

If you would like to have more information about amino acids, you can look at http://www.jomarlabs.com on the internet or call them at 1-800-538-4545.

NUTRITIONAL FACT

Ezekiel flour contains balanced protein, fiber, and vitamins B and E.

God knew that something like this would be too complicated for people to keep track of, so he allowed the Israelites to eat meat, dairy products, and eggs, and he gave them Ezekiel flour. Ezekiel flour has the perfect mix of grains and beans to make complete protein (see Illustration #7, page 38). According to the Mediterranean Diet, we should eat beans and grains daily.

Remember This . . .

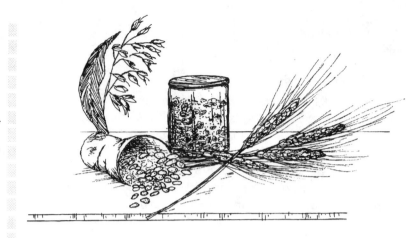

Illustration #7

Dried Beans and Grain—
Beans and grains combine to
form complete protein.

> **I Samuel 17:28, 29** . . . brought bedding and bowls
> and articles of pottery. They also brought wheat and
> barley, flour and roasted grain, beans and lentils, honey
> and curds, sheep and cheese from cows' milk for David
> and his people to eat. For they said, "The people have
> become hungry and tired and thirsty in the desert."

Beans—Our Health Food

David's friends brought him grains, beans, and dairy products—a
perfect complement of proteins to keep his soldiers healthy. The
only additional foods they needed were some fresh greens.

Have you been eating low-fiber foods? Have you ignored whole
grains and beans? Perhaps you need to have some Ezekiel flour
products to restore your health! Beans contain protein, carbohydrates, and fiber. They also contain B vitamins and are low in fat.
Beans are easy to carry around dry without spoiling, and they
have a variety of tastes.

**What Others
are Saying:**

Maureen Salaman: [In Bible times] grains, as well as lentils or
beans were cooked in water or olive oil with onions, leeks, and
garlic, or in butter and, when available, with meat or fish.[2]

Reginald Cherry, M.D.: [Ezekiel 4:9] we see an amazing revelation from the Bible cure. Each specific food contained in the
bread mentioned has particular benefits for our health and for
preventing disease. Of course God knew this, and he provided us
this wonderful bread for our health and healing.[3]

Cheryl Townsley: Dried beans, split peas, lentils, and black-eyed peas are examples of legumes. They have little, if any, fat and are high in fiber. They are a complex carbohydrate high in vitamins and minerals.[4]

Time For Fiber!

Fiber from both beans and whole grains is essential to health. Research done in Houston, Texas, in 1997 showed that fiber from grains, beans, fruits, and vegetables was responsible for low rates of breast cancer among Hispanic women.[5]

NUTRITIONAL FACT

"Legumes," "beans," and "pulses" all mean the same thing. They are the seeds of plants in the same families. Dried peas are also in this category.

DAILY BREAD

BEANS, LENTILS, OR NUTS
Have at least one serving per day.

In societies where there are no refined grains, where the majority of meals and foods are high in natural plant-based fibers, there are also very low rates of degenerative diseases like heart disease, cancer, diabetes, colon cancer, and **diverticulitis**.

Something to Ponder

WHERE DO I GET THIS FIBER?

By following the Mediterranean Diet and eating whole grains frequently during the day and adding in some form of high-fiber beans, legumes, or nuts, you will start getting the kind of fiber required for health. There are many companies that make whole-grain and/or bean products: Eden Foods, Hain's, Westbrae, Cascadian Farm, Amy's, Garden of Eatin', Wanda's, Soy Deli, Turtle Island Foods, White Wave, Lundberg Family Farms, Barbara's Bakery, Arrowhead Mills, and Bob's Red Mill. Many of these products are sold frozen in your health food store or supermarket health food section.

Cascadian Farm, for example, makes a frozen entrée from **bulgar wheat**, lentils, **garbanzo beans**, vegetables, raisins, and seasonings. This is a great meal in itself. All you really need to add is a dark green salad.

diverticulitis: *inflamed pockets in the large intestine*

bulgar wheat: *whole wheat that has been cooked, chopped, and dried. It is easily reconstituted by adding boiling water to it.*

garbanzo bean: *round bean also called 'chick pea'*

BEANS AS MEDICINE

Beans have been shown to reduce serum cholesterol in many studies. Canned beans and even **tofu** are being used to reduce

tofu: *a compressed block of soy protein made from curded, fully cooked soy milk*

body fat: *also called 'lipids'*

all **body fat** in many clinics in the United States and Canada. The old saying still stands: eat a cup of beans a day and lose a pound of weight.

Rex Russell, M.D.: When asked how much fiber we need, I often give the admittedly earthy answer that we need only to look into our toilets. As insoluble fiber passes through the bowel, it takes fat with it into the stool. Fat floats. So floating stools are a good sign that you have enough fiber.[6]

NUTRITIONAL FACT

Beans can reduce your cholesterol and other body fats.

If you are going to eat canned beans, check the sugar content. Please do not eat beans with any sugar in them, as this defeats the purpose of healthy eating. Diabetics may benefit from eating bean fiber but not if it contains sugar.

ON Target:
Chewing all food until it is liquid before swallowing

OFF Target:
Washing partially chewed food down with liquids, especially coffee

Chew It Up!

The most important thing to remember when you switch to a higher fiber diet is that chewing starts digestion. Each time you chew grains until they are fully chewed, you are aiding your digestion and reducing your need for larger quantities of food. Saliva contains the enzyme "salivary amylase," which digests starch. The more you chew each mouthful of starch, the easier it will be to digest it. The chewing also starts all the processes of digestion going in your stomach, pancreas, intestines, and so on.

complex carbohydrates: *sugar and starches found in whole grains, fruits, and some vegetables*

insulin: *a hormone produced by your pancreas that regulates the metabolism of sugar in your body*

Fiber And Diabetes

For years fiber has been used to reduce the risks and symptoms of diabetes. When I worked as a nutritionist in a Toronto clinic we used a specific diet of 80 percent **complex carbohydrates**, 10 percent fat and 10 percent protein to help people with diabetes. Most of the patients reduced their **insulin**, and some didn't need insulin at all when they followed the high-fiber diet.

Do not try a new diet on your own. Always discuss any program with your doctor, especially if you are a diabetic, have a heart condition, or high blood pressure.

Reginald Cherry, M.D.: Fiber is turning out to be a major factor used to lower blood sugar. Fiber has decreased insulin requirements 30 to 40 percent in Type I diabetes. In Type II diabetes, most patients were off insulin in 10 to 20 days in one study.[7]

GTT

In 1924 Dr. Seale Harris recognized that certain individuals secreted excessive insulin in response to eating refined carbohydrates and white flour. He even devised a special blood sugar test called the six-hour **Glucose** Tolerance Test or **GTT** to diagnose **hyperinsulinism** and functional **hypoglycemia**.

Reginald Cherry, M.D.: Beans can also help to stabilize blood sugar levels, reduce the risk of breast and prostate cancers, and lower the risk of heart disease in people with diabetes.[8]

Fiber is essential to your digestive processes. Digestion is less efficient in a low-fiber lifestyle.

BUT BEANS GIVE ME GAS!

Beans are known for giving people gas, which happens because beans are difficult for some people to digest. There are two reasons for this. One is that the fiber in beans causes your body to work better and this creates gas at first. After you have been eating a high-fiber diet for a few days or weeks, this will not happen. The second reason is that there are two complex sugars called raffinose and stachyose in beans that some people cannot digest very well without forming gas. Generally, this is remedied by adding **kombu** to the bean-cooking water or a small amount of **asafoetida** to the food. You can also purchase Beano™ in most stores, which will help you digest many gas-giving foods.

Cheryl Townsley: If you have trouble digesting legumes, try a strip of kombu. Kombu is a sea vegetable sold in dried strips . . . in health food stores or Asian markets. A six-inch strip adds nearly one week's worth of minerals.[9]

What Others are Saying:

glucose: the simple sugar that is the source for the energy in your body

GTT: used as one of the diagnostic tools for diabetes and hypoglycemia

What Others are Saying:

Remember This . . .

hyperinsulinism: a high level of insulin in your body

hypoglycemia: a low level of blood sugar in your body

kombu: a sea vegetable; can be purchased in Japanese or health food stores

asafoetida: an herb from India; generally called "hing" or "yellow powder"

What Others are Saying:

NUTRITIONAL FACT

Beans are excellent for diabetics.

From The Kitchen

clean: Wash off the beans. Pick out any dirt, sticks, or hulls and remove them. Remove any discolored or broken beans.

rehydrated: water is fully soaked up into beans

slow simmer: using a heat low enough that the water bubbles break at a slow rate

soba: flat noodles made from buckwheat flour

whole-wheat udon: flat noodles made from whole grain wheat flour

serotonin: a chemical found in the brain that is essential for relaxation, sleep, and concentration

Cooking Beans

The best way to cook beans to avoid the gas problem is to use the "quick soak" method. This will reduce the amount of complex sugars that ferment and give you gas. Start by using a stainless steel saucepan that has a tight-fitting lid. Add three times as much water as the amount of beans you want to cook. Bring the water to a boil on high heat while you **clean** the beans. Slowly add the beans to the boiling water and boil them hard for 2 minutes. Turn off the heat, cover the beans, and let them sit until they are completely **rehydrated**. The time it takes will vary between bean sizes and could be anywhere from 1½ to 4 hours. When the beans are fully soaked and no longer look shriveled, pour out the water. Add fresh water and bring them to a boil over medium heat. Then reduce the heat to a **slow simmer** until they are fully cooked. Then add seasonings. Do not add salt, tomatoes, or other acids during the initial cooking.

VOILA! INSTANT MEALS!

Many health conscious companies make quick lunch or snack soups or pasta meals in a cup that you just have to add boiling water to and wait 3–5 minutes. This makes it possible to have whole grains and beans ready in just a few minutes. Please look at the label of any meal-in-a-cup-type foods to be sure that they are really made of whole grains and beans. A black bean soup should really have black beans in it, but it should also have whole-grain flour or pasta too. If you are fond of the ramen noodles meals, please buy the ones made of whole grains like **soba** or **whole-wheat udon**.

White Flour Noodles Spell Trouble

If you eat meals of white refined flour noodles, you are only asking for trouble later on. White pasta can raise your blood sugar or **serotonin** levels too high and make you sleepy. They can also strip your body of B vitamins (because B vitamins are required to digest the starch in pasta and grains) by using up your B vitamins and not replacing them as there are no B vitamins in white flour pastas. This could make you feel nervous, edgy, hyper, tired, or lead to exhaustion later in the day.

BEANS UNDER PRESSURE

A pressure cooker may be used to cook large beans, but not the smaller beans like mung beans or lentils. The skins on the smaller beans have a tendency to come off during cooking and clog up the air vent. I generally cook beans in a pressure cooker with an onion, garlic, carrot, bay leaf, and strip of kombu. When you use a pressure cooker the beans don't have to be soaked first, they take less time to cook as well, and they don't cause gas. If you want to cook beans in a pressure cooker, read your pressure cooker's instructions.

PATIENCE IS A VIRTUE: SLOW-COOK BEANS

With the exception of soybeans, it is possible to cook beans without soaking them first. Put them in a pot of water after cleaning them. Use enough water to soak the beans and to cook them. So if you are cooking one cup of beans, you will need at least 3½ to 4 cups of water. Do not add salt or **acid**. Cover the pan. Turn the heat to medium-high and bring the beans to a simmer. This should take around an hour. Turn the heat to low and let them simmer for about 4 hours. I have done this in a slow cooker overnight or during the day and found the beans to be perfectly cooked. Many ethnic recipes for cooking beans and even recipes from famous chefs do not call for soaking the beans first. It might be said, then, that not soaking the beans before cooking is the newest and the oldest trend in cooking them. Please do not add baking soda to beans at any stage of soaking or cooking. This can remove a lot of nutrients from the finished beans.

BEANS FROM A CAN

If you want to use canned beans, check the labels first. Make sure that there is no sugar or **EDTA** in the beans. Wash them off to remove the majority of added salt. Many health food stores have beans in jars and cans with no preservatives or additional ingredients. They often have beans that have been grown without chemicals as well.

EASY BEANS

Cook beans according to the recipe for regularly cooked beans and put them on a paper towel to dry them just enough to no longer be wet. Then put them in a plastic bag or covered refrigerator container in the freezer. Use them in salads, add them to soups and grain dishes, mash them and put them in sandwiches, just keep them handy so you can eat them any time of the day

From The Kitchen

NUTRITIONAL FACT

Beans can be cooked many different ways.

From The Kitchen

acid: *lemon juice, orange juice, vinegar, tomatoes, or tomato juice*

ON Target:
Cooking lots of natural beans

OFF Target:
Cooking beans with salt, sugar, fat, and fatty meats

EDTA: *a preservative*

NUTRITIONAL FACT

Canned beans with no or low salt and no sugar are good for you.

From The Kitchen

 **NUTRITIONAL FACT**

2 Tbsp of lentils = 7.1g
of protein

2 Tbsp of cheddar
cheese = 7.1g of
protein

ON Target:
Eating beans daily

OFF Target:
Eating beans loaded
with salt or fat

☞ **GO TO:**

II Samuel 23:11 (lentil)

 **NUTRITIONAL FACT**

Eat 20–35 grams of
fiber a day.

 **NUTRITIONAL FACT**

Soybeans are the only
beans with complete
protein.

(see Illustration #8, this page). If you freeze several different types of beans you will have lots of variety. It is especially wonderful to have black beans like this that you can defrost and make into black bean dip or add to basic soup, to give you a special black bean soup.

> **Genesis 25:34** Then Jacob gave Esau some bread and some lentil stew. He ate and drank and then got up and left.

Lentils: The Bible's Very First Vegetable

Jacob bought Esau's birthright with a dinner of <u>lentil</u> stew. They had been fighting over who would take over when their father died. Esau had been out in the field and was very hungry, so hungry that he gave up his rightful place in the family for some lentil stew. Lentils are a kind of bean or legume. They are easy to cook and do not require soaking first. They come in red, brown, and green and are shaped like a convex lens. Lentils happen to be the first vegetable mentioned in the Bible.

How Much Fiber Should I Eat?

The recommendation for total fiber in the daily diet is 20 to 35 grams. This will allow for proper daily bowel movements that will assist your body in removing the toxic waste matter excreted in your stools without the excretion of any calcium.[10] Children two years of age and up should increase their dietary fiber intake in an amount equal to or greater than their age plus five grams a day. For example a three-year-old child should have at least eight grams of fiber a day. This should continue to increase until age 20 when the fiber intake should be 25 to 35 grams a day.[11] This includes all fiber from whole grains, beans, fruits, and vegetables. Even as much as a six-gram increase in fiber can reduce **serum cholesterol concentrations**.[12]

serum cholesterol concentrations: *amount of cholesterol in your blood*

Soybeans: They Didn't Have 'Em, But We Do!

Many kinds of beans were eaten in Bible times and still are eaten in the Middle East and the entire Mediterranean region. Soybeans, unfortunately, were not grown in this area during Bible times, according to Bill Shurtleff, the author of many books on tofu and soybeans and an authority on soybeans. Nowadays, there are many kinds of soybeans for your use, and they make a wonderful addition to your life.

The Complete Protein Bean

In 1979 Nevin Scrimshaw and Vernon Young of **M.I.T.** published the results of research showing that soybeans do contain complete protein.[13] They are the only beans known to contain complete protein. This means that they are balanced in amino acids and do not need to be complemented with grains, nuts, seeds, dairy products, or animal proteins. Until this discovery, it was not known why soybeans were so healthy.

M.I.T.: *Massachusetts Institute of Technology*

gluten: *wheat protein*

genistein: *one of the* **phytonutrients** *in soybeans*

T. D. Jakes: Soybean is one of the best proteins for us to eat. There are some veggie-burgers at the supermarket made of soybean, **gluten**, mushrooms, and spices which have an excellent flavor.[14]

What Others are Saying:

Francisco Contreras, M.D.: Soybeans contain **genistein**. This **phytochemical** has an **anti-aggregate** that won't allow small **tumors** to attach themselves to **capillaries**. In this way, the tumors can't get nutrients and, consequently, they can't **metastasize**.[15]

phytochemical/phytonutrient: *plant-based chemical or nutrient*

anti-aggregate: *against clumping together*

tumors: *a growth arising from existing tissue, but growing independently*

capillaries: *one of the minute blood vessels that connect the arteries and veins*

DAILY BREAD

SOYBEANS
Some form of soybean can be eaten daily.

metastasize: *transmitted from one site to another within the body*

> **Genesis 1:12** The land produced vegetation: plants bearing seed according to their kinds and trees bearing fruit with seed in it according to their kinds.

Soybeans Are Important Seeds

Soybeans are the seeds of the soy plant. They are used as food and for oil in North America and throughout the world and have many other industrial uses that make them a valuable cash crop. Soybeans are also very healthy to use as a regular food.

Soybeans Contain Phytoestrogens

isoflavones: plant-based hormone

phytoestrogen: plant-based estrogen, a hormone necessary for women and men

Isoflavones have been in the news lately because they are the newest form of plant-based hormones. Genistein is an isoflavone found in soybeans that is especially beneficial to men and women because it contains **phytoestrogen**. Phytoestrogens have been shown to be effective in both protecting against and treating prostate cancer [16] and in preventing the symptoms of menopause such as hot flashes, memory loss, and night sweats.

What Others are Saying:

phytohormones: plant-based hormones

Francisco Contreras, M.D.: Soybeans also contain **phytohormones** with the "good" estrogenic action without the undesirable effects of the synthetic estrogens. [17]

PHYTO-WHAT?

Oftentimes, there are undesirable side effects with synthetic estrogen pills and creams. These generally do not occur with plant-based estrogens in your diet. Phytoestrogens have been proven useful in offering protection against breast, bowel, prostate and other cancers, cardiovascular disease, brain function, alcohol abuse, osteoporosis, as well as menopausal symptoms. [18]

Something to Ponder

It is the high-soybean diet in the East that is deemed responsible for the low level of menopausal symptoms in oriental women, who traditionally eat a high-soybean, high-fiber diet.

What Others are Saying:

Reginald Cherry, M.D.: Soy products can limit the spread of cancer and can stop its early growth. Tofu and soy burgers are among the sources of this protective food. [19]

How Do You Like Your Soybeans?

Soybeans are eaten as beans in a side dish or as baked beans, the traditional ways of eating any dried beans. I prefer to eat soybeans in the form of tofu, **tempeh**, soyburgers, or tempeh burgers. I also drink soy protein and soy milk–based shakes that are high in isoflavones, especially genistein.

Ezekiel's Punishment Really Is Our Health Food

The mixed fibers from whole grains, beans, and lentils into what we call Ezekiel flour may have been a punishment for Ezekiel, but it is really a wonderful health food for everybody. Because there are so many modern health problems that can be directly related to a low-fiber diet, it is no wonder that people all over the world are rediscovering the special flour blend that has come to be known as Ezekiel flour. God created this special recipe for Ezekiel thousands of years ago, and now it is your special health food.

Study Questions

1. What is different about Ezekiel's bread recipe?
2. Why is Ezekiel's punishment our health food?
3. What are amino acids and why do we need them?
4. What's so great about beans and lentils? Give four examples.
5. Which bean is the most healthful? Why?

CHAPTER WRAP-UP

- For years there has been a controversy in the area of health foods and nutrition about eating beans and grains together to make complementary and complete protein. Ezekiel was told by God how to make grains and beans into a bread that would sustain life for a long time—more than a year, actually. This should tell scientists that God made the food, and he knows exactly how to put it together to be the most healthful. (Ezekiel 4:9)

- Make sure that when you eat beans you also eat whole grains on the same day, not necessarily at the same meal. Try various ethnic dishes that naturally mix beans or lentils and whole grains together as a way to start eating this more healthful diet.

tempeh: *a firm, generally flat, soy product made of fermented soybeans; a vegetarian source of vitamin B_{12}*

NUTRITIONAL FACT

A diet high in soybeans and avocados was very useful in reducing the amount of **NSAIDS** used for treating symptomatic osteoarthritis of the knee and hip.[20]

NSAIDS: *nonsteroidal anti-inflammatory drugs like ibuprofen or naproxen*

NUTRITIONAL FACT

Scrambled tofu or tofu burgers are great for breakfast.

Women with **PMS**, **perimenopause**, or actual **menopause** should eat some soybean products daily to ease their symptoms.

PMS: "premenstrual syndrome," characterized by bloating, crankiness, headaches, fatigue, or water retention before menstruation

perimenopause: the time leading up to the end of the menses when there may be some symptoms like fatigue and weight gain, but there still is menstruation

menopause: the time in a woman's life when menstruation stops, often characterized by hot flashes, fatigue, and weight gain due to hormonal imbalances

- Beans in some form should be eaten daily as part of the Mediterranean Diet. Doing so will improve your digestion and elimination, and reduce your risk for heart disease, cancers, and menopause or PMS symptoms.
- God also made soybeans, even if the Bible does not mention them or if people did not know of them in the Bible lands. They are very healthful and should be included in your diet weekly.

4 DANIEL AND HIS DIET FOR STRENGTH

CHAPTER HIGHLIGHTS

- Daniel and Vegetables
- Raw Vegetables
- Vegetable Fiber
- Colored Vegetables
- The Israelites' Gripe

Let's Get Started

Believe it or not, whole grains, beans, and peas are from the vegetable family. You probably don't think of them as vegetables, but they are. There are a lot more vegetables in the vegetable kingdom than we have discussed so far—root vegetables like potatoes, beets, carrots, and sweet potatoes; bulb vegetables like onions, garlic, and kohlrabi; flowering vegetables like broccoli and cauliflower; head vegetables like cabbage and lettuce; leafy vegetables like parsley, kale, and collards; and hanging vegetables like tomatoes and peppers. There are yellow, orange, red, purple, brown, green, white, and pink vegetables. In short, vegetables are endless in tastes and varieties.

KEY POINT

Vegetables are endless in tastes and varieties.

> **Daniel 1:12, 13** "Please test your servants for ten days: give us nothing but vegetables to eat and water to drink. Then compare our appearance with that of the young men who eat the royal food, and treat your servants in accordance with what you see."

Daniel Put Vegetables To The Test

Daniel asked to eat vegetables in preference to the king's royal food and wine. Why do you think he did that? Because he didn't want to fit in with the Babylonians? Because he missed his regular food? The clue to this strange action is in Daniel 1:3, 4.

> **Daniel 1:3, 4** Then the king ordered Ashpenaz, chief of his court officials, to bring in some of the Israelites from the royal family and the nobility—young men without any physical defect, handsome, showing aptitude for every kind of learning, well informed, quick to understand, and qualified to serve in the king's palace.

Did They Eat Junk Food?

The young men chosen for this assignment were to be the healthiest men among the royalty and nobility, the best learners, the best of all the available young men. This was Daniel and his friends. What made them this way? You got it! Eating mostly vegetables, no wine, no rich foods, and no junk foods. Even when they were put to the <u>test</u> they were ten times better in wisdom and understanding than all the magicians and enchanters in his kingdom.

☞ **GO TO:**

Daniel 1:18–21 (test)

What Others are Saying:

Rex Russell, M.D.: Many studies have shown that if we ate our veggies, as Mom told us, along with more fruit as well, we could avoid or cure several common ailments.[1]

Jack and Judy Hartman: Many of us who desire increased energy should follow the example of Daniel and his friends. We should turn away from the "rich dainties" that so many of us eat and eat more of the vegetables God has provided for us.[2]

Illustration #9

The Vegetables Section—The darkened section of this pyramid represents how much of your diet should be devoted to vegetables.

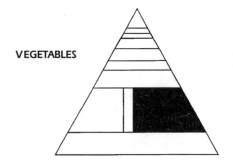
VEGETABLES

How Much Should I Eat?

If you look at the Mediterranean Diet/Bible Diet food pyramid section for vegetables, you will notice it is actually the largest section (see Illustration #9, this page). This means you should eat more vegetables than any other food each day. It also means that you should eat more vegetables than fruit, grains, and animal proteins combined. Whew! That's a lot of vegetables! Isn't it wonderful that vegetables are also the most convenient to carry around and the least expensive to buy?

HAVE SOME MORE!

The average North American eats only the basic seven or eight kinds of vegetables—corn, peas, potatoes, green beans, head lettuce, green peppers, cucumbers, and tomatoes. As recently as 50 years ago, the average person ate more than 20 different vegetables, which they grew and stored or preserved for the winter. Actually, a wider variety of vegetables is available to us today, in most supermarkets, than was available ten years ago. Be adventurous and try a new vegetable!

Mark A. Pearson, D.O.: There is some evidence that a diet with between 5–6 servings of fruits and vegetables a day protects against cancer.[3]

DAILY BREAD

VEGETABLES
Eat mostly vegetables daily.

A Word About Potatoes

Whole, unpeeled potatoes are **real food**. Peeled and deep-fried french fries are not. Baked potatoes are real food, potato chips are not. Homemade scalloped potatoes made from fresh potatoes that have not been peeled and are baked in a low-fat sauce are real food. Packaged, peeled, chemically treated scalloped potatoes are not real food—they are processed food stuffs.

real food: *food in it's natural, healthful state*

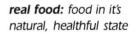

Illustration #10

Potatoes vs. French Fries— Always make sensible choices when selecting food. Ask yourself questions like: Is it high in fats? Does it contain lots of salt? Is it filled with chemicals? If the answer is "yes" to any of these questions, make a healthier selection.

A Not-So-Well-Known Benefit Of Spinach

Your mother, grandmother, and, perhaps, your second grade teacher all told you to "eat more vegetables." Most of you grew up knowing that spinach made Popeye stronger, but do you eat spinach on a regular basis? Do you know that it can prevent macular degeneration, the most common cause of blindness in people over 65?

Fresh Is Best

fresh: *not canned or frozen*

raw: *not cooked or processed (pickles and sauerkraut are processed)*

Fresh vegetables are the best. **Raw** vegetables are excellent snack foods (see Illustration #11, page 53). Each day you need to eat some raw vegetables. The U.S. government says everyone should eat at least 5 half-cup servings of vegetables, and at least one should be raw. This is actually less than the Bible Diet recommends.

Anne and David Frähm: Live foods (foods not already cooked or processed) help keep our bodies strong against disease.[4]

Jack and Judy Hartman: I believe our Creator provided fruit to cleanse our bodies and vegetables to build our bodies. As I've grown older and studied the Word of God, I've come to the conclusion that almost everyone can benefit from eating more fresh vegetables. The Word of God explains how important it is to eat fresh vegetables.[5]

Raw Vegetables Are Essential

enzymes: *substances that start or speed up chemical reaction in your body without being consumed in the process*

Raw vegetables are essential for a vital life. They contain **enzymes** that are destroyed by cooking. Raw vegetables are high in vitamin C, beta-carotene, and phytochemicals. Raw vegetables, along with vegetable oils, fish, beta-carotene, vitamin E, and calcium, have been shown to be responsible for prevention of breast cancer in a study done in Italy between 1991 and 1994.[6]

WARNING

Canned vegetables do not have the same nutritional impact as fresh vegetables do. They also might be loaded with sugar, salt, or other preservatives. Canned vegetables should be your last resort.

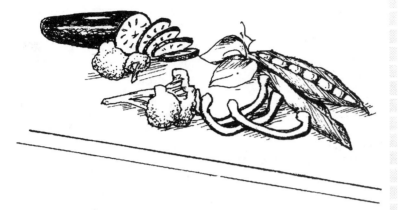

Frozen vegetables can be better for you in the winter if your grocery carries wilted and limp produce. Frozen veggies are picked at their peak of ripeness and **flash frozen**. Don't overcook them. Often they don't need to be cooked any more, just defrosted.

Remember This . . .

The Perfect Snack

It is often easier to eat vegetables raw as snacks. Children love snacks of raw vegetables, especially if they have been included in the preparation of the snacks. I often recommend that people carry raw vegetable snacks with them to eat between meals. If you are out and about, and feel a slump in energy, don't reach for a caffeine-laden drink, reach for some raw vegetable snacks. Go to a supermarket and get a bag of salad greens and some baby carrots. You'll be surprised how much energy eating these will give you.

flash frozen: *frozen quickly*

Anne and David Frähm: Healthy snacks: vegetable pieces (raw), carrots, celery, peppers (green, red, yellow), cucumbers, broccoli, cauliflower, tomatoes. Excellent source of health-promoting vitamins and minerals, especially vitamins A, C, calcium, phosphorus, potassium, and essential amino acids.[7]

What Others are Saying:

ON Target:

Five to ten half-cup servings of vegetables every day

OFF Target:

High fat snacks instead of veggies

 **NUTRITIONAL FACT**

Vegetables contain fiber that is essential for your health.

 **NUTRITIONAL FACT**

Vegetables contain vitamins C and A in the form of beta-carotene

Kcal: kilocalories, a measure of energy, the amount of heat produced by metabolizing food

PEAS FROM THE POD

I love to eat peas in the pod as a snack. They make a good substitute for candy or sugar, they are so sweet tasting. Let your children open the peas themselves and find the surprise of what the peas look like. Did you get one that has big peas or are they really little? Is the pod bigger than the peas inside? What a thrill it is to find a pod that has some peas that are already sprouting inside. Plant these in a pot and see how peas grow. Make eating vegetables fun!

Children Need Vegetables

A study done in Cooperstown, New York, between 1992 and 1993 of 223 children aged two and five showed that intake of vegetables is essential for obtaining the required amounts of vitamin A, vitamin C, beta-carotene, and dietary fiber. This study pointed out that the preschool-aged children naturally choose to eat about 80 percent of the recommended fruit servings and only about 25 percent of the recommended vegetables. They replaced the fruits and vegetables they should be eating with high intakes of total fat and saturated fat.[8] This shows all parents that they must monitor and supervise the foods of their children if they are to obtain a high level of health. Children need to eat at least the recommended servings of three to five half cups of vegetables a day.

What Is A "High-Fiber Diet"?

The general consensus is that a diet of around 35 grams of fiber a day is considered to be a normal high-fiber diet for North Americans. According to David Jenkins of the Department of Nutritional Sciences, Faculty of Medicine, at the University of Toronto, this diet would also include 30 percent fat and 1800 **Kcal** overall.[9]

Why We Need Fiber

Fiber in the form of grains and especially vegetables has been shown to prevent colon cancer, and reduce high cholesterol and high blood pressure. There is so much research out showing that the risks for all diseases go up with a diet low in vegetables, fruits, and whole grains, that anyone who ignores it is asking for trouble.[10] But that's why you are reading this book right now, to change your lifestyle to a healthier one!

> **Proverbs 15:17** Better a meal of vegetables where there is love than a fattened calf with hatred.

Solomon Said!

Solomon, the writer of this section of Proverbs, points out that even a special occasion where they would serve a fattened calf was worthless if there was hatred. A special occasion was a really big deal for them. A meal of vegetables was the general daily fare for most people in Bible times. So he is saying that even a regular meal with love is better than a feast with hatred. The important part of this verse for now is that it lets you understand that the daily fare was a meal of vegetables. Vegetables were their main food! They only ate meat on special occasions. How about you?

They're Everywhere!

All throughout the Bible there are references to vegetables, eating vegetables, and different kinds of vegetables, starting with God's creation of them. This should really be the only reason you need to eat vegetables; they are very important.

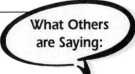
Remember This . . .

Kenneth Cooper, M.D.: At the end of [Dr. Matthew Gillman's] investigation, he determined that for every increase of three servings of fruit or vegetables a day, there was a 22 percent decrease in the risk of all strokes.[11]

What Others are Saying:

Powerhouses Of Phytochemicals

Phytochemical is a big-looking word, but all it means is plant chemicals or ingredients. Often they are also called "phytonutrients," plant-based nutrients. These phytochemicals have been associated with protection from and/or treatments for chronic diseases such as heart disease, cancer, diabetes, and **hypertension** as well as other medical conditions. The foods and herbs with the highest anticancer activity include garlic, soybeans, cabbage, ginger, licorice, and umbelliferous vegetables.[12]

phytochemicals: health-protective substances in plants

hypertension: high blood pressure

Kenneth Cooper, M.D.: Cruciferous vegetables, notably broccoli, brussels sprouts, cauliflower, and cabbage, have been identified as strong anticancer weapons. They are also thought to be protective against other conditions including heart disease, diverticulitis, and constipation.[13]

What Others are Saying:

Antioxidants: What's The Buzz?

The one phytochemical mentioned in the news more than any other is the antioxidant. There are many of them, perhaps 20 are being used in nutritional supplements right now. Cabbage, tomatoes, grape seeds, wheat germ, green tea, black tea, carrots, all dark green, leafy vegetables, and all dark orange vegetables contain antioxidants. Antioxidants are shown to be preventive agents against cancer and heart disease, especially **atherosclerosis.** [14]

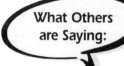

What Others are Saying:

Julian Whitaker, M.D.: Antioxidants like vitamin E, beta-carotene, and **selenium** have also been shown to reduce your risk of heart disease and other degenerative diseases, including cancer and **cataracts**. Can Budweiser do this?[15]

Anne and David Frähm: The carrot is the king of the "cabbage patch" when it comes to waging war on cancer. It is high in beta-carotene, a plant form of vitamin A.[16]

PEPPERS FIGHT CANCER

Research done in Mexico on the effectiveness of the antioxidant **carotenoids** beta-carotene and **xanthophylls** shows that they were able to reduce the **mutagenic** and **carcinogenic** properties of various known mutagens that they introduced. They used extracts of bell peppers, poblano peppers, serrano peppers, and jalapeño peppers, all readily available in most supermarkets—fresh, dried, or in cans.[17]

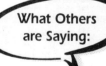

What Others are Saying:

Kenneth Cooper, M.D.: Beta-carotene, which is transformed into vitamin A after it enters the body, is part of the "carotenoid" family of nutrients. Their pigments are the source of the yellow, orange, and green colors in certain vegetables and fruits like carrots, cantaloupe, sweet potatoes, spinach, collard greens, and kale. High blood serum levels of beta-carotene have been linked to lower risk of cataracts, heart disease, and cancers such as rectal cancer, **melanoma**, and bladder cancer. The best way to take beta-carotene into your body is through foods high in this nutrient.[18]

SMOKING DESTROYS ANTIOXIDANTS

Smoking cigarettes, cigars, or pipes, or inhaling secondhand smoke can deplete your body of vitamin C and beta-carotene. This is why it is very important for smokers to eat a lot of deeply colored vegetables, preferably raw, every day. Obviously, it would be better to stop smoking or to stop going to places where people smoke, but that might not always be an option for people.

Julian Whitaker, M.D.: A smoker inhales high levels of free radicals which deplete key antioxidant nutrients like vitamin C and beta-carotene.[19]

DAILY. BREAD

DARK-COLORED VEGETABLES
*Eat as many dark-colored vegetables
as you can each day.*

Colored Vegetables

Dark-colored vegetables have the highest amounts of phytochemicals, especially beta-carotene. Winter squash generally have very dark-colored flesh and are excellent sources for beta-carotene. They are wonderful to have as a basic winter food. Isn't it interesting how the very foods that can be stored and used over the winter are the same foods that contain the precious nutrients you need to be healthy during the winter?

Cheryl Townsley: The more intense the color of the vegetable, the higher the nutrient level.[20]

WINTER SQUASH

Eating winter squash like turban, gold nugget, kabocha, hubbard, butternut, or acorn can increase your resistance to winter colds and the flu. Kids love eating baked squash with a little salt and pepper and butter or olive oil on it. They especially love eating puréed winter squash when it is disguised as pumpkin pie or molasses and honey muffins. Baked squash can also be used as a thickener in soups, stews, and gravies if your family finds squash unacceptable as a vegetable on their plates.

I like to bake a squash in the oven and freeze the mashed or puréed pulp in the amounts I need for my favorite recipes.

BROCCOLI FOR BREAKFAST . . . WHY NOT?

"Broccoli for breakfast" was the headline of an article that appeared in Toronto's *Globe and Mail* newspaper in 1978. It was an interview with me! Yes, I did eat broccoli for breakfast, and I still do. Had some just yesterday. Breakfast is a great time to eat veg-

What Others
are Saying:

NUTRITIONAL FACT

The darker or brighter colored a vegetable is, the better it is for you.

NUTRITIONAL FACT

Beta-carotene, vegetable-source vitamin A, is essential for the health of **mucous membranes**. It counters the effects of aging and air pollution.

What Others
are Saying:

From The Kitchen

mucous membranes:
lining inside your mouth, nose, intestines, anus, and vagina

Something to Ponder

etables. I often eat steamed veggies for breakfast with a boiled egg. Sometimes I put cheese, leftover meat, or even tofu in with the veggies. I especially love potato, carrot, squash, broccoli, green peas, green beans, beets and beet tops, mustard greens, and any combination of these vegetables. When they are steamed, I add some fresh parsley or cilantro, pressed garlic, chopped onion, cumin, butter and/or olive oil, and salt and pepper. I actually mash it all up with a fork and eat it with a spoon. It is delicious! Often I add vegetables to oatmeal while it is cooking and add the fresh parsley at the end. This is more like the kind of food they ate in Bible times.

Often a typical breakfast in Bible times would consist of dark whole grain bread, olives, fresh or dried figs or raisins, cheese—sort of like the feta we have now, or a pressed cottage cheese or cream cheese—cucumbers, garlic, onions, and perhaps parsley or romaine lettuce. A meal like this will give you a really great start to the day without any sugar highs or letdowns.

> **Numbers 11:5** We remember the fish we ate in Egypt at no cost—also the cucumbers, melons, leeks, onions, and garlic.

Repeating Vegetables

All the vegetables the Israelites longed for, in Numbers 11:5, are the ones we call the "repeating" vegetables. Many people find the taste of these vegetables coming up, hence repeating, in the gas released from the stomach for several hours after eating. Cabbage, broccoli, and green peppers are generally in this list, as well as the cucumbers, onion, and garlic mentioned (see Illustration #12, page 59). Guess what? It isn't the vegetables' fault! If you chew each mouthful really well and allow your stomach to have the necessary digestive enzymes by reducing your stress level and, perhaps, taking a digestive enzyme, you will not experience this repeating from these vegetables. It is very important to eat slowly and chew well when eating any food; and these vegetables are no exception. Why do you think God gave us teeth, if not to use them when we eat?

Illustration #12

*Garlic, Leeks, and Onions—
These three vegetables make
up part of the family of
onions—the lily family.*

Cucumbers

Cucumbers have a very high-water content and are eaten often, along with melons, in dry, hot areas. Eating cucumbers is a great way to keep from getting dehydrated in the desert. Cucumbers also contain calcium, iron, phosphorus, potassium, magnesium, vitamin A, and folate as well as **trace** amounts of zinc, copper, and the B vitamins.

trace: very little, as in just a trace

Leeks, Onions, And Garlic

Leeks, onions, and garlic come from the same family. They have been used around the world for thousands of years for healing and for eating, and they make many ethnic dishes taste great.

Reginald Cherry, M.D.: Garlic has demonstrated multiple benefits. It fights bacteria, strengthens the immune system, raises the good (HDL) cholesterol, and has **potent** cancer-fighting effects.[21]

**What Others
are Saying:**

potent: very strong

Francisco Contreras, M.D.: Garlic is known to have therapeutical value in a wide variety of diseases. From an antibiotic (as potent as penicillin or tetracycline), anti-micotic (fungus), anti-viral, to cancer killing powers.[22]

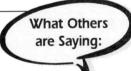

ON Target:
Eating garlic daily

OFF Target:
*Using antibiotics
needlessly*

DAILY · BREAD

GARLIC
Include garlic and onions in your diet daily.

WHAT ABOUT THE SMELL?

Many people can eat raw garlic and have no body odor of garlic. The smell of garlic and onions is "set" by heat and removed by cold. When you peel, cut, or chop garlic or onions, always wash off everything—your hands, knife, and cutting board—with cold water, and they will not smell. If you wash off with hot water you will smell like garlic or onions for several hours, or even days afterwards. Eating garlic that has been heated during cooking will cause a body odor of garlic. This is why French, Italian, and other garlic-spiced cooking is known for causing the garlic odor.

Raw garlic in salad dressings or on bread generally will not give that garlic after-odor. If you want to take garlic supplements, you will want a garlic extract that is not oil-based, since heat is used to extract oils. The aged garlic extract, Kyolic®, has been proven to promote health and have no odor. One capsule or tablet is equivalent to an entire head of garlic, and yet, there is no body or breath odor.

NUTRITIONAL FACT

Garlic can be rubbed on blemished skin or an open cut to aid healing.

What Others are Saying:

Rex Russell, M.D.: Garlic cloves are often used successfully to protect people from infections. It is helpful in treating asthma, diabetes, and high blood pressure. It stimulates the immune system and is also a pain killer. Population studies indicate an inverse relationship between the amount of garlic consumed and the number of cancer deaths in a given population.[23]

STOP THAT BACTERIA!

Research done in India in 1997 and published in the U.S. in 1998 indicated that garlic inhibited the following bacteria: *Staphylococcus aureus, Salmonella typhi, Escherichia coli,* and *Listeria monocytogenes.* Garlic is the most effective against *E. coli.*[24] Garlic is a good preventative for people who live or work in areas where these bacteria might be present. Have you ever noticed that places where outbreaks of bacteria-related illnesses occur are almost always places where garlic is not on the menu and where the people who eat or live there don't eat garlic? When was the last time you heard of a nursing home serving garlic or handing out aged garlic extract tablets or capsules? When was the last time you ate garlic in a fast food burger place?

GARLIC: IS IT USEFUL FOR HEALTH?

There has been a lot of publicity about garlic being useless. Research was done using garlic powder, like from your kitchen, and garlic oil in a laboratory. The research indicated that these two forms of garlic did not reduce cholesterol or high blood pressure.[25] This is no surprise! Garlic has to be vital and alive to do its job! Crushed raw garlic put into capsules did significantly lower total serum cholesterol and **triglycerides** and increased the **HDL-cholesterol** activity. All good results.[26]

triglycerides: the form in which fat is stored in your body

HDL-cholesterol: high density lipoprotein, the "good" cholesterol

AGED GARLIC EXTRACT

Most of the really great garlic research has been done using aged garlic extract. A recent study done at East Carolina University School of Medicine in Greenville, North Carolina, concluded that aged garlic extract reduced **platelet adhesion** by 30 percent in men with high cholesterol.[27] Aged garlic extract also had a positive effect on their blood **lipids** and blood pressure. A recent study published in the journal *Atherosclerosis* indicated that the aged garlic extract Kyolic® provided protection against the onset of atherosclerosis.[28]

platelet adhesion: clumping together of the smallest particles in the blood

lipid: a type of blood fat not soluble in water

Bobbing For ~~Apples~~ Vegetables

There are many kinds of sea vegetables in common use. The most common is **dulse**. It is a reddish-brown color and is often sold dried in seafood markets. Generally it comes from Maine or New Brunswick, where many people eat it fresh or dried as a high mineral snack. It is very salty and should not be consumed regularly, especially if you have high blood pressure or a heart condition. The nutrients in dulse are the minerals iodine, phosphorus, bromine, rubidium, manganese, titanium, along with trace minerals, and vitamins B_6, B_{12}, C, and E.

dulse: a coarse edible red seaweed

Kelp Or Kombu?

Deep sea kelp, which is called kombu in oriental markets, is the highest in iodine and potassium. Kelp has over 200 times more potassium than sodium. That is why kelp powder is often added to salt substitutes to give the salty taste with less sodium than table salt. It also contains **alginates** which can remove toxins from your body like lead, mercury, and cadmium, and some kinds of environmental pollutants. Because kelp is so high in iodine, many people take kelp tablets to stimulate their thyroid gland. This is not a good idea unless you are directed to do so by your health

alginates: the main, slippery part of sea weed that grabs onto toxins and expels them from the body

From The Kitchen

care practitioner, because taking kelp tablets in large doses can often make your thyroid **atrophy**.

Sea Vegetables In Daily Life

Sea vegetables are great to add to many foods such as soups, stews, or cereals. I often add them to cooking grains or beans to aid digestion. Rehydrated sea vegetables can be added to salads or can make a salad on their own as they do in oriental cuisine.

You Decide

How would you rather spend your money: 60¢ for a candy bar that robs your body of calcium, B vitamins, and stimulates your adrenal glands and keeps you wired? Or 60¢ for a few baby carrots, ¼ of a red pepper, and several slices of cucumber, which would give you vitamin C, beta-carotene, potassium, calcium, and magnesium? It's up to you. God gave you a wide variety of vegetables that contain all the nutrients you need to be healthy. Do you choose health?

Study Questions

1. Why was Daniel chosen to be in the King's service?
2. What special favor did Daniel request and why?
3. What part of your diet should be vegetables?
4. Is the color of vegetables important and why?
5. Which vegetables are especially good for your health?
6. Name at least five diseases or conditions that can be improved or prevented by eating vegetables.
7. Name the best ways to get children to eat vegetables.
8. Which vegetables did the Israelites long for in the desert, and why are they healthy for you?

CHAPTER WRAP-UP

- Daniel and his friends refused to eat the king's food and asked for their regular meals, which consisted of vegetables. It also included grains, nuts, seeds, and beans but excluded strong drink and fatty meats. (Daniel 1:3–20)
- God created a wide variety of vegetables for all people.
- Vegetables should comprise the largest group of foods you eat each day.

- Vegetables contain many health-giving properties such as fiber, vitamins, minerals, and antioxidants.

- God gave man a really easy way to tell which vegetables were good to eat by giving the deepest colors to the ones that were essential for health and vitality.

- Even when God was providing food for the Israelites, they longed for their health foods: cucumbers, leeks, onions, and garlic. (Numbers 11:5)

5 SOLOMON'S GARDEN

CHAPTER HIGHLIGHTS

- Nuts and Seeds
- Fruits
- Olives

Let's Get Started

Nuts, seeds, and fruits are the basic crops Solomon grew in his luxurious garden. All of them are amazingly portable and convenient nutrition. Isn't it also amazing that God created these essential foods to taste great! Walnuts are a marvelous Bible food that lowers cholesterol, and they were grown in Solomon's garden. In the mid-1990s grape seeds and skins became the hottest health food supplement of the day. They are filled with **proanthocyanidins**, antioxidants for health, anti-aging, and vitality. Olives—they are fruits you know—are one of the best sources of monounsaturated fatty acids, and they have a large section of the Mediterranean Food Pyramid. Olives and grapes are the health foods of the 21st century, just as they were in Bible times. **Flaxseeds** are not mentioned in the Bible, but flax plants are. They are one of the best sources of omega-3 essential fatty acids.

proanthocyanidin: antioxidant found in grape seeds and skins and in pine bark

flaxseeds: seeds of a plant grown for making linen from the fibrous stems

> **Song of Songs 6:11** I went down to the grove of nut trees to look at the new growth in the valley . . .

Whadduh You, Nuts!

The nuts on Solomon's trees are in the same category as beans and other legumes in the Mediterranean Diet Pyramid (see Illustration #13, page 66). See Chapter 3 for more information about the protein in nuts and seeds. They can be eaten daily along with dried beans and peas. Nuts and seeds also can team up with the proteins of grains and/or beans to make complete protein, which is necessary for optimum health.

KEY POINT

The only nuts that are bad for you are roasted and salted ones, or ones that are rancid due to improper storage.

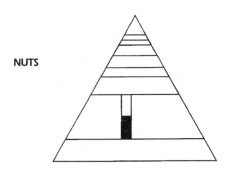

NUTS

Walnuts, almonds, and pistachios were the most common nuts grown in Bible lands, and you can be sure they were in Solomon's garden.

LDL-cholesterol: low
density lipoprotein, the
bad cholesterol

HDL-cholesterol: high
density lipoprotein, the
good cholesterol

Rex Russell, M.D.: Nuts are high in fat and in total caloric content. They have a poor reputation these days because of the fad that fat is always bad.[1]

Walnuts are the nuts that Solomon went down to his garden to see, according to F. Nigel Hepper in the *Baker Encyclopedia of Bible Plants.*

Walnuts Are Healthful

Walnuts have long been used in cookies, sweet rolls, and candies. Today's research indicates that walnuts are useful as part of a low-fat diet, to reduce **LDL-cholesterol** and increase **HDL-cholesterol.**[2]

According to the Bible Diet, we should eat nuts every day, particularly walnuts and almonds, because of their ability to lower our "bad" cholesterol. In addition, nuts are so filling that you may find you lose your desire for high-fat junk foods and large portions.

Anne and David Frähm: Almonds, Brazil nuts, cashews, hazelnuts, peanuts, pecan, pine nuts, pistachios, pumpkin seeds, squash seeds, sunflower seeds, [and] walnuts [are] powerfully nutritious. Rich source of carbohydrate, protein, fiber, B vitamins, and minerals—calcium, iron, phosphorus, and potassium.[3]

> **Genesis 43:11** Then their father Israel said to them, "If it must be, then do this: Put some of the best products of the land in your bags and take them down to the man as a gift—a little balm and a little honey, some spices and myrrh, some pistachio nuts and almonds."

☞ **GO TO:**

Genesis 42–50 (famine)

Exodus 37:19, 20;
Numbers 17:1–9
(almonds)

THE BEST PRODUCTS OF THE LAND

When Jacob wanted to impress Joseph, the Egyptian ruler, he sent pistachio nuts and almonds. Pistachio nuts didn't grow in Egypt, so it was a very special gift. There was a <u>famine</u> in the land of Canaan where they lived and not in Egypt, so they went to Egypt to ask to buy grains.

SCIENTISTS WORK WITH ALMONDS AND WALNUTS

Almonds and walnuts have both been used in research to lower LDL cholesterol and total cholesterol, and to preserve higher levels of HDL cholesterol.[4] Adding <u>almonds</u> and/or walnuts to your diet is very helpful for reducing blood fats.

scleroderma: a disease characterized by hardening of the skin and organs

unsaturated fatty acids: vegetable fats that are liquid at room temperature

Reginald Cherry, M.D.: Almonds (10 per day) or walnuts (10 per day) rank at the top of the list of acceptable nuts in the Mediterranean Diet.[5]

What Others are Saying:

Lots Of Nutrients In Nuts

Nuts contain vitamin E, fiber, and essential fatty acids. Essential fatty acids (EFAs) are very useful for smooth skin and shiny healthy hair. Essential fatty acids are also called vitamin F. Vitamin F has been used for years to reverse an overactive thyroid, to help reverse some of the symptoms of **scleroderma**, to improve immune function, and to improve digestion. The fatty acids found in nuts are **unsaturated fatty acids** and **polyunsaturated fatty acids**, both known to be healthful.

polyunsaturated fatty acids: fat found in corn, soybean, safflower, and some fish oils; may help to reduce cholesterol

chronic fatigue syndrome: an illness that extends over a long period of time, extreme fatigue being one of the many symptoms

Essential Fatty Acids For Health

In a study done in the early 1990s EFAs were used to recover people with **chronic fatigue syndrome** with a 90 percent success rate.[6] EFAs have also been shown to be of use during pregnancy for the development of fetuses and for the prevention of premature births.[7] Essential fatty acids were used with patients with **chronic gastrointestinal disorders** such as **Crohn's disease** and good response was obtained.[8] Essential fatty acid deficiencies have also been implicated in **cystic fibrosis, schizophrenia**, and the tendency to **pressure ulcers**. Essential fatty acids have been shown

chronic gastrointestinal disorders: diseases of the intestines, stomach, mouth, and anus

Crohn's disease: ulceration and inflammation of the digestive system

to increase calcium absorption by preventing the loss of calcium in urine and increasing the depositing of calcium in bones, preventing **osteoporosis**.[9]

DAILY BREAD

NUTS
Have eight to ten nuts a day.

What Others are Saying:

Rex Russell, M.D.: The nut has a lot of the **fat-soluble vitamins** and essential fatty acids that repair damaged cells in the body.[10]

Brazil Nuts For Health

Brazil nuts are high in the mineral selenium. A selenium deficiency can often cause symptoms that are closely related to some kinds of depression. I had a friend who got off a prescription drug for depression, with her doctor's help, by eating Brazil nuts every day. She had a selenium "deficiency"–induced depression!

What Others are Saying:

Reginald Cherry, M.D.: Brazil nuts are high in selenium and can elevate mood. Sunflower seeds and oat bran are also high in selenium.[11]

SELENIUM AND OVARIAN CANCER

Selenium supplementation is being recommended to women with ovarian cancer who are undergoing chemotherapy, to improve their recovery rate.[12] It seems that Brazil nuts and sunflower seeds are useful for more than just elevating mood.

WARNING

Nuts and seeds can go rancid easily, making them dangerous for your health. Purchase nuts or seeds in the shell for your protection. Keep them in the refrigerator or freezer once they are shelled. Many health food stores keep their nuts and seeds refrigerated for this very reason. So be sure to look for nuts and seeds that have been kept refrigerated.

Cheryl Townsley: Seeds, along with nuts, do contain oil. If they are fresh and properly stored, the natural oils will not turn rancid. Buy nuts and seeds in whole form (versus chopped) for longer freshness. Store in the refrigerator or freezer.[13]

Nuts Make Great Snacks

Nuts make great snacks. They can be easily carried in your purse or briefcase. They go well in school lunches. Nuts are a good source of protein and the essential fatty acids so necessary for growth and health. When well chewed, they can relieve the fatigue of low blood sugar and give you a boost of energy as an afternoon snack.

NUT BUTTER

Nut butters have been considered "kid food" for as long as I can remember. I hardly ever ate peanut butter, because I didn't like the way it stuck to my mouth. Then, when I first began to eat natural nut butters as an adult, I was amazed that they didn't stick to my mouth. A lettuce and nut butter sandwich on whole grain bread is a really nutritious lunch or snack for children and adults. I like a sandwich of Maranatha's almond butter and leaf or bibb lettuce on whole wheat bread.

Cheryl Townsley: Nut butters should not contain hydrogenated fats, added sugar, or chemicals. Almond butter is a good replacement for peanut butter. It is lower in fat, easier to digest, and higher in calcium than peanut butter.[14]

> **Genesis 3:18** . . . and you will eat the plants of the field.

Nothing Seedy About This

Seeds grow on plants in the field or in gardens. God gave them to you for your health. All seeds have unsaturated fatty acids, which are also known as vitamin F. Pumpkin seeds are known for their zinc content, which is useful for men's problems and for general healing for everyone. Low levels of zinc in your body signal that you are undernourished and likely to have a **suppressed** immune system. It may mean you get more colds and bouts of the flu than other people or that you tire more easily, or just that you are more susceptible to many diseases. Zinc and vitamin C **lozenges** have become popular for helping with colds and sore throats, and there is research showing that they both work and don't work, so it's up to you if you want to use them. Sunflower seeds are high in cal-

What Others are Saying:

ON Target:
Natural nut butter without sugar or fillers

OFF Target:
Commercial nut butters with sugar, salt, and fillers added

What Others are Saying:

ON Target:
Snacks of nuts, seeds, and fruit

OFF Target:
Nutrientless junk food as snacks

suppressed: subdued, lowered

lozenges: medicated discs that you suck on

cium and magnesium, and are very good for someone who wants to add these nutrients to their diet.

What Others are Saying:

Cheryl Townsley: Seeds help feed the brain and reproductive system.[15]

> **Proverbs 31:13** She selects wool and flax and works with eager hands.

Flaxseeds

Flaxseeds are the latest health food, and one of the oldest seeds referred to in the Bible. The Bible mentions the growing of flax for making linen. The stems were spun into threads that were woven into cloth. Some of the finest cloth in the Bible comes from flaxseeds, and the finest health food comes from flaxseeds, too. Flaxseeds grown for oilseed use (rather than for the flax fiber made into linen) contain omega-3 fatty acids.

TWO KINDS OF FIBER

From The Kitchen

soluble fiber: *fiber that can be easily dissolved*

insoluble fiber: *fiber that is incapable of being dissolved*

mucilage: *one of the seven basic kinds of fiber found in food*

colon: *large intestine*

Flaxseeds contain both **soluble** and **insoluble fiber**. The soluble fiber in flaxseed is **mucilage**, a thick sticky substance. It is similar to the soluble fibers in fruit pectin, oat bran, or mustard seed. A lot of people make a morning "tea" of flaxseeds and boiling water to supply this mucilaginous fiber to their diets and prevent constipation. When I was at a health spa, once, we were awakened each morning with a steaming cup of flaxseed and lemon juice tea.

The insoluble fiber in flaxseeds is similar to wheat bran and is helpful for regulating bowel movements. This part of flaxseed contains lignan and cellulose which hold water in the stool allowing it to move through the **colon** more quickly.

The National Cancer Institute included flaxseeds in a study of foods that have cancer-fighting ability. The other foods were garlic, licorice root, vegetables from the parsnip family, citrus fruits, and soybeans. All were found beneficial to fighting cancers.

What Others are Saying:

Rex Russell, M.D.: Recent studies show that flaxseed causes some breast cancers to shrink. It also lowers the incidence of breast cancer among women who are more susceptible.[16]

EATING FLAXSEEDS

Flaxseeds can be added whole to baked goods. There are many commercial breads that contain whole flaxseeds. Just remember to chew them well for the most benefit. They can also be freshly ground in a seed mill or blender and used in baked goods, on cereals, or in protein shakes. Many companies produce flaxseeds already ground and nitrogen sealed to preserve freshness. Keep ground flaxseeds in the refrigerator or freezer.

Flaxseed bread is a great way to add these wonderful seeds to your diet. Some Roman Meal™ breads and cereals have flaxseeds in them.

Pamela Smith: Flaxseed has the highest content of vitamin E of any known seed. It excels in complete **bulk fiber**, is easy to digest, is high in complete protein, and rich in minerals and oil.[17]

What Others are Saying:

bulk fiber: fiber that aids in digestion by providing bulk in the intestines

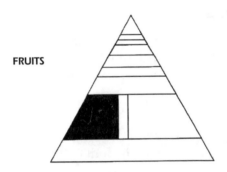

FRUITS

Illustration #14

The Fruit Section—The darkened section of this pyramid represents how much of your diet should be devoted to fruit.

Fruit In The Mediterranean Diet

Fruits are so important in the Bible or Mediterranean Diet that they have their own section in the food pyramid (see Illustration #14, this page). Some form of <u>fruit</u> should be eaten daily for really vibrant health. There are many kinds of fruits. Some grow on vines like grapes and kiwi. Some grow on bushes like blueberries, raspberries, gooseberries, currants, and huckleberries. Some grow on the ground like strawberries. And still others grow on trees like apples, pears, oranges, bananas, mangoes, grapefruit, avocados, apricots, peaches, and plums, just to mention a few. With so many choices, it should be easy to select some fruit each day.

☞ **GO TO:**

Isaiah 16:9, 10 (fruit)

NUTRITIONAL FACT

Avocadoes, tomatoes, and olives are all fruits.

Illustration #15

Basket of Fruit—Any fruit a
day, not just apples, can keep
the doctor away

This Won't Hurt A Bit

We have all heard the expression, "An apple a day keeps the doctor away," but do we really believe it? Most people don't take it seriously enough to have fruit every week let alone daily (see Illustration #15, this page).

> **Isaiah 5:2** In that day the Branch of the Lord will be beautiful and glorious, and the fruit of the land will be the pride and glory of the survivors in Israel.

**What Others
are Saying:**

cerebrovascular:
pertaining to the blood
vessels supplying the
brain

mortality: death rate

Jim Shriner: Fruit in the morning is a good colon cleanser, so eat some every morning.[18]

FRUIT AND CEREBROVASCULAR DISEASE

A 20-year study of diet, lifestyle, and **cerebrovascular** disease (CVD) in Spain indicated that as the general public became more aware of the need to eat more fruits and fish and decrease wine consumption, the rates of CVD decreased measurably. In people over 45 years of age the decline in **mortality** by CVD decreased by 22 percent.[19] Here is an example of the saying that some fruit a day keeps the undertaker away, not just the doctor.

> **Song of Songs 2:5** Strengthen me with raisins, refresh me with apples, for I am faint with love.

Grapes Or Raisins?

Grapes grow on vines in a vineyard. When grapes are dried in the sun, or any other way, they are called raisins. Raisins are perfect for carrying around as a fruit snack while traveling, working, or going to school. Grapes, raisins, and apples are high in fiber and natural sugars and can provide an energy boost anytime, not just when you are "faint with love."

Reginald Cherry, M.D.: Grapes contain ellagic acid. This compound blocks enzymes that are necessary for cancer to grow, thus slowing the growth of tumors. Grapes also contain compounds that can prevent blood clots. Another substance in grape skins (resveratrol) prevents the deposit of cholesterol in arteries.[20]

GRAPES ARE GREAT!

Scientists are working to extract **resveratrol** from grapes to use as an anticancer agent.[21] This could be very promising for those people who have cancer in their family history. There are many "health" diets that prescribe drinking grape juice or eating grapes as part of the diet. Grapes contain small amounts of protein and fiber, vitamins A and C, calcium and magnesium, phosphorus, and very small amounts of zinc, manganese, iron, and copper. One cup of grapes has about 6 **mcg** of **folic acid**, a nutrient essential for pregnant women. Raisins have high amounts of iron in them because they are concentrated. The best way to find out how much iron you need is to consult a doctor who practices natural medicine.

> **Matthew 7:16** By their fruit you will recognize them. Do people pick grapes from thorn bushes, or figs from thistles?

Figs Are Fantastic!

Figs are high in fiber; this makes them healthful for preventing cancers of all kinds. So much research is being published these days that shows we all need to eat more fruits than we do, it is impossible to include it all here. Eating more fruits, especially high fiber ones, can lower cholesterol, reduce blood pressure, and prevent many different types of cancers, including breast cancer.

☞ **GO TO:**

Isaiah 5:2, 4;
    Isaiah 18: 5 (grapes)

I Chronicles 12:40
    (raisins)

What Others are Saying:

ON Target:
Eating fruit more and wine less

OFF Target:
Drinking wine instead of grape juice

resveratrol: *a chemopreventive agent found in grapes and other food*

mcg: *micrograms, a small unit of measure*

folic acid: *if begun before pregnancy, 400 mcg a day in the diet of a pregnant woman can prevent neural tube birth defects,*

mg: *milligram*

☞ **GO TO:**

Luke 21:29 (figs)

pharyngeal cancer: *cancer of the passageway extending from the nose to the voice box*

flavonoids: *crystalline compounds found in plants*

anti-atherosclerotic: *"against atherosclerosis," the most common type of hardening of the arteries*

In one study it was shown that low fruit and vegetable intake and high meat intake were directly responsible for **pharyngeal cancer**.[22] Fruits and other plant materials high in **flavonoids** are **anti-atherosclerotic** components of your diet.[23]

> **I Chronicles 12:40** Also, their neighbors from as far away as Issachar, Zebulun and Naphtali came bringing food on donkeys, camels, mules and oxen. There were plentiful supplies of flour, fig cakes, raisin cakes, wine, oil, cattle and sheep, for there was joy in Israel.

CAKE OF FIGS OR RAISINS

Figs and raisins have been pressed into cakes or strung to dry since before Bible times. We still see figs being sold in this way in grocery stores, especially in Italian and Greek markets. These cakes mentioned in the Bible were not the kind of cakes we think of as a dessert. Just like you can have a cake of soap, which is a pressed form of soap, you can also have a cake of figs or raisins.

Other Fruits In Health News

cognitive behavioral deficits: *memory and understanding ability that fades with age*

incontinence: *involuntary loss of urine*

kegel: *exercises that work the muscles used in urination*

carcinogens: *agents capable of producing cancerous changes in body tissues*

Of all the fruits we know about, the strawberry is getting the most press. Research indicates it is responsible for retarding age-related **cognitive behavioral deficits**. Strawberries were tested along with spinach and vitamin E supplementation; they all helped in reversing the decline of central nervous system (CNS) functioning.[24] This means that if you are concerned about losing your thinking ability or nerve functions, you will want to make sure that you eat strawberries and spinach on a regular basis. No matter how much they cost in the store, doing without them will cost more. Strawberries are even touted for having a flavonoid that is useful in preventing breast cancer.

Cranberries are useful for reversing bladder infections. Many nursing homes recognize this about cranberries and on a regular basis give the juice to people prone to bladder infections.

Black cherry juice is known to reverse **incontinence** in women, especially when **kegel** exercises are done as well.

What Others are Saying:

Francisco Contreras, M.D.: Tomatoes, strawberries, pineapple and dried chili contain the phytochemicals p-coumaric acid and chlorogenic acid that block the marriage of molecules that form **carcinogens**.[25]

Pamela Smith: Kegels are a miracle exercise and easy to do. . . . aim for ten to twenty-five repetitions two or three times a day. To do Kegels, firmly tense the muscles as if you are stopping the flow of urine. Hold for as long as you can, working up to eight to ten seconds, then slowly release the muscles and relax.[26]

Francisco Contreras, M.D.: Citrus fruits and blackberries contain flavonoids and prevent **carcinogenic hormones** from being introduced into the cells.[27]

carcinogenic hormones: hormones that cause cancer

Tomatoes Are Fruits Too

Tomatoes are really fruits, even though we consider them to be vegetables. Eating tomatoes weekly can help reverse **prostate** problems for men. They are high in lycopene, an antioxidant, as well as the provitamin A compounds beta-carotene and gamma-carotene.

prostate: a male gland at the base of the bladder

A Nutritional Sweetness

Snacks of fruit are very healthful and taste good too. When you or your children want a sweet snack, consider eating a piece of fresh fruit instead of candy, cakes, or cookies. It will increase your level of health and reverse the downward spiral of poor health that eating junk foods causes.

> Would you rather spend 60 cents on a candy bar that robs your body of calcium and damages your teeth, or an apple or pear that can bring a sparkle to your eyes and energy and health to your body?

Something to Ponder

T. D. Jakes: Snacks can be any fat-free food or a fruit such as a banana, pear, apple, etc.[28]

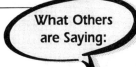

Rex Russell, M.D.: Dried fruit has a high concentration of minerals (iron, copper, potassium), fiber, and beta-carotene.[29]

Olives: The Green And Black Fruits

Yes, olives are really fruits; even in Bible times they were considered fruits. Olives and olive oil are so important in the Bible Diet that they have their own section in the food pyramid (see Illustration #16, page 76). Olives and/or olive oil should be eaten daily for the best of health.

Illustration #16

The Olive Oil Section—The
darkened section of this
pyramid represents how
much of your diet should be
devoted to olive oil.

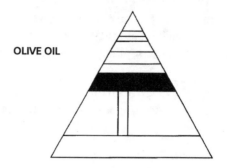

OLIVE OIL

> **Deuteronomy 28:40** You will have olive trees through-
> out your country but you will not use the oil, because
> the olives will drop off.

What A Curse!

*You will have olive trees whose fruit drops off before being harvested
and pressed into oil*, was among the curses given in Deuteronomy.
This would really be a curse—to see your crop fail before your
eyes (see Illustration #17, page 77).

The Green And Black Of It

brine: *salt water that is
used to preserve many
fruits and vegetables*

Green olives are really the unripe fruit and the black ones are
ripe, that is the difference between the two kinds. Many olives are
cured in salt **brine**, oil, or both as a way to preserve them. Some
olives are cured with spices, lemon peel, or hot peppers. Olives
are aged for different lengths of time so that the fresher ones have
a milder taste and the aged ones are saltier and more concentrated in taste.

Olives contain a high amount of salt. Always wash olives
off with water before eating them.

The Good Fats

atherogenetic: *having to
do with the arteries*

Olives contain monounsaturated fatty acids which have been
shown to protect the LDL from being broken down into harmful
components. This has been correlated with lowered rates of coronary heart disease (CHD), **atherogenetic** disease, and the prevention of cardiovascular diseases.[30]

Rex Russell, M.D.: . . . olive oil is very healthful. It contains anticancer properties, leads to more efficient **cardiac** contractions and does not lead to **vascular disease**. Olive oil apparently promotes healing of atherosclerotic plaques.[31]

It's The Phenolics That Do It

There are eight different **phenolic** compounds in olives and olive oil that are antibacterial, antifungal, **antimicrobial**, and antiviral. The phenolic compound that proved to be the most effective is oleuropein. This bitter property in olives has been shown to inhibit the growth of many bacteria, including *Escherichia coli, Klebsiella pneumoniae, Aspergillus flavus, Aspergillus parasiticus,* and *Bacillus cereus.*[32] It also delayed the growth of *Staphyloccus aureus, Clostridium botulinum,* and *Samonella enteritidis.*[33] These bacteria and viruses are among the most troublesome and destructive factors known to mankind. They can cause illnesses from simple digestive disturbances to death.

OLIVES DESTROY THE DANGERS OF EATING OUT

Over the last 10 years, many people have had *E. coli* and *Salmonella* poisoning from eating in restaurants or from catered picnics or parties. In most cases, either of these problems might have been avoided if people had consumed olives and olive oil as a regular part of their diets. Because olive oil and garlic are in the Mediterranean diet, most people in the Mediterranean do not get ill from these kinds of agents. If more people would add olive products into their North American diet, there might be less problems here as well.

What Others are Saying:

cardiac: *heart*

vascular disease: *having to do with the circulatory system*

phenolic: *aromatic*

antimicrobial: *against small life forms that cause diseases including parasites*

ON Target:
  Using olive oil for most or all cooking

OFF Target:
  Using animal fats for cooking

NUTRITIONAL FACT

Olives contain compounds that are very healthful.

DAILY BREAD

OLIVES
Eat olives or use olive oil daily.

ON Target:

Adding olives to salads and sandwiches, using olive oil

OFF Target:

Using hydrogenated fats such as shortening and margarine

Deuteronomy 8:8 . . . a land with wheat and barley, vines and fig trees, pomegranates, olive oil and honey, a land where bread will not be scarce and you will lack nothing; a land where the rocks are iron and you can dig copper out of the hills.

Do What God Says

The Israelites went through testing by God in the desert where he took care of them, even though they didn't always like what he brought. God reminded them to praise him and keep his commandments and they would one day see the promised land, a land where everything would be wonderful, where they would never lack anything. There would be the things that Israelites loved most including olive oil. That's how important olive oil is.

What Others are Saying:

Reginald Cherry, M.D.: Olive oil is good for you—it may lower blood fats. Some studies suggest that it may also lower blood pressure.[34]

> **Judges 9:8, 9** One day the trees went to anoint a king for themselves. They said to the olive tree, "Be our king." But the olive tree answered, "Should I give up my oil, by which both gods and men are honored, to hold sway over the trees?"

King Olive Tree

fable: a story about people using nonhuman characters

This **fable** compared the murder of Jotham's family by King Abimelech to the olive trees. In this way Jotham revealed that Abimelech "gave up his oil," or killed his family, so that he could hold sway over all the people of Shechem.

Even though, in this fable, the olive tree refused to be anointed king over the trees, many people think the olive is king of the trees anyway. Olives contain a bitter property that is considered to be the king of all healing materials. This bitter substance is called **oleuropein**. It is in the olive fruit, the olive branches and bark, and in the olive leaves. Olive leaf extract is used currently for healing, especially for getting rid of viruses and parasites.

> **Revelation 22:2, 3** On each side of the river stood the tree of life, bearing twelve crops of fruit, yielding its fruit every month. And the leaves of the tree are for the healing of the nations. No longer will there be any curse.

Olive, The Tree Of Life?

Could olive trees be the tree of life mentioned in Revelation? It certainly seems to have all the properties spoken of. The leaves really could be used to heal the nations because they work against bacteria, viruses, microbes, and parasites. The main health curses we have today are the viral diseases of Herpes I and II and shingles. Olive leaf extract is known to eradicate these viral problems.[35]

Olive Leaves Keep Salt Away

If you are worried about consuming the salt in preserved olives, it might be a good idea to take an olive leaf extract supplement to be sure you are getting the benefits of the olive tree. Olive leaf extract is touted as giving you more energy as well as getting rid of bacteria, molds, viruses, and parasites.

Study Questions

1. What did Solomon grow in his garden? And why are they important for you?
2. Most people have read that eating fat is bad for them, but nuts contain a different fat that is actually good for you. How does this conflict make you feel about eating fat? Name three nuts mentioned in the Bible and what there is about them that makes them healthy enough to include in your diet.
3. Why is it important to eat fruit daily?
4. Which diseases are helped or prevented by fruits? What do you have to do to get the health benefits of these fruits?
5. Which three foods that we think of as vegetables are really fruits? How can you incorporate them into your diet?
6. Which parts of the olive tree are used for health and healing? Do you think that the olive is the tree of life?
7. Name the disease-fighting properties of olives. How is this related to North America and the Mediterranean region?

- Solomon grew nuts and fruits in his garden; both are part of a healthy diet. (Song of Songs 6:11)

- Walnuts, almonds, flaxseeds and other nuts and seeds are rich sources of EFAs (essential fatty acids) that are essential for healthy skin, hair, and arteries.

- Fruits are an important part of your daily diet. They are high in antioxidants and fiber.

- Grapes, figs, dates, strawberries, mulberries, cherries, apricots, melons, and other fruits are filled with minerals and multiple nutrients. They can help to prevent many kinds of cancers. (Genesis 1:11, 12)

- Olives and olive oil contain compounds that are known to be antiviral, antimicrobial, and antibacterial. The Bible mentions them in many places as trade items. People in Bible times used the oil for lamps and for eating and cooking. They also ate the olive itself.

6 MILK AND CURDS

CHAPTER HIGHLIGHTS

- Milk
- Drinking Milk
- Mother's Milk
- Fermented Dairy Products
- Solid Dairy Products

Let's Get Started

Dairy cattle were first domesticated for milk production in 3000 B.C. in Macedonia. In the first century A.D. Virgil wrote *Georgics* in which he is quoted as saying, "Camel's, goat's, and ewe's milk is for humans, cow's milk is for calves."[1] This will give you some idea of how long the battle against cow's milk has been going on! For nearly 2000 years people have said that cow's milk is bad for you, but it is still being served all over the world. There is even research that indicates cow's milk may be good for you. Very seldom do people in the West drink camel's or ewe's milk, but we do drink goat's milk. Let's just examine the facts of milk and dairy products, and you can make your own decision.

> **Genesis 18:8** He then brought some curds and milk and the calf that had been prepared, and set these before them. While they ate, he stood near them under a tree.

Moooooooooo!

Abraham had a feast prepared for three guests who appeared. This is very traditional in the Middle East, even today. He served them <u>meat and milk</u> together because this was also traditional; God had not yet outlawed having milk and meat together. It is supposed that at least two of the three men were really angels, so Abraham would have served the best food he had.

☞ **GO TO:**

Exodus 23:19; 34:26; Deuteronomy 14:21 (meat and milk)

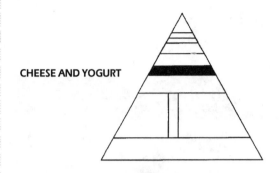

CHEESE AND YOGURT

Low to moderate intake of dairy products contributes to the healthfulness of the Bible Diet (see Illustration #18, this page). Milk is consumed in moderation and almost always in the form of soft or aged cheeses and yogurt. The increase in plant foods like vegetables, fruits, and whole grains, as the major foods in this diet, allows for the moderate consumption of dairy products. In populations where the Mediterranean Diet is followed, chronic-disease rates are low and life expectancies are long.[2]

Dairy products—mostly cheese and yogurt—have their own section in the Mediterranean Diet Pyramid. It is a smallish section compared to the ones for vegetables, fruits, and grains, but it is still sizeable. When you look at the pyramid you can see the amount of dairy products you should have in relation to the other foods—not very much!

**What Others
are Saying:**

Pamela Smith: Skim or low-fat dairy products are excellent low-fat sources of protein.[3]

> **Isaiah 55:1** "Come, all you who are thirsty, come to the waters; and you who have no money, come, buy and eat! Come, buy wine and milk without money and without cost.

Why Milk?

summons: a calling

The Israelites were in exile, and all of Isaiah 55 is a **summons** for them to return to Jerusalem. Wine and milk were used as symbols of abundance, and it was free! What a great place!

Milk is one of the few concentrated sources of a wide variety of nutrients. After all, it is the food for babies. Milk contains protein, calcium, phosphorus, sodium, and twice as much potassium as sodium, magnesium, zinc, copper, vitamin A, small amounts of vitamins B_1, B_2, B_3, B_6, B_{12} and C, as well as B_9 or folate, amino acids, and monounsaturated fatty acids along with saturated fats. (For definitions to these nutritional terms, see the *Glossary of Nutritional and Medical Terms* at the back of the book.) The amino acid **tyrosine** is only found in meat and milk. It is essential for the normal functioning of the **thyroid gland**.[4] This makes dairy products almost essential for vegetarians, unless they are taking an amino acid supplement that contains tyrosine. Tyrosine is also noted for helping to reverse depression.

DAILY BREAD

DAIRY PRODUCTS
Consume dairy products daily.

There are many different kinds of animals that give milk. Cow's and goat's milk are used for drinking and making cheeses and yogurts more than any other kind of milk (see Illustration #19, page 94).

> **Deuteronomy 27:3** Write on them all the words of this law when you have crossed over to enter the land the Lord your God is giving you, a land flowing with <u>milk and honey</u>, just as the Lord, the God of your fathers, promised you.

A Land Flowing With Milk And Honey

There are at least 18 references to *a land flowing with milk and honey* in the Bible, and each time it connotes richness. Why do you think God used milk to give the idea of richness? Perhaps because it is a rich food. It is what we have done to milk that makes it less nutritious than God originally intended. We have over bred cattle, forced them to give more milk than is natural, filled them with antibiotics and other drugs, and even given them hormones to produce more milk. Is it any wonder that so many people are allergic to it or that so many people think milk is not healthful?

God designed milk to be the perfect food for **mammals**. Humans are mammals and give milk for their young.

tyrosine: acts as a mood elevator

thyroid gland: regulates metabolism

NUTRITIONAL FACT

Dairy products are a great source of nutrients, especially calcium and protein.

Something to Ponder

☞ **GO TO:**

Deuteronomy 31:20; Deuteronomy 26:9, 15 (milk and honey)

mammals: animals with spines that have self-regulating body temperature, hair, and females that produce milk

> **Proverbs 27:27** You will have plenty of goats' milk to feed you and your family and to nourish your servant girls.

BAAAAAAAH!

Goat's milk was one of the most common milks used in the Bible Diet and is still popular. It was even given to the servants to drink. Many cheeses, like feta for example, are still made with goat's milk. People who have trouble digesting the protein in cow's milk can often digest the protein in goat's milk without a problem. This is because the protein molecules in cow's milk are larger than the protein molecules in goat's milk. Goats are smaller animals than cows and their milk has the genetic message of growth for a smaller animal, so many people find that it is less stressful on them to use goat's milk products.

Not only is goat's milk easier to digest, but it is also a healing agent. For example, goat's milk has long been held out as a cure for arthritis. In fact, many people with arthritis keep their **inflammation** down by drinking a quart of goat's milk every day. Hildegard of Bingen—an abbess of a convent—used goat's milk for many different cures in the Middle Ages.

inflammation: localized heat, redness, swelling, and pain; the result of irritation, injury, or infection

What Others are Saying:

Hildegard of Bingen: Whoever has an unhealthy lung shall drink enough goat's milk and be cured.[5]

ANOTHER BAAAAAH!

In Bible times, as today, people in the Mediterranean area ate cheese that is made from sheep's milk. Many of the cheeses found in Italian and Greek stores, such as feta and asiago, are made of goat's and/or sheep's milk. Just read the labels on some of the cheeses at your favorite store or gourmet market, and see if you can find sheep and goat cheeses.

☞ **GO TO:**

Judges 5:25 (milk)

> **Judges 4:19** "I'm thirsty," he said. "Please give me some water." She opened a skin of <u>milk</u>, gave him a drink, and covered him up.

Milk: To Drink Or Not To Drink!

In Judges 4:19 when Sisera, a commander of a Canaanite army, was hiding in the tent of Jael, a woman who was not his wife, he asked for water to drink. Jael gave him milk instead. Although the milk may have helped him fall asleep, it was not essential to the story.

Whether or not you should drink milk is still a question after thousands of years. Why is that, you ask? Perhaps it is something that was carried over from the Romans! Or could it be because many people have trouble digesting milk for many different reasons.

Pamela Smith: Although they get a bad rap these days, dairy foods are a treasure chest of protein, calcium, and other body building nutrients.[6]

Milk Allergy

Some people are actually allergic to the protein in milk which causes acute **gastrointestinal** disturbances like cramping, diarrhea, constipation, and even vomiting in some cases. Others get allergic symptoms to milk the same as they would to any other substance that causes allergies. (Some other allergy-causing foods are peanuts, soybeans, chicken, oranges, shrimp, and other seafoods.) In a true, classic case of food allergy, the immune system overreacts, and mistakenly identifies innocent compounds in foods as enemies, like bacteria and viruses. This mistake throws the immune system into a chain reaction of alertness. It produces antibodies called *immunoglobulin E* (or IgE) to launch an attack on the false threats (antigens), releasing **histamines** and other chemicals that provoke symptoms of allergies. Traditionally, only reactions that involve IgE are considered truly allergic reactions.[7]

gastrointestinal: stomach, small and large intestines, colon, rectum, liver, pancreas, gallbladder

histamines: chemicals secreted by the immune system that act on many different body tissues

Lactose Intolerance

Some people don't have the ability to digest the milk sugar called lactose because they are low in lactase, the enzyme needed for milk digestion. This is called being "lactose intolerant." Often, as people age, they lose their ability to produce lactase in their small intestine, and become unable to digest milk. Many more Caucasians are able to digest milk than people of Asian and African ancestry.

> **I Corinthians 9:7** Who tends a flock and does not drink of the milk?

Milk Nay-Sayers

There are those who would have you believe that milk is not good for you, but people have been drinking milk and eating dairy products ever since Bible times. Does this sound like a

dangerous food? There is a very strange situation in our schools all over the United States; soft drinks are being consumed instead of milk. Many soft drink companies are even supporting the schools with equipment and money along with soft drink dispensing machines. Elementary, middle, junior high, and high school students are consuming three to five cans of soft drinks per day. The phosphorus and sugar in soft drinks can rob your body of calcium. In fact, a study published in 1997 indicated that adolescent females were taking in less and less calcium from 1980 to 1992. Since 1992, it has gone down even more.[8] Calcium and magnesium are necessary for the relaxation of muscles.

What Others are Saying:

Anne and David Frähm: In the United States, where we experience high rates of osteoporosis (weakening of the bones due to calcium loss), the recommended daily allowance (RDA) [for calcium] has recently been raised from 800 to 1,200 milligrams.[9]

Other Sources Of Calcium

collard greens and kale: green leafy vegetables

There are other dietary sources of calcium. Salmon, sardines, or mackerel with the bones, dried figs, tofu and other soybeans, turnip greens, **collard greens, kale,** and broccoli are all great sources of calcium. Just the foods kids and teenagers eat a lot of, right? Wrong! Now you can begin to see why God created milk to make into yogurt and cheese. It was so adults and children would get enough calcium and protein in their diets, even if they aren't eating right but use dairy products. It would be much better for growing children (including teenagers), to consume dairy products daily rather than soft drinks. I don't drink milk, but I do eat cheese and yogurt.

What Others are Saying:

Reginald Cherry, M.D.: Calcium can help decrease tumor formation and may decrease uptake of a fatty acid that causes tumor formation (alpha linoleic acid).[10]

Greens And Milk

bioavailable: able to be utilized by your body

boron: a mineral found in dark-green, leafy vegetables

Adelle Davis, the mother of modern nutrition, used to advise people to eat dark-green, leafy vegetables cooked in milk, or sprinkled with lemon juice. She felt that the nutrients were more **bioavailable** this way. She was right! Calcium can be absorbed and utilized in your bones more efficiently if you also eat **boron** with the calcium. This is why so many supplements that say they will prevent or reverse osteoporosis contain boron.

Calcium in Some Common Foods

Milk, low fat, 1 cup	297 mg
Cheddar cheese, ½ cup	476 mg
Cottage cheese, low fat, ½ cup	69 mg
Tofu, ½ cup	130 mg
Chickpeas, ½ cup	38 mg
Fig, dried, one	27 mg
Oatmeal, cooked, ½ cup	107 mg
Almonds, ½ cup	195 mg
Sesame butter, tahini, 1 tablespoon	64 mg
Sardine, with bone, 1 ounce	54 mg
Broccoli, raw, ½ cup	20 mg
Spinach, cooked, 1 cup	245 mg
Lettuce, iceberg, ½ cup	6 mg
Lettuce, leaf, ½ cup	19 mg
Kale, cooked, ½ cup	47 mg

SOURCE: USDA Nutrient Data Laboratory, www.nal.usda.gov/fnic/foodcomp/

NUTRITIONAL FACT

Adults need from 1000 to 1500 mg of calcium daily. Two glasses of milk, a handful of almonds, a serving of cooked oatmeal, and a serving of spinach would do.

Jim Shriner: The latest research has shown that the mineral boron, found in leafy vegetables and most fruits, will help improve your mental agility.[11]

What About Milk And Kidney Stones?

Many people with kidney stones, which are made of calcium, have been advised to stay away from drinking milk. Research done at the Department of Food Science and Human Nutrition at Washington State University with adult subjects who had a tendency to form kidney stones showed that drinking milk did not increase their risk of forming kidney stones.[12] This is excellent news for those with kidney stones or the tendency to get them.

If you have kidney stones and were told to avoid milk, please check with your doctor or specialist before you consume it. Write down the reference for the above study (from the endnotes) and show it to your doctor.

What Others are Saying:

Something to Ponder

WARNING

What Others are Saying:

> **Matthew 21:16** "Do you hear what these children are saying?" they asked him. "Yes," replied Jesus, "have you never read, 'From the lips of children and **infants** you have ordained praise'?"

Breast Milk

Should Children Be Breast-fed?

In many areas of the Mediterranean region children are breast-fed until they are old enough to feed themselves, often until five or six years of age. (Many people do this in North America, too!) All mammals can breast-feed their young. If a mother is healthy, breast-feeding is the best way to nourish her children.

Joe S. McIlhaney, M.D.: Breast-feeding is superior to bottle feeding a newborn baby. Studies show that babies who are breast-fed tend to be healthier, have a lower mortality rate, seem to develop better physically and mentally, and have fewer problems with allergies later in life. In addition, other studies show that babies who nurse have greater **immunity** to **respiratory** and digestive tract disease than babies who do not. Also, babies who nurse seem to have straighter teeth and better mother/child bonding.[13]

What's So Good About Breast Milk?

Breast milk was designed by God to feed children. It contains the exact amount and kind of protein and other nutrients that a growing child needs. It also has the proper amount of bacteria-producing elements that aid in digestion and contribute to the balance of **microflora** in the infant's intestine. Even formula that was supplemented to have the same composition as breast milk did not function as effectively.[14]

Breast Milk Builds Immunity

Breast milk contains nutrients that build up your **immune system** by supporting the growth and health of your **thymus gland** and **spleen**. A healthy thymus gland can prevent infections and many immune and autoimmune diseases such as **AIDS** or cancer. A healthy spleen can help to prevent infections by secreting a substance called tuftsin that stimulates **macrophages** in the liver, spleen, and lymph nodes. Macrophages are essential in protecting against invasion by microorganisms as well as cancer.[15] Mother's milk also contains essential fatty acids that contribute to prostaglandin production that help to build a healthy cardiovascular system in the newborn baby.[16]

Rex Russell, M.D.: Breast-fed children have a special resistance to many childhood diseases. This is because the early milk or colostrum sets up the infant's **immunoreactive** system.[17]

immunoreactive: a properly functioning immune system

NUMBER ONE UNDER THE SUN

The most important thing you can do for your immune system is to avoid contact with the sun on your skin for more than 5 or 10 minutes at a time. In other words, wear protection against the sun even when driving to the store. Use a natural moisturizer that has sun protective factor (SPF). Whatever you do, don't sunbathe! If you are very fair or have an autoimmune disease, you might want to consider buying clothes that are sun protective.

WHAT'S THE SKINNY?

Your skin is the largest immune system organ in your body. It contains **Langerhans cells** which are part of your immune system. Your skin has macrophages the same as your thymus and spleen do. These macrophages in your skin can be damaged by harsh cosmetics, fragrances, chemicals, and sun exposure and other sources of radiation. In order for the macrophages to work, they need to be functioning fully. Use cosmetics that contain **beta-1, 3-D-glucan** on your face and hands, such as Nayad® Essentials. This will fill your macrophage cells with the very nutrient that they need to function effectively and efficiently: beta-1,3-D-glucan. Each macrophage cell, whether in your skin or in the rest of your immune system, has a receptor site for beta-1,3-D-glucan.[18] Without this substance your immune system will not be able to work. Beta-1,3-D-glucan comes from the cell walls of baker's yeast, and in milder amounts from various mushrooms like maitake, shitake, and reishi.

Langerhans cells: immune cells in the skin, named after the discoverer

beta-1,3-D-glucan: extracted from the cell wall of baker's yeast, immune enhancer

Colostrum, The Miracle In Mother's Milk

Colostrum is also called the "first milk" because it is in the first milk secreted after the birth of any mammal. This substance has been highly researched and is shown to contain all the elements necessary for combating viruses, bacteria, yeasts, toxins, **allergens**, and other foreign substances. Colostrum stimulates your body's own immune response so that it is better able to fight off invaders on its own.[19]

allergens: substances that provoke allergic responses

HEALTHY INTESTINES NEED HGF

Colostrum contains **hepatocyte** growth factor (HGF), which is an important factor in the growth of the intestinal cells in new-born babies. HGF helps to prevent intestinal problems during all stages of life, from infancy into old age.[20]

LACTOFERRIN COMES FROM COLOSTRUM

Lactoferrin is one of the hottest substances in the health food industry along with colostrum and beta-1,3-D-glucan. They all stimulate the immune system to function better. Lactoferrin has been shown in studies to be good for diabetics who suffer from infections.[21] Lactoferrin from **bovine** colostrum has antiviral and antifungal properties.[22] Human breast milk contains colostrum and is known to be antiviral and antifungal; therefore, it makes sense that the colostrum of other mammals would have the same properties.

What Others are Saying:

Joe S. McIlhaney, M.D.: I believe that breast-feeding is the best of two choices but that either choice is acceptable.[23]

Remember This . . .

A really good diet while pregnant and breast-feeding can help keep your baby's immune system healthy. If a breast-feeding mother consistently eats a good diet that contains all of the required nutrients for health, her breast milk will provide the best food to keep her baby healthy, strong, and disease resistant.

What If You Were Bottle-Fed?

If you were bottle-fed, as I was, what can you do? The best thing you can do for yourself is to follow a really good diet. Eat a lot of veggies every day, especially dark-green, leafy ones. Stay away from alcohol, tobacco, **MSG** and other food enhancers or additives; don't eat processed foods of any kind; don't eat any rancid fats, **beef tallow**, **suet**, or **lard**; eat a lot of fresh foods (especially fruits and veggies) daily; keep away from animal products with antibiotics or hormones in them; eat only whole grains, and eat them in moderation; make veggies the largest portion of your daily food intake, and you will do a lot for your immune system. You might also want to take proven immune-enhancing supplements like Kyolic® (the odorless garlic extract), colostrum, lactoferrin, or Macroforce™ (a purified beta-1,3-D-glucan immune enhancer), or even the herbs astragalus or echinacea. Exercise daily if you want to keep your immune system working well; just don't overdo it because that will suppress your immune system.

> **Isaiah 7:15** He will eat **curds** and honey when he knows enough to reject the wrong and choose the right.

Fermenting Helps

In order to make curds, milk has to be soured or curdled with acid. You probably have done this by adding lemon or orange juice to milk to watch it form curds. In Bible times and today, many people curdle the milk to keep it longer without having to refrigerate it. The curds were eaten by adults, children drank milk. Adults know right from wrong, or at least they are supposed to. When the Christ Child was to come, as the reference in Isaiah 7:15 points out, he would have baby food—milk—until he became an adult. Then he would be given curds.

In order to store milk and keep it fresh during Bible times, it was fermented so that the fermentation would keep it from going bad so quickly. Many people in the Middle East, even today, do not have refrigeration and rely on using fermented or curded dairy products. When milk is left outside of refrigeration it picks up various yeasts and bacteria in the air. They can sour the milk in an undesirable way and cause health problems. Therefore, specific agents are used to make the milk sour or ferment so that it will not go bad and cause health problems. Many dairy products are made of fermented cow's or goat's milk. Yogurt, kefir, buttermilk, cottage cheese, and other cheeses, as well as most butter, are all made from fermented milk.

curds: solid pieces, formed when milk protein is **curdled** with acid and then heated.

curdle: to "curd" or to form curds

ON Target:
 Breast-feeding your baby

OFF Target:
 Worrying about whether you were breast-fed instead of following a good diet

---

Maureen Salaman: The butter [according to the King James Version—New International Version uses "curds"] referred to in Genesis 18:8 appears to have been a thick sour milk called *Laban*, a semifluid similar to yogurt or kefir.[24]

What Others are Saying:

> **Isaiah 7:21, 22** In that day, a man will keep alive a young cow and two goats. And because of the abundance of the milk they give, he will have curds to eat. All who remain in the land will eat curds and honey.

Prosperity!

Milk and honey were both symbols of prosperity in the Bible. However, Isaiah mentions milk and curds in this prophecy, to point out that they will have to return to the simple diet of those who live off the land.

Something to Ponder

What's So Good About Yogurt?

Yogurt with live culture and fresh fruit added can reduce serum LDL-cholesterol levels in three weeks.[25] Live culture–containing yogurt reduces the occurrences of many women's problems, when eaten daily. Pasteurized yogurt, without live culture, does not help.[26] Yogurt contains both the curd and the **whey** so it is high in many B vitamins as well as protein.

What Others are Saying:

whey: *clear, yellowish liquid released when curds are made; generally thrown away*

Pamela Smith: Milk, cheeses, and yogurts are loaded with calcium and magnesium that keep your blood pressure more stable and [when you are pregnant] build your baby's skeletal system while keeping yours strong and intact.[27]

Yogurt Can Be Good Or Bad For You

Real, true, natural, plain yogurt is good for you. It must contain a live fermenting agent or culture called *Lactobacillus acidophilus* or *Bifidobacterium bifidum*, or both. If the package does not clearly say that there is "live culture," "live bacteria," or live *L. acidophilus* in the yogurt or yogurt tablets, it does not contain the health-giving properties of natural yogurt.

Bad-for-you yogurt contains white sugar, jam or fruit preserves made with white sugar, artificial colors and flavors, and no live culture.

What Others are Saying:

Maureen Salaman: Beware of flavored yogurt which often contains sugar and adds up to anywhere from 60 to 120 extra calories to an 8-ounce container. Better to slice up a small piece of fresh fruit into yogurt if you need a sweetener.[28]

Yogurt For Life

There are two kinds of bacteria—good and bad. Your intestines are supposed to have good bacteria—intestinal flora—in them to help with digestion. Antibiotics kill all the bacteria—both the good and the bad. This can cause diarrhea, unless you take some good bacteria—a **probiotic**, generally yogurt. Yogurt can restore the good bacteria that was destroyed by the antibiotics, while the antibiotics destroy the bad bacteria that made you sick.

Remember This . . .

probiotic: *Greek for "for life," a form of "good" bacteria*

Don't Leave Home Without Them

Many things can upset the delicate balance in your gastrointestinal (GI) tract. Some of them are bad water or poor hygiene, too many sweets or starchy foods, too many alcoholic drinks, food allergies, excessive stress, environmental toxins, parasites, viral illnesses, and overgrowth of undesirable bacteria or yeast. When you travel to third world countries where "it isn't safe to drink the water," you will want to begin taking yogurt capsules before you go and continue to take them while you are there and even after you return. Doing so does not give you license to be foolish, but it will help to keep you from getting **tourista** while you are there. Kyo-dophilus® is a brand of probiotic capsules that do not need to be refrigerated, so they are excellent to take with you on trips to Mexico, India, China, or anywhere that bacteria in the water and food might be different from in your hometown. Actually, it is great to take them camping too, because the water might have different bacteria than you are used to.

Cheese: Can You Stomach This?

The story of how cheese was discovered is an old one. A soldier was taking some milk to a friend a few miles away. He had a goat-stomach bag in which he carried water, so he decided to put the milk into it instead. He strapped it onto his horse and rode to the friend's house. When he got there, the milk had soured and formed curds. He got so mad he stepped on it and pressed the curds into a fresh cheese. Why did cheese curds form in this stomach bag? The stomach acid still in the bag, from when it belonged to a goat, caused the milk to curdle. Acid—stomach acid, specifically—is used to curdle milk and make it into cheese. The stomach acid from cows is called "rennet" and is used to make most cheeses. At markets, during the Middle Ages and as recently as the 1940s, cooks could buy strips of stomach lining from which to make cheese. Today, we just buy rennet in a package or tablet. There is also vegetarian rennet available for those who do not wish to mix meat with milk or who want to stay strictly vegetarian.

Little Miss Muffett Was Here

In the nursery rhyme, Little Miss Muffett sat on a tuffet eating her curds and whey. She could have been eating yogurt or what we call cottage cheese. The curds are the solid part and the whey is the liquid which is drained off when acid forms the curds. In creamed cottage cheese, cream or milk is added to the whey to

ON Target:
Eating healthy yogurt weekly

OFF Target:
Eating sweetened yogurt anytime

tourista: *popular name for illnesses caused by higher bacteria counts*

KEY POINT

From animals, rennet is a curdling agent for milk.

Illustration #19

Milk and Dairy Products—It is important to have a moderate amount of milk and dairy products daily.

make it creamy. Whey is generally yellow and transparent in color. You can see how this works if you add some lemon juice or vinegar to milk and watch the acid make curds in the milk. Rennet is a much stronger curding agent than lemon juice or vinegar, so it makes firmer curds. If we added the curds from cottage cheese to yogurt we would *really* have curds and whey, just like Miss Muffett!

What Others are Saying:

Jim Shriner: A healthy, well-balanced breakfast could be as simple as a small cup of fresh fruit, a glass of nonfat milk, or a low-fat yogurt and fruit, and a slice of wheat toast.[29]

Job 10:10 Did you not pour me out like milk and curdle me like cheese, clothe me with skin and flesh and knit me together with bones and sinews?

Cheese Is Generally Well Pressed

When rennet is added to milk, whether it be whole, skimmed, or low-fat, it causes the milk to curdle. The whey is drained off and used for other purposes. The curds, which are just protein and fat along with the minerals in milk, are cooked and stirred and then pressed in a form or mold. Some cheeses are left in a cool place to age like cheddar and blue cheese. Some are called semi-soft and are not aged, but are generally cooked longer to make them sort of rubbery. Job used the example of making cheese when he was talking to God to describe a lengthy and complicated process.

Dr. Mary Ruth Swope: Cheeses were made from the milk of several animals [in Bible times]. Soured milk which formed hard lumps was dried in the sun, and curds produced were used in cooking.[30]

A Little Goes A Long Way

When you use whole milk to make cheese, you remove some of the liquid. This makes the same volume of what is now cheese have a higher concentration of fat and other nutrients than it did when it was milk. Therefore, cheese generally has more calories than milk, so you don't need to eat a lot at one time. Cheese and yogurt are a daily part of the Bible Diet. This does not mean you should drink a glass of milk at every meal, but cheese or yogurt in small amounts can be eaten daily, especially if you have some of it in the form of low-fat or nonfat cheese or yogurt.

Remember This . . .

> **I Corinthians 3:1, 2** Brothers, I could not address you as spiritual but as worldly—mere infants in Christ. I gave you milk, not solid food, for you were not yet ready for it. Indeed, you are still not ready.

Milk In The New Testament

In Bible times drinking <u>milk</u> was exclusively for infants while different forms of milk—yogurt, cheeses, or butter—were for adults. Because milk was for infants, the use of the term "milk" in referring to one's spiritual life meant that he or she had not become a mature Christian.

Today we often call a new Christian a "baby" Christian. They have only learned a small amount about following Christ. They have only consumed milk, not solid food.

"Solid food" was reserved for adults, or for those who had progressed in their spiritual life to become Christians of sound judgment and discernment—those who could distinguish good from evil. Solid spiritual food for a Christian comes after years of reading the Scriptures, attending Bible study, and living the life Jesus described for mature Christians in the New Testament (see GWBI, page 292).

☞ **GO TO:**

Hebrews 5:11–14 (milk)

Study Questions

1. Why is it a good idea to have dairy products daily?
2. There has been a controversy over what kind of milk and for how long?
3. Why is mother's milk so important for health?
4. What current "health food" was eaten in Bible times as part of the Bible Cure?
5. What are some reasons for eating fermented milk products?
6. In what situation did New Testament people consider it acceptable to drink milk?

CHAPTER WRAP-UP

- Milk is mentioned throughout the Bible, especially the milk of goats, sheep, and cows.
- Milk and milk products are high in protein, calcium, magnesium, and have small amounts of the B vitamins.
- Mother's milk is considered the best food for babies to be the healthiest. Many herbs and supplements can be used to restore the immunity of those who were not breast-fed.
- Cheese and yogurt are recommended as daily foods in the Bible Diet.
- Milk in the form of yogurt can be healthful for all sorts of intestinal problems and may also help to lower cholesterol levels.
- If cheese is to be a regular part of your diet, it is best to eat small amounts at a time and to try to have more of the lower fat or part-skimmed varieties.
- In Bible times drinking milk was considered an activity for infants, not adults. (I Corinthians 3:1, 2)

7 FISH FOR FIVE THOUSAND

CHAPTER HIGHLIGHTS

- Fishing
- Fish in the Mediterranean Diet
- Fish Is Good for You
- Eating Fish

Let's Get Started

Because the Mediterranean area surrounds the Mediterranean Sea, fish play a major role in the Old Testament and in the New. Fishing was an important occupation for some of Jesus' disciples, so much so that he even talked with them about being "fishers of men." Because of this, the fish is a symbol that refers to Christ. Fish and fish oils have been shown to be very healthful for your body and mind. Perhaps the people of the Mediterranean knew how healthful fish is, and that is why they ate it almost daily in some form or another (see Illustration #20, this page).

 GO TO:

Mark 1:16–18; Luke 5:1–3 (fishing)

Illustration #20

A wide range of fish in the Mediterranean—Fish are in the sea and rivers of the Mediterranean region.

> **Matthew 4:18–20** As Jesus was walking beside the Sea of Galilee, he saw two brothers, Simon called Peter and his brother Andrew. They were casting a net into the lake, for they were fishermen. "Come, follow me," Jesus said, "and I will make you fishers of men." At once they left their nets and followed him.

Catch Any?

Fishing was a good job because people ate so many kinds of fish, so often, that a fisherman could earn a living if he could catch fish. It was hard work, but it was steady. Jesus picked his disciples from fishermen. Peter, who was a fisherman when Jesus asked him to be a disciple, later became one of Jesus' leading disciples. He even wrote I and II Peter in the New Testament (see GWBI, pages 304–308).

There are 50 different types of fish mentioned in texts dating from before 2300 B.C. There are 40 species found in the inland waters of the Middle East, 22 of which are peculiar to Palestine and Syria (see Appendix A), and of these 14 are known only to the Jordan river system (see Appendix A). That was a good variety of fish.[1]

Before eating any fish that you catch in your local waterways, check with the Wildlife Department to see if the fish are safe to eat.

> **Ezekiel 47:9, 10** Swarms of living creatures will live wherever the river flows. There will be large numbers of fish, because this water flows there and makes the salt water fresh; so where the river flows everything will live. Fishermen will stand along the shore . . . there will be places for spreading nets. The fish will be of many kinds—like the fish of the Great Sea.

Something to Ponder

If you dislike fish, you may not have cooked it properly, or it may be that you have not found a variety you like. By eating different varieties of fish, you can find a kind that you like. You are likely to find at least 10 different varieties at your local market in any season.

> **Matthew 14:16–21** Jesus replied, "They do not need to go away. You give them something to eat." "We have here only five loaves of <u>bread and two fish</u>," they answered. "Bring them here to me," he said. And he directed the people to sit down on the grass. Taking the five loaves and two fish and looking up to heaven, he gave thanks and broke the loaves. Then he gave them to the disciples, and the disciples gave them to the people. They all ate and were satisfied, and the disciples picked up twelve basketfuls of broken pieces that were left over. The number of those who ate was about five thousand men, besides the women and children.

☞ **GO TO:**

Mark 6:30–44; Luke 9:10–17;
  John 6:1–15 (bread and two fish)

Miracle Fish

The story about how Jesus multiplied the barley loaves and fish is something most children accept, but adults sometimes doubt its plausibility. The story is of some importance because it is in all three **Synoptic gospels** as well as John, so it is repeated four times. In II Kings, Elisha multiplied 20 <u>loaves</u> of barley bread but no fish. The story of Jesus' miracle, which does include multiplying fish, builds on Elisha's miracle. The gospel passages set the stage for Jesus to be called the <u>bread of life</u> later on.[2] Fish played a very important part in the lives of Jesus' disciples—they were fishermen. Fish was a very important food for them and for all people of the Mediterranean. Fish can and should play a very important part in your life too.

☞ **GO TO:**

II Kings 4:42–44 (loaves)

John 6:32–49 (bread of life)

Synoptic gospels:
Matthew, Mark, and Luke

Illustration #21

Basket of Bread and Fish—They all ate and were satisfied, and the disciples picked up twelve basketfuls of broken pieces that were left over (Matthew 14:20).

Fish In The Mediterranean Diet

Fish should be eaten almost daily when you are following the Mediterranean or Bible Diet. Its section on the food pyramid is a bit bigger than dairy products but not much (see Illustration #22, this page). This means that you might want to eat some form of fish or fish oil every day. Sound impossible? Try cooking with fish flakes or using fish broth in cooking. If you are fond of dried (though not salted) fish, they make good snacks; so does canned fish like the old standbys of tuna, salmon, and mackerel. Tuna can even be purchased in snack packs that can be easily opened for a school lunch. I ate a tuna sandwich almost every day for lunch during high school and had lots of energy to do well in school, sing in the school choir, take private singing lessons and practice every day, sing in a church choir, and to be on the school-governing board as well as hold an office in the church youth group. I think the tuna did it, along with the breakfast I ate, which I'll tell you about in Chapter 9.

Illustration #22

The Fish Section—The darkened section of this pyramid represents how much of your diet should be devoted to fish. This is the last section of the daily foods.

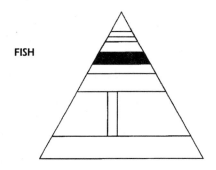

FISH

DAILY   BREAD

FISH
Eat some form of fish daily.

NUTRITIONAL FACT

Eating fish daily can provide essential fatty acids.

The Thick And Thin Of Fish

Fish come from either salt or fresh water. Farm-raised fish are generally freshwater fish. Look for the "naturally raised" label on farm-raised fish to be sure that they are not loaded with antibiotics or growth hormones. Most fish are categorized as either round fish or flatfish. A good example of a flatfish is the flounder, which is so flat that it has both eyes on one side of its head. It swims

GOD'S WORD FOR THE BIBLICALLY-INEPT

along like a great oval platter. An example of a round fish is the salmon, which has an eye on either side of its head.

Take a field trip to a fish market or look up various types of fish in a book as a family project to become more familiar with different kinds of fish. You might even want to go to a Greek, Egyptian, or other Middle Eastern restaurant, and order a traditional fish dish to taste different types of fish in their original recipes from the Mediterranean. Many Italian restaurants have fish flown in from the Mediterranean region that might even be the same as those eaten in Bible times.

Something to Ponder

> **Matthew 7:9, 10** "Which of you, if his son asks for bread, will give him a stone? Or if he asks for a fish, will give him a snake?"

The Fat And Thin Of Fish

In this passage, Jesus helps people to understand just how senseless it is to doubt God's love. In essence, Jesus says to doubt that God has your best interests at heart is as unthinkable as giving your son a stone when he asks for bread or a snake when he asks for fish.

Speaking of fish, did you know there are three classifications of them? The classifications are: lower fat, fatty, and high fat. The lower-fat fish have less than 5 grams of fat in a 3½-ounce, cooked serving. The fatty fish have more than 5 grams of fat in a 3½-ounce, cooked serving. The high-fat fish, like Pacific herring, Atlantic mackerel, pompano, salmon, sardines, and shad, have more than 10 grams of fat for a 3½-ounce, cooked serving. The fatty and high-fat fish have the largest amounts of **omega-3 essential fatty acids**. Some lower-fat fish, such as trout, whitefish, sablefish, and tuna, also have omega-3 fatty acids. Even when canned, these fish still contain omega-3 fatty acids.

Fatty fish are naturally that way. The term fatty fish does not refer to breaded and deep fried, greasy fish.

KEY POINT

Fat in fish is not always bad.

omega-3 essential fatty acids: fatty acids, found mostly in fish, that can't be made in your body

WARNING

Fishy Fat

Fish Type	Examples
Lower fat	Atlantic cod, flounder, haddock, halibut, lingcod, monkfish, perch, pike, pollack, red snapper, rockfish, sea bass, smelt, rainbow trout, yellowfin tuna
Fatty	freshwater bass, bluefish, carp, catfish, mullet, orange roughy, shark, swordfish, tilefish, bluefin tuna
High fat	herring, Atlantic mackerel, pompano, sockeye salmon (red), sardines, shad

SOURCE: USDA Nutrient Data Laboratory, www.nal.usda.gov/fnic/foodcomp/

What Others are Saying:

Jim Shriner: If you want more omega-3, the fatty acid found in fish, which has been shown to be effective in preventing heart disease, eat more fish.[3]

> **Luke 5:6** When they had [put their nets into deep water as Jesus told them to], they caught such a large number of fish that their nets began to break.

Why You Need Fish

selenium: a mineral that inhibits the oxidation of fats

alpha-linolenic acid: an essential fatty acid found in fish, canola oil, flaxseeds, and walnuts

EPA: eicosapentaenoic acid, essential fatty acid in fish

DHA: docosahexaenoic acid, essential fatty acid in fish

Fish and fish oil are important parts of a healthy diet. Fish provides animal protein and can be easily prepared. Tuna fish, oysters, and clams contain the mineral **selenium**, oysters and crabmeat contain high amounts of the mineral zinc, and sardines, herring, salmon, mackerel, and tuna contain vitamin D. All these nutrients are essential for good health! (For more information about eating shrimp, clams, and oysters, Chapter 11 deals with clean and unclean foods.) Fish contains omega-3 fatty acids, especially **alpha-linolenic acid**, eicosapentaenoic acid (**EPA**), and docosahexaenoic acid (**DHA**).

What Others are Saying:

Kenneth Cooper, M.D.: Increase your intake of deep-water fish, such as salmon, tuna (white), herring, mackerel, and trout. These fish contain significant amounts of the omega-3 fatty acids, which include the all-important EPA acid or eicosapentaenoic acid. An abundance of these in the diet has been linked to lower levels of blood lipids, including triglycerides.[4]

FISH OIL CAN CHANGE YOU

A recent study showed that infant formula supplemented with DHA-rich EPA from low fish oil (oil with 10 percent EPA) could have the same health benefits as breast milk.[5] This is great news for women who are not able to breast-feed for whatever reason. Pregnant women with a family history of **cerebral palsy (CP)** should be certain to include fish in their diets to help prevent the occurrence of cerebral palsy in their children. In a study done in Greece, the mothers of children with CP were found to consume less fish and grains and more meat than control groups. The control groups were comprised of mothers and children who did not have CP. It was found that during pregnancy those mothers ate more fish and cereal products as well as less meat than the mothers whose children had CP.[6]

Julian Whitaker, M.D.: The omega-3 oils are especially important in pain prevention and control, as they have anti-inflammatory, pain-relieving properties.[7]

FISH OIL HAS ANTI-INFLAMMATORY PROPERTIES

Fish and fish oil are shown to be effective **anti-inflammatory agents** in cases of asthma and **rheumatoid arthritis**.[8] Feeding fish oils to laboratory animals during an experiment reduced **acute** and **chronic** inflammatory responses, improved their survival to external poisons or toxins, and improved their immune response. Fish oil has been used clinically in acute and chronic inflammatory conditions and even has had good response in inflammation following transplants.[9]

Julian Whitaker, M.D.: A component of omega-3, EPA, works on a similar, but more selective, pain-relieving principle as aspirin and other **NSAIDS**: it shuts down the production of pain and inflammation-causing **prostaglandins**.[10]

FISH
Three to four ounces of fish is considered a serving.

ON Target:
Eating fish daily during pregnancy

OFF Target:
Eating no fish during pregnancy

cerebral palsy (CP): a disease characterized by impaired muscular power and coordination

What Others are Saying:

anti-inflammatory agents: substances that counteract inflammation

rheumatoid arthritis: inflammatory arthritis, an autoimmune disease

acute: comes on quickly, has limited duration

What Others are Saying:

chronic: persists or recurs over an extended period

NSAIDS: non-steroidal, anti-inflammatory drugs like ibuprofen

prostaglandins: hormone-like substances

Reginald Cherry, M.D.: Certain oily fish such as tuna, salmon, and cod may lower the tendency to develop blood clots and heart disease.[11]

FISH FEEDS YOUR BRAIN

You've probably heard at some time in your life that "fish feeds your brain," and now we have the scientific evidence to back up all the old wives' tales about this. A study in Switzerland indicated that two to three portions of fatty fish per week, which comes to 1.25g EPA + DHA, is good for your heart and brain. When these fatty fish were consumed with a high-saturated-fat diet (mostly from animal products), then the fish nutrients were not as efficient as they were when other sources of omega-3 fatty acids (mostly from flaxseed and canola oil) were eaten instead of the animal fats. Low amounts of DHA in the diet have been associated with reduced functioning of the brain, **retina**, **spermatozoa**, and visual impairment in newborns.[12]

DAILY BREAD

FISH / FISH OIL
Eat fish or take fish oil daily.

Kenneth Cooper, M.D.: It's long been known that consumption of the omega-3 oils found in deep-water fish such as salmon and tuna is associated with a lower risk of heart disease. Now a study reported in 1995 in the **JAMA** suggests that these fatty fish oils may provide protection from deadly **cardiac arrhythmia**, or irregular heartbeats.[13]

FISH IS GOOD FOR YOUR HEART

Arrhythmia and **sudden cardiac death** have been studied around the world, and as few as one to two meals a week of one of these fish can lower the risk from these two causes.[14] A Japanese study even suggested that overweight **hypertensives** would do better to follow a weight loss program that included one meal a day of omega-3-rich fatty fish to reduce their blood pressure and reduce their risk of a cardiovascular accident.[15]

If you suspect that you have high blood pressure, please see your doctor before you do any home remedies. You can always eat fish, but don't start taking fish oil capsules without checking with your doctor first.

☞ **GO TO:**

John 21:12–14 (fish)

> **Luke 24:41–43** . . . [Jesus] asked them, "Do you have anything here to eat?" They gave him a piece of broiled <u>fish</u>, and he took it and ate it in their presence.

Eating Fish

Fish For Breakfast?

Both times Jesus ate or gave fish to his disciples, it was for breakfast. Many peoples around the world eat fish for breakfast. In England eating kippered herring, pilchards, or sardines for breakfast is considered common. Eating fish for breakfast would be better than some of the highly sugared, highly refined stuff (I can't really call it "food") that many people eat for breakfast. Try giving yourself or your family a tuna- or salmon-salad sandwich for breakfast and see how much better they think during the day. Have some sardines or herring in low-fat sauce on whole grain toast for breakfast; you might be surprised at your new-found energy. Eat some broiled fish and a salad for breakfast. Eating these kinds of meals will really feed your brain. The junk food won't! Eating fish at any meal is a good idea.

ON Target:
Fish for breakfast with whole grains or vegetables

OFF Target:
Sugary cereals or toaster snacks for breakfast

DAILY BREAD

Keep easy-to-open canned fish in your purse, desk, or car for a quick snack.

 NUTRITIONAL FACT

Fatty fish can be an important part of a low-fat diet.

T. D. Jakes: When I know I can't stop eating something, I've learned not to even start. I get the broiled fish.[16]

What Others are Saying:

Eating Fish—Eating Out

broiled: cooked about six inches above or below a fire

baked: cooked in an oven or sealed up in foil or parchment paper

poached: cooked in simmering liquid

When you are eating out, always look for simply prepared fish on the menu. Fish is healthiest for you when it is **broiled, baked,** or **poached**. Deep-frying and frying are not healthy ways to cook fish. A clear fish soup such as bouillabaisse would be a good substitute. Fish chowder is generally loaded with cream and/or bacon, which puts it in the category of being high in animal fats that are not omega-3 fatty acids. Many restaurants have fish that comes to them already breaded and frozen, ready to be deep fried. This is not a good choice. However, breaded, deep-fried fish with the breading removed might be a good way to get some fish into your diet to start. You can be sure that when the children of Israel were wandering in the desert and longed for leeks, garlic, cucumbers, and fish, they were not talking about fast-food fish dinners!

What About The Fishy Smell?

From The Kitchen

When you cook fish, it should be over medium heat or at least six inches from the broiler or heat source. If it smells fishy—really, really fishy—in your house, you are not cooking it right or you have purchased fish that is not very fresh. Cooking fish on high will cause the fibers to shrink and allow all the vital juices to fall into the fire or the pan which will smell fishy. It will also make the fish dry out and become fishy smelling. Adelle Davis, the mother of modern nutrition, used to say that if fish smelled fishy, you were doing something wrong with the cooking or the shopping.

It's All In The Eyes

gills: the breathing vents of a fish

When you purchase a whole, fresh fish, the eyes should be clear and firm. The flesh should be firm and not smell of fish at all. The **gills** should be pink and firm. The skin should not be covered with anything. When you purchase fish that is already filleted or cut into steaks, ask to see the box or wrapper and look for any preservative chemicals that the pieces might have been dipped into. If you are at all worried about preservatives, it is better to get the fish cut in front of you than to purchase already cut-up portions.

ON Target:

Buying only fresh fish

OFF Target:

Buying old smelly fish

Study Questions

1. Why do you think fish play an important role in the New Testament stories about Jesus?
2. Fish is healthy for you to eat. What makes it so?
3. What are the best kinds of fish to eat for health? Do you eat them?
4. There are at least four medical/health conditions that can be helped by fatty fish. What are the diseases, and why are they mostly modern diseases?
5. What are the best ways to cook and eat fish? Share some recipe/cooking ideas that come to mind after reading this chapter. Look at some historical books, like *The Life and Times of Jesus*, or *Food in History*, or *Apicius: Cookery and Dining in Ancient Rome*, to get some ideas about the foods that were eaten in Bible times and how they differ or compare with the recipes we use today.
6. When is a good time to eat fish? Give some examples of when you eat fish and how you felt.

CHAPTER WRAP-UP

- The Old and New Testaments both have miracle stories wherein loaves of bread were multiplied, but only Jesus multiplied bread and fish. (Matthew 14:16–21)
- Fish is an important part of a healthy diet and plays an important role in the Mediterranean or Bible Diet.
- Many health problems previously connected with aging can be helped by eating fish and fish oils.
- Components in fish oils are now being used to reduce pain when there is also inflammation.
- Fish can be eaten any time of the day. Many people around the world eat fish for breakfast, just as Jesus and his disciples did. (Luke 24:41–43; John 21:12–14)

8 THE PASSOVER FEAST—BITTER HERBS AND UNLEAVENED BREAD

CHAPTER HIGHLIGHTS

- History of the Passover Feast
- The King of Herbs
- Dandelions and Chinese Parsley
- Greens And Bitter Herbs

Let's Get Started

Of all the foods mentioned in the Bible, there are a few that are very important to health, both physical and mental. Garlic, fish, olive oil, and **bitter herbs** are among the most important. With just these foods you can live for a long time and live well. (Olive leaves are bitter herbs, but they were covered in the fruit chapter because olives are fruits.) The Passover Feast consists of roasted lamb, bitter herbs, and <u>unleavened bread</u>. The bitter herbs play an important role in the spiritual significance of the Passover. They are also an essential part of the healing and healthfulness of the Passover.

> **Exodus 12:8** That same night they are to eat the meat roasted over the fire, along with bitter herbs, and bread made without yeast.

Passover Feast And Bitter Herbs

God gave the children of Israel a feast to commemorate the time when they were slaves to Egypt and made to work bitterly. During the Passover Feast, which is called the **Seder**, they remember their slavery with blessings and with the eating of bitter herbs. The bitter herbs include parsley, chicory, endive, and dandelion greens (generally, parsley is used in North America). The bitter herbs are called **maror**. They are dipped in salt water to remember the tears that were shed during this hard labor. Next, the maror are dipped in **haroset**—a plate of chopped or grated apples, nuts, wine, and

bitter herbs: *dark green, leafy vegetables; parsley, watercress, Romaine lettuce, dandelion greens*

☞ **GO TO:**

Exodus 13:3–10;
  Exodus 23:15;
  Exodus 34:18;
  Deuteronomy 16:1–8
  (unleavened bread)

Seder: *meal eaten on the first night of the Passover Feast*

maror: *the green, bitter vegetable that stands for bitterness in the Passover Feast*

haroset: *reminder of the mortar used in Egypt*

spices to remind them of the brick-and-mortar work they did for the Egyptians. Each time they dip the bitter herbs, they then eat them to "swallow the past bitterness."

Many Jews, non-Jews, Christians, and non-Christians still commemorate the Passover in the spring. This is a good time to cleanse your body or let it rest after a winter of inactivity and heavy food. You can find the **Passover Haggadah** for Christians in many Christian bookstores and the many different Jewish ones, from ancient texts to very modern texts, in Jewish bookstores and gift shops. Moreover, there are many sites on the World Wide Web; just search for the words "Pesach," "Passover," or "Haggadah."

What Others are Saying:

Cheryl Townsley: Endive is high in vitamin A and works very well in ridding the body of infections. It is high in iron and potassium. It is best eaten raw.[1]

> **Numbers 9:11** They are to celebrate it on the fourteenth day of the second month at twilight. They are to eat the lamb, together with the unleavened bread and bitter herbs.

God Knows About Bitter Herbs

The children of Israel ate bitter herbs at the Passover to commemorate the bitterness of having been slaves in the past, before they were able to flee. God's instructions were to eat the herbs along with roasted lamb and unleavened bread. This seems rather peculiar at first because, generally, the Hebrews ate very little meat; it was not an everyday food. But God's instructions make more sense in light of the fact that nutritionists and scientists now know bitter herbs stimulate the liver and other organs to produce **enzymes** that digest meat fat. How thoughtful of God to give a recipe that would prevent high cholesterol and gallbladder problems.

enzymes: *protein modifiers that initiate or increase the rate of chemical reactions in the body without being used up in the process*

If you want to start adding bitter herbs into your diet, start cooking with herbs such as parsley, basil, oregano, marjoram, thyme, and savory (see Illustration #23, page 111). Once you are used to the wonderful flavors they offer, start adding them fresh, as garnish to food that has been cooked. Chopped, fresh parsley and watercress make a wonderful "power" garnish on soups, stews, salads, even oatmeal. Be adventurous and add fresh thyme or basil to your food.

From The Kitchen

Illustration #23

Dried Herbs—Dried herbs are used for cooking in almost all cuisines. Fresh herbs are also eaten as flavoring and for health benefits.

chlorophyll: pigment responsible for the green color in leaves, it is high in magnesium and trace minerals

Why Are They So Green?

Why are the bitter herbs green? They contain **chlorophyll**, which makes them green. Chlorophyll protects you from cancer by retarding growths, and it keeps many toxins from causing health problems, especially **Salmonella and Drosphila**.[2] Chlorophyll can also protect you from environmental cancer-causing substances.[3]

Salmonella and Drosphila: health-endangering bacteria

Reginald Cherry, M.D.: Most plants [contain] chlorophyll [which] **detoxifies** blood, helps heal **bedsores**, and is a **growth deterrent**.[4]

What Others are Saying:

The Best Times For Bitter Herbs

Bitter herbs should be eaten daily. There are many times when it is imperative to eat dark green, bitter herbs. That is whenever you eat fatty sources of protein such as a cheese sandwich, steak dinner, pork roast, etc. Never eat a burger without really green lettuce. Never eat a meat, egg, or cheese anything without bitter herbs. If you are eating eggs Benedict, please make sure that you eat green things. If you are in a restaurant, do as I do, and ask for some fresh parsley to go with it. Your liver will thank you. Dark green lettuce goes great with peanut butter, sesame butter, cheese, and even sardines. Have a salad of mixed greens daily. Never let a day go by without eating something dark green and leafy.

detoxifies: removes poisons

bedsores: sores from lying in bed

growth deterrent: substance that discourages tumors

Try some of those mixed baby greens in the grocery store. Use them as the base of a salad. Add some tomatoes, cucumbers, celery, red and green peppers, parsley, watercress, romaine lettuce, black olives, and perhaps some tuna, salmon, or chicken. Use a

From The Kitchen

Illustration #24

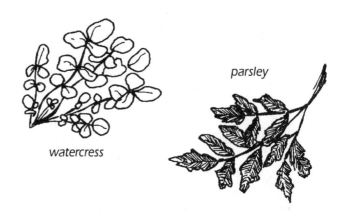

parsley

watercress

The Bitter Herbs Parsley and Watercress—Bitter Herbs have been used for health food for thousands of years. Of course they didn't call it "health food" then; it was their regular food!

low-fat dressing or no dressing. Have some whole-grain bread, rolls, or bread sticks. A salad like this and whole-grain toast or rolls is a really great supper meal. It's best to have your lightest meal of the day at the end of the day when you aren't going to need as many calories; that's why salad is great for supper. This will make it easier to get to sleep because you will be finished digesting before bedtime.

Parsley, The King Of Herbs

ON Target:
Eating bitter herbs daily

OFF Target:
Eating pale vegetables that should be green

Parsley is the bitter herb that I consider the king of herbs because of all the great things it can do for your health (see Illustration #24, page 112). For years tea made from dried parsley has been used to reduce kidney stones. Parsley also contains substances that prevent multiplication of tumor cells. It is also known to relieve gas and stimulate normal digestion.[5] Because it contains chlorophyll, parsley can sweeten your breath. It can even dispel breath problems from strong-smelling foods like garlic and onions. This is why you find it on your plate in a restaurant. It is not just a decoration. It is meant to cleanse your mouth to make you ready for the new taste of the next course.

ON Target:
Eating parsley with everything

OFF Target:
Not eating the parsley in a restaurant

What Others are Saying:

Cheryl Townsley: Parsley is a blood purifier and a stimulant to the bowel. It is high in iron and rich in copper and manganese. Many kidney complaints will decrease when parsley is added to the diet.[6]

Parsley, A Powerhouse Of Nutrients

Something to Ponder

Parsley is high in iron, potassium, and vitamins A and C. It is a powerhouse of health and healing. If you could choose only one herb to take on a desert island, parsley would be the most useful. Garlic would be the most useful vegetable.

DAILY BREAD

PARSLEY
Eat parsley daily.

> **Psalm 104:14** He makes grass grow for the cattle, and plants for man to cultivate—bringing forth food from the earth . . .

Dandelion, The Not-So-Lowly Weed

Dandelion leaves have been used for many years as a **spring tonic**. They are reputed to flush the sludge of winter from your liver. This was a lot more popular in times when it was not possible for most people to get fresh vegetables in the winter, especially dark green leafy ones. Many people in the northern areas of the country ate a lot of preserved foods, meats, dried fish, potatoes, beans, breads, and biscuits with gravy, with almost no green vegetables or salads during the long winters. Some people were able to store and use dark orange squashes, carrots, and **rutabagas**, which helped provide much needed vitamin A. In those days, large quantities of butter and heavy creams were included in the daily foods, so cleaning out the liver from all this fat was a really great idea to keep them healthy. Eating the first greens of the season was a spring-tonic ritual in many northern towns, especially eating dandelion greens.

I still eat dandelion greens, though I buy the commercially grown ones, because most places let dogs and other animals in their yards. If you have a fenced in yard and no animals, go for it! Eat the first-sprouted leaves of your dandelions. Your neighbors will think you are really great, digging up the dandelions and ridding the area of what they think are pests. Once the plants begin to flower, they become even more bitter than in the spring and you might want to stop eating them. If you want to gather your own dandelion greens, pick them in the early spring before they flower and in areas away from animals and exhaust. Wash the leaves well. Eat them raw in a salad or steamed lightly. According to most reference books, *Taraxacum officiale* was probably the bitter mentioned in the book of Numbers, and this *Taraxacum officiale* is the very one that grows so freely in our lawns!

spring tonic: special food or drink that helps clear your body of winter heaviness and sludge

rutabagas: a type of yellow-fleshed turnip that is generally larger than white turnips

 *From The Kitchen*

Dandelion Power

bile: *a yellow substance secreted by the liver to help digest fats*

Dandelions are often thought of as the bitter herb that was mentioned in the Bible to be eaten with the Passover Feast because they are found in pastures and fields all over the Middle East. They clean your bloodstream and liver and encourage the production of **bile**. They are also known to reduce **serum cholesterol** and **uric acid**.[7]

serum cholesterol: *cholesterol found in your blood*

uric acid: *leftover substance from faulty metabolism of proteins, often causes gout*

Chinese Parsley, Cilantro, Or Coriander: What's In A Name?

This dark green vegetable has a lot of names. In Chinese medicine and cooking it is called "Chinese parsley." In Spanish or Mexican medicine and cooking it is called "cilantro." North Americans know it as the green leaves of the "coriander" plant.

dental amalgams: *composition dental fillings containing mercury*

endocrine glands: *ductless glands like the thyroid, adrenal, ovary, testis, and Isles of Langerhans in pancreas*

intractable: *stubborn, difficult to cure*

Recent research in Japan has shown Chinese parsley to be of great benefit in removing mercury from the tissues and organs of people who have had their **dental amalgams** removed from their mouth and their cavities filled with synthetic materials. The strong bluish light that is used to cure the synthetic fillings was found to cause the free-floating mercury (liberated during drilling) to be deposited in the lungs, kidneys, **endocrine glands**, liver, and heart. This happened even when a dental dam was used and precautions were taken to keep the patient from mercury exposure. This mercury then contributed to **intractable** infections. The mercury deposits were removed from these people in the study by the oral intake of a 100 mg tablet of Chinese parsley four times a day.[8] This is really great news for people who have had their mercury fillings removed, thinking that their health would improve, and yet found it to be worse. The study showed that when bacteria in the body was surrounded by mercury, it could not be successfully treated with any kind of antibiotic. The Chinese parsley removed the mercury and relief came right away.

What Others are Saying:

Francisco Contreras, M.D.: Among the vegetables that best provide minerals are broccoli, spinach, watercress, coriander, lettuce, parsley, sweet peppers, tomatoes, chili peppers, prickly pears, and mushrooms.[9]

In With The Chinese Parsley, Out With The Lead

Chinese parsley can help your body excrete lead as well. High levels of lead in your body can cause mental retardation, loss of feeling in your fingers and toes, impotence, and even loss of balance. Gasoline no longer has lead in it, but you might still be affected by it or by lead paint from your childhood toys or from stripping paint from a surface that contained lead-based paint.

Something to Ponder

Lead has a half-life of 52 years, which means that it takes 52 years for lead to break down and be excreted. Many children from inner cities (where there is lead in the air from industrial pollution) are considered retarded or simple-minded when in reality, they are suffering from an overload of lead. Before computers, when all printing was done with lead type, printers, typesetters, and proofreaders used to suffer from lead poisoning because of the lead type they used and touched frequently. In the 1960s many hyperactive children in England were found to have very high lead levels from the industrial pollution and from the smoke of cigarettes that were being smoked by their parents. Once the lead was removed from their bodies, with sodium alginate from sea weed, they were no longer hyperactive.

Many ethnic foods contain coriander or Chinese parsley, especially Mexican, Southwestern, East Indian, Chinese, and other oriental foods. Look for recipes that contain Chinese parsley or cilantro, and include them in your regular, weekly diet.

GET YOUR LEAD LEVELS CHECKED

If you even suspect that you have had contact with high levels of lead from paint or other sources, please see your doctor. A nutritional hair analysis will show if lead is in your system and a blood test will show if it is in your blood. Eating dark green, leafy vegetables, especially cilantro, will help remove the lead. So will **sea vegetables** (which are also green, leafy vegetables), garlic, egg yolks, beans, and **cruciferous** vegetables like broccoli, cabbage, kale, and collard greens.

From The Kitchen

sea vegetables: contain the heavy metal–removing agent sodium alginate

cruciferous: vegetables with four-petaled flowers, suggesting a cross pattern

Swiss chard: very leafy green or deep reddish-green vegetable

---

Cheryl Townsley: **Swiss chard** is high in vitamins C and A, potassium, sodium, and calcium. It is helpful to the digestive system.[10]

What Others are Saying:

> **Isaiah 66:14** When you see this, your heart will rejoice and you will flourish like grass; the hand of the Lord will be made known to his servants, but his fury will be shown to his foes.

Grass And Herbs: Not Just For Cows

Grass grows almost anywhere. When you "flourish like grass" you will be really healthy, and growing under all circumstances. This is because grass and all greens are high in chlorophyll and minerals. This is why so many people drink green juice, or juice made from green plants, especially grasses. It is a very powerful kind of "health food" that you can make yourself if you have a juicer. There are many companies that provide powdered green drinks that you just mix with juice or water to get the benefits of the high mineral content of greens. Many of these green-drink powders are made with alfalfa, barley grass juice, wheat grass juice, sea algaes, **blue-green algaes**, parsley, and often contain garlic, carrot, or **kelp** powder. If you have trouble eating greens every day, you might want to start out by having a green drink. Once you start to feel more energy, you will be convinced to eat more greens too.

blue-green algaes: fresh water chlorella or spirulina; compact nutritional powerhouses

kelp: a deep-water sea vegetable

Remember This . . .

> Eating greens is very important. You may also take a green powder drink such as Kyo-Green; Barley Green; Green Magma; ProGreens; Futurebiotics Superfood Powders of Alfalfa, Barley, and Chlorella; or Nikken Emerald Harvest.

Algae Is Good For You (Never Mind How It Looks)

Green algae and blue-green algae have been the subject of much research showing that they, too, are green plants with curative powers. Chlorella, a green algae, has been shown to prevent stress-induced ulcers.[11] Chlorella was also shown to contain an antitumor factor.[12] Another popular algae is spirulina; it has exhibited antioxidant protection and has also been shown to reduce allergic reactions.[13] Those people with **multiple sclerosis** have been shown to have a longer remission of symptoms when they are eating spirulina.[14]

multiple sclerosis: also called MS; a disease that causes neural and muscular impairments

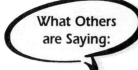

What Others are Saying:

Reginald Cherry, M.D.: Spirulina detoxifies blood and stimulates production of the body's most powerful antioxidant, superoxide dismutase.[15]

ALGAE IS GREAT FOR VEGETARIANS

A strict vegetarian who eats no animal products is called a "vegan." Vegans are often deficient in vitamin B_{12} because it generally comes from animal sources. There are two vegetarian sources of this vitamin. One is the fermented soybean product from Indonesia called "tempeh" and the other is green algae.[16] Vegans would do well to include these two foods in their diet.

Popeye's Choice

Spinach is a really dark green, leafy vegetable. It is high in iron, folic acid, vitamins A and C, and minerals. It is often classified as a bitter herb; just eat some raw to find out why. Spinach is added to a lot of foods in classical French cooking that are traditionally high in fat such as **quiche**, omelettes, fish, or veal. Anything with spinach in French cooking is called Florentine. Spinach will help your body digest the fat in these high-fat foods and prevent health problems. Many of these recipes go back to Bible times. The two most popular types of quiche, asparagus and spinach, were in the first cookbook ever written, which was published around the time of the life of Jesus.[17]

quiche: *a pie made of egg, cheese, and cream; eaten as a meal*

> Spinach is very high in **oxalic acid**. If you have kidney problems, please see your doctor before you start to eat spinach or take powdered spinach in large amounts.

WARNING

Pamela Smith: Spinach, this dark green leafy [vegetable], provides a bumper crop of vitamins A and C along with folic acid. It also gives you valuable magnesium.[18]

What Others are Saying:

Cheryl Townsley: Spinach . . . promotes the health of the **lymphatic**, urinary, and digestive systems.[19]

oxalic acid: *found in rhubarb and spinach, not suitable for people with kidney problems*

> **Hebrews 6:7** Land that drinks in the rain often falling on it and that produces a crop useful to those for whom it is farmed, receives the blessing of God.

Green Grasses

Barley grass, wheat grass, and other cattle foods were considered useful crops in Bible times and today. Whereas in the early part of the century grasses were considered to be only cattle food, they are now considered health food because of their high nutritional

lymphatic system: *a series of vessels throughout your body that provide lymph fluid to nourish your cells and clean out waste matter*

content. The wheat and barley grasses that are used in green-drink powders are the leaves of the same plants that produce the seeds, which are harvested to be used as whole grains.

Greens And Eye Problems

In the last few years, much research has been done on the dietary habits of the elderly. A landmark study of almost 900 people, ages 55 to 80, was done in Boston. They were broken into two groups: the control group had not been diagnosed with eye problems, the other groups had. The study was to assess their dietary habits over an undisclosed period of time, to assess the similarities in the diets of the people with and without eye problems. Of the group with eye problems, 356 of them had been diagnosed within one year of the study with an advanced stage of **age-related macular degeneration** (AMD). The results were startling, but to be expected. Those who were not diagnosed with age-related macular degeneration had the highest intake of the **carotenoids**, **lutein**, and **zeaxanthin** due to a high frequency intake of dark green leafy vegetables, specifically spinach and collard greens. The study showed that taking vitamin E and/or vitamin C in the form of supplements did not have any affect on AMD.[20] If you want to be able to see better when you are older, eat spinach and collard greens! Another study done in the same clinic showed that women who smoked 25 or more cigarettes a day were also at risk for age-related macular degeneration.[21]

age-related macular degeneration: the most common cause of blindness in the elderly

carotenoids: a class of compounds related to vitamin A

lutein: a carotenoid

zeaxanthin: a carotenoid

What Others are Saying:

Remember This . . .

bilberry: an eye-building herb

DNA: deoxyribonucleic acid, that part of your cells that contains the genetic or inherited blueprint

Kenneth Cooper, M.D.: [To fight cataracts and age-related macular degeneration,] concentrate on these foods: kale, collard greens, spinach, mustard greens, okra, broccoli, and Brussels sprouts.[22]

A green drink or green-drink powder with spinach and broccoli is still considered food, not a supplement. Therefore, drinking a green drink will be of some help in fighting AMD. There are many supplements that contain **bilberry** and the ingredients of spinach and broccoli that are the most helpful: xanthophylls, lutein, and zeaxanthin. These will be very useful in fighting AMD.

GREEN AND MEAN (AGAINST CANCER)

Folic acid–rich foods have been shown to prevent cancers. The foods that are high in folic acids are green vegetables, legumes, and whole grains. According to a recent study, when a person is deficient in folic acid, there is damage to the **DNA** that resembles damage in cancer cells.[23]

How Bitter Herbs Can Help

The Bitter Herb	The Help
Parsley	stimulates digestion
	dissolves kidney stones
	deodorizes breath and body
	dispels gas
	breaks up fat
Endive	rids body of infection
Dandelion	spring tonic
	breaks up fat
	cleans bloodstream
	encourages bile production
Chinese parsley (cilantro)	removes heavy metals
	breaks up fat
Kelp	stimulates energy production
	removes heavy metals
	breaks up fat
Spinach	breaks up fat
	prevents blindness in the elderly
	cleans lymphatic system
	prevents neural tube birth defects
Chlorella	prevents stress ulcers
	prevents tumors
Spirulina	reduces allergic reactions
	aids MS remissions

ON Target:
Eating spinach, collard greens, or other sources of lutein and zeaxanthin daily

OFF Target:
Smoking and eating no greens

Francisco Contreras, M.D.: Broccoli, cauliflower, Brussels sprouts, turnips, kale, turnip greens, and **bok choy** are the most highly regarded anti-cancer foods.[24]

Green Foods Fight Birth Defects And Vascular Disease

The folic–acid–rich foods, which include leafy greens, were also found to prevent several kinds of birth defects, including **neural tube defects**, or to reverse the incidents of vascular disease in women.[25] If you are planning to become pregnant or if you suspect you have **vascular disease**, please go and have your folic–acid levels checked. Your doctor may want to prescribe a folic–acid supplement. You would also be wise to keep track of your intake of folic acid and make sure that it is at least 400 mcg daily.

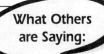

What Others are Saying:

bok choy: *a Chinese green with white stems and green leaves*

neural: *of or pertaining to nerves or the nervous system*

vascular disease: *disease of the circulatory system*

How Does This Relate
To The Mediterranean Diet?

From The Kitchen

Eating dark green, leafy vegetables is an important part of the Mediterranean Diet. This is partly why the vegetable section on the pyramid is the largest section, to show the importance of eating a lot of vegetables, including dark green, leafy ones. Try adding garnishes of parsley or watercress to every meal. Make sure that the entire family eats green things; it is very important. At my home we even put chopped fresh parsley on popcorn or scrambled eggs. Be creative in the ways you can get something green in every meal. Make your own alfalfa or other sprouts for some additional green foods.

Study Questions

1. What Jewish feast includes bitter herbs and why? Why are they important for you to eat today?
2. Which important bitter herb grows nearly everywhere? Name some local places where it grows so you know where to harvest them in the spring.
3. Name four health benefits of eating dark green leafy vegetables. How are you going to add them to your diet?
4. Which two bitter herbs are easy to add to everything? Can you think of any benefits to doing this? Why do you suppose people ate more greens during Bible times?

CHAPTER WRAP-UP

- The Passover Feast or Feast of Unleavened Bread is significant for more than spiritual reasons. God uses it to point out that everybody should eat bitter herbs with rich proteins. (Exodus 12:8 and Numbers 9:11)

- There are many references to plants, grasses, and green leaves in the Bible. (Psalm 104:14, Psalm 23:2, and Isaiah 66:14)

- Green leafy vegetables and herbs play an important role in daily life.

- Science and medicine have taken a great interest in green plants (including algae).

- The Bible Diet includes eating dark green leafy vegetables, often called bitter herbs, on a daily basis.

9 ALL THE FAT IS THE LORD'S

CHAPTER HIGHLIGHTS

- God's Prohibition of Fat
- Fat
- Eating Meat
- Chickens and Eggs
- Clean and Unclean Meats

Let's Get Started

Many people talk about the low-fat or nonfat craze, but in Scripture God gave strict orders about the kind of fat that can be eaten by his people. This mostly pertains to the hard fat around the organs of beef, lamb, sheep, goat, and pigs. There are fats that are good for you and fats that are not so good. As it turns out, the fat that God told his people to stay away from is the same fat that today's scientists say you shouldn't eat. That never changes. The Bible Diet is not really a low-fat diet as much as it is a high-vegetable, low-*animal*-fat diet, which is different. The Mediterranean Food Pyramid shows that to be really healthy, you should eat fatty fish, olive oil, and cheese or yogurt every day (see Illustration #2, page 7).

> **Leviticus 3:14–17** From what he offers he is to make this offering to the Lord by fire: all the fat that covers the inner parts or is connected to them, both kidneys with the fat on them near the loins, and the covering of the liver, which he will remove with the kidneys. The priest shall burn them on the altar as food, an offering made by fire, a pleasing aroma. All the fat is the Lord's. This is a lasting ordinance for the generations to come, wherever you live: You must not eat any fat or any blood.

☞ **GO TO:**

Exodus 29:13; Leviticus
7:22–27 (fat)

hydrogenated fat: oil
that has been made hard
by adding hydrogen to it

rendered: melted down

suet: hard fat from beef
cattle used in cooking
much like lard is

What Others
are Saying:

NUTRITIONAL FACT

Some whole-grain
crackers and baked
goods contain hydro-
genated fat and/or
palm kernel oil, a
saturated fat.

What Others
are Saying:

No Fat Allowed!

God instructed the Israelites to burn the <u>fat</u> that surrounded the organs like a cushion and the fat that was inside the body cavity of the animals, as a food offering to him. This fat, referred to in the passage from Leviticus, is the same fat that is used to make lard. It is very hard fat and is the major animal fat that is known to cause a lot of health problems. Hard fat is very difficult to digest. Shortening is made of vegetable oil that has hydrogen added to mimic this hard fat, or lard. Shortening or **hydrogenated fat** is also hard to digest and can turn to fat in or on your body, which is true for any hydrogenated fat products like margarine and many processed foods. The most common place to get lard is from pigs. The hard fat is **rendered** to remove the fibrous material and the remainder is chilled to form lard. Sometimes acid, like lemon juice or citric acid, and salt is added, but it is still the forbidden fat. The same forbidden fat is called **suet** when it comes from beef cattle. This is also very hard to digest. North Americans generally don't use the hard fat from goats, sheep, lambs, or deer.

Cheryl Townsley: Don't eat hydrogenated fats. These fats in-clude margarine, shortening, and processed foods containing hy-drogenated fats. These fats work like plastic in the body. They are toxic and impossible to digest.[1]

Burn The Fat

The instructions were to burn the hard fat as an offering to God. This meant that it would belong to the Lord and not to the people. Why do you think God would declare he should get the very worst fat for humans to eat? Why was the aroma pleasing to God? Could it be because the smell reminded him that nobody was eating it?

Always remove the visible fat from animal proteins before cook-ing them, only God gets to have burned fat. Remove all the lard, bacon fat, and shortening from your recipes; replace them with butter, olive oil, or canola oil.

Today's animals live in a polluted environment, and some of the toxins produced from living in a polluted world are stored in their fat. Burning, not eating animal fat, also protects us from con-suming toxins found in animal fat.

Francisco Contreras, M.D.: In the United States, 70 percent of all deaths are related to excessive consumption of fat, sugar, and salt.[2]

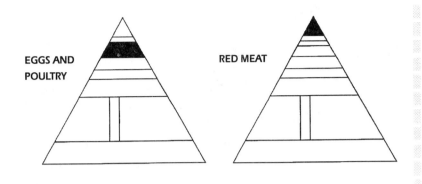

EGGS AND POULTRY

RED MEAT

Illustration #25

Eggs and Poultry Section, Red Meat Section—The darkened section of the pyramid on the left represents how much of your diet should be devoted to eggs and poultry, while the darkened section of the one on the right represents how much of your diet should be devoted to red meat. For the complete pyramid, see page 7.

Red Meat: Be Careful With The Stuff

The Mediterranean Diet encourages low consumption of red meat, animal products, saturated fats, hydrogenated fats, and refined carbohydrates. It encourages high consumption of fruit, vegetables, and whole grains. Research has shown that high consumption of red meat is associated with increased risks of coronary heart disease (CHD) as well as colon and other cancers. A high animal-protein diet of mostly red meat is also responsible for calcium losses in the urine, which leads to osteoporosis.[3] The Mediterranean Diet suggests that red meat be eaten a few times per month, while eggs and poultry can be eaten as often as a few times per week (see Illustration #25, this page).

Julian Whitaker, M.D.: The low-fat craze has missed the mark. The truth is that fat, consumed in moderate amounts, is important to the body. Fat slows the release of sugar into your bloodstream, helping to sustain energy. Fat is necessary for the absorption of vitamins A, E, D, and K, and beta-carotene, and for the formation of all cell membranes.[4]

What Others are Saying:

Fat Gets A Bad Wrap

Fat has gotten a lot of bad publicity in the last eight to ten years. It was always considered important for weight loss until North Americans developed a fat phobia—yes, a fear of fat! Fat is essential for the breakdown and absorption of the fat-soluble vitamins A, D, E, and K. If you follow a very low-fat diet, you will quickly become deficient in these vitamins. Your hair, skin, and nails will become dry, flaky, and lusterless. Many diet programs that recommended no fat have changed to low fat because people on no-fat diets were beginning to look like dried-out prunes. What's the sense of losing weight if you wind up looking like a prune in the process?

Unsaturated fatty acids are essential for proper functioning of the glands and organs in your body. Your thyroid gland will actually overfunction without vitamin F, or unsaturated fatty acids, in your diet.

Fat keeps you from getting hungry too soon by slowing down the digestion process. If you eat a really low-fat or no-fat diet, you will be hungry all the time.

DAILY BREAD

FAT
Eat some form of the good fat daily.

What Others are Saying:

Maureen Salaman: So far as calorie content is concerned, all classes of foods are not created equal. One gram of fat contains nine calories whereas one gram of carbohydrates or protein contains four.[5]

> **Ezekiel 39:19** At the sacrifice I am preparing for you, you will eat fat till you are glutted and drink blood till you are drunk.

Fat Has A Purpose

Ezekiel is trying to tell the Israelites that they might have to endure a punishment that includes eating fat (and he means the forbidden fat) and drinking blood, also forbidden, if they don't change their ways. If they ate fat until they were glutted, that would be a lot of fat! In a normal diet, fat tells you when you have eaten enough. (I'm referring to fat in general, not the forbidden fats lard and suet.) When you feel satisfied after eating two cookies made with butter and eggs, it is because of the fat. If you eat cookies with no fat, you might find yourself eating a lot more before you feel full or satisfied. This means that you will consume a lot more calories, in the form of starch and sugar, when there is no fat. These calories from sugar and flour are really **empty calories** if you are eating refined flour and sugar, which will put fat on your body very fast. This is why a low-fat or nonfat diet could be unhealthy, even though fat has nine calories to every one calorie of starch or carbohydrate. Because fat keeps you from eating too many empty calories, you will also have less calories in your diet from either fat or starch by following the Bible Diet.

empty calories: energy from food with no nutritional value, only calories

GOD'S WORD FOR THE BIBLICALLY-INEPT

Jim Shriner: Fat has more than twice the calories per gram that protein or carbohydrates have.[6]

Fat Can Make You Fat

Animal fats have been shown to be responsible for many health problems including atherosclerosis and prostate, colon, rectal, pancreatic, breast, and skin cancers.[7] Eating too much fat can indeed cause a person to "get fat." The proportions of fat to other foods and to the amount of exercise are the important comparisons. If most of your calories come from fat, then you will become fat. If most of your calories come from other sources, you have less chance of getting fat. You will also stand a chance of getting fat if you do not exercise, no matter how many calories you have from any source. Just because you have a lean body or low body fat does not mean that fat is not being deposited in your arteries. Many slender people have high accumulations of fat in their arteries. Fat is displaced from your body, including your arteries, by fiber from grains and vegetables along with using up the energy from the fat during your daily life or through an exercise program. This is why eating vegetables, especially bitter herbs which are known to break up fat, is so important.

To lose weight you must eat lots of vegetables and fruits and reduce your intake of animal fats. This, along with exercise, will help burn up the fat stored in your body. Do not try to lose weight by cutting out all fat and protein; this is not healthy.

Jim Shriner: In their attempts to lose weight, some Americans have tried cutting fat completely out of their diet. This is not the answer. I recommend a person never allow their daily fat intake to drop below fifteen to twenty percent of their total calorie intake.[8]

There are many kinds of weight-loss diets. There are diets with only fat and protein and no carbohydrates; diets with small amounts of carbohydrates at only one meal; diets where you eat only certain kinds of protein based on the chemical **purine**; diets based on your blood type; and low-calorie or low-fat diets. Whether you're looking for a sensible diet for health, or a diet for weight loss, follow the Bible Diet. Do not follow a diet that only contains vegetables and no protein sources; all the nutrients are necessary for health (see Illustration #26, page 126).

What Others are Saying:

ON Target:
Eating monounsaturated fats like olive oil

OFF Target:
Eating mostly fatty animal foods like burgers and steaks

WARNING

What Others are Saying:

Something to Ponder

purine: *an organic, colorless compound*

How Much Protein Do You Need?

Protein is generally calculated by kilograms of body weight. Adults should have around 0.8 grams of protein per day for each kilogram (2.2 pounds) of body weight. Infants and growing children need more protein than adults, and older adults need less than younger adults. Infants can often require up to 2 grams per kilogram of body weight or between 13 to 14 grams a day. A 120-pound teenager would require around 64 grams and a 160-pound adult would require around 70 grams. This includes protein from all sources, not just animal sources.

If you are under a lot of stress (such as from an accident, flood, or death of a loved one), you might need more protein to repair your body. If you are pregnant or **lactating**, you will want to make sure that you are getting adequate amounts and even add a little extra plant-based protein. A 3-ounce serving of fish contains about 20 grams of protein, two eggs contain about 15 grams of protein, one cup of tofu (a soybean product) contains about 20 grams of protein, 3 ounces of white-meat chicken contain about 18 grams of protein. By eating several 3-ounce servings of protein or 2 eggs, it is possible to maintain the required amount of protein each day. Servings of 3 or 4 ounces of protein food are a lot smaller than what most people eat at one time. Consider that a can of tuna fish is 6 or 6½ ounces; this will give you some idea of the size of a 3-ounce serving—about half a can of tuna fish.

lactating: producing milk for breast-feeding

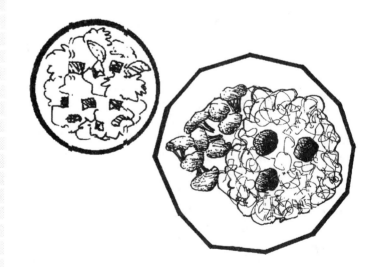

Illustration #26

Plate of Spaghetti—This is a balanced meal. The vegetables (i.e., the salad and broccoli) make up the largest amount of food while the whole grain pasta (a source of carbohydrates) makes up the second largest. The meat in the meatballs makes up the smallest food group—4 ounces of meat or less.

Serving of Food	Grams of Protein
Cheddar cheese, ½ cup	16.0
Cottage cheese, ½ cup	13.0
Black beans, ½ cup cooked	8.0
Tofu, ½ cup	10.0
Lentils, ½ cup cooked	9.0
Avocado, ½	2.5
Lean Ground Beef, 3 ounces	21.0
Chicken, light meat, ½ cup	20.0
Chicken, dark meat, ½ cup	18.0
Almonds, ½ cup	12.0
Halibut, 3 ounces	22.0
Salmon, 3 ounces	21.0

What Others are Saying:

Reginald Cherry, M.D.: While protein is essential to our health, we should limit our protein intake to 10 to 15 percent of our total calories. Excessive amounts of protein can lead to kidney problems, high cholesterol levels, and heart disease, as well as other health-related problems.[9]

I Timothy 4:1–5 The Spirit clearly says that in later times some will abandon the faith and follow deceiving spirits and things taught by demons. Such teachings come through hypocritical liars, whose consciences have been seared as with a hot iron. They forbid people to marry and order them to abstain from certain foods which God created to be received with thanksgiving by those who believe and who know the truth. For everything God created is good, and nothing is to be rejected if it is received with thanksgiving, because it is consecrated by the Word of God and prayer.

What To Do?

Look again at the Mediterranean Food Pyramid in the first chapter (on page 7). You will see that no foods are left out of this Bible Diet. You are not being told not to eat something. The Mediterranean Diet shows that red meat should be eaten no more than a few times a month. Sweets, eggs, and poultry can be eaten a few times per week. Fish, cheese, and yogurt can be eaten daily. The Mediterranean Diet is the same diet that was followed for thousands of years. This is the Bible Diet of the Bible lands. It is sensible and fits in with both the Old and the New Testament regulations about clean and unclean foods.

You have the option of eating foods that were considered unclean if you want to, but they are not required to be eaten. Even though beef—"oxen" as they called them—is considered clean, that doesn't mean you need to have it daily. Just a few times a month is the maximum—the same frequency at which the Israelites of old would have eaten beef or lamb—at a special holiday, banquet, party, or wedding. The Bible Diet says eating red meat is acceptable, but you don't have to eat it if you don't want to. You do, however, have to eat vegetables and whole grains if you want to be healthy.

Mary Lynn, a publisher in New Mexico, used to tell me that meat should be like a **condiment** that goes along with the other foods. If you think of meat this way, you will have a good idea of how much to eat daily.

Remember This . . .

condiment: a seasoning for foods such as mustard, catsup, or pickles

To Beef Or Not To Beef? That Is The Question

Beef and other animal products contain vitamin B_{12}. There are a few nonanimal sources of B_{12} like tempeh, a fermented soybean product. However, the easiest and most foolproof way to ensure your adequate intake of B_{12} is to eat animal products. Vitamin B_{12} is needed to prevent some types of anemia, and it is also required for proper digestion and absorption of foods. It is especially essential for the metabolism of fats and carbohydrates. Vitamin B_{12} is also associated with preventing nerve damage and otherwise protecting the nerves. Lack of adequate B_{12} is associated with faulty memory and learning. This is why it is often given to older people who suffer from some form of memory impairment or even **dementia**.

dementia: a permanent acquired impairment of intellectual function

Often people with a vitamin B_{12} deficiency have a shuffling gait when they walk. Other characteristics of being low in B_{12} are tiredness, general weakness, poor appetite, speaking difficulties, pernicious anemia, nervousness, neuritis, brain damage, and growth failure in children. This makes vitamin B_{12} a really important part of your diet.

MEAT FOR BREAKFAST

When I was in high school I did not like eating cold cereal or sweet things for breakfast, like pancakes or french toast, at least not during the week. My mother was at a loss about what to have available for me for breakfast. One day I just said that leftovers from dinner the night before would be fine. She thought I should have some meat so she got me a pound of ground beef. She then divided it into six servings and individually wrapped them and put them in the freezer. Each day for breakfast I would have all the leftover vegetables, any gravy leftover, and a very small patty of ground beef, which I cooked up. I felt great and never had mid-morning slumps. Even then I ate vegetables for breakfast!

From The Kitchen

If you have a steak or some other serving of meat that is over 4 ounces, do not have any more fat or animal proteins for the rest of the day. Stick to veggie proteins.

Remember This . . .

> **Isaiah 10:14** . . . as men gather abandoned eggs, so I gather all the countries; not one flapped a wing, or opened its mouth to chirp.

Which Came First: The Chicken Or The Egg?

There is evidence that eggs were eaten in Bible times because, as seen above, there are references to eggs in the Bible. The eggs they had were from both domesticated birds and wild birds as this passage points out. However, the Bible doesn't say which came first, the chicken or the egg. Perhaps they were created at the same time, but I suspect that the chicken came first. The chicken was created and then it laid an egg, just like Adam was created and then had offspring. Of course, who can be sure?

Young Jewish boys used to discuss, as part of their schooling, whether it was lawful for a chicken to lay an egg on the Sabbath, because no work was to be done on the Sabbath. So you can be sure that eggs were part of the Jewish diet.

Maureen Salaman: Eggs are mentioned in various parts of the Scriptures, and it is common knowledge that they were eaten in Old and New Testament times, when available.[10]

What Others are Saying:

How Much Can I Have?

The Mediterranean Diet suggests that you eat poultry and eggs a few times a week. When you are eating a diet high in vegetables (especially soybeans), whole grains, nuts, and seeds, a few times a week you can supplement these vegetable proteins and fats with animal protein, such as that which comes from poultry and eggs.

From The Kitchen

What Others
are Saying:

You don't want to eat eggs every day, but a few a week are generally recommended (see Illustration #27, this page). Eggs contain
choline and **inositol** which feed your brain in such a way as to
allow you to think better. Eggs do contain cholesterol, but they
also contain **lecithin**, which helps the cholesterol to be used up.
Cooking eggs on medium or low heat is advised to prevent the
protein from becoming too tough or from releasing sulfurous compounds, which could cause gas and are difficult to digest.

All protein foods should be cooked on medium or low heat. If
you are broiling meat, fish, or cheese, always keep it six inches
from the heat source. Meat and eggs should be cooked through
but never blackened.

Eggs—The Perfect Food?

For many years eggs were considered the perfect food. Consequently, eggs were the standard on which to base all proteins.
This meant that any proteins for human consumption had to "measure up" to the complement of protein in eggs, or it was judged
inadequate. In other words, each protein food was assigned a "protein efficiency ratio" (PER), and because eggs contained 100 percent of the amino acids for complete protein, they were given the
number 100. Fish, milk, meat, and soybeans also have a PER of
100. All other protein foods have a PER of less than 100.

Maureen Salaman: If any food can be called perfect, the egg
can, inasmuch as it contains all the amino acids essential to our
health. Over and above its protein richness, the egg boasts many
vitamins and minerals. Few foods are as digestible, contain as few
calories, and cost as little per unit weight.[11]

> **Matthew 23:37** "O Jerusalem, Jerusalem, you who kill the prophets and stone those sent to you, how often I have longed to gather your children together, as a hen gathers her chicks under her wings, but you were not willing."

Eggs make a great snack or main meal. Consider having eggs for dinner when you are in a hurry or want a light meal. To "hard" cook an egg, place it in a pan and fully cover it with water that is the same temperature as the egg. (More water is OK.) Bring it just to the boiling point over medium heat. This should take about 15–20 minutes. Remove it from the heat and cool it under cold water. Refrigerate the hard-cooked eggs immediately.

From The Kitchen

What About The Chickens?

In Bible times many people were in touch with the elements and their surroundings. Examples of animals were used for clarification in many stories. This passage from Matthew 23:37 uses the example of a hen gathering her chicks under her wings to give the all-encompassing feeling of how God wants to shelter the people spoken to here.

NUTRITIONAL FACT

Really fresh eggs have not formed an air pocket inside and, when hard boiled, the shell will be more difficult to remove.

Grain-fed, chemical-free, antibiotic-free chickens and eggs are the best kinds to eat. There is much controversy about whether the skin on chickens and the yolks of eggs are okay to eat. Research has shown that chicken with and without the skin have about the same health benefits. There is a lot more fat in and around the skin, so if you are watching your fat intake, you will have to count this extra fat. For example, 100 grams of roasted white-meat chicken without the skin has 173 kilocalories and 4.5 grams of fat, while 100 grams of roasted white-meat chicken with the skin has 222 kilocalories and 10.85 grams of fat. Just remember that the measurement in grams is a weight measurement and **muscle** weighs more than fat, so you are getting more fat per weight than you would muscle for the same weight.

muscle: the part of the animal that is eaten

ONE PICTURE'S WORTH A THOUSAND WORDS

Look at the pyramids at the beginning of this chapter (page 123). You will see that poultry and eggs have a small section. Red meats have an even smaller section. Poultry, which includes chicken, duck, geese, and other birds, can be eaten a few times a week. Eggs, which include scrambled, boiled, or poached as well as eggs used in cooking (in baked goods, as a thickening agent in sauces,

Many foods have eggs hidden in them like ice cream and muffins.

coney: hyrax or rock badger, some people think it is a guinea pig

☞ **GO TO:**

Leviticus 11:1–8;
   Deuteronomy 14:9,
   10; Deuteronomy
   14:11–18 (unclean)

and in custards—both sweet and savory), can be eaten a few times a week.

> **Deuteronomy 14:4–8** These are the animals you may eat: the ox, the sheep, the goat, the deer, the gazelle, the roe deer, the wild goat, the ibex, the antelope, and the mountain sheep. You may eat any animal that has a split hoof divided in two and that chews the cud. However, of those that chew the cud or that have a split hoof completely divided you may not eat the camel, the rabbit, or the **coney**. Although they chew the cud, they do not have a split hoof; they are ceremonially unclean for you. The pig is also unclean; although it has a split hoof, it does not chew the cud. You are not to eat their meat or touch their carcasses.

Keep It Clean

The Israelites were told not to eat hard fat, blood, or certain meats. These meats were considered to be <u>unclean</u> for a variety of reasons. They were also not to eat anything found dead—no road kill.

> **Acts 10:10–15** He became hungry and wanted something to eat, and while the meal was being prepared, he fell into a trance. He saw heaven opened and something like a large sheet being let down to earth by its four corners. It contained all kinds of four-footed animals, as well as reptiles of the earth and birds of the air. Then a voice told him, "Get up, Peter, kill and eat." "Surely not, Lord!" Peter replied, "I have never eaten anything impure or unclean." The voice spoke to him a second time. "Do not call anything impure that God has made clean."

Are These Rules For You?

There are those who say that everyone should be a vegetarian, there are those who say we should follow the clean and unclean food instructions of Deuteronomy and Leviticus, and there are those who say everyone should do neither of these choices. All base their ideas on something they have read in the Bible. It is up to you to follow these rules in the way that you feel comfortable.

Let me say, however, that there are often several reasons for not eating animals that the Old Testament calls unclean. They might be carriers of diseases or fleas that bring the plague, they might eat rotting foods that could carry bacteria or viruses with them, or they may simply be high in fat. I have known many people who do not eat fish without scales and fins such as shrimp and lobster, nor would they eat pork. They were healthy without them. You may have known any number of people who eat pork and lobster, and they also are healthy.

Study Questions

1. Why does the Bible say, *All the fat belongs to the Lord?*
2. Which fats are prohibited to the Israelites and where do you find these fats in our foods today?
3. Why don't we just quit eating fat altogether?
4. What does the Bible Diet say about eating eggs and poultry, and when should we eat them?
5. Which foods are to be eaten a few times a week? Are you eating more of them than you need to? Are you willing to cut back to be healthier? When do you pledge to do this?
6. Which foods in your diet are clean, and which foods in your diet are unclean? Does it matter?

CHAPTER WRAP-UP

- God prohibited the Israelites from eating the hard fat found around the organs. (Leviticus 3:14–17)

- The hard fat and all visible fat on meat was to be burnt as an offering that would please God. (Leviticus 3:14–17)

- Chicken and eggs do have a place in a healthy diet and can even be part of a reduced fat diet for weight loss.

- Nutritionists recommend that 15 to 20 percent of your calories come from fat and that 15 to 20 percent come from proteins.

- The rest of your calories should come from the carbohydrates in whole grains, vegetables, and fruits. This is about the same percentage as in the Bible Diet.

- The New Testament says that it isn't necessary anymore to be concerned with the clean and unclean foods. (Acts 10:10–15)

10 SWEETS, SALT, WATER, AND WINE

CHAPTER HIGHLIGHTS

- Land of Milk and Honey
- Sweets and Sugar
- Salt
- Liquid Life
- Wine Is a Mocker

Let's Get Started

Sweets and alcohol are the last two food sections of the Mediter-ranean Diet Pyramid (see Illustration #28, page 137). The Medi-terranean Diet allows sweets to be eaten a few times per week, but this does not necessarily mean what you think it means, as you will see. Salt and water are essentials of life, so they must also be covered. Lastly, alcohol is a tricky subject, but after reading this chapter, you will have a better understanding of how it fit into the diet of people in Bible times, and how it should fit into yours.

> **Exodus 3:8** So I have come down to rescue them from the hand of the Egyptians and to bring them up out of that land into a good and spacious land, a land flowing with milk and honey.

Land Of Milk And Honey

There are two kinds of honey mentioned in the Bible. One is the kind you know of that comes from honey bees and the honey-comb. The second is "honey" that comes from a syrup of fruits or **carob pods.** Date honey is made from **reduced**, pressed dates, just like maple syrup is the boiled or reduced sap of maple trees. It is boiled or just set out in the sun to allow some of the liquid to evaporate. Date honey and carob honey (or carob syrup) are still popular in the Middle East.

carob pods: *high-fiber, bean-like pods grown on trees of the locust family in the Middle East; also called "St. John's bread" after John the Baptist*

reduced: *when water added during pressing is boiled off, reducing the volume*

Something to Ponder

The most interesting thing about the way Mediterranean people have been eating this sweet "honey" since Bible times is that they always have it with some form of protein such as milk. This is because this kind of honey, as well as honey from bees, is little more than carbohydrates. Honey contains so little protein, it can't be measured. It also contains no fat. Eating straight carbohydrates was not done in Bible times, and it shouldn't be done today either. To redress the situation, Arabs always have milk, or some other form of protein, along with their honey.[1] How fitting that the latest health food information agrees with what was being done in Bible times!

> **Psalm 19:10** They are more precious than gold, than much pure gold; they are sweeter than honey, than honey from the comb.

Milk And Honey: A Marvelous Match

Psalm 19:10 compares the sweetness of honey, which is very sweet, with the sweetness of the Lord's revealed laws, which are even sweeter than honey. God's laws were really sweet to them and should be to you as well.

Honey can be eaten directly from the honeycomb. This unrefined honey is from honey bees and is very sweet, a little bit sweeter than honey made from dates might be. Protein and sweets together are the newest health food necessity. Because North Americans have been eating so many refined sugars and carbohydrates over the years, there is an epidemic of people who react very quickly to sugar. These people find that they should always eat some form of protein with fruit or other sweets. Generally, nutritionists suggest that protein (from low-fat cheese or in a few nuts) be eaten with fruits and other sugars to avoid the sudden rush of blood sugar. People in Bible times tried to avoid the very same sort of reaction by having <u>milk and honey</u> together.

This is why the many Bible references to a "land of milk and honey" meant the place mentioned would be paradise—nobody would get sugar rushes or other health problems from eating honey by itself because there would also be milk products like cheese and yogurt to balance the honey, since honey (and honey from the comb) were very sweet. A place with both would be a really excellent place to live; it would have all the essential foods provided by God.

☞ **GO TO:**

Leviticus 20:24;
   Numbers 13:27;
   Deuteronomy 6:3;
   Joshua 5:6; Jeremiah
   11:5; Ezekiel 20:6
   (milk and honey)

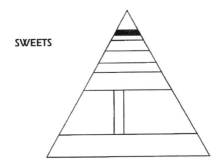

SWEETS

Illustration #28

The Sweets Section—The darkened section of this pyramid represents how much of your diet should be devoted to sweets. This is the last section of daily foods.

Sweets In The Mediterranean Diet

Sweets, other than fruit, are allowed when you are following the Mediterranean Diet or Bible Diet (unless you react to sweets that is). It is best to train your taste buds to want fruits of some kind when you want something sweet, rather than refined sugar. The more complex the sugar is, the slower it enters your bloodstream; and the slower it enters your bloodstream, the less likely you are to have a "sugar rush." If you want to have a muffin, for example, bake your own out of whole-grain flours. This way you will be able to monitor the amount of sugar you are getting.

They Don't Make 'Em Like They Used To

Until about the 1970s, muffins were considered a healthy food. A dozen muffins had two tablespoons of sugar, and so they were considered healthy snacks. Then came the muffin popularity, and stores that sold muffins popped up everywhere. In order to sell enough to make it a viable business, they added more sugar. Recipes for homemade muffins are being influenced too. Nowadays, a recipe for a dozen homemade muffins calls for about one cup of sugar. This is indicative of how the taste for sweets has really grown in North America. Don't believe any of the estimates about how much sugar the average person consumes in a year; most estimates are far behind the actual consumption. Sugar consumption has changed all over North America. In the 1940s and 1950s, for example, schools gave children snacks of graham crackers and milk, or fruit. Now they serve soft drinks in the schools. Soft drink companies are even paying for school equipment (like basketball hoops and team scoreboards) and putting soft drink machines in

ON Target:
Eating fruits when you want something sweet

OFF Target:
Eating sweets instead of fruit

the schools. Many school children consume five soft drinks a day on the average.

> **Isaiah 55:2** Why spend money on what is not bread, and labor on what does not satisfy? Listen, listen to me, and eat what is good, and your soul will delight in the richest of fare.

If You Know What's Good For You . . .

God designed your body to function from the fuel in whole grains, fruits, vegetables, and proteins (see Illustration #29, page 139). Man designed the refined foods that so many people eat today, like sugary snacks, white flour breads, and soft drinks. Do you spend your money on white bread, which is not really bread because it isn't whole grains? Do you eat mostly the foods that are good? Too many people take the foods that God designed for human bodies and change them in such a way that they are causing countless health problems. There are many foods that fit into this category: refined grains, refined sugars, margarine and other hydrogenated fats, and processed foods filled with unhealthy fats and chemicals.

Sugar By Any Other Name

Sugar has a lot of different names. Look for these on products that you buy: sucrose, dextrose, fructose, maltose, corn syrup, brown sugar, honey, and high-fructose corn syrup. You will be getting sugar in products with those ingredients. The more natural sugars are fruit juice, honey, brown rice syrup, dehydrated cane juice, evaporated cane juice, barley malt syrup, and fruit purées. The more natural sugars are not refined, so they contain the B vitamins and minerals in the original food. The sugar source in its natural state has fiber in it as well. B vitamins, minerals, and fiber are all used to help your body assimilate the sweet part efficiently. When sugar is refined and the vitamins, minerals, and fiber are removed, it is more difficult for your body to handle.

There are many brands of natural foods that contain **organic** cane sugar or **dehydrated cane juice** that contain less sugar, and therefore less sweetness, and no chemicals or additives. Even my local supermarket carries Natural Choice Organic Sorbet and Howler Rainforest Sorbet, both made with natural ingredients and thus less-processed, more natural sugar.

organic: grown without pesticides or artificial fertilizers

dehydrated cane juice: dried juice of the sugar cane plant

 *From The Kitchen*

Cheryl Townsley: Although no sweetener at all is best for the body, if you choose to have a sweet baked food item, it is important to know which sweeteners are less harmful.[2]

What Others are Saying:

There are two kinds of carbohydrates: simple and complex. Simple carbohydrates are often called simple sugars. They are fructose (fruit sugar), sucrose (table sugar), and lactose (milk sugar). Complex carbohydrates are found in vegetables, whole grains, dried peas, and dried beans. Both sugars are converted into **glucose** in your body. The simple sugars go directly into your bloodstream causing a rise in blood sugar. The complex carbohydrates are called "slow release" because they release sugar more slowly than simple sugars do.

Remember This . . .

glucose: the sugar that fuels your body and brain

Cheryl Townsley: Honey is a simple carbohydrate, which means it enters the bloodstream quickly.[3]

What Others are Saying:

IS SUGAR BAD FOR YOU?

Natural sugar in moderate or low doses, as prescribed by the Mediterranean Diet, along with a low animal-fat, natural diet, is not bad for you. What is bad for you is a diet with very little nutrients, very little whole foods, lots of stimulants like caffeine and nicotine, lots of sugar, and no vegetables, especially no green vegetables.

Cheryl Townsley: Sugar was a big contributor to my emotional and mental problems.[4]

Dr. Mary Ruth Swope: Limit the amount of desserts, cookies, and other sweets served to your children. Instead, give them nuts, seeds, and dried fruits like raisins, apricots, etc.[5]

insulin resistance: body cells are unresponsive to insulin

Carbohydrates And Syndrome X

Syndrome X is one of the latest diseases to come along in medicine, it was first written about in 1988. Syndrome X is also called **insulin resistance** syndrome. Many people who have syndrome X develop **NIDDM** later. Syndrome X is characterized by **hyperlipidaemia, hypertension, obesity, cardiovascular disease**, and insulin resistance.[6] Much research has been done on syndrome X and diet over the last two years, and most of the results point to a high-fat, refined-sugar diet as being partly responsible for the syndrome.[7] Insulin resistance has become a predictor for cardiovascular disease[8] and coronary artery disease.[9] Syndrome X is even present in children as young as 9 years old. In one study, a program that used a special diet and exercise program proved to be the best treatment, but most of the children were not eager to comply with this program even though it could prevent major disease symptoms.[10] A low-fat, complex-carbohydrate diet, much like the Bible Diet, was found to be the most effective treatment for syndrome X.

NIDDM: non-insulin-dependent diabetes mellitus, diabetes that doesn't require the person to take insulin either orally or by injection

hyperlipidaemia: high blood fats

hypertension: high blood pressure

obesity: overweight

cardiovascular disease: disease of the heart and/ or circulatory system

Reginald Cherry, M.D.: Fiber is turning out to be a major factor used to lower blood sugar.[11]

> **Isaiah 44:12** He gets hungry and loses his strength; he drinks no water and grows faint.

It's Simple: Food = Energy

Food supplies the energy to run your body. If you eat no food, you will have no energy. If you get hungry and don't eat, you'll lose your strength. It's as simple as that! If you follow the Mediterranean Diet, you will have strength, energy, and be on the path to a healthy life. The more you eat denatured or refined foods, the more you will have low energy, loss of strength, and diseases that might have been prevented with a more appropriate lifestyle.

HOW CAN I TELL WHAT'S BAD FOR ME?

By keeping a log you can easily tell what you are doing right or wrong in your diet. Write down what you eat and when you eat it. Write down how you feel. After a week or so you should begin to see some patterns.

Once you can assess your lifestyle and your energy levels, you can pretty much see what you are doing right or wrong.

Questions To Ask Yourself

- Did I eat breakfast?
- Did I eat lunch?
- Did I get tired?
- Did I have a mid-morning or mid-afternoon slump?
- Was I too tired to fix dinner at the end of the day?
- Did I lose my temper?
- Did I crave anything with sugar, carbohydrates, alcohol, caffeine, or nicotine?
- Did I want or have a candy bar or coffee to "perk me up"?
- Did cheese give me a headache?
- Did I eat green or orange vegetables?
- Did I have raw vegetables?

> **Matthew 5:13** "You are the salt of the earth. But if the salt loses its saltiness, how can it be made salty again? It is no longer good for anything, except to be thrown out and trampled by men."

Salt In The Bible Diet

Although salt is used in the Bible many times to mean something essential or stable, it does not have a section on the Mediterranean Diet Pyramid. Salt is to be used in small amounts, and should never be used during cooking. This means you can add small amounts of salt to your food at the table but not on a regular basis. You will want to keep away from processed foods that are typically high in salt, sugar, and hydrogenated fats. These refined and processed foods are not part of a healthy diet anyway. Stick to fresh vegetables, raw or lightly steamed; small amounts of cheese or yogurt; broiled, baked, or poached fish; olive oil as a dressing; beans; peas; tofu; nuts; and fresh or dried fruits for your daily diet. This will automatically give you a low-salt diet. Only the cheese, and perhaps the yogurt, is likely to contain salt.

> **Job 6:6** Is tasteless food eaten without salt, or is there flavor in the white of an egg?

How Salty?

In Bible times salt was the main preservative of fish and meat. For hundreds of years salt has often been an ingredient of the **brine** used in meat-smoking processes. Recently, in the last 50 years or so, salt has become an addiction for many people. You've probably seen people put salt on their food even before tasting it. They know there will never be enough salt for them. Perhaps you are one of these people. Many women are addicted to salt and prefer salt over sugar any day. Most **natural practicing doctors** will tell you that when you have either exhausted or overactive adrenal glands, you will have low blood pressure, and you will crave salt. You might also crave salt if you are low in iodine, because most salt has iodine added to it. For many people, salt is their only source of iodine.

Rex Russell, M.D.: It is easy to become addicted to salt. Enough evidence of possible health risks exist to make it advisable for most people to cut back on their use of salt.[12]

How Much Can You Have?

You need some salt in your diet, because it is a valuable mineral that will help keep the fluid balanced in your body. It is only when you start to take in too much that it becomes a problem. Sodium chloride, regular table salt, is also useful to maintain normal stomach, nerve, and muscle functions. Excessive sodium intake can lead to **edema**, high blood pressure, potassium deficiency, and liver and kidney disease.

SHOULD YOU CUT BACK?

In a study done with elderly people, many people who did not have a history of hypertension, but had a high-sodium intake, had strokes.[13] Because this was the case, it was suggested that all elderly people evaluate the amount of salt in their diets and reduce any excess intake. This would mean not using salt in cooking and adding very little to food at the table. It would also mean eliminating those foods high in salt such as bacon, ham, potato chips or pretzels, and using sodium-reduced crackers, juices, and salad dressings when possible. Always consult with your doctor if you are planning to make some dietary changes. If you suspect that you are eating too much salt or sugar, have your doctor prescribe a visit with a nutritionist or dietitian who can evaluate your diet.

Pamela Smith: Excessive **sodium** is indicated in many diseases, especially high blood pressure and kidney disease. Excessive salt causes temporary buildup of body fluids in your system. This makes it difficult for your heart to pump blood through the cardiovascular system, and the results may be high blood pressure or excessive swelling.[14]

What's It Taste Like?

Many habits that you may have can dull your taste buds. Drinking very hot or very cold liquids, eating very hot or very cold foods, eating spicy-hot foods, smoking cigarettes, **mouth breathing**, low zinc in your diet, and B vitamin deficiencies all can play a part in some part of your mouth or tongue becoming unable to taste well. There are five basic tastes: salty, sweet, bitter, pungent, and sour. Each taste is experienced in a different place on your tongue. If you have desensitized your tongue and/or your taste buds, you may want to add enough salt so that you can taste it, when really you are adding too much.

Test yourself out. Ask a child to taste some of your food, before you add salt, and get his or her reaction. Then you taste it. Next add salt until it is the taste you like and ask the child to taste it again. Note the child's reaction. Did he or she think it was too salty the way you like it? Children are often sensitive to strong tastes because they have not yet engaged in habits that would destroy their sense of taste.

What Others are Saying:

sodium: sodium chloride, table salt

mouth breathing: regularly breathing through your mouth instead of your nose

From The Kitchen

What Others are Saying:

Remember This . . .

Kenneth H. Cooper, M.D.: People who have high blood pressure should severely restrict their salt intake. One reason for this restriction is that a number of problems have been linked to high salt intake, including loss of calcium and bone deterioration, stroke, heart enlargement, kidney stones, and asthma. [15]

Salt sensitivity and insulin resistance are often related in both hypertensives and nonhypertensives. In fact, one study even suggested that salt sensitivity actually contributed to insulin resistance, and that this could lead to cardiovascular disease.[16] This finding would suggest that everybody should restrict their salt intake to the lowest required amount. Give up the salty snacks! Give up adding salt to store-bought foods, because they are already high in salt. Use reduced salt items when appropriate and eat more potassium-rich vegetables and fruits, such as bananas, potatoes, red and green peppers, and tomatoes.

> **I Samuel 30:11, 12** They found an Egyptian in a field and brought him to David. They gave him water to drink and food to eat—part of a cake of pressed figs and two cakes of raisins. He ate and was revived, for he had not eaten any food or drunk any water for three days and three nights.

Water: Liquid Of Life

Water makes up a large percentage of your body weight and volume. There are so many figures about how much of a human body is water, somewhere between 70 and 90 percent, that it is hard to say for sure. Even if 50 percent of your body was water, it would still be a large percentage of your total weight. Without water you will dry up (see Illustration #30, page 144). This is what was happening to the Egyptian in the quote from I Samuel; he was **dehydrated.**

dehydrated: dried up

Kenneth H. Cooper, M.D.: Water, even more than food, is necessary to sustain life. Everyone should drink the equivalent of at least eight 8-ounce glasses of water per day.[17]

What Others are Saying:

How Much Should You Drink?

Eight 8-ounce glasses is the least amount of water you should drink every day. There are weight loss plans that suggest drinking a gallon of water every day, but that is very difficult to do. As soon as you get up in the morning, drink a large glass of fresh water. Always let the water run for a while, so that you aren't drinking water that was in the pipes overnight. Many of the pipes used in modern kitchens can allow water to leach out chemicals that you don't want to be drinking if water is left standing in the pipes. When you go to bed drink a large glass of water. That makes two of the required eight glasses of water. Drink an additional glass after each meal; that's three more. Then drink at other times during the day. I always carry a bottle of water with me in my purse or car. You can always stop at a convenience store and purchase a bottle of fresh water so there is no excuse for not having water. The more you drink, the better you will feel!

KEY POINT

Eight 8-ounce glasses is the least amount of water you should drink every day.

Maureen Salaman: To remove impurities that had accumulated in my body over the years, I stepped up my water drinking from six glasses to nearly nine. Many authorities feel that such a move is necessary to **detoxify** the body.[18]

What Others are Saying:

detoxify: remove impurities

> **Isaiah 44:12** He gets hungry and loses his strength; he drinks no water and grows faint.

AND IF YOU DON'T DRINK IT?

Your body will respond to low water levels in a lot of ways—lower energy and reduced performance, inability to concentrate, and irritability, just to name a few. Please don't wait until you feel thirsty to drink. By then you really need the water; you might even be dehydrated already.

Remember This . . .

Drink regularly! Mountain bikers and hikers know that it is essential to drink whether they are thirsty or not, especially when exercising. Because of this they always carry water so that they can drink on a schedule. When doing any exercise that might make you sweat and, therefore, lose water, it is essential to drink frequently before, during, and after. If you work out in a gym or do anything aerobic, you need more water. If you take walks, you need more water. Everyday you require at least eight 8-ounce glasses of water; when you exercise, you need even more.

GETTING UP AT NIGHT

If you find yourself getting up at night to urinate, you will want to have a thorough checkup at your family doctor. Generally, having to urinate is not the real reason people get up at night. There are many health problems that might be diagnosed early, if you mention getting up at night to urinate to your doctor.

> **Proverbs 20:1** Wine is a mocker and beer a brawler; whoever is led astray by them is not wise.

Wine Is A Mocker!

Yes, wine and beer have been leading people astray for a long time. Even in Bible times people were picking fights because they drank too much wine or beer. All through the Bible there are warnings against being drunk. Much research has been published, lately, showing the health benefits of drinking wine. However, the same benefits can come from other fruits and vegetable juices just as well. You can also drink non-alcoholic wine. If you do, select a non-alcoholic red wine, which contains beneficial substances.

Rex Russell, M.D.: The University of Wisconsin recently reported that bioflavins in wine are good for the vessels and for the heart, that is true . . . [bioflavins] are found in higher concentrations in juices, fruits, and vegetables than in wines.[19]

Alcohol And B Vitamins

Wine and other alcohol misuse can produce deficiencies of the B vitamins, especially B_1 and B_3. Low amounts of vitamin B_2 have been associated with a desire to drink wine or other alcoholic beverages. During the early days of vitamin therapy, and again today, many natural practicing doctors treat alcoholics with injections of B vitamins, especially B_2, because it makes people lose their taste for alcohol.[20]

> **Ephesians 5:18** Do not get drunk on wine, which leads to debauchery. Instead, be filled with the Spirit.

All The Benefits, None Of The Hassle

Although there are many passages in the Bible where people drink wine, there are many passages warning against getting drunk. Many companies produce wine without alcohol. The benefits of wine come from the skins and seeds, not from the alcohol. This is why so many health food stores sell capsules of grape seed and grape skin extract—they are powerful antioxidants! If you want to experience how wine can be of benefit to your health, you can easily purchase one of these products, which contain all the benefits of wine without the alcohol. Or, better yet, eat grapes—skins, seeds, and fruit.

Study Questions

1. What were the different kinds of honey used in the Middle East and where did they come from? Why did they always mention milk and honey together?
2. How many sweets should we eat? Which are the best forms of sweets to eat? How will this information allow you to change your diet?
3. What health problems are attributed to eating salt and how can you reverse them? Why do you think that people could eat more salt in Bible times than we can now?

4. What is the most important liquid for health? When should you drink it? Why do you think there has been more emphasis on drinking water in the last five years?
5. When are the most important times to drink wine? What does your church say about drinking wine? How do you feel about that now?
6. What are the benefits of wine, and which foods have the equivalent nutrients?

CHAPTER WRAP-UP

- The Bible has many references to the land of milk and honey. It was a phrase that meant the land was rich and balanced. (Exodus 3:8)

- Sweets are not forbidden on the Mediterranean Diet/Bible Diet. It is suggested they be eaten a maximum of a few times per week. Eating fruit is okay anytime.

- Salt was essential in Bible times, but it is not as essential today because we consume it in so many different vegetables. For some people salt causes health problems. (Matthew 5:13)

- Water is the most essential liquid in any diet; six to eight glasses should be drunk each day. (Isaiah 44:12)

- Wine is not an essential food for modern people. Although wine is part of the Mediterranean Diet, experts concede it is not the alcohol that is the healthy part of wine; it is the bioflavins, which are also found in the skins and seeds of grapes and other fruits.

Part Two

GOD'S WORD ON GOOD HEALTH

REVEREND FUN

11 ALL FOOD IS CLEAN

CHAPTER HIGHLIGHTS

- Cleanliness Rules
- Peter's Vision
- Safe Food Handling
- Mildew Regulations

Let's Get Started

Chapter 9 touched on <u>clean and unclean</u> foods. Jews were not supposed to eat the meat or flesh of many animals, fowl, and birds. Clean land animals, the Law read, chewed their **cud** and had a split hoof. Unclean land animals either chewed cud but did not have a split hoof, or had a split hoof but did not chew cud. Examples of unclean animals are pig, camel, rabbit, and coney. Animals living in the waters that did not have fins and scales—trout, lobster, shrimp, scampi, octopus, clams, oysters, mussels—were also considered unclean. Many Jews, even today, do not eat these foods.

In the New Testament Peter had a vision of a new way of looking at these prohibitions, as God showed him that all foods were clean. Although the clean and unclean foods were prescribed by God for spiritual reasons, recently, scientists have found the unclean foods to actually be unhealthy.

☞ **GO TO:**

Leviticus 11:1–47 (clean and unclean)

cud: *food regurgitated from the first stomach to the mouth to be chewed again*

> **Deuteronomy 14:6–10** You may eat any animal that has a split hoof divided in two and that chews the cud. However, of those that chew the cud or that have a split hoof completely divided you may not eat the camel, the rabbit or the coney. Although they chew the cud, they do not have a split hoof; they are ceremonially unclean for you. The pig is also unclean; although it has a split hoof, it does not chew the cud. You are not to eat their meat or touch their carcasses. Of all the creatures living in the water, you may eat any that has fins and scales. But anything that does not have fins and scales you may not eat; for you it is unclean.

Are You Eating Unclean Foods?

The unclean animals of the Old Testament are the same animals that could carry disease, harbor bacteria, or have rotted flesh inside them that would taint the meat. These animals are generally **scavengers**. In this day and age, when so many foods are becoming contaminated because of handling problems, it would be wise to avoid meats that are likely to be contaminated before or while being slaughtered. If you know where your meat is coming from and it is raised under the strictest standards, the need for concern may be less.

Something to Ponder

Because rabbits look as if they are chewing things, ancient peoples thought they were chewing their cud. They did not chew their cud, they didn't even have cud! Cud-chewing animals have more than one stomach, and rabbits have only one stomach.

What Others are Saying:

Rex Russell, M.D.: The differences between clean and unclean animals appear to be related to their primary food source and to their digestive systems. Scavengers that eat anything and everything are unclean, not suitable for food, according to the Bible.[1]

Dr. Mary Ruth Swope: Jesus would not have eaten pork in any form—not even barbecued or grilled on an open pit. Our favorites of baked ham, broiled pork chops, fresh pork with sauerkraut, or even the famous BLT (bacon/lettuce/tomato) sandwich would all have been "unclean" to Jesus.[2]

Blech!

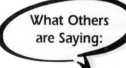

ON Target:

Eating a wide variety of foods and lots of vegetables

OFF Target:

Eating pork and other scavenger animals frequently

Much animal meat is tainted with new contaminants that did not exist in Bible times. Generally, animal producers use these contaminants to make animals grow faster, protect them from some real or imagined infection, and to make them fatter and therefore weigh more. Many of these chemicals and additives can cause allergic reactions in people who eat the meat. They often cause other health problems and many of them are dangerous to the environment if they are not properly taken care of.

In the last 10 years or so antibiotics have been forbidden in slaughtered animals, so meat producers have stopped feeding them to animals a few days before they are sent to the killing plant. Many people feel that the overuse of antibiotics in meat and dairy products was responsible for so many people being

Something to Ponder

allergic to antibiotics, especially penicillin, and that this also contributes to **antibiotic resistant** strains of bacteria. Perhaps if meat producers and packers followed God's instructions for raising, killing, and processing animals found in the Bible, we would not have this problem. One can only speculate that if modern man had not raised, killed, and processed "unclean" animals, they would not have needed to use as many antibiotics and other chemicals.

antibiotic resistant: when bacteria have mutated in such a way that there is no antibiotic that will eradicate them

Anne and David Frähm: Current practices in livestock and poultry management are producing meat products that are laden with production chemicals and drugs that undermine human health. These substances, unlike bacteria, which can be killed by cooking, remain in the animal products when consumed by humans.[3]

What Others are Saying:

Where's The Beef?

Meats that are raised without the use of chemicals, antibiotics, hormones, steroids, or other growth hormones are generally called **organically grown**. Some farmers also feed their livestock organically grown food, which results in meat that is cleaner and has less contamination.

organically grown: grown or raised without petrochemicals

Cheryl Townsley: There are meat producers that use no chemicals or steroids. The animals and the grains are grown without exposure to chemicals. These meats are definitely preferable to the more commonly sold meats. They are more flavorful and healthful. Many health-food stores provide this natural meat.[4]

What Others are Saying:

 **NUTRITIONAL FACT**

Most states have laws prohibiting the use of antibiotics three days before the slaughter of animals used for eating.

> **Acts 10:9–16** Peter went up on the roof to pray. He became hungry and wanted something to eat, and while the meal was being prepared, he fell into a trance. He saw heaven opened and something like a large sheet being let down to the earth by its four corners. It contained all kinds of four-footed animals, as well as reptiles of the earth and birds of the air. Then a voice told him, "Get up, Peter. Kill and eat." "Surely not, Lord!" Peter replied. "I have never eaten anything impure or unclean." The voice spoke to him a second time, "Do not call anything impure that God has made clean." This happened three times, and immediately the sheet was taken back to heaven.

☞ **GO TO:**

Acts 11:4–10; Matthew
15:10, 11, 18
(unclean)

**Something
to Ponder**

If you are allergic to antibiotics or **petrochemicals**, consider
eating only organically grown meats and dairy products.

Peter's Vision

Peter followed the Jewish laws of the time and did not eat any
<u>unclean</u> or impure animal products. Jesus had already been teach-
ing his followers that it was not what they ate but what they said
that made them clean or unclean. This vision appeared to Peter to
reinforce Jesus' teachings (see Illustration #31, this page).

Jesus was a practicing Jew, so he followed the clean and unclean food rules, but he was more concerned with spiritual
health. Jesus said that following the "rules" set out in the
commandments was more important than mindlessly following rituals. He taught that all people should be more concerned with what they said and did to themselves and others
than with observing conventional customs.

> **Mark 7:18–23** "Are you so dull?" he asked. "Don't you see that nothing that enters a man from the outside can make him 'unclean'? For it doesn't go into his heart but into his stomach, and then out of his body." (In saying this, Jesus declared all foods "clean.") He went on: "What comes out of a man is what makes him 'unclean.' For from within, out of men's hearts, come evil thoughts, sexual immorality, theft, murder, adultery, greed, **malice**, **deceit**, **lewdness**, envy, **slander**, **arrogance** and folly. All these evils come from inside and make a man 'unclean'."

malice: *a desire to harm others*

deceit: *misleading people*

lewdness: *obscene, being preoccupied with sex and sexual desires*

slander: *making false statements about another that might hurt their reputation*

arrogance: *being overly convinced of one's own importance*

Jesus' Response

You do not have to follow the rules set up for the Israelites in Old Testament times for the sake of following the rules. Jesus declared that you should be more concerned with what comes out of your mouth than with what goes into it. However, if you want to be really, really healthy, you will want to pay attention to why these foods were unclean. Scavengers eat rotting and infected foods. They were designed by God to be the garbage collectors of the world. It is your choice if you want to pollute your body and make yourself sick from eating these foods. I almost never eat pork and the other unclean meats for health reasons. I don't want to be sick!

Rex Russell, M.D.: In the United States, three of the six most common foodborne parasitic diseases of humans are associated with pork consumption. In Japan, the source of these infections was traced to the flesh of pigs, bears, horses, raccoons and foxes. All of these animals are listed in Scripture as putrid or unclean.[5]

What Others are Saying:

HELP, THIS SCARES ME!

If you find this frightening, you should! There are so many sources of parasites today that it has become big business to sell potions and supplements to rid your body of them. What can you do? Stay away from any unclean foods, including spoiled foods. Eat only wholesome foods that have been raised chemical free and wash off your vegetables with soap and water. Include those foods and herbs in your diet that have been shown to clean out your body or kill various parasites. These foods include garlic, onions, bitter herbs, papaya seeds, pumpkin seeds, olives, olive oil, and olive leaves. Stay away from refined sugar and white flour products (they are considered garbage anyway), as they can reduce

NUTRITIONAL FACT

Abdominal cramps and pain, constipation, diarrhea, fatigue, fever, flatulence, food allergies, headaches, hives, indigestion, and lower back pain are symptoms associated with parasitic infection.

the effectiveness of your immune system. When your immune system is not functioning fully, you can be even more susceptible to parasites and illnesses. If you even suspect that you have a health problem related to your consumption of these unclean foods, please see your doctor for testing and treatment.

> **I Timothy 4:3–5** They forbid people to marry and order them to abstain from certain foods, which God created to be received with thanksgiving by those who believe and who know the truth. For everything God created is good, and nothing is to be rejected if it is received with thanksgiving, because it is consecrated by the Word of God and prayer.

THIS IS CONFUSING!

Even in New Testament times there were people saying that you shouldn't eat this or that because it wasn't clean by Old Testament standards. Often people interpret this passage to mean that they shouldn't be vegetarians, since that is forbidding them from eating any meat. The Old Testament says to keep away from "unclean" animals, not meat in general, and Jesus says it doesn't matter as much as how you act toward others.

> **Colossians 2:16** Therefore do not let anyone judge you by what you eat or drink. . . .

Pray A Lot

If you decide to eat these foods that are unclean or impure to Jews, just be sure to receive them with thanksgiving and pray over them. I would also suggest you eat raw or odorless garlic, pumpkin seeds, olive oil, and take olive leaf extract. If you have chosen to eat any foods that others find objectionable, remember that only God can judge you. It is your right to choose to eat these foods or to eat meat at all.

JUST TRY IT

If these "unclean" foods are in your diet on a regular basis and you feel really great, don't be too concerned. However, if you eat these foods and you have headaches, unexplained muscle pain, fever, or swelling on a regular basis, or you just don't feel really great, go off them for two weeks. If you begin to notice that you feel better, stay off them. It really takes much longer to get rid of parasites, and you must see your doctor for treatment. However if the antibiotics they use to kill the bacteria in the "unclean" animals is causing you health problems, then you will notice a lifting of your energy right away. Wouldn't you rather feel great than eat something that made you feel bad?

> **Romans 14:20** Do not destroy the work of God for the sake of food. All food is clean.

All Food Is Clean

It seems obvious that by the time this verse was written in Romans, the New Testament Christians were going around and around about this matter of clean and unclean foods, so I don't expect it to be solved here either.

> **Exodus 30:18–20** Make a bronze basin, with its bronze stand, for washing. Place it between the Tent of Meeting and the altar, and put water in it. Aaron and his sons are to wash their hands and feet with water from it. Whenever they enter the Tent of Meeting, they shall wash with water so that they will not die. . . .

Wash Those Hands And Feet

Hand <u>washing</u> was both a common practice and ceremonial ritual for 3,500 years after God gave these instructions to Moses. God gave Moses instructions for washing hands and feet, and for washing clothes of wool, linen, anything woven or knitted, and leather. The clothes-washing instructions were for removing contaminants and for general purification. Hand washing was for sanitation and ritual purification.

A Reason For Sadness

For many years autopsies were performed on dead women by doctors who left the autopsy room and went in to examine pregnant women in another hospital ward. One out of every six of these women died. The physicians thought it was due to unrelenting constipation, bad air, or some other thing wrong with the women. In the 1840s, after Ignaz Semmelweis instituted a process of hand washing between the autopsies and the pelvic examinations, the death rate was one in every forty-two. After a

☞ **GO TO:**

Exodus 29:4; 40:12; Leviticus 8:6 (washing)

ON Target:
Washing your hands before handling food or eating

OFF Target:
Eating with dirty hands

month of the practice, the death rate was one in every eighty-four. This is most astonishing! And yet Dr. Semmelweis was ridiculed for his idea. He was shunned and eventually left the hospital in disgrace.

S. I. McMillen, M.D.: Many centuries before Semmelweis, however, God gave to Moses detailed instructions on the safest method for cleansing the hands after handling the dead or the infected living. Semmelweis's method went a long way in preventing many deaths, but it would not be accepted in any hospital today.[6]

You Wash Your Hands Before?

I am really strict about hand washing. I always wash my hands after touching a dog, cat, horse, or other animal. I also wash my hands in the ladies' room before I go into the cubicle and after I come out. I often get a lot of strange looks when women see me washing and then going into the toilet. I realize that when I am out in public shopping and touching objects that an infected person could have touched, I could actually contaminate myself if I didn't wash my hands before using the toilet. Moses told Aaron to wash before and after entering the Tent of Meeting. There must be some message for everybody in this.

> **Deuteronomy 23:12, 13** Designate a place outside the camp where you can go to relieve yourself. As part of your equipment have something to dig with, and when you relieve yourself, dig a hole and cover up your excrement.

Safe Food Handling

You Are Clean—Hah!

Almost weekly you see some TV special talking about the importance of hand washing in the bathroom and the kitchen. They always show the bacteria on the kitchen sponge and cutting board. In a kitchen that looks spotless, there is always the most bacteria on the cleaning rag because someone forgot to wash it out with soap and water after doing the dishes and wiping the counter. Several times a year you hear about an epidemic in a nursing home, day care, or hospital, because someone made a sandwich on a cutting board that had held raw chicken without washing it in between (see Illustration #32, page 159). We still don't have complete sanitation and safety in our houses!

Illustration #32

Cutting Board with Bleach—
After cutting meat, be sure to
sanitize the cutting board
with a chlorine solution.

This Is Not The Same Clean

Although this chapter starts with "all food is clean," it does not mean that all food is bacteria free. That is up to the person raising the animal, killing the animal, cleaning the animal, preparing the animal, cooking the animal, and serving the animal. It is essential to take charge of your health by frequent hand washing and by following the cleanliness rules in the Food Safety list (shown below). As far as whether you should eat the foods declared "clean" and "unclean," that is really up to you.

Food Safety

The Food Safety and Inspection Service of the U.S. Department of Agriculture recommends:

ON Target:
Washing your hands
frequently, especially
before preparing
food

OFF Target:
Going to bed or
brushing your teeth
without washing
your hands

- Hands should be washed, gloved or not, for 20 seconds before beginning preparation; after handling raw meat, poultry, seafood or eggs; after touching animals; after using the bathroom; after changing diapers; or after blowing the nose.
- Always wash your hands, counters, equipment, utensils, and cutting boards with soap and water immediately after use.
- Counters, equipment, utensils, and cutting boards can be sanitized with a chlorine solution of 1 teaspoon liquid household bleach per quart of water.
- Thaw food in the refrigerator, never on the counter.

If you are interested in all of their recommendations, you may contact the USDA Meat and Poultry Hotline at 1-800-535-4555. Or look at their website at: http://www.fsis.usda.gov/[7]

Taking a probiotic
daily is helpful for
people who travel or
have to be in unclean
environments.

Dig A Hole

God told his people to bury their excrement. This, too, is something relatively new. You probably remember from history classes reading about people throwing human waste out of windows into the streets of Europe. A lot of the basic rules of cleanliness and sanitation that we follow today come from the Old Testament. Many people are alive today because some ancestor followed God's instructions and washed his hands and buried his excrement. Many places in the world use human excrement for fertilizer on crops. Eating fruits and vegetables fertilized this way can cause major intestinal upsets. This is one of the reasons we get "tourista" or traveler's disease in other countries.

**What Others
are Saying:**

NUTRITIONAL FACT

When traveling in
other countries,
always drink and
wash with water that
has been boiled or is
safe bottled water.

S. I. McMillen, M.D.: Up to the close of the eighteenth century, hygienic provisions, even in the great capitals, were quite primitive. It was the rule for excrement to be dumped into the streets, which were unpaved and filthy. Powerful stenches gripped villages and cities. It was a heyday for flies as they bred in the filth and spread intestinal diseases that killed millions. Such waste of human lives could have been prevented if Europe had only taken seriously God's provisions for freeing man of diseases. With a single sentence the Bible pointed the way to deliverance from the deadly epidemics of typhoid, cholera, and dysentery.[8]

> **Leviticus 14:35** . . . the owner of the house must go and tell the priest, 'I have seen something that looks like mildew in my house.'

Regulations About Mildew

Mildew is something that we don't think too much about and yet various kinds of mildews and molds in houses are causing serious problems for a lot of people. God gave Moses and Aaron information about how to deal with mildew in the house and on clothes that still is useful today.

> **Leviticus 14:37** He is to examine the mildew on the walls, and if it has greenish or reddish depressions that appear to be deeper than the surface of the wall, the priest shall go out the doorway of the house and close it up for seven days.

Sorry, We're Out

When mildew was found, people were to tell the priest and leave the house so he could come in and examine it. If someone was in the house, he may be declared unclean. When the priest did find mildew, he closed up the house for seven days. If the mildew had spread by the time the priest returned, the house had to be cleaned by either scraping off the mildew and even the plaster, or replacing the contaminated stones with clean ones. If the mildew returned the entire house had to be torn down and replaced. All the contaminated matter was to be removed and placed in a designated place outside of town.

What Others are Saying:

S. I. McMillen, M.D.: Could submitting to a code of "restrictive" rules lead to freedom from sicknesses? Could this promise remain pertinent even in the twentieth century? Yes! Medical science is still discovering how obedience to the ancient prescriptions saved the primitive Hebrews from the scourges of epidemic plagues; and medical research is constantly proving the timeless potency of the divine prescription for modern diseases.[9]

Is Your Home Dangerous?

Should the priest be coming to your home, day care center, or office to look for mildew? The most common illnesses associated with mildew or mold in the home or workplace are asthma, wheezing, headaches, and **sick building syndrome**. Children with mold allergies often develop persistent cold-like symptoms in a moldy environment.[10] In a recent study, children with asthma were very susceptible to **alternaria** even in the desert.[11] The indoor pollution and **sick building syndrome symptoms** were often found to be caused by one or more of three common molds—aspergillus, cladosporium, and penicillium. These microfungi were most prevalent in damp buildings and buildings with basements, especially basements that had standing water.[12] In the places that had air conditioning, the symptoms were not as great as they were in nonair-conditioned places.

sick building syndrome: illnesses that develop because impure air is allowed to circulate from room to room

alternaria: a common mold

sick building syndrome symptoms: headaches, coughing, sinus problems, stomachaches, and rashes

If more schools followed God's instructions about mold and mildew, perhaps there would be less absenteeism and better grades. If children are being subjected to mold and mildew at day care or school, they could be developing reactions that would make it difficult to concentrate, stay awake, or be alert. It might also influence their health by compromising their immune systems, allowing them to be more susceptible to colds, the flu, asthma, or bronchitis.

What Others are Saying:

Francisco Contreras, M.D.: Our homes often lack adequate ventilation so that pure air is limited and harmful elements can reach very high levels. The danger represented by indoor contaminants is aggravated by the lack of information about the problem.[13]

Stachybotrys, The New Scourge?

scourge: pestilence

A new **scourge** has been causing severe health problems and even death in many areas of the country, especially to young infants. It is a mold, called *Stachybotrys*, that grows on wood or paper that has gotten wet. It is generally black (though not all black mold is *Stachybotrys*.) and slimy and often has white edges. This mold is causing **Pulmonary Hemosiderosis**. Infants and children as well as adults around the country are becoming very ill and even dying from the toxins this mold produces. *Stachybotrys* can also produce inflammation in the intestines, stomach, lungs, and throat, and can suppress the immune system.[14] If you suspect that you have this mold, ask the health department to check it and call in some professional help to clean it up.

Pulmonary Hemosiderosis: *bleeding in the lungs*

Remember This . . .

Most walls are made of plaster that is covered with paper; this is called wallboard or plasterboard. Ceiling tiles made of cellulose, newspapers, cardboard boxes, wall paneling, and cotton items are all possible places for this mold to grow if they get wet for at least a week.

WHAT CAN YOU DO?

Always keep your house, office, and school areas clean and free from mildew, mold, and other fungi. Use approved air cleaners, air conditioners, and dehumidifiers. If there is water damage, clean it up immediately; seek professional help to do this if the damaged area is large. Some studies have shown that raw garlic, onions, and green onions can inhibit the growth of aspergillus, so you might want to be sure you are eating these foods if you come into contact with mildew or mold.[15] The best thing to do is call the board of health to inspect the mold. Then do whatever they suggest. Follow the instructions God gave Moses and Aaron, and have the walls scraped or removed. If the water damage has been very bad from a flood, leak, or other water damage, you might have to tear the house down and rebuild, as God prescribed in Leviticus.

Let's Wrap It Up!

The information in this chapter might be somewhat scary. Just remember that when you live in the West, you live in one of the cleanest countries possible. There is no longer excrement in the streets. Doctors and nurses always wash their hands between seeing patients and before any surgical procedure. Your food is not allowed to be fertilized with human excrement. And even though many people are trying to separate church and state, be happy that this is one of the areas where they have not succeeded.

ON Target:

Cleaning up water spills or floods immediately

OFF Target:

Ignoring mold or mildew in any place in your house

Study Questions

1. Name some "clean" and "unclean" animals. Name one unclean animal that many people eat. Why do you think that some animals are still considered unclean today?
2. What was Peter's vision and why was he so shocked about it?
3. What two cleanliness rules did God institute that are still in use today?
4. List some things that you should do when selecting and preparing food.
5. What is the name given to foods that are grown without pesticides and chemicals? Do you think this is necessary?
6. What did God say to do about mold in your house?

CHAPTER WRAP-UP

- God gave the Old Testament Jews special rules regarding which foods to eat, calling some foods "clean" and others "unclean." (Deuteronomy 14:6–10)
- Many of the foods that were considered "unclean" in Bible times are still not considered clean today because of parasites.

- God gave Peter a vision. All foods were to be considered "clean" because they were made clean by God. (Acts 10:9–16)

- Jesus instructed his disciples to pay more attention to what they say and how they treat people than to whether they are following rituals. (Mark 7:18–23)

- God instructed Moses and Aaron to wash their hands on many different occasions. This was a cleanliness ritual, but it was also very practical and hygienic. (Exodus 30:18–20)

- Raw meat can contaminate objects in the kitchen, and everything that touches it should be washed carefully with soap and water, preferably hot water, and chlorine bleach.

- The rules regarding mildew are just as important and necessary today as they were in Moses' time. You don't usually "call in the priest" to look at the mildew, but you should call the health department.

12 ELIJAH AND AHAB

CHAPTER HIGHLIGHTS

- Elijah
- The Angelic Remedy
- Ahab
- Diets for Depression
- When to Eat?
- Herbs and Other Things That Help

Let's Get Started

Depression is not a modern disease, and using diet and nutrition is not a new way of dealing with depression. Elijah had depression and Ahab had **sullenness**. God chose nutrition and diet therapy to help these two overcome their problems. You will be able to do the same thing once you read this chapter.

sullenness: a type of depression

> **I Kings 19:35** Elijah was afraid and ran for his life. When he came to Beersheba in Judah, he left his servant there, while he himself went a day's journey into the desert. He came to a broom tree, sat down under it and prayed that he might die. "I have had enough, Lord," he said. "Take my life; I am no better than my ancestors." Then he lay down under the tree and fell asleep.

Elijah's Story: Does This Sound Familiar?

Have you ever felt stressed out? Have you felt that people were chasing you, after you, or bugging you to do something, be somewhere, go somewhere, when all you really wanted to do was lie down and escape in a nap? Are there times when you just wish the world would stop or go away and leave you alone? Or perhaps you wish you weren't even here to be caught up in all this running around, schedules, and frantic lifestyle. This used to be called "a case of the blues." Now experts are discovering that brain chemicals are involved. You could be suffering from depression. There are many levels of depression, and Elijah had one of them. He was so far down that he wanted God to take his life.

Cheryl Townsley: I cried out in front of the mirror; I just let go. The reflection of "ugliness" was too much. I could no longer deal with my life and the mess I had made of it. I slowly, hopelessly swallowed the pills.[1]

Clinical Depression Symptoms

ON Target:
Checking with a professional if you have depression symptoms

OFF Target:
Ignoring the symptoms of depression

According to the American Psychiatric Association, in its Diagnostic and Statistical Manual of Mental Disorders (DSM-IV), there are eight primary criteria for diagnosing depression. If you have even three of these symptoms, please go directly to your family doctor and discuss this with him or her. Many disorders have some of these symptoms, so only your doctor can really diagnose if you have depression and need medication.

Depression Symptoms

insomnia: chronic inability to sleep

hypersomnia: excessive sleep habits

1. Poor appetite accompanied by weight loss, or increased appetite accompanied by weight gain
2. **Insomnia** or **hypersomnia**
3. Physical hyperactivity or inactivity
4. Loss of interest or pleasure in usual activities, or decrease in sexual drive
5. Loss of energy, feelings of fatigue
6. Feelings of worthlessness, self-reproach, or inappropriate guilt
7. Diminished ability to think or concentrate
8. Recurrent thoughts of death or suicide

> **I Kings 18:46** . . . he ran ahead of Ahab all the way to Jezreel.

Woe Is Me

Elijah ran in front of Ahab's chariot. This appears to be symptom number three: physical hyperactivity. He also had feelings of worthlessness and self-reproach, loss of energy, hypersomnia, and thoughts of death. There also could have been a diminished ability to think and a loss of pleasure in usual activities, though it is not really clear. Of these eight symptoms you need the presence of five to have the diagnosis of clinical depression, which means if Elijah were alive today, he would most likely be on antidepressants.

Herbert Wagemaker, M.D.: My patients often see themselves through the prism of distortion. Their minds lie to them. They begin to see themselves as no good, as failures, as bad.[2]

What Others are Saying:

A Sliding Scale

Depression can range from mild feelings of depression to serious considerations of suicide. Elijah had serious considerations of suicide and even asked God to take his life. With mild depression, often called **dysthymia**, the symptoms are less serious clinically but are still very serious to the person with the symptoms.

dysthymia: *mild depression, used to be called "depressive personality" or "depressive neurosis"*

Dysthymia Symptoms*

1. Low self-esteem or lack of self-confidence
2. Pessimism, hopelessness, or despair
3. Lack of interest in ordinary pleasures and activities
4. Withdrawing from social activities
5. Fatigue or lethargy
6. Guilt or ruminating about the past
7. Irritability or excessive anger
8. Lessened productivity
9. Difficulty concentrating or making decisions

* You must be depressed most of the time for at least two years and have at least three of these symptoms to have mild depression.

WARNING

Remember This . . .

Herbert Wagemaker, M.D.: Self-esteem has to do with our own history, with how we see our successes and failures. Self-esteem also has to do with how we see others relating to us. How do they see us? What do they think of us? We often see ourselves through the eyes of others. Sometimes these eyes are harsh, judgmental, demanding. Sometimes they are loving, accepting. And sometimes we mistake or distort what these "other" eyes see.[3]

Do not attempt to diagnose or treat yourself. See your doctor for an assessment, and then work with him or her on a recovery program that includes a good diet, medicinal herbs, or medications.

No Better Than His Ancestors

Even Elijah in his despair and depression was judging himself against his ancestors. He was beaten, scared, and depressed, and all he could think of to tell God was that he wasn't as good as the rest of his family, as if they were judging him. Studies of college students with depression have indicated that a lifetime exposure to interparental violence is associated with depression, anxiety, interpersonal problems, and violence. Indeed, it seems that if you have parents who are constantly making cutting remarks to each other, displaying physical and verbal aggression to each other, and even acting out physical and sexual abuse on you, you will end up no better than your ancestors. You will become just like them unless you get some help.[4] Another study showed that children with a depressed parent had a 40 percent chance of experiencing an episode of major depression before turning 20.[5] If you have a parent with depression, no matter how minor, please see your doctor for an assessment. It is up to you to become better than your ancestors.

Depression is a real illness, it is not caused by a lack of discipline, failure, laziness, or punishment from God. Do not be ashamed if you have any of the symptoms listed here. You will have more cause for shame if you do not seek treatment than if you do. Once you are treated you will be a healthy person on medication. If you are not treated, you could be hiding at home or causing trouble in public. What a waste!

Cheryl Townsley: My health continued to decline. I became emotionally depressed and mentally muddled. Forest [her husband] would make me promise each morning that I would be there when he came home that night. He knew that if I gave my word I would keep it and not try another suicide attempt . . . at least that day.[6]

What Others are Saying:

I Kings 19:5–8 . . . All at once an angel touched him and said, "Get up and eat." He looked around, and there by his head was a cake of bread baked over hot coals, and a jar of water. He ate and drank and then lay down again. The angel of the Lord came back a second time and touched him and said, "Get up and eat, for the journey is too much for you." So he got up and ate and drank. Strengthened by that food, he traveled 40 days and 40 nights until he reached Horeb, the mountain of God.

Angelic Help

When Elijah was depressed and wanted to die, God sent an angel to feed him (see Illustration #33, this page)! That's right! He sent whole-grain bread baked on coals and water. Whole-grain bread of wheat and/or barley contains carbohydrates which can improve your blood sugar levels and lift your spirits. Whole grains also contain folate or folic acid, selenium, vitamin B_3, and vitamin B_5; all of these nutrients are known to help prevent or reverse several different kinds of depression. (Please do not begin to eat vast quantities of bread if you have depression, as this would be very foolish. Instead, see your doctor.)

Rex Russell, M.D.: If you feel sick, eat. You do not get extra "macho" points by making yourself suffer.[7]

FOOD: THE BASIC UNIT OF ENERGY

God designed your body to run off food, and a constant supply of food is needed. If you do not eat, you will not have enough fuel to operate your body or your mind. When the basic unit of fuel in your body, blood sugar, gets low, you can have depression, just like Elijah. It is essential to eat frequently to avoid drops in your blood sugar. Studies have indicated that a carbohydrate-rich and protein-poor diet is one of the best for people who have depression or a tendency toward depression.[8] The carbohydrates should be in the form of fruits, vegetables, soybeans, and whole grains to supply the nutrients essential to help overcome depression. Omega-3 polyunsaturated fatty acids can also help reverse some forms of depression.[9] Omega-3 fatty acids are found in fish and flaxseeds. (See Chapters 5 and 7 for more information.)

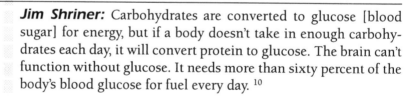
Jim Shriner: Carbohydrates are converted to glucose [blood sugar] for energy, but if a body doesn't take in enough carbohydrates each day, it will convert protein to glucose. The brain can't function without glucose. It needs more than sixty percent of the body's blood glucose for fuel every day. [10]

The angel that appeared to Elijah was pretty smart, smart enough to bring the food God wanted Elijah to have. Are you that smart? Do you feed your body the food that God meant for you to have to be healthy? Do you eat several meals a day? Do you have a balance of lots of vegetables, fruits, whole grains, beans, nuts and seeds, olives and olive oil, dairy products, and fish? Do you eat to sustain your body? Or do you eat to satisfy a craving for sweets, fat, and salt? Does your lifestyle put you in danger of having Elijah's type of depression?

> **I Kings 21:4, 5, 7** So Ahab went home, sullen and angry because Naboth the Jezreelite had said, "I will not give you the inheritance of my fathers." He lay on his bed sulking and refused to eat. His wife Jezebel came in and asked him, "Why are you so sullen? Why won't you eat?" Jezebel his wife said, "Is this how you act as king over Israel? Get up and eat! Cheer up, I'll get you the vineyard of Naboth the Jezreelite."

Ahab: Eat, Eat, Eat!

Judging from the above scripture, the remedy for depression and ill humor seems to be eating. How interesting that two men, Elijah and Ahab, who were fighting with each other both had health or mental problems that could have been remedied by eating. Of course, Ahab's wife wasn't exactly implying that eating would cheer him up. Rather, she was saying that he should not be sullen but take action and since he couldn't or wouldn't, she would get him the vineyard he wanted. She knew this would cheer him up.

The Most Incredible Diet!

You probably have guessed by now that the diet Elijah and Ahab ate was the Mediterranean or Bible Diet. It is a diet with small, frequent meals—generally six meals, or three small meals and three snacks. The food is in its natural state, not refined or processed, so there are only whole grains, lots of fresh vegetables and fruits, dairy products, olives and olive oil, fish, chicken and eggs, and small amounts of red meat and sweets.

If you eat when your body runs out of energy or just before that happens, you will have plenty of energy, and you will eat just the right amount of food. If you eat only enough to take care of your energy needs at that time, you will not eat too much and what you do eat, you will use, and it will not turn to fat. Your brain will have a constant supply of the correct fuel for functioning efficiently.

Once you keep your blood sugar from going too high or dropping too low, you will be surprised at how some forms of depression will just lift. If you have any kind of depression or even suspect that you do, please talk to your doctor for an assessment. Let your doctor monitor your diet change. Also, let your doctor know before you go off any medication.

KEY POINT

The Mediterranean Diet is one with small, frequent meals—generally six meals, or three small meals and three snacks.

Remember
This . . .

KEY POINT

Eating foods in the two bottom sections of the Mediterranean Diet Pyramid (see Illustration #2, page 7) every day can help you get the fuel you need to stay healthy.

W. David Hager, M.D. and Linda Carruth Hager: The neurotransmitter serotonin plays a critical role in an individual's mood. Increasing serotonin by dietary means or by using antidepressants can improve mood and depressive symptoms. The best sources of serotonin are bananas and meat, especially turkey. Carbohydrates are necessary to enhance the absorption of serotonin by the body.[11]

How Often Should I Eat?

Most people will need to eat every three or four hours in the beginning. This will keep your blood sugar levels stable, and your energy levels up. Eating this regularly will constantly feed your brain with the brain foods it needs (see Illustration #34, this page). The whole-grain carbohydrates will provide the pathways for all the brain chemicals you will need to be healthy. You must make sure that you eat dark green, leafy vegetables and dairy products to provide the folate and tryptophan that your body needs.

People often tell me that they don't have time to eat. What so many people don't realize is that the time they spend eating will greatly reduce or eliminate the time they waste in depression (see Illustration #35, page 173). Hopefully, with this in mind, you can see how eating is worth whatever time it takes.

Illustration #34

Breakfast, Lunch, and Dinner—Eat at least three times a day to be healthy. The food you eat is the fuel that runs your body, including your brain. Eating nutrient-filled, natural food at least three times a day will feed your brain so it can function at its optimum level of efficiency.

Illustration #35

Food and Mood—Eating healthily will oftentimes put you in a good mood, while not eating healthy can set you up for depression.

KEY POINT

What so many people don't realize is that the time they spend eating will greatly reduce or eliminate the time they waste in depression.

Put Down That Chocolate Bar

There is no sugar mentioned in the Bible except that found naturally in fresh fruit. This means that there is no sugar on a daily basis. The instructions are to have sweets no more than two or three times a week (see Illustration #2, page 7). This includes all forms of sugar, such as sweetened coffee and tea, hot chocolate, doughnuts, soft drinks, ice cream, candy, artificially sweetened gums and candies, cake, pie, etc. When you remove sugar and sweetened foods from your diet altogether, you will have less trouble with depression, especially if you follow the Bible Diet. Keep away from low-fat diets if you have depression because research has shown there is a direct relationship between decreases in dietary fats and decreases in energy and/or in moods. The best fats are the olive oil and the omega-3 fatty acids which have been explained in previous chapters.[12]

Cheryl Townsley: I was eating less and gaining weight. Emotionally I was out of balance. I would cry over everything. This woman who in the past had coolly and calmly presented multimillion-dollar computer proposals to vice presidents could not handle a phone call. . . . We decided to plunge ahead full force with this "nutritional approach." We were motivated by my life-and-death situation. Within a few weeks we began to see significant changes. Within six months I had lost most of my excess weight, my skin had cleared, my emotions had begun to stabilize, and I had begun making decisions. These changes felt enormous compared to where I had been.[13]

What Others are Saying:

ON Target:
Eating fruits as your major sweets

OFF Target:
Eating sugary foods daily

Eating artificial sweeteners can reduce your calories, but it still makes you want sweets.

I Samuel 16:14, 23 Now the spirit of the Lord had departed from Saul, and an evil spirit from the Lord tormented him. Whenever the spirit from God came upon Saul, David would take his harp and play. Then relief would come to Saul; he would feel better, and the evil spirit would leave him.

Music Lifts And Depresses The Soul

despondent: feeling dejected or disheartened

In Bible times it was well known that the right kind of music, played in the right manner, could lift the spirits of a person who was **despondent**, sullen, fearful, or depressed. It still works today. Generally, classical music does this, but many other kinds of music will too.

Remember This . . .

It is almost certain that a teenager who constantly listens to music with a rock beat that has negative messages in the words, especially words that say "kill yourself" or "women are stupid" or any of the many other negative phrases that are in rock music today, will eventually find himself in a sullen or depressed state. Many precious children are selling their souls into the slavery of negative thinking and depression, because they are bringing themselves into a deep negative state with their music and not getting out of it. This negative state might even be an evil spirit brought on by the words of the music itself.

WARNING

There are many musicians who record songs even they don't believe in, as long as it sells. Such songs could be the very ones that might destroy your mind or your hearing.

What Others are Saying:

Pamela Smith: Pay close attention to the warning signs of physical and emotional exhaustion. Take an hour's soak in the tub. Beg your husband [or wife] for a back and foot rub. Play relaxing music.[14]

The Mozart Effect

The music of Mozart is now being touted as promoting learning and creativity as well as increasing positive moods and promoting relaxation. If you are depressed, start with some Mozart!

Music Soothes The Soul

Many classical music pieces were composed as church music and are extremely uplifting. There are even modern Christian pieces that will do the same, as long as they don't have the kind of rock music that can bring you down. Let yourself go into the spirit of the music when listening to religious music; it is intended to praise God, and praising God is always helpful for dispelling depression.

> **Proverbs 17:22** A cheerful heart is good medicine, but a crushed spirit dries up the bones.

Just Get Over It

According to Proverbs, a cheerful heart is good medicine. This is wise counsel for everyone, and especially for people who are suffering from depression and who need to work at being positive and cheerful. People used to tell a person with depression to "just get over it" or "cheer up," thinking he or she might just snap out of it. There are times you might be feeling low when a change of heart, taking some positive action, laughing at a joke or story, or listening to music will change your attitude. But there may be other times when your depression is more serious, and it's important to remember that before true depression can be helped, a chemical change must take place in your brain.

Don't let well-meaning friends make you feel worse than you already do because you can't force yourself to cheer up. If you would like to start the healing process by changing your diet, see your doctor or a nutritionist. If you want to start by taking antidepressants, see your doctor and perhaps when you start feeling better, you can begin changing your diet. When you have been on antidepressants for a length of time and then change your diet, you will begin to feel well enough for your doctor to reduce your prescription.

Cheryl Townsley: Most healthy people have learned to laugh and keep things in perspective. They don't take themselves too seriously. They acknowledge their blessings. It's not easy to see the humor in a current situation. This is especially true if the situation is painful or difficult.[15]

ON Target:

Eating small, frequent meals, including the foods that help with depression and listening to uplifting music

OFF Target:

Missing meals, eating lots of sugar and caffeine and/or listening to abrasive music

ON Target:

Encouraging your friends to seek help if they seem depressed

OFF Target:

Putting your friends down when they have trouble coping with life

Remember This . . .

What Others are Saying:

> **Proverbs 4:20–22** My son, pay attention to what I say; listen closely to my words. Do not let them out of your sight, keep them within your heart; for they are life to those who find them and health to a man's whole body.

Prayer

The words of Solomon can be health to your whole body if you keep them in your heart. This theme is followed throughout the entire Bible. Prayer is good for you. God answers prayers in *his* time, *you* must just keep praying.

> **James 5:13–16** Is any one of you in trouble? He should pray. Is anyone happy? Let him sing songs of praise. Is any one of you sick? He should call the elders of the church to pray over him and anoint him with oil in the name of the Lord. And the prayer offered in faith will make the sick person well; the Lord will raise him up. If he has **sinned**, he will be forgiven. Therefore **confess** your sins to each other and pray for each other so that you may be healed. The prayer of a **righteous man** is powerful and effective.

sinned: *morally missed the mark*

confess: *admit the truth, acknowledge*

righteous man: *a morally right person*

GROUP PRAYER AND PRAYER GROUPS

Praying alone may not be suitable for you; you will need to have others pray for and with you. This is why there are prayer groups, prayer circles, and **prayer warriors**! Both the Old and New Testament churches were founded on and filled with prayer. This verse in James explains the basis of healing: Recognize that you have missed the mark, confess it, ask for God's forgiveness, and then let go of it.

prayer warriors: *people who pray fervently for others every day*

What Others are Saying:

Rita Bennett: If the depression is too deep, and he is too debilitated to pray himself, the prayer partners may need to allow him to simply rest while they do the praying. If the person is suicidal, check with your pastor for guidance or referral.[16]

Herbs And Other Things That Can Help

Besides eating small, frequent meals, avoiding sugar, caffeine, nicotine, and alcohol, there are other nutrients that can help. Vitamin B_6 (pyridoxine), B_{12} (cyanocobalamin), and B_9 (folate) have been used to help with depression.[17] A lack of the mineral selenium can cause depression-like symptoms. Selenium has a very small dose requirement, so please check with a nutritionist to see if you are taking the correct amount. The amino acid tyrosine has been used for depression for over 20 years, though it is not recommended for people who are taking an **MAO inhibitor**. The product **5-HTP** (5-hydroxytryptophan) has been used for depression, fibromyalgia, obesity, sleep disorders, and aggressive behavior.[18] The herb **St. John's wort** is being used for depression and is especially effective when formulated into a tablet with other ingredients such as the herb Kava Kava, which is an antianxiety agent. St. John's wort has been used for hundreds of years for many illnesses including depression.[19]

Julian Whitaker, M.D.: Since B$_6$ is needed for the production of the neurotransmitter serotonin, a deficiency can result in depression and mental confusion. Good sources of B$_6$ are bananas, chicken, fish, eggs, oats, soybeans, tomatoes, salmon, kale, kidney beans, peanuts, and walnuts. Deficiencies of B$_{12}$ can cause a loss of balance, numbness or weakness of the limbs, irritability, and mild depression. B$_{12}$ is only found in animal (lean meat, fish) and dairy (milk, cottage cheese, yogurt) products.[20]

Magnets: They're Not Just For The Refrigerator Door

For thousands of years, magnets have been used for healing. You will probably remember hearing about the "lodestone," which was a magnetic stone on which sick people were placed to become well. The idea is that a magnet replaces the magnetic pull of the earth that is lost by being out of balance. Modern scientists realize that magnets contribute to increases in blood circulation, thereby reducing healing time and accelerating feelings of well-being. In Israel magnets are being used with great success for people with mania as well as depression.[21]

Julian Whitaker, M.D.: The research is equally clear that electromagnetic fields speed up the healing of bone fractures and soft-tissue injuries to a remarkable degree, and can be effective in treating stress-related disorders, including anxiety, insomnia, and depression, even in patients resistant to drugs.[22]

What Others are Saying:

ON Target:
Asking your doctor to work with you on taking herbs and vitamins for depression

OFF Target:
Forgetting to tell your doctor that you are starting to experiment with herbs for depression

What Others are Saying:

Study Questions

1. What happened to Elijah, and why is he important in this chapter?
2. What did the angel tell Elijah, and why is it important to you?
3. Name some symptoms of depression.
4. What are the two most important things you can do for yourself if you think you have depression?
5. How did David help Saul with his depression? Which music do you find helps you feel more positive?

CHAPTER WRAP-UP

- Elijah was under a great deal of stress that he couldn't handle. He became fearful and ran for his life when he was threatened. (I Kings 19:3–5)

- Elijah didn't notice how stressed out and depressed he was becoming; he went off by himself and asked God to take his life.

- Twice God sent an angel to Elijah to give him food and water to regain his strength.

- Ahab's wife, Jezebel, realized that Ahab was sullen and needed to eat. (I Kings 21:4, 5, 7)

- God provided you with all the nutrients you need to be healthy, including those that cure many different diseases. These nutrients are in the vegetables, fruits, dairy products, fish, olives, meats, and grains that he created for your body to eat.

13 FOOD CRAVINGS, WEIGHT LOSS, AND EATING DISORDERS

CHAPTER HIGHLIGHTS

- Manna from Heaven
- Wrong Food at the Wrong Time
- Weight Loss
- Poor Body Image and Out-of-Control Eating

Let's Get Started

Of all the problems that plague modern man, weight loss, weight gain, and out-of-control eating are near the top of the list. There was a time when being plump was a sign of wealth and prosperity; now most people think of plump people as lacking in self-control.

Why has the size, shape, and flexibility of your body become a subject for discussions, diets, loathing, and concern? Something is out of balance in a society where people are more concerned with how thin they look than with helping neighbors or spending time with God every day. Some people feel that it is the influence of the "me generation" of the 1960s and 1970s. There are many other reasons for society's obsession with thinness, some spiritual and some biochemical. Could the food you eat (or don't eat) be causing the real problem? The Bible is filled with people who have weight problems, eating problems, and even eating disorders.

> **Psalm 78:23–25, 27, 29** Yet he gave a command to the skies above and opened the doors of the heavens; he rained down **manna** for the people to eat, he gave them the grain of heaven. Men ate the bread of angels; he sent them all the food they could eat. He rained meat down on them like dust, flying birds like sand on the seashore. They ate till they had more than enough, for he had given them what they craved.

manna: miracle food that God supplied daily, it was oily and had the taste of coriander seeds

☞ **GO TO:**

Exodus 16:4, 5 (raining down)

Numbers 11:4–6 (craved)

Numbers 11:18–22 (meat)

Numbers 11:20 (nostrils)

Is This All We Get?

When Moses led the Israelites into the desert, God provided for them by <u>raining down</u> manna from heaven every night except on the Sabbath. On the sixth day he sent double the amount because Jews were not supposed to do any work on the seventh day, the Sabbath, and gathering the manna would have been considered work. They grumbled and mumbled about having to eat the stuff and <u>craved meat</u>, garlic, leeks, cucumbers, fish—all the foods they had eaten in Egypt and now didn't have. So God made them eat birds until it "[came] out of [their] <u>nostrils</u>," just so that they would learn to like the manna and be obedient.

> **Matthew 4:3** The tempter came to him and said, "If you are the Son of God, tell these stones to become bread."

☞ **GO TO:**

Genesis 3:1–24 (Adam and Eve)

Numbers 11:4–6 (Israelites)

Matthew 4:1–4 (Jesus)

Matthew 4:11 (angels)

Don't Fall For It

<u>Adam and Eve</u> were tempted by forbidden food, and eating it got them in big trouble. The <u>Israelites</u> were tempted by the fancy food they had eaten before they went into the desert. The devil tempted <u>Jesus</u> to turn stones into bread, which was the first of three temptations he had to endure when he was in the desert.

Being tempted by food is nothing new, and look at some of the consequences for failing to resist this kind of temptation. Adam and Eve caused the Fall of man, and the Israelites were forced to eat until it oozed from their noses. Jesus, however, did not fall for the temptation, so the devil left, and <u>angels</u> came to Jesus' aid.

What Others are Saying:

T. D. Jakes: Remember, you are not the enemy. You're a victim of a tempter who has been around for a long time. Food was the first thing the devil used to tempt Eve. Adam didn't hold up against the temptation when Eve said, "Look at what we can have if we eat this food." And eating something they shouldn't had fatal consequences. Eating the food God had made for them would have kept Adam and Eve where they wanted to be.[1]

Something to Ponder

Are you also tempted by foods? Most of the foods that tempt people consist of fat, carbohydrates, caffeine, or sugar (which also includes alcohol). The Israelites had perfect food, and yet they wanted meat, fish, and vegetables. At least they craved for decent food, while most North Americans crave salt, fat, sugar, starch, or all of the above. How long has it been since you heard someone say, "I really **crave** a piece of lettuce?" Probably never! People only crave those foods that will give them a quick fix, a lift, perk them up.

How Your Body Works

God created your body, and God created food for your body. In Chapter 12 you learned that an angel told Elijah to eat several times a day. This gave him strength and self-confidence. Your body is the same. It is essential to eat only the food you need just before you are going to need the energy the food produces. You also need to eat only the foods that contain the nutrients and energy you need. This sounds simple, doesn't it? It is.

FOOD = ENERGY

NO FOOD = NO ENERGY

 **NUTRITIONAL FACT**

Many health problems are related to changes in blood sugar.

It's Very Simple

All the parts of your body—skin, hair, organs, muscles, even your brain—need energy to function. All food changes into the basic unit of energy once it is in your body. This basic unit of energy is called blood sugar. Blood sugar feeds every part of your body so it can function; without this energy nothing will work. When your blood sugar goes up it is called **hyperglycemia**; when it drops down it is called **hypoglycemia**.

hyperglycemia: high blood sugar

hypoglycemia: low blood sugar

Florence Littauer: Physical problems repeat themselves. In my family, diabetes and hypoglycemia have appeared many times in each generation as far back as we can trace.[2]

What Others are Saying:

What Does It Feel Like?

When your blood sugar drops down it is very uncomfortable. The symptoms could be allergies; anger; anxiety; depression; crying spells; confusion; compulsive eating; lack of coordination; cravings for sugar, starches, or alcohol; exhaustion; drowsiness; headaches; fears; forgetfulness; incoordination; **indecisiveness**; irritability; nervousness; nightmares; poor concentration; sighing and yawning; staggering; twitching and jerking of the muscles; weak spells; lack of sex interest; insomnia; and even tremors. You might get very sleepy or glassy-eyed when you eat too much, which makes your body produce too much blood sugar, or when you eat too seldom, which causes your blood sugar to drop and produce no

indecisiveness: can't make a decision

energy for your body. Either way, eating too much or eating too seldom is bad for your body.

DO YOU TAKE SUGAR?

Eating sugar can be the main way to cause these fluctuations in energy/blood sugar. All food turns into blood sugar, but sugar can, in some people, cause a greater rise in blood sugar. Insulin is released from the pancreas to use up the blood sugar. If the meal is large, has a high-starch content, contains a high amount of sugar, or contains alcohol, the blood sugar levels can go very high which causes a high amount of insulin to be released. This insulin uses up the blood sugar more quickly and the levels will fall quickly, causing hypoglycemia. Hypoglycemia can also occur when an insulin-dependent diabetic takes too much insulin.

ON Target:

*Eating **whole** foods*

OFF Target:

Eating sugary foods and drinks

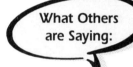

whole: *complete, not refined*

> If you have any of these symptoms or have blood sugar problems in your family, see your doctor for a six-hour, oral glucose tolerance test (GTT) to determine the cause of the problem.

What Others are Saying:

Dr. Mary Ruth Swope: Sugar causes a rapid rise in blood sugar levels—sometimes causing a person to swing from hypoglycemia to diabetes within a one-hour period (or less). Headaches, fatigue, forgetfulness, irritability, and blurred vision can result.[3]

> **Isaiah 44:12** He gets hungry and loses his strength; he drinks no water and grows faint.

Wrong Foods At The Wrong Times

When you get hungry and begin to feel a loss of strength, this is generally when your blood sugar levels have dropped because you have eaten no food. You have actually gone too long without eating at this point. This is when many people crave sweets, caffeine, alcohol, or nicotine. When you feel hungry and know that you need to eat something, eat food that does not contain sugar or caffeine (see Illustration #36, page 183). In the long run this will give you more energy and help to stabilize your energy levels. If you choose sweets or caffeine to perk you up, you could drive your blood sugar levels higher, only to have them fall again very soon. Pay attention to when you eat and what you choose to eat when you have gone without eating long enough to "lose your strength."

Some soft drinks contain sugar and caffeine. This is a double whammy that can stimulate your blood sugar levels to go out of control.

WARNING

T. D. Jakes: I used to think I was too busy to eat breakfast, but breakfast is a significant meal. It helps to regulate you so you will eat at the proper times throughout the day.[4]

What Others are Saying:

The mother of modern nutrition, Adelle Davis, used to say: Eat breakfast like a king, lunch like a prince, and dinner like a pauper. This was her idea of how to be healthy. It is good advice to follow because it will give you the most food when you need the most energy.

Remember This . . .

Yeah, Yeah, But I Want To Know About Weight Loss

Many people who are trying to lose weight think they can cut down on calories by cutting out breakfast and lunch. This is a grave error! Doing so can set up a really big stress in your body that makes you crave sweets, starches, and perhaps alcohol. God designed your body to run on the fuel of foods like fish; whole grains; vegetables; dark green, leafy vegetables; squash; meat; milk; cheese; and olives and other fruit. These foods contain the nutrients necessary for health and energy. If you do not eat the right foods at the right time, your body will make you crave the foods that will turn into fat in your body.

NUTRITIONAL FACT

Foods like lettuce, celery, parsley, cabbage, and broccoli do not trigger severe blood sugar swings.

*metabolism: the physical
and chemical processes
involved in the
maintenance of life*

Jim Shriner: Let's take a closer look at how important breakfast really is. Think about it: you've just come off a seven-to-eight-hour period of sleep where there was no food available in your stomach to be converted to energy. Within only minutes of waking up, your body will be in search of vital nutrients. As soon as you get up in the morning and get moving, your metabolism begins to rise, and just by eating a well-balanced breakfast, you can boost your daily **metabolism** by as much as fifteen percent. That could mean burning as many as two hundred to three hundred more calories per day! Still thinking about missing breakfast?[5]

Do Yourself A Favor: Eat Breakfast!

Breakfast is the most important meal of the day. Eating breakfast is how God meant for you to get the fuel to run your body every day. If you do not eat breakfast, your brain may get so little fuel that you are unable to think correctly, and you may choose to eat the wrong foods or not to eat at all, which in turn will set you up for craving sweets, starches, and high-calorie foods. Or, you may lose control altogether and just keep eating and eating and eating.

**What Others
are Saying:**

T. D. Jakes: Most people who do not eat breakfast eat more and more later in the day. The evening is their ravenous time.[6]

Pamela Smith: Breakfast is important to "break the fast" your body has been in during the hours of night rest. Think of your body as a campfire that dies down during the night. In the morning it needs to be stoked up with wood to begin burning vigorously again. Without stoking, the fire will die down with no flames or sparks. Your body is very similar—it awakens in a slowed, fasting state and needs breakfast to rev the body into high gear, allowing better nutrient utilization for you.[7]

**Something
to Ponder**

Mood swings or energy slumps at mid-morning and mid-afternoon are often a reaction to dropping blood sugar levels. If you have either of these problems, try eating a breakfast that does not contain any sugar or caffeine. After a few days you will feel really strong and energetic all day long with no drops in energy or concentration.

> **John 21:12, 13** Jesus said to them, "Come and have break-fast." None of the disciples dared ask him, "Who are you?" They knew this was the Lord. Jesus came, took the bread and gave it to them, and did the same with the fish.

FISH OR BREAKFAST? WHY NOT?!

When the disciples came back from a fishing expedition, on shore Jesus had a fire ready to cook the fish. He asked them to bring some of their catch and have breakfast with him. Jesus gave fish to his disciples for breakfast. Fish and barley bread would be a great breakfast. It is worth noting that Jesus did not eat sugar-coated cereal, or anything similar, but rather real whole foods—foods that would stimulate his metabolism and give him energy with-out the energy fluctuations that sweets cause. A small steak and a salad would be a great weight loss breakfast, because it would contain protein, vegetables (including dark green, leafy ones), and no sugar, especially if you have no dressing on the salad.

Broiled fish or even tuna fish salad is great for breakfast. Either will give you the correct kind of protein and nutrients that you need for thinking and concentrating. Don't fall into the cold cereal or sugar-laden, quick-breakfast habit if you want to have lots of energy. Who said you had to eat pastries, pancakes, or cold cereal for breakfast? Surely not the Bible.

Eat A Little Food A Lot Of Times

Small, frequent meals of low-calorie whole foods are the best way to lose weight. Eat a baked potato for breakfast with some low-fat yogurt and chopped, fresh parsley. Then for lunch or dinner eat the 4-ounce piece of meat and some vegetables with lemon juice or fresh herbs. For supper eat the salad with some avocado, a boiled egg, or a small amount of low-fat cheese. Generally, this would have been one meal, right? Baked potato, steak, veggies, and salad would all have been eaten at one sitting before you real-ized that this was going to cause you to gain weight. Now that you know you can eat these foods throughout the day, you will soon begin to lose weight. Between meals eat low-calorie snacks to keep your energy up—things like whole grain crackers, of which you only need three or four with some low-fat cheese or peanut butter (see Illustration #37, page 187). A snack of a hard-cooked egg and lettuce is also great. Any veggies can be eaten as snacks as long as they are *au naturel*, not coated with anything. Even dill pickles and a few almonds would be a good snack.

Remember This . . .

What Others are Saying:

ON Target:

Eating small frequent meals

OFF Target:

Going more than five hours without eating

acute psychotic state: state in which a person hears voices and sees things that are not really there

nitrates: compounds used in curing meats; can lead to nitrosamines which are known to cause cancer

nitrites: compounds used in curing meats, similar to nitrates

What Others are Saying:

MSG: monosodium glutamate, a preservative or flavor enhancer in many foods; often causes allergic reactions or water retention

T. D. Jakes: Always carry a couple of snacks with you so you won't get hungry. It isn't good to go too long without food.[8]

Herbert Wagemaker, M.D.: Hypoglycemia is the opposite of diabetes, and though it usually occurs in diabetics, it also appears in nondiabetics. Some patients with this condition may be suffering from bipolar illness, experiencing the delusions, the hallucinations, and the excitement associated with an **acute psychotic state**. They may complain of feeling faint, of feeling shaky or weak, or of having headaches. Patients respond to diet regulation, eating high-protein snacks and meals five times a day rather than three, and cutting back on sugary foods.[9]

THESE FOODS CAN MAKE YOU THIN

The foods mentioned in the Bible Diet are the foods that make you thin, when eaten in moderation and frequently during the day. There is no secret to weight loss. A sensible diet of nutritious foods at the right time in the right amounts will allow your body to obtain its optimum weight. Follow the basic rule: If God made it, eat it; if man made it, leave it. This means do not eat processed foods; artificial sugars or sweeteners; processed cheeses or meats; foods filled with preservatives like **nitrates, nitrites**, or **MSG**; partial foods like white-flour products or instant mashed potatoes; anything with sugar added; anything with salt added; anything with fat as the first or second ingredient; or anything that promises it has had the calories removed. Look at the Do Eat/Don't Eat chart on page 187 for more ideas.

Kenneth H. Cooper, M.D.: A major reason for poor eating discipline is that most people have a relatively weak belief in the need for good eating—and as a result, they possess few defenses against the distractions and temptations that often get in the way of a healthy diet. Yet the problem most people have with sticking to a good, healthy diet goes far deeper than merely failing to abide by good intentions. The real difficulty is that they have never understood that their eating habits should reflect their deepest beliefs about life. In other words, they have failed to learn that the right kind of food can transform them into the energetic, healthy people they are meant to be. It's only with such an understanding about the connection between basic values and eating habits that a person is likely to experience lasting, beneficial dietary change.[10]

But I Need A Special Diet

If you eat these whole, natural foods that God made for your body and eliminate anything that has chemicals or preservatives, or has been processed, you will not need a restrictive diet. When you begin to add daily stretching, walking, and gentle exercises to this regime of whole food—when you follow the Bible Diet—you will not need a special diet.[11]

DO EAT	DON'T EAT
100 percent whole grain bread, bagels, crackers, pretzels, pasta	White flour bread, bagels, crackers, pretzels, pasta
Romaine, leaf, Mesclun Mix, escarole	Iceberg lettuce
Yogurt, cream cheese, low-fat cheese	Processed cheeses, cheese food
Unsweetened whole grain cereal	Sugar-coated, refined cereals
Fresh or frozen veggies	Canned veggies
Veggies with a drizzle of olive oil	Canned veggies with margarine
Broiled, baked, roasted meats; fish	Breaded, deep-fried meats; fish
Steamed, baked potatoes	Breaded, deep-fried potatoes
Fresh potatoes with skin on	Peeled, packaged potatoes
Homemade macaroni and cheese	Packaged white macaroni and cheese
Sweet red, green, and yellow peppers	Candy snacks
Frequent snacks, regular meals	No snacks, poor meals
Fresh fruit snacks	Fruit roll-ups
Protein snacks	Carbohydrate only snacks
Beans, soybeans, tofu, tempeh	Canned, sweetened baked beans
Whole grain cookies	Low-fat, refined flour cookies

Neva Coyle: Do I ever overeat? Probably, although I can't remember when I've done so. I don't overeat regularly—certainly not as much as I did when I was dieting. There's just no need for it anymore. For the most part I choose healthy, wholesome foods. I eat marvelous fresh vegetables and luscious fruits. I choose whole-grain breads and low-fat whole-grain crackers. But the most miraculous thing of all is—I eat without guilt.[12]

> **I Samuel 1:2, 5–8, 17–20** He had two wives; one was called Hannah and the other Peninnah. Peninnah had children, but Hannah had none. But to Hannah he gave a double portion because he loved her, and the Lord had closed her womb. And because the Lord had closed her womb, her rival kept provoking her in order to irritate her. This went on year after year. Whenever Hannah went up to the house of the Lord, her rival provoked her till she wept and would not eat. Elkanah her husband would say to her. "Hannah, why are you weeping? Why don't you eat? Why are you downhearted? Don't I mean more to you than ten sons?" Eli [the priest] answered [Hannah's prayer], "Go in peace, and may the God of Israel grant you what you have asked of him." She said, "May your servant find favor in your eyes." Then she went her way and ate something, and her face was no longer downcast. Elkanah lay with his wife, and the Lord remembered her. So in the course of time Hannah conceived and gave birth to a son.

Eating Disorders In The Bible

anorexia nervosa:
disorder wherein the person refuses to eat, suffers from underweight, poor body image, and other symptoms including lack of circulation

According to Isaac Schiff, M.D., and Morty Schiff in the medical journal *Fertility And Sterility*, Hannah had the eating disorder **anorexia nervosa**. Partly it was brought on by the torment she received from Elkanah's other wife, Peninnah, and partly it was brought on by refusing to eat. First she was not able to conceive and this caused her to stop eating. Because she was being tormented by her rival she also quit eating. Because she was not eating she was unable to conceive. The Schiffs speculate that God closed Hannah's womb, because she was listening to her tormentors instead of him. When Hannah became able to praise God and turn her situation over to God, she was able to eat again. Once she ate and gained her strength, she conceived and gave birth to a son.[13]

This is one of the first references to an eating disorder that is brought on by being tormented or teased. Modern psychiatrists and psychologists have developed many ways to treat eating disorders. Hannah's prescription—eat something and turn your infertility over to God—was simple and very much in line with the recommendations of the Bible Diet.

Something to Ponder

Eating a really good diet, small frequent meals, and avoiding caffeine and sugar are the first steps to working on overcoming eating disorders and infertility. In order for your body to function, it needs a wide variety of nutrients—all of which come from food. Avoiding food can cause many health problems due to depriving your body of nourishment.

Remember This . . .

Joe S. McIlhaney, M.D.: Menstruation can be erratic or absent [with eating disorders] even though weight is normal. This does not permanently damage one's body, but pregnancy is often impossible.[14]

What Others are Saying:

What Are Eating Disorders?

There are several kinds of eating disorders. Anorexia nervosa is an eating disorder wherein the person with it cannot or will not eat. Bulimia nervosa is a disorder wherein the person often eats to excess and then purges the excess food with laxatives of many different kinds or by forced vomiting. In rare cases the person exercises excessively to purge the body of extra food. There are many theories about why these disorders exist. Natural practicing doctors and nutritionists have found that low levels of certain minerals like zinc, chromium, or copper can cause a distorted mental image of what someone sees in the mirror. Unstable blood sugar has also been known to contribute to the lack of self-confidence that often triggers one of these disorders. Critical adults or self-criticism can often lead a child into an eating disorder as a way of exhibiting power over either themselves, adults, or their parents.

ON Target:
Eating nutritiously when you're sad

OFF Target:
Not eating when you're sad

Sometimes there might be a personality clash in the **family dynamics**. I counseled a family once where the teenage daughter was an anorexic. She was very outgoing, loved bright colors, and excelled in sports. Her mother, father, and two older sisters had the personality type that always wore grey, dark blue, or black clothes, didn't like to create waves, stayed in the background, were fussy about details, and put the more outgoing daughter down for her **gregarious** ways. Her grandmother was just like she was. While

family dynamics: interaction between members of the family

gregarious: outgoing

the grandmother was in the house, she was a normal teenager. When the grandmother died, she had no one to relate to, and she developed an eating disorder. She was also low in some important minerals, and she very seldom ate vegetables or protein but did eat a lot of carbohydrate foods due to her athletic involvement— a real setup for developing an eating disorder. I gave her some books and tapes on personality and temperaments, which she found helpful for understanding why they were treating her so differently. She left home and went to live with another person who could relate to her, changed her diet, and became a normal teenager.

> **Colossians 3:21** Fathers, do not embitter your children, or they will become discouraged.

Bitter? Who's Bitter?

How many children drink soft drinks and eat sugary snacks all day long? The average amount of soft drinks per day for high school students is 10 cans. That's a lot of sugar! When a family consistently consumes high amounts of sugar and low amounts of nutritious foods, there can be many kinds of behavior problems. The parents might be cranky and nit-picky, or constantly criticize the children. Often parents can have attacks of anger and hostility that will embitter the children. Some parents can be so busy with their lives that they ignore their children and when they do talk to them, they are critical and disapproving. If a child (or even an adult for that matter) is already down on himself or herself, poor nutrition and belittling influences at home, school, or work can be the perfect setup for an eating disorder.

Something to Ponder

Many people consider ignoring children to be the worst kind of abuse, followed by belittling them, criticizing them, beating them, fighting in front of them, and being an alcoholic. Ephesians 6:4 says *Fathers, do not exasperate your children.* This is really good advice to all parents and prevents children from needing to feel powerful by withholding food.

What Others are Saying:

Florence Littauer: I have increasingly encountered women who have suppressed the truths of the past and who have denied that childhood deprivations or abuse have anything to do with their chronic headaches or eating disorders.[15]

> **Proverbs 3:27** Do not withhold good from those who deserve it, when it is in your power to act.

IT'S UP TO THE PARENTS

The most important job of parents is to encourage their children, discipline them, and not to withhold good from them when they deserve it. When your child comes home with an 85 percent on a test, do not complain that he or she should have gotten 100 percent; give praise for a job well done. Then help them with their school work so that they will be encouraged to get a 100 percent the next time. It is very important for all people to receive praise and encouragement for a job well done, not just criticism for the things they do wrong.

IT'S NOT JUST CHILDREN

Adults can have eating disorders too. Anyone with low self-esteem, a weight problem, poor nutrition, a habit of dieting, exercise mania, or critical friends, parents, or coworkers can begin to suffer from an eating disorder. Many women, large and small, find solace in eating too much and then vomiting or taking harsh laxatives or "cleansing" herbs to purge their bodies of the extra weight.

Neva Coyle: The clinical stereotype of a bulimic is a woman, usually a young woman, who keeps her weight down through binge/purge practices. I've met more than a handful of slim women who suffer from the practice of bulimia. However, no one really mentions the larger woman who keeps her weight where it is through the same destructive practices.[16]

> **Psalm 107:17–22** Some became fools through their rebellious ways and suffered afflictions because of their **iniquities**. They loathed all food and drew near the gates of death.

Who Is Rebellious?

Many times children and teenagers will rebel against their parents in the only way they know how—by not eating, or by eating more than they should. This can also be carried into adulthood. Tendencies to eating disorders are passed on through family life. Often if a mother is a perfectionist and obsessed with dieting, her daughters and sometimes her sons will develop eating disorders.

ON Target:
Praising your children for things they do well

OFF Target:
Always criticizing your children

NUTRITION FACT

Eating small, frequent meals of real food can reduce the cravings for binging and thereby reduce the need to purge.

What Others are Saying:

iniquities: *wickedness, sinfulness, and grossly immoral acts*

Oftentimes children have a need to please and to be in control at the same time. So a child could 'clean up his plate' in order to please and then vomit to be in control of his eating habits.

Rita Bennett: Characteristics of an anorexic or bulimic person: self-hate/form of suicide, low self-esteem, paradoxical need to please and power play to be in control, fear of rejection and failure, perfectionism, suppressed rage, sometimes a desire to be a child or infant again. A high percentage of people with eating disorders have incest or sexual abuse histories.[17]

TOUGH STUFF

There are no solutions that will work for every person with an eating disorder. Some people may just have an imbalance of serotonin, which causes depression and may lead to an eating disorder. In one study, a serotonin-active antidepressant was suggested to correct eating disorders.[18] This type of antidepressant could be a prescription drug, St. John's wort, or 5-HTP; please consult a doctor if you feel this would be of benefit.

A hair analysis from a reputable nutritionist or doctor who is skilled in the correct interpretation of the lab work can assess any mineral imbalances or toxic metal levels, many of which can contribute to eating disorders. A psychologist can often help with family dynamic problems. A family study of Dr. Kevin Leman's *Birth Order Book* or any number of different books on temperaments or personality types can help a family accept a member who has an eating disorder and find ways to relate to him or her. This kind of family involvement can go a long way in raising self-esteem and releasing rage.

Florence Littauer: As you look through your family's background, be alert to signs of negative patterns that need to be changed so that the REAL YOU can stand up.[19]

Is It In Your Family?

Many families have patterns, habits, or lifestyles that get passed on from generation to generation. If someone in your family has an eating disorder, here are some questions to answer that can begin the healing process:

- What does he or she do that is typical of a person with an eating disorder?
- Is he or she the first child?

- Does he or she have a different personality type than that of the other family members?
- Does he or she have an addiction to sugar and junk foods, or perhaps even alcohol?
- Are the parents too busy to pay attention to the children?
- Did or do the parents allow the oldest child to be the responsible one, robbing him or her of a childhood?
- Do the parents pay so little attention to food that many family members end up going without eating when they are young?
- Do the parents provide regular meals for the family and a stable home life?
- Does the family eat mostly nutritionless foods?
- Is there a really strong spiritual family life?
- Does the family pray together and read the Bible together?

KEY POINT

If you even suspect that one of your friends, family members, or neighbors has an eating disorder, please get help for them.

Anne and David Frähm: Remember, it's not what you eat five percent of the time that'll do you harm, but the food you feed your body the other ninety-five percent of the time.[20]

What Others are Saying:

Study Questions

1. What are some examples of being tempted by food in the Bible? Why is it important to know about them?
2. What are two opposite blood sugar conditions and how can you avoid them?
3. What did Jesus give to the disciples for breakfast? Why do you think he did so?
4. Name some foods you usually eat that are not healthy for you and healthy foods you can eat instead. Why do you think God created food that was not good for health?
5. What medical problems did Hannah have, and what do they mean to people now? Why was Hannah considered to have an eating disorder?
6. What are two common eating disorders and who gets them? Why do eating disorders exist?

CHAPTER WRAP-UP

- God provided manna for the Israelites while they were in the desert and they wanted to have other foods. They were sent there because of disobedience to God, and they didn't trust God to give them food. They became more disobedient when they began to grumble and complain about the manna. (Psalm 78:23–25, 27, 29)

- Adam and Eve were tempted by food and caused the Fall of man. (Genesis 3:1–24)

- Jesus was tempted by the devil, who used food as a way to get Jesus to turn stones into bread. Jesus was able to resist this temptation. (Matthew 4:1–4)

- Every part of your body needs blood sugar to function. Healthy food is the source of the most stable blood sugar.

- Eating several times a day, either three meals and three snacks or six small meals, is the best way to have lots of energy.

- Hannah was an example of a woman who suffered from an eating disorder and also infertility; she was restored to good health and fertility by prayer and eating regularly. (I Samuel I:1–20)

14 CURSES AND WASTING DISEASE

CHAPTER HIGHLIGHTS

- Fungus
- The Yeast Syndrome
- Curses and Cures
- Prayer

Let's Get Started

There are many places in the Bible where people are cursed with plagues and diseases because of disobedience. Many times God prescribed a special diet, like he did for Ezekiel (see Chapter 3). The curses in Deuteronomy 28 are for disobedience. The Israelites seemed very headstrong and often disobedient to God. The really good news is that the diet God prescribed in the Bible for the Israelites' disobedience is the exact same diet that is prescribed by physicians today. Could it be that North Americans are just as disobedient as the Israelites were? Or perhaps even more disobedient?

> **Deuteronomy 28:15, 20–22** However, if you do not obey the Lord your God and do not carefully follow all his **commands** and **decrees** I am giving you today, all these **curses** will come upon you and overtake you. The Lord will send on you curses, confusion and **rebuke** in everything you put your hand to, until you are destroyed and come to sudden ruin because of the evil you have done in **forsaking** him. The Lord will plague you with diseases until he has destroyed you from the land you are entering to possess. The Lord will strike you with **wasting disease**, with fever and inflammation, with scorching heat and drought, with **blight** and **mildew**, which will plague you until you perish.

commands: orders

decrees: an authoritative order having the force of law

curses: an appeal or prayer for evil or injury to befall someone

rebuke: to reprove sharply or reprimand

forsaking: giving up, abandoning

wasting disease: illness that gradually deteriorates the body, sapping strength or energy

blight: adverse environmental condition such as air pollution or plant disease

mildew: fungi or yeast-type mold

☞ **GO TO:**

Leviticus 13:47–59;
14:33–57; Haggai
2:17 (mildew)

NIV: *New International Version*

Candida albicans: *a* **pathogenic**, *yeast-like fungi; mildew is also a fungi*

pathogenic: *capable of causing disease*

fungi: *plural for more than one fungus*

What Others are Saying:

KEY POINT

Remove leftovers from the fridge before they go moldy.

 **NUTRITION FACT**

Blue cheese contains the mold penicillin; **camembert cheese** contains the mold *Candida albicans*.

camembert cheese: *a soft, ripe, aged cheese*

thrush: *the candida problem that is in the mouth, throat, and lungs*

Whew!

The **NIV** translation of the Bible calls this section "Curses for Disobedience." Whew! That is really a heavy curse, and yet I have met thousands of people who are suffering from this today. This modern disease or curse is called "the Yeast Syndrome" or **Candida albicans**. Mildew is so gross a thing that there are entire sections in the Bible under the ritual laws (see GWBI, pages 36–37) that deal specifically with mildew and cleansing yourself and your house from mildew.

Is There A Fungus Among Us?

Mildew and blight are both **fungi** that can damage your crops, your house, and your body. It has been so since Bible times! In the late 1970s, C. Orian Truss began talking about how a specific fungus or mold called *Candida albicans* can affect your body and mind. People used to joke about there being a "fungus among us" without realizing the seriousness of this particular mildew and the many different kinds of health problems that are possible once this fungus is allowed to overrun one's body.

William Crook, M.D.: In the late fall of 1979, I learned from C. Orian Truss, M.D. of the relationship of *Candida albicans*, a common yeast, to many chronic illnesses. Then, following his recommendations, I began treating some of my difficult patients with a special diet and a safe antifungal medication. Nearly all were adults with complex health problems, including headache, fatigue, depression, irritability, digestive disorders, respiratory disorders, joint pains, skin rashes, menstrual disorders, loss of sex interest, recurrent bladder and vaginal infections and sensitivity to chemical odors and additives. Almost without exception, they improved. And some improved dramatically.[1]

What Can Mold And Mildew Do?

If you have yeast syndrome—a kind of immune suppression—it is important to avoid exposure to mold and mildew, as they can make a bad situation worse. Many people with AIDS have suppressed immune systems; they also have raging candida problems like **thrush**. Small children often get thrush due to *Candida albicans* overrun, especially if they are allergic to dairy products and are being given cow's milk nonetheless. Studies of children with persistent cold-like symptoms found that they were very sensitive to molds in the environment.[2] They often had the additional symptoms of bloodshot eyes, mouth breathing, **rhinorrhea**, nasal voice, **postnasal drip**, and headache.

William Crook, M.D.: I began to see and help many patients with candida-related health problems. The great majority were women and over three-quarters were in their thirties. Their complaints included fatigue, irritability, PMS, headache, and depression. Most gave a history of recurrent vaginal infections, loss of libido, painful intercourse, and recurrent urinary tract infections[3] . . . Many different factors play a part in making you sick. Yet I am convinced that repeated courses of broad spectrum antibiotics are the main "villain." These antibiotics cause yeast overgrowth in your intestinal tract and vaginal yeast infections. And these infections, like a stream cascading down a mountain set off disturbances which can make you feel "sick all over."[4]

SICK ALL OVER

Many people who are bothered by the candida problem report feeling "sick all over" most of the time. Many diagnosed diseases or disorders also can be influenced by candida. A course of treatment for candida problems can often be helpful in treating a score of other health problems like hyperactivity, memory loss, learning difficulties, muscle pain (even **fibromyalgia**), **PMS, impotence**, fatigue, **MS, psoriasis, autism**, the list goes on and on.

If you want more information on this health problem, please see your doctor. If your doctor is not familiar with these kinds of problems, and you think you might be suffering from a yeast-related illness, look for a doctor who can treat you.

> If going into a house with a basement or an old barn or garage makes you feel queasy, swimmy-headed, or gives you a headache or runny nose, have yourself checked out for yeast problems.

How Do I Get This?

According to Dr. Crook, there are many things that can contribute to your becoming susceptible to yeast problems. Taking broad spectrum antibiotics and/or birth control pills are really major ways to start the vicious cycle that becomes the **yeast connection**. The antibiotics kill all the good "germs" along with the bad. This allows the yeast that is in the air and on everything to multiply in your body until it is out of control.

If you also have a diet rich in yeasts, fermented foods, sugar,

---

refined carbohydrates, or have exposure to chemicals or molds, you can expect that your immune system will not be able to handle all of this, and the yeasts will multiply (see Illustration #38, page 199). In the act of multiplying, the yeasts make some **gross toxins**, the most common of which is alcohol, which further suppress your immune system, and you will likely begin to get any number of symptoms that come when your immune system is not functioning 100 percent. Doctors have various names for all these symptoms, but most of them are related to poor immune functioning. Nutritional deficiencies, food and **inhalant** allergies, not enough exercise, and emotional stress or deprivation also contribute to this downward cycle.

Antibiotics can be life saving. Taken on a regular basis, however, they can suppress your immune system and allow a yeast problem to develop. Always take **acidophilus culture** or live yogurt when you are taking antibiotics; this will prevent the antibiotics from causing diarrhea, and will help to prevent yeast overgrowth.

gross toxins: crude poisons

inhalant: something you breathe in

Remember This . . .

acidophilus culture: the good bacteria that makes yogurt

> **Mark 12:28–31** One of the teachers of the Law came and heard them debating. Noticing that Jesus had given them a good answer, he asked him, "Of all the commandments, which is the most important?" "The most important one," answered Jesus, "is this: 'Hear O Israel, the Lord our God, the Lord is one. Love the Lord your God with all your heart and with all your soul and with all your mind and with all your strength.' The second is this: 'Love your neighbor as yourself.' There is no commandment greater than these."

Not Enough Love

Of all the causes for candida that Dr. Crook mentions in *The Yeast Connection*, the one I have found to be the most common is not enough love. We would do well to take Jesus' words to heart—loving God, your neighbor, and yourself are the most important commandments—because he may have had our health in mind when he said so.

I have counseled many women with candida problems who felt they were not loved as children. In some cases the mother had another baby while the first was still an infant; in others the parents had wanted their child to be a different sex; sometimes the

parents were not ready to have children and said so while the child was in the womb, making him or her feel unloved before being born; and in still others the mother had tried to abort the child. There are many ways to make a child feel unloved. They are children, after all, and do not think as adults do.

ON Target:
Loving God, yourself, your family, and your neighbors

OFF Target:
Being unloving to any child

> **Deuteronomy 29:5, 6** During the forty years that I led you through the desert, your clothes did not wear out, nor did the sandals on your feet. You ate no bread and drank no wine or other fermented drink. I did this so that you might know that I am the Lord your God.

The Cure!

The NIV Bible calls this passage from Deuteronomy the "Renewal of the Covenant." When the Israelites were disobedient, they were cursed with wasting diseases; when they decided to obey and renewed their covenant with God, he gave them the cure for the curses—eat no fermented foods, drink no fermented drinks, and go to a place where there is no mold. This is exactly the same cure for the yeast problem! You must also eat foods that improve your immune system and foods (not necessarily the same foods) that destroy the fungus. Among these foods are garlic, yogurt, and olive oil.

Reginald Cherry, M.D.: We may be disobedient by eating foods that are unhealthy for us, such as foods high in saturated fats. Or we may not be exercising and staying physically fit. Perhaps we have allowed sin, unforgiveness, worry, cares, or stress to work their destructive attacks on our bodies.[5]

Things To Avoid

If you think that you might be suffering from too much yeast, mold, or fungus in your body, see your doctor for a test. You can also start a special diet that is designed to prevent the yeast from multiplying. This is a diet with no yeast; no fermented foods such as wine, beer, or vinegar; nothing made with vinegar such as pickles, mayonnaise, and other salad dressings; no cheeses (except for cottage cheese which is not fermented); and no bread or crackers made with yeast and no soft drinks (see Illustration #39, page 201). Many people find they can't have sugar, not even fruit, for a period of time because yeast and other fungi love to grow on fruit and fruit juices. Many people do not eat any grains or carbohydrate vegetables like corn, peas, lima beans, and potatoes.

Experience this yourself by going off all these foods for at least a month and then gradually adding in one new food a week. If your symptoms start to subside while you are off the offending foods and return when they are added back in, you have the answer to your problem!

*Remember
This . . .*

Foods To Avoid	Foods To Eat Instead
Bread made with yeast	Unleavened bread
Cheese	Soy & almond cheeses
Leftovers	Freshly made foods
Vinegar	Lemon juice
Pickles	Fresh cucumbers
Dried & fresh fruits	Vegetable sticks
Canned vegetables	Fresh vegetables
Rollmop herrings	Fresh fish
Bagels, sweet rolls, pastries, etc.	No-yeast crackers
Beer, wine	Water
Soft drinks	Unsweetened herbal teas
Coffee, tea	Water
Fruit juice	Water
Fast food hamburgers	Broiled meat and no bun
Corn chips and salsa	Veggies and salsa

Illustration #39

*Mug of Tea—Unsweetened
herbal tea makes a healthy
substitute for soft drinks!*

Maureen Salaman: During the time I was able to hang in there on the diet [of mostly fruits], I experienced every diabolical digestive disturbance because I am a Candida sufferer. Candida, a yeast overgrowth in the intestines and elsewhere in the body, can cause illness or, in some cases, death. Individuals with *Candida albicans* must go easy on the intake of sugars, even fruit.[6]

**What Others
are Saying:**

Well, What CAN I Eat?

Just eat whole natural foods (see Illustration #40, this page). Avoid sugar and sugar-laden foods, refined foods, and processed foods. Have small amounts of fish, meat, yogurt, cottage cheese, or nuts and seeds every day. Add to this a lot of raw and steamed vegetables. You may have butter, olive oil, or flaxseed oil on them. Put raw garlic on everything! So a great breakfast would be fish and a salad, or eggs and veggies. Even tofu and veggies is great for you. Generally, almond- or soy-milk cheeses are not fermented so experiment with eating these. After a few days or weeks you will start to feel better.

Illustration #40

*Foods for the Immune
System—Garlic, yogurt,
parsley, and fish can help to
build up your immune
system.*

Nutritional Supplements That Help

- Odorless garlic extract
- Low-dose B complex vitamins, three times a day
- Colostrum or lactoferrin[7]
- **Biotin**
- Olive leaf extract
- Acidophilus liquid or tablets/capsules
- Probiotics
- **Melaleuca**[8]
- **Beta-1,3-D-glucan**

ON Target:
Avoiding fermented foods and drinks; eating fresh food

OFF Target:
Consuming pizza, hamburgers, luncheon meats, soft drinks, beer, or wine

> **Ephesians 6:2, 3** "Honor your father and mother"—which is the first commandment with a promise—"that it may go well with you and that you may enjoy long life on the earth."

A Grimm Lesson

One of Grimm's fairy tales is about a woman whose father-in-law lived with her and her husband, because he had nowhere else to live. The woman—a modern lady—thought her father-in-law was getting in the way of her happiness, so she and her husband led him to a stool in a dark corner of the kitchen and told him that he would eat his meals there in an earthenware bowl. One day, the old man's hands trembled, he dropped the bowl, and it broke. The woman responded by saying, "If you eat like a pig, you must have a trough." So she and her husband made a trough for him to eat out of. Now the couple had a four-year-old son whom they loved very much. One day they noticed him playing with some bits of wood and asked him what he was doing. "I'm making a trough," he replied, "to feed you with when I get big."

This fairy tale keenly illustrates how disobeying the fifth commandment can affect our well-being. Reginald Cherry thinks disobedience can remove us from God's "hand of protection."

What Others are Saying:

Reginald Cherry, M.D.: When a person is physically ill, the devil may indeed be attacking—and there also may be other causes for that illness. For example, I sometimes explain to patients that they may have come out from under the umbrella of protection that God has placed over his children. When we are disobedient or ignorant of God's will for our lives, we can remove ourselves from God's hand of protection.[9]

If you find yourself saying negative things about your parents, your childhood, or how your parents brought you up, you are not honoring them. Work with your pastor, your prayer group, or healing group on forgiving your parents and letting go of the negativity. Things will go better for you.

Something to Ponder

> **Hebrews 12:15** See to it that no one misses the grace of God and that no bitter root grows up to cause trouble and defile many.

Bitter Root

Remove bitterness from your heart; see that no bitter root grows to keep you from God. Love God, forgive others, love yourself and others—love and forgiveness will remove bitterness and improve your immune system. When you can do this, you will be much closer to total health.

Florence Littauer: Do you have some pain that needs to be healed? Do you have some heavy chains that need to be broken? Do you have some roots that need to be dug up?[10]

What Others are Saying:

> **James 5:13–16** Is any one of you in trouble? He should pray. Is anyone happy? Let him sing songs of praise. Is any one of you sick? He should call the elders of the church to pray over him and anoint him with oil in the name of the Lord. And the prayer offered in faith will make the sick person well; the Lord will raise him up. If he has sinned, he will be forgiven. Therefore confess your sins to each other and pray for each other so that you may be healed. The prayer of a righteous man is powerful and effective.

Pray For Each Other

It is very important to pray for those who are sick. If they have sinned, they must confess it and then be forgiven through prayer. This is the work of prayer groups, elders, and healing ministries in many churches. Even if you are not a member of their church, they are obligated to pray for you believing that you will be healed. Confess your sins—the times that you missed the mark. Confess when you cheated on your taxes, took too much change at the grocery, yelled at your children for no reason, belittled your husband, wife, children, or mother-in-law. Any time you were not 100 percent loving to God, your neighbor, or yourself is a sin to be confessed.

Reginald Cherry, M.D.: So we may diagnose the physical illness, but we also need spiritual insight to understand that a physical attack on our bodies comes from the realm of darkness. Medical diagnosis is not enough in understanding our illness. We also must not be ignorant of the devices of the devil.[11]

ON Target:

Having your pastor or prayer warriors pray for your healing

OFF Target:

Belittling yourself for being weak; not praying for healing

> **Matthew 22:37–39** Jesus replied: " 'Love the Lord your God with all your heart and with all your soul and with all your mind.' This is the first and greatest commandment. And the second is like it: 'Love your neighbor as yourself.' All the Law and the Prophets hang on these two commandments."

Body, Mind, And Spirit

Healing encompasses the body, mind, and spirit of a person. If you have anger or hatred in your heart, you might have a suppressed immune system. This can make you more susceptible to all kinds of illnesses. Do not hold onto anger or hold something against a person; confess it and let it go. God will forgive you, and you should forgive yourself. Eat sensibly, pray without ceasing, and remember to forgive all people (including yourself). This will put you on the road to a healthy body, mind, and spirit.

Study Questions

1. Why did God curse the Israelites? And with what?
2. If the Israelites were disobedient and God cursed them with mildew and wasting diseases, what do you think is happening in the world today that has brought back the curse of mold and mildew even more widespread than in Bible times? Relate this to a modern plague.
3. What foods did God keep from the Israelites in the desert that are good to stay away from for the modern yeast and fungi plague? What do you imagine modern people have in common with the Israelites, that they would both receive the same curses on their health and bodies?

4. What else can you do to improve your immune system and your health? Why do you think so many people are reluctant to look at their own level of health and try to assess what God wants for them in their lives? (I assume that they are reluctant because there are so many sick people who are suffering from faulty-lifestyle related illnesses.)

CHAPTER WRAP-UP

- God found the Israelites to be disobedient because they turned away from him. (Deuteronomy 28:15)

- God put a curse on the Israelites because of their disobedience. He sent on them mold and mildew along with other curses. (Deuteronomy 28:20–22)

- The curse of blight and mildew is very similar to a modern illness that has many symptoms. The mildew or fungus that is the scourge of modern civilizations is *Candida albicans,* often called the "yeast syndrome."

- God forbade the Israelites from eating bread, wine, and other fermented foods and drinks. Staying away from these foods and drinks will help you to overcome the health problems related to mold and mildew. (Deuteronomy 29:5, 6)

- Many outside substances—fermented food, junk food, preservatives, mold on leftovers, and various yeasts and molds—can affect your immune system and allow your body to have too much candida in it. Lack of love can also have a great effect on your immune system, causing suppression that can also lead to a wide range of symptoms and diseases.

- Prayer can do a lot toward healing all afflictions. (James 5:15, 16)

15 GOD'S SACRED TEMPLE

CHAPTER HIGHLIGHTS

- Your Body Is God's Temple
- A Poultice of Figs
- Forgiveness
- WWJD?
- Rainbow of Hope

Let's Get Started

Many external substances such as mildew, mold, air pollution, noise pollution, overcast skies, and unkind words can affect your body. You are also affected by the thoughts you put into your mind and the words that come out of your mouth. God has given many herbs and foods that can help you find health in your body and mind. God has also given complete instructions on how to know him. He created your body to be turned over to him as a <u>temple</u> for him to dwell in.

☞ **GO TO:**

I Corinthians 6:19 (temple)

> **I Corinthians 3:16, 17** Don't you know that you yourselves are God's temple and that God's Spirit lives in you? If anyone destroys God's temple, God will destroy him; for God's temple is sacred, and you are that temple.

Your Body Is God's Temple

God created you in his image, you bear his image in your body, in your cells, in every part of you. This alone should be enough to make you want to respect your body and take care of it. Most people take better care of their car or truck than they do their body and yet their car or truck was not made in the image of God. When you feed your sacred temple of God less than nutritious food, you are defiling it; you might actually be destroying it. What you do to your body, whether it be smoking, drinking alcohol, eating junk food, being angry, or telling lies, directly affects the temple that God has given you. Is this any way to treat the temple you have been entrusted with?

KEY POINT

Every day ask God for direction in your life.

Smoking, alcohol, sugar, and excess animal fat have all been shown to destroy your body.

ON Target:
Offering your body and mind to God every day

OFF Target:
Forgetting about God

☞ **GO TO:**

Romans 6:13 (offer)

**What Others
are Saying:**

**Remember
This . . .**

hypertension: *high blood pressure*

aorta: *the main trunk of the body's arteries*

Cheryl Townsley: In other areas of my life I had learned that *what you deposit is directly related to what is available for withdrawal.* I understood this principle in the realm of banking, but I had no comprehension of it in regard to health or other less tangible areas of my life.[1]

Maureen Salaman: The more vegetables and fruit we eat in their natural state—the way God made them—the closer our diet comes to perfection.[2]

> **Romans 12:1, 2** Therefore, I urge you, brothers, in view of God's mercy, to offer your bodies as living sacrifices, holy and pleasing to God—this is your spiritual act of worship. Do not conform to the pattern of this world, but be transformed by the renewing of your mind. Then you will be able to test and approve what God's will is—his good, pleasing and perfect will.

You Can Become A Temple

By offering your body to God, you can become a sacred temple. Every day you must <u>offer</u> up your body and mind to God. A really simple way to do this is to say, "God, I offer you my body and mind today, to do with as you will." Or, "My body is your body, Oh God." You don't have to say much; just offer your body to God first thing in the morning and in the evening before going to bed. This will bring you closer to God, and remind you of your sacred responsibility to care for his temple.

Rex Russell, M.D.: Alcohol damages all cells. Even a small amount of alcohol weakens the heart muscle. Abstinence from alcohol strengthens the heart's contraction ability unless permanent damage has already been done.[3]

Hypertension can be aggravated by drinking coffee, adding salt to food, and excessive use of alcohol. Eating fish and flax oils will help to reduce high blood pressure.[4] Eating garlic on a regular basis can reverse the aging process of your arteries by keeping the **aorta** elastic and less stiff.[5] Even keeping your bones in great shape is possible. Research shows that elderly people who eat high-calcium foods and take a vitamin D supplement or get adequate sunlight exposure can reduce osteoporosis and hip fractures. Of course, scientists suggest reducing caffeine intake as a preventative.[6]

God gave you the choice to choose the foods you eat and the habits you develop and keep. It is up to you to decide which things you do that are damaging your body and which things you could add to your lifestyle or **habits** that will build up your body to become a glorious temple of God. By following all the recommendations in the first half of this book you will be well on your way to building up a clean and beautifully functioning temple for God to inhabit.

Cheryl Townsley: I began to explore my feelings. I found that many of my mind-sets and emotional reactions were merely habits. The good news about habits is that they can be changed. The bad news is that changing habits takes time.[7]

> **II Kings 20:1–5, 7** In those days Hezekiah became ill and was at the point of death. The prophet Isaiah son of Amoz went to him and said, "This is what the Lord says: Put your house in order, because you are going to die; you will not recover." Hezekiah turned his face to the wall and prayed to the Lord, "Remember, O Lord, how I have walked before you faithfully and with wholehearted devotion and have done what is good in your eyes." And Hezekiah wept bitterly. Before Isaiah had left the middle court, the word of the Lord came to him: "Go back and tell Hezekiah, the leader of my people, 'This is what the Lord, the God of your father David, says: I have heard your prayer and seen your tears; I will heal you. . . .'" Then Isaiah said, "Prepare a poultice of figs." They did so and applied it to the boil, and he recovered.

A Poultice Of Figs

Many fruits and vegetables are made into **poultices** or **plasters** for healing. Some draw out poisons, which could have been the case with the poultice of figs in II Kings 20. Some bring heat to the skin on the surface and increase the blood flow to the area, as a mustard plaster does. Aloe vera gel from the leaf is used to relieve the sting of burns and speed healing. Comfrey leaves are used to draw out poisons. Even ginger root can draw out a **sebaceous cyst**.

> **Matthew 6:14, 15** For if you forgive men when they sin against you, your heavenly Father will also forgive you. But if you do not forgive men their sins, your Father will not forgive your sins.

Forgiveness

☞ **GO TO:**

Colossians 3:13
(forgive)

ON Target:
Forgiving everybody for every little thing against you

OFF Target:
Holding on to resentment and bitterness

Jesus makes it clear in Matthew 6:14 and 15 that it is essential to <u>forgive</u> anyone who sins against you. If you cannot do so, God won't be able to forgive you. This is a basic theme in Jesus' teachings—you must forgive others when they have sinned against you. You have all heard this before, but how hard it is to do! It doesn't matter who has sinned against you—your father, mother, aunts, uncles, the grocery store manager, your first grade teacher—you must forgive them all.

Practice Forgiveness

Each time you have a memory of something hurtful that someone did to you, just forgive them. Turn it over to God. I remember hearing in a sermon that C. S. Lewis, the great Christian writer, spent 25 years trying to forgive someone. You must forgive people whether you want to or not. The very practice of doing it when you least want to is an act of forgiveness to yourself.

What Others are Saying:

molested: harassed sexually

Mark Pearson: Often people block their healing—by clinging to resentment. I ministered to a man who had been sexually abused as a child. One day one of the people ministering to him asked him if he had forgiven the person who had **molested** him. "No," he responded. "I hate him!" He was reminded that our Lord tells us to forgive others and pray for those who persecute us. Indeed, Jesus said that if we do not forgive others, we ourselves will not be forgiven. Forgiving the mán who molested him had not been easy, but it had brought healing.[8]

ON Target:
Using natural remedies for simple problems

OFF Target:
Refusing to seek the opinion of a qualified doctor before doing any natural treatments

> **Matthew 18:21, 22** Then Peter came to Jesus and asked, "Lord, how many times shall I forgive my brother when he sins against me? Up to seven times?" Jesus answered, "I tell you, not seven times, but seventy-seven times."

WWJD?

What would Jesus do? is always the perfect question to ask when you want to find total health. What would Jesus do in this situation? When someone sins against you, you must forgive them; this is exactly what Jesus said to do. It is a simple act but not always easy. When somebody cuts in front of you on the road, don't get angry; forgive them. Say out loud, "I forgive you for doing that." When your child spills his milk, say to him, "I am not mad at you, I forgive you for having an accident. Please clean it up." Then give him a hug, and you will both be on the way to better health. If you are tempted to eat something that you know is bad for you, just ask yourself WWJD? He would not have eaten junk food or gotten drunk. Especially since there was no junk food, and we know that he spoke against <u>drunkenness</u>.

☞ **GO TO:**

Luke 21:32–36 (drunkenness)

> **Colossians 3:5–10** Put to death, therefore, whatever belongs to your earthly nature: sexual immorality, impurity, lust, evil desires, and greed, which is idolatry. Because of these, the **wrath** of God is coming. You used to walk in these ways, in the life you once lived. But now you must rid yourselves of all such things as these: <u>anger, rage</u>, **malice**, slander, and filthy language from your lips. Do not lie to each other, since you have taken off your old self with its practices and have put on the new knowledge in the image of its Creator.

wrath: *divine retribution for sin*

☞ **GO TO:**

Ephesians 4:31 (anger, rage)

malice: *a desire to harm others or to see others suffer*

Turn To God

God makes it quite clear that you are not to take part in anger, rage, malice, and many other actions and reactions that we now call "stress response." If you really expect to spend time with God and to be healthy, you are to get rid of any worldly ways. Most of the actions and emotions that God tells man not to take part in are those of the "fight or flight" response. This response occurs when you do not follow a sensible diet, eat too much sugar and caffeine, and allow your blood sugar to go way up and then to drop way down creating a stress that triggers the "fight or flight" response. The "fight or flight" response is also a response to the failure to handle stressful situations in your life.

Perhaps you are doing more than your body can handle, perhaps you are not eating right, perhaps you are not sleeping enough, perhaps you are in over your head. You can "put to death" these stresses in your life by turning them over to God.

Cheryl Townsley: When I was tempted to explode or isolate myself emotionally, I took time and dealt with the issue. In the past, I usually suppressed my emotions.[9]

Anger And Rage

type A behavior: *typical behavior of heart attack personality*

Of all negative emotions anger and rage can do the most damage to your body. Research is showing that the **type A behavior**, thought to be responsible for heart disease and heart attacks can now be called "type anger." Scientists have found it is anger that damages the heart muscle, not the other behaviors of a type A personality. Even infants can cause damage to their heart muscles, over time, if left to cry so long that they become angry frequently.

Kenneth H. Cooper, M.D.: A failure to handle the pressures of life can increase cholesterol, blood pressure, and other risk factors linked to heart disease.[10]

Mark Pearson: Increasingly, articles are being published both in medical journals and in the popular press demonstrating the relationship between sickness and the inappropriate handling of emotions. Bitterness, resentment, anxiety, inappropriately expressed anger—all of which the Scripture calls sin—besides harming others, harm ourselves, spiritually, emotionally and physically.[11]

> **Genesis 9:13–16** I have set my rainbow in the clouds, and it will be a sign of the covenant between me and the earth. Whenever I bring clouds over the earth and the rainbow appears in the clouds, I will remember my covenant between me and you and all living creatures of every kind. Never again will the waters become a flood to destroy all life. Whenever the rainbow appears in the clouds, I will see it and remember the everlasting covenant between God and all living creatures of every kind on the earth.

The Rainbow Of Hope

The rainbow appears after storm and rain. It takes the sun shining on the wetness to form a rainbow. Each time you feel gray or stormy remember the rainbow and the hope it brings to you. Let the rainbows in your life remind you that God has a covenant with you. If you keep his commandments and follow his precepts and advice, you will see the rainbow and be reminded that God loves and cares for you and has given instructions for you to feel really great.

W. David Hager, M.D., and Linda Carruth Hager: The Lord stands ready and more willing than we can ever know to meet us at the point of our deepest need. Will you trust him? Step off the banks and move into the ongoing river of his love.[12]

What Others are Saying:

Study Questions

1. Why is your body a temple?
2. When it comes to healing, what is the role of God, and what is the role of medicines or remedies?
3. Why was Jesus so adamant about forgiving? Why should you be too?
4. Which emotions can harm your body? How do they do this?

CHAPTER WRAP-UP

- You were created in the image of God. The Bible tells you that you are to be a temple of God. (I Corinthians 3:16)

- God often instructed his prophets to use common substances for healings. He instructed Isaiah to use a poultice of figs to cure a boil. (II Kings 20:1–5, 7)

- Over and over again Jesus talked about the importance of forgiveness. He even said we should forgive our brother seventy-seven times. (Matthew 18:21, 22)

- Jesus warns everybody about the use of anger, rage, and other negative emotions. (Colossians 3:5–10)

- God gave the Israelites a rainbow to remind them of his covenant with them. (Genesis 9:13–16)

16 AND JESUS WENT A'WALKIN'

CHAPTER HIGHLIGHTS

- Jesus the Walker
- Benefits of Walking
- Adam and Eve
- Walking Distance
- Walking Tips

Let's Get Started

Deciding what kind of exercise to do can be confusing—should you walk, bicycle, lift weights, do aerobics? What you do is really up to you, but why not start with walking. Walking is easy to do, does not require any special equipment, can be done in almost any environment, and it's free! Jesus and his disciples walked everywhere they went. Everybody knows how to walk, but in this chapter you will learn the correct way to walk for health.

> **Matthew 4:18–20** As Jesus was walking beside the Sea of Galilee, he saw two brothers, Simon called Peter and his brother Andrew. They were casting a net into the lake, for they were fishermen. "Come, follow me," Jesus said, "and I will make you fishers of men." At once they left their nets and followed him.

Jesus The Walker

Jesus and his disciples walked because they didn't have automobiles, airplanes, or subways (see Illustration #41, page 216). He walked up on a <u>mountainside</u> to deliver the Sermon on the Mount. Jesus <u>walked</u> frequently with his disciples even after he returned to the world after his resurrection. What other choice did they have? The only other modes of transportation were donkeys, donkey carts, and boats. Often he took a boat but according to Scripture, more often he walked.

☞ **GO TO:**

Matthew 5:1 (mountainside)

Luke 24:13–29 (walked)

Illustration #41

Map of First-Century Palestine—Jesus and his disciples
walked from the Dead Sea to
Galilee in their ministry
travels.

ON Target:

Walking to the store
and taking the stairs
whenever possible

OFF Target:

Avoiding exercise

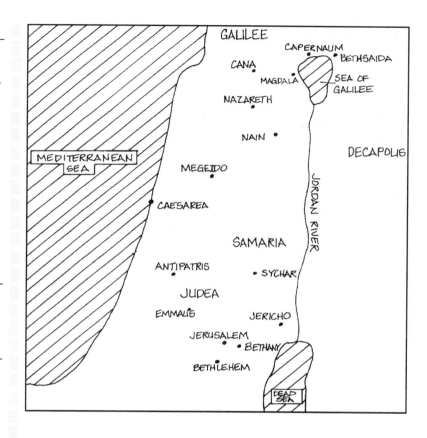

**chronic obstructive
pulmonary disease:**
persistent difficulty in
breathing because lung
tissues cannot function
effectively; emphysema or
severe asthma

**benign prostatic
hyperplasia:**
enlargement of the
prostate gland including
overproduction of
prostate cells

What Others
are Saying:

Walking Is Great!

If you don't exercise at all, and you start to do regular walking,
you will soon find yourself feeling better, even if you didn't think
you felt bad in the first place. A recent study of patients with
chronic obstructive pulmonary disease (COPD) showed that
when COPD sufferers added walking and cycling to their daily
lifestyle, they had increased muscle strength, got out of breath
less, and enjoyed an improved quality of life.[1] Men with **benign
prostatic hyperplasia** who walked two to three hours a week
had a 25 percent lower incidence of urinary tract symptoms.[2] Walking helped to improve the bone mineral density after hip surgery
in both men and women.[3]

Jim Shriner: If you are really overweight, or out of shape, a good
walking program might be all you should be doing right now.
Walking could be enough to get you into your personal training
zone very easily.[4]

WHAT ELSE DOES IT DO?

Walking is an excellent exercise to help relieve the symptoms of **fibromyalgia**, along with physical therapy, massage, and relaxation techniques.[5] Although it is often difficult for people with fibromyalgia to do any exercise because of the chronic pain and fatigue associated with the disease, it will improve their well-being in many ways. Walking can help remove some of the pain caused by the **lactic acid** that is trapped in the muscles. When a person with fibromyalgia starts a walking program, it may be painful and difficult; but with regular walking, the pain decreases, the heart rate improves and there will be an increase in stamina and energy. Regular walking can reduce high blood pressure and increase blood flow in the arms and legs for older **hypertensives**.[6] Daily walking was shown in another study to increase bone mineral density in postmenopausal women.[7] When bones lose their density there will be a problem with osteoporosis.

Weight-bearing exercise, especially walking, can help restore calcium to bones, increasing their density and helping to prevent osteoporosis and breaking bones. Did you know many women have a greater need for exercise after menopause than before? After hearing all this, how can you not walk?

> **John 4:3–5** When the Lord learned of this, he left Judea and went back once more to Galilee. Now he had to go through Samaria. So he came to a town in Samaria called Sychar, near the plot of ground Jacob had given to his son Joseph.

Not Your Everyday Stroll

The distance between Judea and Galilee could be as much as 50 miles depending on where they went in each place. Do you ever walk that far just to see friends? Or to do your work? Yet, in Jesus' day walking was the usual mode of transportation. In many places in the world, walking is still the main mode of transportation; perhaps you can make it your main transportation (see Illustration #42, page 218).

ON Target:
Asking your doctor if you can exercise by starting a walking program

OFF Target:
Sitting in a chair or on the couch every night, instead of walking

fibromyalgia: chronic, achy, muscular pain

lactic acid: by-product of muscle use that often causes temporary pain when trapped in muscles

Something to Ponder

hypertensives: people with high blood pressure

KEY POINT

A great way to get into the discipline of walking is to get a dog that insists on being walked every day!

Illustration #42

Walking in Bible Times—In Bible times people walked everywhere!

Francisco Contreras, M.D.: The fact is that little exercise is needed to get more out of our bodies. One of the easiest and most accessible exercises is walking. To keep yourself in good physical condition, you should, on average, walk briskly from 25 to 60 minutes 3 times a week; that's not asking much at all![8]

ON Target:
Walking to church or friends' houses

OFF Target:
Taking the car everywhere you go

> **Genesis 3:8** Then the man and his wife heard the sound of the Lord God as he was walking in the garden in the cool of the day. . . .

God Walked Too!

From the verse in Genesis 3:8 it appears that even God liked to go walking. When you go out walking, consider it your daily time with God. Take a tape recorder every now and then and listen to uplifting songs. Make your walking time your time with God.

Make It Really Count

When you walk, it is important to do so at a brisk pace. Start by walking a little more with everything you do. Take the stairs for one flight instead of the elevator or escalator, park your car a few yards farther from the store. Walk to the post office or visit a museum or art gallery for additional walking. Many older adults start a walking program by joining the "mall walkers" in their favorite shopping mall. Because it's enclosed, bad weather is never an excuse. Once you are in the habit of walking more, pick up the pace a little each time that you walk. Walking is best for your body if you can increase your pulse a little. Obviously you need to take your pulse when you are resting so you can tell what your resting pulse is. (For instructions, see the Pulse Chart, this page.)

What Others are Saying:

T. D. Jakes: "E" is for seizing "extra" opportunities to strengthen your energy and burn off extra calories. It includes taking the stairs over the elevator. It includes parking further from the door and allowing yourself to walk. It includes picking up the pace just a bit when you walk and never driving the car when your destination is within a mile of you.[9]

Pulse Chart

- Sit in a comfortable chair for at least ten minutes, until you are relaxed.
- Place your fingertips on your throat next to your Adam's apple or voice box.
- Swallow to find the location of the center of your throat.
- Using your fingertips, feel around in the area of your neck beside the Adam's apple until you find a beating pulse.
- Look at a clock with a second hand and count the number of beats or pulses for one full minute. That will be your resting pulse.
- You can also count the beats for 15 seconds and multiply by four to get the one-minute pulse.
- A true resting pulse of 60 to 75 first thing in the morning (before you get out of bed) is the general range for an adult. If this pulse is closer to 100, see your doctor.
- A first-thing-in-the-morning pulse of 100 or more calls for a visit to your doctor.

KEY POINT

Ask your doctor what your normal resting and exercise pulse should be.

ON THE PULSE OF IT

Once you know your resting pulse, take your pulse before you walk. Check it while you are walking, and then when you are finished. Ask your doctor what your normal resting and exercise pulse should be. This way you will know how high you can increase your pulse for your age or health level.

Julian Whitaker, M.D.: The most important thing is to get your body moving enough to raise your pulse a bit above the resting level.[10]

Good Exercise Choices

Walking	Tennis	Stationary Bike
Gardening	Bicycling	Treadmill
Aerobics	Stair Climbing	Swimming
Dancing	Golfing	Weight Lifting
Bowling	Ping Pong	Heavy House Cleaning

 DAILY BREAD

WALKING
Walking in the morning and evening can be part of your time with God each day.

WALKING THE STRAIGHT AND NARROW

When you decide to start walking for exercise, check out your equipment. First look at your shoes. Do not wear shoes that are run over or uncomfortable. Wear shoes with firm but flexible soles and low or no heels. The heels of your shoes should fit snugly around your heels. If they don't, purchase some heel grips for inside your heels. They are very inexpensive and can keep you from getting blisters while you walk.

Once you have comfortable shoes and an outfit that allows you to move freely, it is time to begin. Start by stepping forward with one foot. Your heel should touch the ground first and the rest of your foot should be rounded to allow you to rock up onto the ball of your foot. Walking coaches often describe the posture of the foot during walking as being like the rockers of a large rocking chair. Each time you place your heel down, rock up onto the ball of your foot. Keep doing this with your knees slightly bent and your body lifted high as if you were going to float off at any minute. Rock onto one foot and then the other until you are walking briskly. Your arms should be swinging, left arm forward when the right foot is forward, right arm forward when the left foot is forward. This is just the natural way to walk. If you have any doubts, look at a young child. Do not roll your feet to the side. Keep both feet pointed straight ahead, as if you were walking along either side of a narrow, drawn line. Don't let your feet point to the left or right, just keep them straight ahead.

DON'T FORGET TO BREATHE

When you are walking along briskly, take slow deep breaths in and out as you walk along. You should be able to feel your heart rate increasing a little, and be a little out of breath, but still able to carry on a conversation. Brisk walking is an **aerobic** activity that increases your oxygen intake, and this will happen best if you concentrate on doing gentle deep breathing.

Julian Whitaker, M.D.: Current recommendations for aerobic activity are for 20 to 30 minutes at least three days a week. You should aim to work at a level where you feel that your breathing is heavier but where you can still hold a conversation.[11]

What Others are Saying:

Study Questions

1. Why do you think Jesus and his disciples walked everywhere?
2. What is the best way to start exercising? Are there exercises that you are doing now that can be increased to improve your health level? What are they?
3. Children are generally more active. How has your attitude about exercise changed since you were a child and why?
4. What are some of the health benefits that can be gained by exercise and walking in general? Does your church have an exercise group? If not, when are you going to start one?

CHAPTER WRAP-UP

- When Jesus began his ministry he called fishermen to walk with him. (Matthew 4:18–20)
- Walking is a great form of exercise for you today.
- Jesus and his disciples often walked 40 to 50 miles to get to the places they visited. (John 4:3–5)
- Walking can improve a person's general health, and it can improve some specific health problems. It is one of the best overall exercises.
- God used to walk with Adam and Eve in the Garden. (Genesis 3:8)

17 FEASTING, FEASTING, FEASTING

CHAPTER HIGHLIGHTS

- Seven Feasts
- Well-known Feasts
- Relaxed Eating
- God's Disapproval
- Your Body's Design

Let's Get Started

The Bible has many passages about <u>feasts</u>. Many people assume feasting means to eat a lot, but this is not always the case with the "feasts" mentioned in the Bible. There were seven feasts specifically for the Israelites. They were often warned against drinking <u>too much</u> and overindulging in food, because this is what Romans and pagans did. Feasts were used to honor religious remembrances, for weddings and funerals, and for other special occasions. In the New Testament, Jesus warns people to keep away from overindulging in alcohol, anger, vile talk, hatred, and unforgiveness. This chapter will explore not only what the Bible says about feasting but also what nutritionists say about it. Too much feasting, specifically eating too much, can actually cause food sensitivities, exhaust your body, and prevent you from being able to handle stress.

GO TO:

Genesis 26:30; Psalm 81:3; Matthew 26:5 (feast)

Proverbs 23:20 (too much)

> **Leviticus 23:1, 2** The Lord said to Moses, "Speak to the Israelites and say to them: 'These are my appointed feasts, the appointed feasts of the Lord, which you are to proclaim in the assemblies.'"

Seven Feasts

God gave the Jews seven <u>appointed feast</u> days to observe forever: Passover, Unleavened Bread, First Fruits, Pentecost, Trumpets, Atonement, and Tabernacles. All of them required special eating and feasting except for the Feast of Atonement, when they were to deny themselves. They were required to do no work, and this meant no eating.

GO TO:

Leviticus 23 (appointed feasts)

Feasts With Lots Of Eating

To the Hebrews a feast was not simply a meal with lots of food, the way it was for the Romans. The seven feasts were festivals—religious remembrances—and sometimes they made animal sacrifices to God. These feasts included special meals and often lasted for several days, but people did not eat a huge amount or drink too much. Feasts were held for special occasions, such as the one held to commemorate Isaac's being <u>weaned</u>, funerals, and weddings. As a matter of fact, Jesus performed his first miracle at a <u>wedding</u> feast when he turned water into wine.

☞ **GO TO:**

Genesis 21:8 (weaned)

John 2:1–11 (wedding)

> **Exodus 12:14–16** This is a day you are to commemorate; for the generations to come you shall celebrate it as a festival to the Lord—a lasting ordinance. For seven days you are to eat bread made without yeast. On the first day remove the yeast from your houses, for whoever eats anything with yeast in it from the first day through the seventh must be cut off from Israel. On the first day hold a sacred assembly, and another one on the seventh day. Do no work at all on these days, except to prepare food for everyone to eat—that is all you may do.

The Feast Of Unleavened Bread

The feast that non-Jews are the most familiar with is the Feast of Unleavened Bread which begins with the **Passover** meal. For seven days they may not eat anything with **leavening** in it. Besides yeasted breads that includes vinegar, corn syrup, brown sugar (because it may contain yeast), baking soda and powder, and more strict Jews even omit beans, peas, grains, corn, and seeds. There is a special meal at the beginning of the period called the "Seder." The Seder is a family ritual to remember the time when the Israelites had to leave in a hurry and did not have time to let the yeast work in their bread, so they ate unleavened bread. During this meal they do not eat any foods with leaven or yeast or anything that might ferment and become leaven. Wine drinking is part of the remembrance, and so are other ritual foods like bitter herbs, boiled eggs, and lamb shanks, which are eaten along with the **matzah.**

Passover: "Pesach," commemorates the flight of the Jews from Egypt

leavening: any substance such as yeast, sour dough starters, or cream of tartar, used in batter to produce fermentation

matzah: unleavened bread, like a large cracker

> **Leviticus 16:29–31** This is to be a lasting ordinance for you: On the tenth day of the seventh month you must deny yourselves and not do any work—whether native-born or an alien living among you—because on this day atonement will be made for you, to cleanse you. Then before the Lord, you will be clean from all your sins. It is a sabbath of rest, and you must deny yourselves; it is a lasting ordinance.

ON Target:
Setting aside a day for atonement

OFF Target:
Ignoring your sins

You Call This A Feast?

The Day of Atonement is one of the feasts required by God, and during it there is no eating at all! This day of at-one-ment is marked by a series of five restrictions, or afflictions: 1) no eating or drinking, 2) no bathing, 3) no anointing of the body with oil, 4) no wearing of leather shoes, and 5) no sexual relations. This is a day when they are to remember their sins, ask for forgiveness, and **repent**. It's definitely not what we normally consider a feast. It is, however, a festival, with services in the synagogue, reading from the holy books, and lighting of candles.

The Day of Atonement: also known as "Yom Kippur"

repent: changing one's conduct or heart, to turn away from sin

What used to be called a "feast" in Bible times is now called a "potluck." Every church seems to have what they call the "famous ____ potluck," and they insert the name of their denomination in the middle of this phrase. I have heard people from at least four different protestant denominations say that their denomination is famous for their potlucks. It seems that eating before, during, and after religious occasions is something that was started in Old Testament times and has carried on until today.

Something to Ponder

WHY FEAST?

In Bible times the feasts were held at certain times of the year, especially before and after harsh weather. First, a feast was held to prepare for winter when people didn't go out as often. Then a feast was held after winter was over, to thank God for getting them through it. Feasts also were held on many important occasions like birthdays, marriages, and harvests. Often, during these nonreligious feasts, there would be much drinking of wine and eating of rich food.

ON Target:
Eating moderately at feasts

OFF Target:
Stuffing yourself

> **Amos 5:21; 6:1, 4, 6, 7** I hate, I despise your religious feasts; I cannot stand your assemblies. Woe to you who are complacent in Zion, and to you who feel secure on Mount Samaria. You lie on beds inlaid with ivory and lounge on your couches. You dine on choice lambs and fattened calves. You drink wine by the bowlful and use the finest lotions, but you never grieve over the ruin of Joseph. Therefore you will be among the first to go into exile; your feasting and lounging will end.

They Ate On A Couch

☞ **GO TO:**

Mark 14:1–5; Luke 22:14–16 (reclining)

ON Target:
Feasting with a purpose

OFF Target:
Feasting just to overeat

During Old and New Testament times, Israelites, Romans, and most of the known world ate reclining on a kind of couch. In fact, Jesus and his disciples were <u>reclining</u> at the Last Supper. This means that when they had a special feast or banquet, they were relaxing while they ate. They were fully engrossed in eating and fellowship. Times were different then. They weren't distracted by the evening news on TV as many people are today. When you are under stress or tension, your digestion slows down. Today people might do well to do nothing else when they eat except relax, enjoy the company of friends and family, and leave the worries of the world behind. This would really help improve digestion, stress levels, and family relations. Perhaps if everyone did nothing else while eating, there would be less need for antacids and digestive aids.

Forget God, Let's Eat

Many of the Israelites who belonged to the house of Joseph (because they were his descendants) had given up on God and were feasting without the religious aspect. They were eating and drinking to excess because they were separated from God. Many of the feasts, holidays, celebrations, and even the clean and unclean food rules were given to them in hopes of making them remember God. It didn't work. They just became more sinful and **gluttonous**. Sounds a bit like the modern-day Christmas celebration, doesn't it?

gluttonous: *consuming large, immoderate amounts of food and drink*

What Others are Saying:

Julian Whitaker, M.D.: People who achieve a high level of wellness consistently make healthy choices.[1]

Illustration #43

Too Much Food—Don't overindulge at meals. Eating moderate amounts of food at all times is the key to being and staying healthy.

When the Israelites began to drink wine, eat lots of food, and forget God during religious feasts and at other times, they were in a lot of trouble. God sent them away so that they had to stop eating and drinking so much. God knew that eating too much was bad for their bodies and forgetting him was bad for their hearts and minds.

Remember This . . .

> **Proverbs 23:20, 21** Do not join those who drink too much wine or gorge themselves on meat, for drunkards and gluttons become poor, and drowsiness clothes them in rags.

Why Can't I Eat That Anymore?

How interesting it is that the writer of Proverbs places eating too much and drinking too much in the same category. So do many people concerned with health. Eating and drinking too much can overload your body and cause many health problems. Stuffing yourself at any meal whether it be a feast, potluck, Sunday dinner, or breakfast is not good for your health. Each time you eat a big meal you ask your body to go into the stress mode. Eventually this can overwork your body to such an extent that it starts to break down (see Illustration #43, this page).

Such A Comfort

A person may be tempted to overeat because doing so **subconsciously** reminds him or her of what it felt like to be a bottle-fed baby. Often a mother will insist or encourage her baby to drink a certain number of ounces, whether the baby wants to or not, which leaves the baby with a full tummy and that groggy feeling that comes from eating too much. When a baby is fed in mother's arms, the baby also begins to equate eating too much, and feeling full and groggy, with comfort and mother's love. This can cause a lifetime of eating for comfort.

What Others are Saying:

T. D. Jakes: "T" is for the "temperance" you have to use in learning to stop eating before your stomach inflates and your body wants to go to bed. We have often conditioned ourselves to eat more than we need, into the oblivion of indulgence.[2]

It Makes Me Feel Strange

Food sensitivities often can be the result of eating too much at one time, or generally eating too much. It has been known for 30 years that if you eat the same foods over and over, day after day, you can develop sensitivities to that food. Food sensitivities can then cause health problems such as headaches, joint pains, overweight, skin rashes, sinus problems, indigestion, depression, achy muscles, fatigue, and fluid retention. Many people inaccurately refer to "food sensitivities" as "allergies." With a true allergy there is some form of swelling; with food sensitivities, you may not even know that you are being affected by the food.

ON Target:

Taking the time to hold a baby during feeding

OFF Target:

Lulling a baby to sleep with a bottle

What Others are Saying:

Cheryl Townsley: What about depression, mood swings, memory loss, inability to concentrate or focus? What many people consider to be abnormal mental health may be a sign of neurologic stress from food allergies.[3]

SYNDROME X

Oftentimes, overeating at feasts can lead to chronic overeating. This is probably the worst sin you can commit against your body. First of all you will eat way more than your body can handle, which can cause digestive upsets. Secondly, if you eat more calories than you use or work off during exercise, you will gain weight and even cause health problems that can lead to cancer. Thirdly, there is a danger of developing Syndrome X, a condition with the "cluster" symptoms of hypertension, glucose intolerance, high

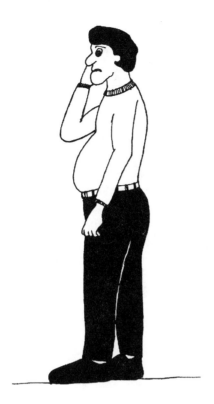

blood fats, and obesity.[4] Chronic overeating, feasting, and **pigging out** are partly responsible for the epidemic levels of type II diabetes (or "adult-onset diabetes") in North America (see Illustration #44, this page).

Reginald Cherry, M.D.: Avoid excess calories. Too many calories may increase the risk of colon, uterine, and esophageal cancer.[5]

What Others
are Saying:

Okay, So What Should I Do?

Break the connection between good times and food. If you are going to go to a feast, potluck, or dinner party, eat a little something before you go so that you won't be so hungry that you "pig out" on too much of everything. Never eat a big meal when you have not eaten for more than four hours. This could be a disaster for your body, mind, and health. Eat slowly by chewing every mouthful well; this will show respect for your digestive organs. Remember Horace Fletcher, who went around the country in the early 1900s telling people to chew every mouthful until it was liquid—"fletcherizing" they called it.[6]

🍎 **NUTRITIONAL FACT**

Many people think they are suffering from the flu when actually they have food sensitivities.

Remember that God made your body to live sensibly, eat sensibly, and pray sensibly. When you are involved in a feast, always make sure God is there, first, before any food. Don't be like the disobedient children of God who forgot him and got involved with eating and drinking too much. Even over-eating healthy food is still overeating.

What Others are Saying:

T. D. Jakes: I find it depressing when I do something against my better judgment, so I take my own low-fat food to parties. It keeps me from a relapse into my old bad habits. Sometimes you have to nibble on something to keep others from feeling like you have broken fellowship. Our society is food-oriented, and some people make you feel like you haven't celebrated until you "break bread" together.[7]

ON Target:

Eating before a feast or party so you won't pig out

OFF Target:

Fasting before a feast or party, and then stuffing yourself

Study Questions

1. What are the appointed feasts, and why did God give them to the Israelites?
2. What sort of feasting did the children of God do on Yom Kippur?
3. What was dangerous about the feasting of Old Testament times? How do you do the same things?
4. What are some of the health problems that can be associated with overindulgence in food, and what can you do to overcome them?
5. What was the real reason for most of the feasts? What part should God play in your feasts today?

CHAPTER WRAP-UP

- God gave instructions to the Israelites for seven appointed feasts spaced throughout the year as a way for them to remember God. (Leviticus 23:1, 2)

- Each of the feasts is really a festival and includes the public reading of the holy books, services at home, in the synagogue, or both.

- The Feast of Unleavened Bread which starts with Passover (Pesah), and the Day of Atonement (Yom Kippur) are the two of the seven feasts that Christians know most about.

- There are many verses in the Bible that indicate God was not happy about the way Israelites were doing their feasting. (Amos 5:21; 6:1, 4, 6, 7)

- God did not intend for you to eat more than your body was designed to hold or use. Many diseases such as cancer, digestive disturbances, and allergies can come from overeating.

18 FASTING, FASTING, FASTING

CHAPTER HIGHLIGHTS

- Four Fasts
- Two Types of Fasting
- Spiritual Reasons
- Health Reasons
- Keep It Secret

Let's Get Started

There are many kinds of fasts. When you go in for a physical check up, the doctor will often ask you to fast from food after 9 P.M. and from liquids after midnight. Perhaps you didn't know you were fasting during these times, but you were!

When the Jews fasted in Old and New Testament times, most of the time it was from sunrise to sundown, very seldom was it for 24 hours. This is still done during some religious fasts. Muslims fast in this same manner during their fast of **Ramadan**. The medical journals contain dozens of studies that show health problems directly related to eating a big meal after the Ramadan practice of eating no food from sunrise to sundown. But the muslims aren't the only ones who do this. No matter who you are, it's a bad idea.

Ramadan: Muslim fast of eating no food or drink from sunrise to sundown

> **Jeremiah 36:9** In the ninth month of the fifth year of Jehoiakim son of Josiah king of Judah, a time of fasting before the Lord was proclaimed for all the people in Jerusalem and those who had come from the towns of Judah.

Fasting From What?

A day of fasting was proclaimed because of a national emergency which historians suspect to have been the Babylonian attack of

☞ **GO TO:**

II Chronicles 20:1–4
(together)

ON Target:
 Supervised fasting in a
 group

OFF Target:
 Fasting without
 guidance

major fasts: all eating
and drinking was
prohibited 24 hours a day

minor fasts: all eating
and drinking was
prohibited from sunrise to
sunset

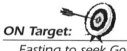

**What Others
are Saying:**

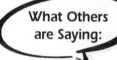

ON Target:
 Fasting to seek God

OFF Target:
 Fasting to feel "high"

605 B.C. Fasting was used as a way to bring the people <u>together</u>, to petition the Lord to help them. Fasting was not used for health purposes but for religious purposes. Apparently, they were allowed to have water during this kind of fast, but no food (see Illustration #45, page 235).

> **Zechariah 8:19** This is what the Lord Almighty says: "The fasts of the fourth, fifth, seventh, and tenth months will become joyful and glad occasions and happy festivals for Judah. Therefore love truth and peace."

Four Fasts

Fasts were normally for commemorating historical occurrences. These four mentioned in Zechariah were to commemorate, respectively, the destruction of the first temple, the destruction of the second temple, the destruction of Jerusalem, and the destruction of the independent Jewish state in ancient times.[1] Although originally these fasts were to be **major fasts**, the latter two eventually became **minor fasts**. Holy texts, readings, and prayers of petition were regular parts of the proclaimed fasts.

T. D. Jakes: Many people are discovering the pleasure of fasting and are renewing the biblical observance of using the day of fasting to pray and seek direction from the Lord.[2]

> **Matthew 4:1–4** Then Jesus was led by the spirit into the desert to be tempted by the devil. After fasting forty days and forty nights, he was hungry. The tempter came to him and said, "If you are the Son of God, tell these stones to become bread." Jesus answered, "It is written: 'Man does not live on bread alone, but on every word that comes from the mouth of God.'"

A Whole 40 Days!

Forty days without eating is about how long it takes to use up all the stored energy in your body. This is not recommended for most Westerners. With the introduction of junk foods, soft drinks, processed foods, air pollution, and high stress levels, most Westerners are not in good enough shape to do a 40-day fast and remain healthy afterward. The medical journals are filled with articles reporting hundreds of negative health results because of the

Illustration #45

*Water Pot and Ladle—
Although some Biblical
fasting required refraining
from drinking water during a
fast, during non-fasting times
it is best to drink six to eight
8-ounce glasses of water
daily.*

Ramadan fasting that Muslims do. They only fast for one month, and then it is only from sunrise to sunset. This creates a great stress on human bodies, especially if, after not eating during the day, one eats a large meal after sundown.

If you decide that you want to try fasting in order to seek the Lord, please do it sensibly! Start by outlining how you will do it, which will be covered in depth in this chapter. Write it down. Then go see your doctor for a physical, show him the outline of your fasting plan, and then ask your doctor to approve your fast. Even if you decide to go to a clinic or retreat to do your first fast, let your doctor know and get his approval.

Acts 13:2, 3 While they were worshiping the Lord and fasting, the Holy Spirit said, "Set apart for me Barnabas and Saul for the work to which I have called them." So after they had fasted and prayed, they placed their hands on them and sent them off.

Why Fast?

Basically, people fast for either religious or health reasons. People who fast for religious reasons do so to get closer to God, to ask for forgiveness, to petition God for something, to confess sins and repent before God, to wait on God for an answer to a petition (as in Acts 13), or just to feel God's presence with them. Some call this last sort of fasting "practicing the presence of God." These are the same reasons people fasted in Bible times.

People who fast for health reasons do so to have blood tests

ON Target:
*Consulting your doctor
before a complete
fast*

OFF Target:
Fasting with coffee

ON Target:
Reading the Scriptures and resting while fasting

OFF Target:
Being under stress while fasting

Something to Ponder

What Others are Saying:

NUTRITIONAL FACT

Fasting one day a week, when properly done, can improve your health.

totally healthy: *having no diagnosed diseases or disorders*

juice: *the liquid part of fruits and vegetables*

clear liquids: *vegetable broth, pure water with lemon juice, flavored and unsweetened mineral water*

pure water: *water with no chlorine or other chemicals in it*

done, to clean out the "sludge of winter," to remove toxins or heavy metals, to improve digestion, to give the body a rest from eating and digesting, to stimulate healing, to test for allergies or sensitivities, or to get over a specific sickness which is generally coupled with prayer, repentance, and forgiveness. When you fast from food, your body doesn't have to concentrate on all the bodily functions that go with eating, digesting, and eliminating. Instead, your body can use its energy for other purposes such as healing and spiritual matters.

Fasting eliminates a host of concerns that normally go with eating—where to eat, what to eat, when to eat, etc. It gives you more time for meditating, reading Scripture, and petitioning God.

Cheryl Townsley: Regular fasting is one of the easiest ways to cleanse the body. When we stop eating, we transfer all of the energy used to process food into eliminating body toxins. Fasting one day a week (for twenty-four to thirty-six hours) totals fifty-two days a year of cleansing the body. Those fifty-two days become days of rest—cleansing restoration for the body, mind, and soul.[3]

DAILY BREAD

FASTING
Each day fast from 9 P.M. until breakfast the next morning.

I Don't Know About This . . .

You have already been doing a mini-fast almost every day! You go from sometime in the evening, say dinnertime, to the first meal of the day called breakfast ("break the fast"). So, you are already going without food for eight to twelve hours, depending on whether you snack after dinner or before bedtime. The Jews most often fasted from sunrise to sunset. That is about the same time you already fast, but at the other end of the day. Hopefully, knowing this will help to calm any fears you may have about fasting.

START SLOW!

If you are **totally healthy**, you might want to start with just taking **juice**, **clear liquids**, and **pure water** all day long for a period of 24 to 36 hours (see Illustration #46, page 237). Your first food

Illustration #46

*Fruit and Vegetable Juice—
Provided you are totally
healthy, start fasting by
drinking only fruit and
vegetable juice for a period
of 24 to 36 hours.*

after this period should be something light like a fruit plate or a
salad plate with just veggies and some lemon juice, and perhaps a
touch of olive oil. Then you can eat something more substantial
after that for the next meal. If you are **not totally healthy**, say you
have diabetes, hypoglycemia, cancer, arthritis, high blood pressure, asthma, kidney disease, heart disease, or any other health
problem, see your doctor first! Then, when you get the OK, start
slowly and keep your doctor informed of what you are doing.
Likewise, if you are fasting for spiritual reasons, inform your pastor, minister, or priest in case you have a need to call them, just as
you might call your doctor, but about spiritual, emotional, or
mental problems.

not totally healthy:
*have a diagnosed or
suspected disease*

Rex Russell, M.D.: Hippocrates, the father of medicine, used
fasting to combat disease 2,400 years ago. The ancient Ayurvedic
healers of the Hindu religion prescribed fasting weekly for a healthy
digestive system. Most nationalities, religions and languages have
a tradition of fasting handed down from their ancestors.[4]

**What Others
are Saying:**

THE FIRST DAYS

Prepare by reading Scripture and praying about the wisdom of
fasting. Then write out what you plan to do and accomplish. This
would include the number of days for each phase as detailed ear-
lier, the time limit you are setting for the fast, and your method of
coming off the fast. On the first day of preparation abstain from
eating fat, meat, and all animal products, including milk and eggs.
On the second day eliminate all foods made of grains, including
gravy, bread, crackers, and pretzels. On the third day begin to drink
several more glasses of water than you usually would and eat only
raw fruits and vegetables. On the fourth day switch to fruit and
vegetable juices. Use juice that is as fresh and unprepared as possible and dilute it half and half with pure water. Stay away from

juice with salt, EDTA, or preservatives. Eliminate all caffeine as well. Drink some diluted juice every hour or two throughout the day and night as long as you are awake. If you feel hungry, drink a little juice or water and breathe deeply several times to relax your digestive organs. On the fifth day you can go to only water if you wish. This can be maintained as long as you feel healthy. If you begin to feel really, **really hungry**, go off the fast.

Many people feel really terrible the first day or two of a juice or water fast. This is to be expected if you have a blood sugar problem, eat poorly, or have been around toxic substances (see the following chart). It is also to be expected if you have been addicted to any foods or substances like caffeine, nicotine, sugar, salt, wheat, or dairy products. This period of feeling terrible is called "withdrawal." It generally takes at least three days for withdrawal effects to go away. Exercise, do deep breathing, relax, and drink a lot of pure water.

Some Toxic Substances

- Tobacco smoke
- Acrylic and gel finger nails
- Alcohol
- Gasoline fumes
- Aluminum cooking pans
- Mold
- Cleaning fluids
- Deodorant with zinc or aluminum
- Exhaust fumes
- Preservatives
- Heavy metals like lead and mercury
- Hair dyes and perms

GET ME OFF OF THIS, FAST!

To go off a fast, just reverse the process. Drink juices for a day. Then eat fresh fruit and veggies. The following day add in grains and on the last day add in meat, eggs, fish, and milk.

If you are on water and feel great and then upon eating fruits and veggie juices you begin to experience strange symptoms, like headaches, a runny nose, coughing, or pain anywhere, you might have a food allergy or sensitivity. Go back on the water

really hungry: stomach rumbling, sick feeling, after a few days on water only

Remember
This . . .

until the symptoms clear up. Then take the diluted juice of only one fruit. If adding the juice causes no change in how you feel, you may add in another type of juice the next time you take juice. Continue to add one new juice each time. When you begin to eat solid foods, eat one type of food at a time. Add a new food, if you wish, each time you take some sustenance. If you come across a juice, vegetable, grain, or other substance that makes a really noticeable change in how you feel, you will be well on your way to discovering what is making you sick. (This is called "food challenging" and is a very popular way to test for food allergies or sensitivities.) See an allergist with this information for confirmation or a remedy. Be suspicious of any of the following: dairy products, corn and corn syrup, wheat, sugar, eggs, chicken, oranges, pork products, preservatives, peanuts, and potatoes. But that's not to say other foods or substances won't cause an allergic reaction; they might.

Rex Russell, M.D.: Don't expect mental miracles on your first fast. Addiction and withdrawal symptoms (irritability, anger, headaches, and so on) could override any first-time benefits. Examples of fasting's positive effect on the mind, however, are even more striking.[5]

> **Leviticus 16:29–31** This is to be a lasting ordinance for you: On the tenth day of the seventh month you must deny yourselves and not do any work—whether nativeborn or an alien living among you—because on this day atonement will be made for you, to cleanse you. Then, before the Lord, you will be clean from all your sins.

FASTING CURES

Many Christians believe that diseases and unclean states are caused by sins; this is why so many churches require a confession of sins before a healing service or prayer for healing. Atonement and repentance are very important parts of a cleansing fast for spiritual or physical healing. In the last 30 years I have heard of many people who have been cured of many different diseases by fasting. **Schizophrenia** and **rheumatoid arthritis** are the most popular diseases for using fasting, because often they can be caused by food allergies. Migraines, stomach problems, allergies, sinus conditions, hyperactivity or **ADD**, various types of cancer, MS, de-

schizophrenia: *disease that includes disordered thinking and perception, emotional changes, behavioral disturbances, and loss of contact with reality*

rheumatoid arthritis: *inflammatory arthritis*

ADD: *Attention Deficit Disorder; central nervous system disorder causing a variety of learning and behavior problems*

pression, Parkinson's disease, and even Alzheimer's disease all have been reported to have been cured by fasting or fasting and prayer together. All of these fasting cures were done in clinical settings with supervision.

> **Matthew 6:16–18** When you fast, do not look somber as the hypocrites do, for they disfigure their faces to show men they are fasting. I tell you the truth, they have received their reward in full. But when you fast, put oil on your head and wash your face, so that it will not be obvious to men that you are fasting, but only to your Father, who is unseen; and your Father, who sees what is done in secret, will reward you.

The Reward Of Fasting

When Jesus speaks of fasting to know God, he speaks of the rewards that God will bring you. They are peace, joy, love, forgiveness, and the wonder of knowing God in a new and refreshing way. Just be sure that when you fast, you do it sensibly. God is not impressed with <u>foolishness</u>.

☞ **GO TO:**

Proverbs 26:3
(foolishness)

Study Questions

1. What does the Bible say about fasting?
2. What were the different fasts that were followed in Bible times? Why are they of importance today?
3. Which fasts are done today by Christians and for what reasons? Do you think it is effective to do these kinds of fasts?
4. What is the right way and what is the wrong way to fast?
5. Why do you think Jesus said for people to keep their fasting secret from all but God?
6. Have you ever considered fasting? Discuss your reasons for wanting to do so and the outcome of this.

CHAPTER WRAP-UP

- God assigned four fasts to the Israelites that were to be joyful experiences. (Zechariah 8:19)
- The Jews observed two kinds of fasts. Major fasts required no food or drink for 24 hours. Minor fasts required no food or drink from sunrise to sunset.

- Fasting was done for spiritual reasons in Bible times, especially to receive information from God. (Acts 13:2, 3)

- Fasting is also done for health reasons. Through the ages many nationalities have fasted as a group for spiritual and health reasons.

- Jesus warned people to fast in silence if they were doing a spiritual fast, because it is between the one who is fasting and God. (Matthew 6:16–18)

GLOSSARY OF NUTRITIONAL AND MEDICAL TERMS

acid. A chemical compound, often sour to the taste, that has a low pH. Many fruits have a high acid count, especially lemon, which accounts for its tart or sour taste. Acid is the opposite of alkaline which has a high pH.

acidophilus culture. An agent used to make yogurt. It is also available in capsules, liquid, and powder. Acidophilus is used to change the bacteria in the intestines. Many illnesses occur when dangerous bacteria get out of balance in the intestines. Taking acidophilus culture can replace the 'good' bacteria destroyed by antibiotics. Many B vitamins need intestinal bacteria in order to be absorbed. Candida albicans lives in gastrointestinal areas of the body that are depleted of the 'good' bacteria, which can be replaced by taking acidophilus.

acute. An acute illness occurs quickly, lasts relatively short periods of time, and goes quickly.

age-related macular degeneration (AMD). In some people the macula of the eye begins to degenerate with age causing blindness. This condition is the main cause of blindness in people over 55 years of age in the U.S. It may occur gradually or suddenly. Research has shown that people who regularly eat spinach, broccoli, and collard greens have less possibility of having this develop than people who do not eat these foods regularly. It is good for all people who have eye problems to eat beta-carotene in their food.

AIDS. Stands for acquired immune deficiency syndrome. A disease of the immune system which compromises the body's ability to defend itself from outside invaders.

alpha-linolenic acid. An Omega-essential fatty acid found in canola oil, flaxseed oil, and walnut oil.

amaranth. A cereal grass that grows in farms and waste places. It is high in protein and being used around the world to make a high protein food, especially in places where there is drought.

amino acids. The building blocks of all cells. These nutrients are essential for life in it's simplest form.

arteriosclerosis. *See* **atherosclerosis/arteriosclerosis**.

antioxidants. Any substance that inhibits or blocks harmful reactions with oxygen.

artificial sweeteners. Sweeteners that have been manufactured from other foods to taste sweet but have less calories than sugar or honey. Many artificial sweeteners have been found by people to cause adverse reactions, especially saccharine and aspartame. The most common complaints are diarrhea, headaches, stomach problems, swimmy headedness, irritability, and faintness.

asafoetida. A yellow powder obtained from the roots of several different plants. It is used in East Indian medicine as a digestive aid. Many health food stores sell this product also known as hing or yellow powder. It can also be purchased at East Indian stores.

atherosclerosis/arteriosclerosis. These diseases are characterized by a buildup of deposits on the inside of the artery walls, which can cause a thickening or hardening of the arteries. In arteriosclerosis the deposits are made up of mostly calcium. In atherosclerosis the deposits are made up of mostly fatty substances. Both of these conditions involve high blood pressure, and can ultimately lead to angina, heart attack, stroke, and/or sudden cardiac death.

B-complex vitamins. Vitamins are organic substances that are essential for life and health. B complex vitamins are essential to help maintain the health of your nerves, eyes, skin, hair, liver, mouth, brain, and gastrointestinal tract. The B complex is composed of B1 or thiamine, B2 or riboflavin, B3 or niacin (niacinamide, nicotinic acid), B5 or pantothenic acid, B6 or pyridoxine, B12 or cyanocobalamin, folic acid (previously called B9), choline, inositol, biotin, and PABA (paraminobenzoic acid. Brewer's yeast, a byproduct of the brewing industry, is a source of most of the B complex vitamins B12 is found mostly in animal products but can also be found in soy bean tempeh, kelp, and alfalfa. *See also* **vitamins.**

beef tallow. The fat in cattle that is found around the organs, especially the kidneys. It is often used for deep frying foods in fast food restaurants. This is one of the fats that God told the Israelites not to eat.

beta-1,3-D-glucan. A component of the cell wall of bakers yeast. This is one of the most researched natural chemicals for the immune system. Many pharmaceutical companies sell this in injectable form to use for shrinking tumors.

beta-carotene. A precursor of vitamin A known to destroy free radicals and carcinogens. Beta-carotene is found in dark orange and dark green foods.

bilberry. A fruit that is used extensively in Europe, the U.S., and Canada to improve eyesight.

bok choy. A Chinese vegetable used in stir fry dishes and many other Chinese meals. It has many leaves growing from one stem, much like celery. It has very white stems and very dark green leaves. The stems stay crunchy when cooked, therefore giving a crispness to many dishes.

bran. The outer layer of many grains including wheat, rice, and oats. A very essential fiber for aiding digestion.

bromine. A heavy, volatile, corrosive, reddish-brown, nonmetallic liquid element, having a highly irritating vapor. It is often used in producing gasoline antiknock mixtures, fumigants, dyes, and photographic chemicals.

buckwheat. A three cornered grain that is really the seed of a plant in the rhubarb family. It is green when dried but is often toasted to become brown before being eaten. Toasted buckwheat cook up like most grains and cam be used with rice in many dishes such as stuffed cabbage, peppers, or squash. It give a stronger taste and many people find that when buckwheat is used in this way it gives the idea that meat is included.

bulgar wheat. Wheat that has been cooked, chopped, and dried. This makes an easy grain to prepare since it is already cooked. Simply pour two cups of boiling water over one cup of bulgar wheat, cover, and leave for 45 minutes to an hour and it will be ready to add to salads, cereals, or serve as a mail dish with vegetables.

calcium. A mineral that is essential for the health of teeth, bones and gums. Calcium is found in dairy products, the edible bones of salmon and sardines, almonds, and dark green leafy vegetables.

carbohydrates. Mostly of plant origin, this substance provides your body with energy. The best sources for carbohydrates are whole grains, fruits, and starchy vegetables such as corn, peas, beans, and potatoes.

carcinogenic hormones. Hormones that cause cancer.

carcinogens. Substances that are capable of causing cancerous changes in your body.

carob pods. The fruit of a tree that grows wild in most of the Bible lands. The pod is very fibrous and contains large very hard seeds. Many people toast the powder of ground carob pods or beans to use as a chocolate substitute. It does not contains the caffeine-like substance that cocoa beans do. Carob pods are a good source of calcium and other minerals.

carotenoids. A class of compounds that are related to Vitamin A. Some even act as precursors to vitamin A. Beta-carotene is the best known carotenoid.

cellulose. Plant fiber that is essential to a healthy digestive system.

chlorogenic acid. A phytochemical found in tomatoes thought to prevent cancers.

cholesterol. A necessary component of cells manufactured by all creatures with backbones. *See also* **LDL cholesterol** and **HDL cholesterol**.

choline. A nutrient beneficial for your nerves, brain, gallbladder, and liver, found in eggs and soybeans.

chronic fatigue syndrome. There are many theories of how this debilitating disease is contracted, and they are just theories, no one really knows for sure. Most speculate that the Epstein-Barr virus is responsible, others feel it is the aftermath of a shock or some stress. The only thing that medical and scientific people agree on are the symptoms. They also agree that the symptoms, persistent fatigue that is not relieved by bed rest and that reduces your average daily activity by at least 50 percent for at least six months, must be present for the diagnosis to be chronic fatigue syndrome. The other symptoms are: aching muscles and joints, anxiety, depression, difficulty concentrating, fever, intestinal problems, headaches, irritability, mood swings, muscle spasms, upper respiratory tract infections, sensitivity to light and heat, sleep disturbances, sore throat and/or swollen glands, and extreme and debilitating fatigue.

complete protein. Containing all the essential amino acids in a nearly equal complement.

Crohn's disease. Chronic and long-lasting ulceration of a section or sections of the digestive tract. The symptoms are similar to ulcerative colitis with one exception, in Crohn's disease all the layers of the intestinal tract are involved. The symptoms include loss of weight and appetite, abdominal pain, general malaise, diarrhea, and rectal bleeding.

cruciferous. Forming a cross. These plants have a leaf pattern that forms a cross.

dementia. Irreversible deterioration of intellectual faculties with accompanying emotional disturbances resulting from an organic brain disorder.

detoxify. To remove toxins and other waste matter from your body. There are many methods including fasting, nutritional supplements, herbs, injections, chelation, and colonics. The best method is to eat a high fiber diet and reduce animal products. Include those vegetables that are known to help remove foreign matter from your system like cabbage, broccoli, sea vegetables, beets, water cress, dandelion, daikon radish, parsley, and beans, especially soybeans.

DHA. Docosahexaenoic acid, essential fatty acid in fish.

diabetes. There are two kinds of this disease: diabetes insipidus (which is rare) and diabetes mellitus(which is common). The mellitus type is divided into two different kind types: Type I , often called insulin-dependent or juvenile diabetes, and Type II, often called non-insulin dependent or adult onset. All types of diabetes are related to the rise and fall of blood sugar and insulin in the body and require supervision by your doctor.

diverticulitis. A condition in which the mucus membranes that line the large intestines become inflamed and form pockets or pouches in the intestinal walls which trap food and then become further inflamed or cause infection.

EDTA. A solution used to remove toxins, especially lead and arterial fat, from your body. The letters stand for: ethylenediaminetetraacetic acid.

EPA. Eicosapentaenoic acid, essential fatty acid in fish.

endocrine glands. Those glands in your body that secrete directly into your blood stream. They are thyroid, adrenal, islands of Langerhans (in the pancreas), ovary (female only) and testis (male only).

enzymes. A protein-based substance found in every cell of every living plant and animal, including the human body. Enzymes are essential for health and are found mostly in raw and unprocessed foods.

essential amino acids. Tryptophan, leucine, isoleucine, lysine, valine, threonine, methionine, and phenylalanine.

essential fatty acids (EFAs). Fatty acids that are essential for life and cannot be manufactured in the body. They are considered the building blocks of which fats and oils are composed. Every living cell needs EFAs. There are two categories of EFAs: omega-3 and omega-6. Included in the omega-6 groups are linoleic and gamma-linolenic acids found mostly in raw nuts and seeds, legumes, and unsaturated oils such as borage, grape seed, sesame, and soybean. The omega-3 groups include alpha-linolenic and eicosapentaenoic (EPA) fatty acids found mostly in fresh deep-water fish, fish oil, flaxseed oil, and the vegetable oils canola, flaxseed, and walnut.

estrogen. One of a number of hormones made in women's bodies that regulate the female cycle.

fat. An oily solid or semisolid that is the main part of many animal tissues.

fat-soluble vitamins. Vitamins that can be absorbed in your body when there is fat present in the same meal as the vitamins are take. They are vitamins A, D, E, and K.

fiber. The indigestible part of plants.

fibromyalgia. A disease that is characterized by chronic achy muscular pain that has no obvious cause. Often depression, anxiety, irritable bladder, and impaired coordination are also involved. There are also nine pairs of 'tender points' that are abnormally tender to the touch that help your doctor make the diagnosis. They are around the lower vertebra of the neck, at the insertion point of the second rib, around the upper part of the thigh bone, in the middle of the knee joint, in muscles connected to the base of the scull, in the muscles of the neck and upper back, in muscles of the mid-back, on the side of the elbow, and in the upper and outer muscles of the buttocks. A visit to your doctor for a diagnosis is a good idea if you have any of these symptoms.

flavonoids. Crystalline compounds found in plants.

folic acid. If begun before pregnancy, 400 mcg a day in the diet of a pregnant woman can prevent neural tube birth defects.

food allergies. An irritation of your body tissues or an inflammation caused by a specific food. There are many different symptoms that can occur including migraine headaches, diarrhea, eczema, hyperactivity, anginalike symptoms, and even a flare-up of rheumatoid arthritis. Some symptoms can occur within 20 minutes of eating the offending food. Others may be chronic or take longer to be detected.

free radical. A highly reactive molecule that can bind to and destroy body components. Free radicals produce 'oxidative' damage in your body that can contribute to aging, heart disease, and cancer. This is why you need to take antioxidants to prevent this damage from occurring. Eating processed foods, rancid fats, and being in polluted environments can contribute to free radical damage.

gamma-carotene. One of the many carotenoids. Part of the vitamin A complex. Included in this group are beta-, alpha-, and gamma-carotene, lutein, and lycopene. All are considered to be antioxidants.

genistein. One of the phytonutrients in soybeans.

glucose tolerance test (GTT). A test that is helpful in determining is a person has diabetes of hypoglycemia. The test is administered after overnight fasting. The person is given a solution to drink and blood is drawn at frequent intervals over six hours to test the rise and fall of blood sugar.

HDL cholesterol. High density lipoprotein, the good cholesterol.

high blood pressure. A term used to indicate when the normal blood pressure of 120/80 is exceeded. The elevation is significant of many health problems including risk for strokes and cardiovascular diseases. Borderline high blood pressure is 120-160/90-94, mild is 140-160/95-104, moderate is 140-180/105-114, and severe is 160+/115+.

histamines. Compound responsible for producing allergic reactions. This is why you take antihistamines for allergic reactions.

immune system. That system of your body whose job it is to identify and eliminate foreign substances such as bacteria. The liver, spleen, thymus, bone marrow, and lymphatic system all play vital roles in the proper functioning of your immune system.

inositol. A nutrient beneficial for nerves, hair growth, and fat metabolism, found in eggs, soybeans, molasses, and whole grains.

iodine. A mineral needed in trace amounts to help your body metabolize fats. It is useful for the functioning of your thyroid gland and to prevent goiter. Good sources of iodine are saltwater fish, seafood, kelp, and iodized salt. It is also found in minute amounts in asparagus, dulse (a sea vegetable), garlic, lima beans, mushrooms, sea salt, sesame seeds, soybeans, summer squash, Swiss chard, and turnip greens. Many foods can inhibit your body's ability to utilize iodine when eaten in large amounts. These foods are Brussels sprouts, cabbage, cauliflower, lake, broccoli, peaches, pears, raw spinach, and turnips.

iron. A mineral needed in your body to produce hemoglobin (blood cells) and to add oxygen to your red blood cells. Prolonged use of antacids, excessive coffee or tea consumption can often result in an iron deficiency. Iron is found in eggs, meat, fish, poultry, green leafy vegetables, whole grains, almonds, avocados, beets, brewer's yeast, dates, dulse, kelp, kidney and lima beans, lentils, millet, peaches, pears, dried prunes, pumpkins, raisins, rice and wheat bran, sesame seeds, soybeans, and watercress.

isoflavone. Plant-based hormone.

kegel. Exercises performed by women that have been shown in medical reports to reduce the problem of incontinence, or urine loss.

LDL cholesterol. Low Density Lipoprotein or "bad" cholesterol.

lecithin. A component of all cells, made of choline and inositol.

lignin. A type of fiber that is good for lowering cholesterol and helping to prevent gallstones. Found in Brazil nuts, carrots, green beans, peaches, peas, potatoes, strawberries, tomatoes, and whole grains.

lutein. A carotenoid.

lycopene. One of the more than 10,000 phytochemicals found in tomatoes. It plays an important role in preventing cancers especially of the lungs and prostate. Lycopene also is a defender against ultraviolet skin damage.

lymphatic system. The system in your body that circulates a clear fluid called lymph that nourishes tissues and return waste matter to your bloodstream.

lysine. An amino acid that is thought to block the herpes simplex virus from causing cold sores and herpes sores.

macrophage. The cells in your immune system that do the majority of it's work. The name means 'big eater.' The macrophage have long 'arms' that pull in toxins and eat or otherwise destroy them.

magnesium. A mineral that is vital to health. It assists calcium and potassium to be used by your body. A deficiency of magnesium can interfere with the transmission of nerve and muscle impulses, causing irritability and nervousness. A deficiency is often implicated in certain heart conditions such as sudden cardiac arrest and hypertension. Asthma, chronic fatigue, chronic pain syndromes, depression, insomnia, irritable bowel syndrome, and pulmonary disorders are associated with a magnesium deficiency. Many forms of hyperactivity in both children and adults are thought to be magnesium deficiencies such as ADD and ADHD. Magnesium is found in dairy products, fish, meats, seafood, apples, apricots, avocados, bananas, brewer's yeast, brown rice, cantaloupe, dulse, figs, garlic, green leafy vegetables, kelp, lentils, lima beans, millet, , nuts, soybeans, tofu, watercress, and whole grains.

manganese. A mineral that helps to prevent repetitive strain injuries and tennis elbow. Manganese is needed in small amounts to allow protein and fat metabolism. It is found in avocados, nuts and seeds, sea vegetables, blueberries and blueberry leaf tea, egg yolks, legumes, dried peas, whole grains, and green leafy vegetables.

menopause. That time in a woman's life when her hormonal levels change to stop her monthly periods.

minerals. Non-living elements that are essential to the functioning of the human body.

monounsaturated fat. Fat that is found in butter, olive and canola oil that is thought to be helpful in lowering cholesterol levels.

natural practicing doctor. A doctor who uses natural methods as his or her first choice when dealing with any health problem of disease. Oftentimes they use this in conjunction with prescription medicines. This is called complimentary medicine.

omega-3 essential fatty acids (EFAs). Found in raw nuts and seeds, legumes, grape seeds, soybeans, and other vegetable oils.

organically grown. A term used to mean grown without the use of any farm chemicals that are produced from coal tar or petroleum. Plant and animal based pesticides and fertilizers are often used.

p-courmaric acid. A phytochemical found in tomatoes thought to help prevent cancers by interfering with certain chemical unions that can create carcinogens.

perimenopause. That time in a woman's life leading up to the ending of menstruation. It is characterized by many symptoms due to hormonal imbalances such as fatigue, mood swings, erratic menstrual periods, and often heavy flow during menses.

pH. A scale used to measure the relative acidity or alkalinity of substances. The scale runs from 0 to 14. A pH of 7 is considered neutral. Numbers that go down from 7 are considered increasingly acidic. Numbers going up from 7 to 14 are considered increasingly alkaline.

phosphorus. A mineral needed for tooth and bone formation., cell growth, contraction of the heart muscle, and kidney function. It is found in asparagus, bran, brewer's yeast, corn, dairy products, eggs, dried fruits, garlic, legumes, nuts, sesame seeds, sunflower seeds, pumpkin seeds, salmon, and whole grains.

phytic acid. A type of fiber found in.

phytochemical. Health-protective substance in plants.

phytoestrogens. Plant-based hormonal substances.

phytohormones. Plant-based hormones.

phytonutrient. Plant-based nutrient.

polyunsaturated fats. Come from vegetable sources.

polyunsaturated fatty acids. Fat found in corn, soybean, safflower, and some fish oils; may help to reduce cholesterol.

potassium. Mineral essential for muscle function.

premenstrual syndrome (PMS). This is a condition that occurs to women younger than those who are in menopause and is characterized by symptoms ranging from tiredness, crankiness, and often short temper. It is generally relieved with a natural diet and mineral supplementation.

protein. The basic element of all plant and animal tissues.

provitamin A. A chemical that can be converted into vitamin A.

respiratory system. That part of your body involved in the process of breathing, the intake of oxygen and the expulsion of carbon dioxide.

rubidium. A basic element found in nature.

saturated fat. Fat that is solid at room temperature. It is generally found in animal sources although coconut oil is also solid at room temperature.

schizophrenia. A disease characterized by disordered thinking and perception, emotional changes such as tension and/or depression, behavioral disturbances ranging from catatonia to violent outbursts, delusions, and loss of contact with reality. Generally a person with this disease is in a world of his or her own.

scleroderma. Literally means hardening of the skin.

selenium. A mineral that prevents the breakdown of fats.

serum cholesterol. Concentrations: amount of cholesterol in your blood.

sodium. Sodium chloride, table salt.

starch. A carbohydrate found in plants.

thymus gland. A gland located just below the thyroid, behind the breast bone, that is an important part of your immune system.

thyroid gland. A gland located at the base of your throat that is responsible for metabolism in your body. It is often called the body's internal thermostat.

titanium. An element used in paint pigment.

toxins. Foreign matter that enters your body. They could come from air and water pollution, bacteria pollution, or ingesting substances that are not part of your body's required nutrients such as lead, aluminum, air-borne pollens, and viruses.

triglycerides. The form in which fat is stored in your body.

unsaturated fatty acids. Vegetable fats that are liquid at room temperature.

vascular disease. A disease of the circulatory system.

vitamins. A substance required in small quantities for life and health.

xanthophylls. A class of carotenoids found in dark green leafy vegetables especially spinach and collard greens. They are reported to be useful in preventing and perhaps reversing many eye conditions including macular degeneration.

zeaxanthin. One of a class of xanthophylls known to prevent eye problems.

zinc. A mineral essential for overall heath. It is especially necessary for the health of the prostate gland and the growth of the reproductive organs. It promotes wound healing and a healthy immune system. A zinc deficiency is often indicated in loss of the sense of taste. It is found in brewer's yeast, dulse, egg yolks, fish, kelp, lamb, legumes, lima beans, liver, mushrooms, pecans, oysters, pumpkin seeds, sardines, seafood, soy lecithin, soybeans, sunflower seeds, and whole grains.

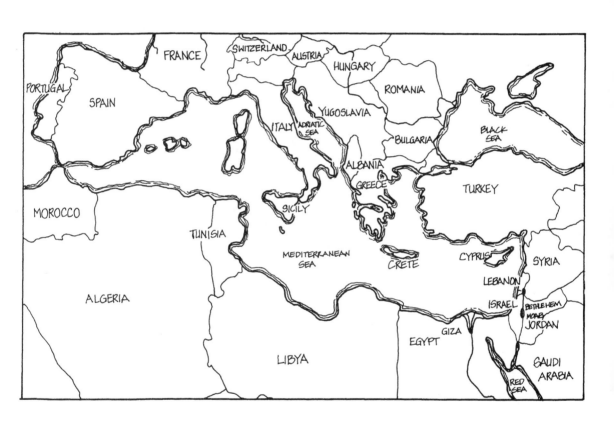

APPENDIX B — THE ANSWERS

CHAPTER ONE

1. God gave us fruits, nuts, seeds, and plants in the Garden of Eden, and all of these foods are available to us today. We in America have the additional benefit of foods that are imported to us directly from the Mediterranean region.
2. After the Flood, God allowed man to eat animal products such as meat, fish, and eggs. These foods were eaten on special occasions like weddings and feasts, and during special religious observances like Passover. I do my best to follow the Bible's example by eating small portions of meat only on special occasions like parties and weddings, or after church on Sundays.
3. An easy way to tell what to eat and when is to follow the Mediterranean Food Pyramid. This is a visual representation of the healthiest diet, which has been followed since Bible times in the Mediterranean region. We can also tell which foods to eat by reading about the foods that are mentioned in the Bible. Sometimes I eat ice cream more than once a week, mainly because I don't eat other sweets and really enjoy ice cream once in a while. When I do have ice cream, I get a brand that doesn't have any chemicals in it. I try to buy the kind of ice cream or sorbet that is made with natural sugars or with no sugar at all, and I always have fresh fruit with it.
4. The Mediterranean Diet Pyramid is a pictorial way of showing which foods are part of a healthy diet. The main groups are grains; fruits, beans, legumes, nuts, and vegetables; olive oil; cheese and yogurt; fish; followed by poultry; eggs; sweets; and red meat.
5. I eat mostly vegetables, nuts, beans, seeds, and whole grains. I eat fruit, dairy, and eggs frequently but not daily. I also have olive oil daily even if it is just in cooking. I have the other foods once or twice a week but not on the same days. If I have eggs for breakfast or lunch, I do not also have poultry or meat in the same day. Sometimes I have tuna fish and egg salad in a sandwich for lunch. When I have this, I have red peppers, olives, onions, garlic, and parsley or cilantro in it with it, and lettuce on the sandwich, so that actually I get a very small amount of egg or tuna. I never eat pork unless it is hidden in foods that I eat when I'm out somewhere, but on occasion I do eat shrimp in a green salad. The Bible Diet tells me to eat mostly vegetables and grains, so that's what I do!
6. We should have only small amounts of fatty foods like red meat, poultry, eggs, and sweets.

CHAPTER TWO

1. Grains can be eaten at any time during the day. I like to eat them for breakfast, snacks, lunch, and dinner. I recommend three or four servings a day.
2. Grains provide fiber that can eliminate constipation and other problems with digestion. They also provide protein and vitamin E for the good health of arteries, skin, hair, and other mucuos membranes. Grains provide energy—fuel for the body. They reduce your risk for many types of cancers and the kind of heart disease common to women after menopause.
3. Whole grains were eaten in Bible times. They ate wheat, spelt, millet, and barley. I try to eat only whole, unprocessed grains. I especially like to have brown rice, whole wheat, and spelt, and I often have barley crackers or barley soup. Millet is also great to put into soup or to eat for breakfast, and I often do that too.
4. Jesus and Elisha probably multiplied barley bread, as it was the bread of the common people. The bread they had in Bible times was a heavier, coarser bread than we have today. Usually it was not baked in a loaf pan like we use today. Bible bread was round and flat, much like many European breads still are. They also had unleavened bread, which is something like crackers.

CHAPTER THREE

1. Ezekiel's bread recipe contains several grains, beans, and legumes. This is unique, as most breads only contain one grain and no beans.
2. Ezekiel was told to eat Ezekiel Bread as punishment, but the remarkable thing is that Ezekiel Bread is really healthy stuff! Its mixture of grains, beans, and lentils gives us complete protein that could sustain us even if we ate nothing else. Of course, I would want to eat vegetables, but if I had to choose just one food, I would choose Ezekiel Bread.
3. Amino acids are the building blocks, the smallest components of protein. There are a great many of them and some can only be obtained from food. We need them to rebuild our bodies, keep us healthy, and give us strength.
4. Beans and lentils are great because they are inexpensive, can be stored without refrigeration, cook easily, and are very healthy. Beans are filled with fiber and carbohydrates for proper digestion and energy. They also contain protein. Beans can help reduce cholesterol and other fat levels in the body, reduce all kinds of cancers, heart disease, diabetes, and diverticulitis.
5. Soybeans are the most healthful bean because they contain complete protein, so they don't have to be complemented with a grain to be healthful. They also contain fiber and phytoestrogens. Soybeans can be made into many different products including tofu, tempeh, and soy milk.

CHAPTER FOUR

1. The king was looking for the best, brightest, most alert, most fit young men; Daniel and his friends were all that and more. The king found these Hebrew young men to be in better shape than his own men.
2. Daniel asked that he be allowed to eat the same food that he generally had been, which was much different from the food that the king provided for his regular men. Because Daniel was used to eating mainly vegetables, grains, beans, and no alcohol, the king's guards were suspicious of him. The king usually fed all his men rich meats, desserts, and lots of alcohol.
3. The largest percentage or portion of my diet should be vegetables. This means that I should eat as much of all the others foods combined as I do vegetables each day, even more than 5 half-cup servings. Vegetables are important in my diet because they contain fiber, vitamins, minerals, and other phytonutrients.
4. The color in vegetables makes a wonderful display of God's handiwork when arranged beautifully on a plate, serving dish, or buffet. God created the colored vegetables to show me easily which vegetables were

best for me to eat. The darker or richer the color is, the more nutrients God put in the vegetable. This makes it easy for me to select the healthiest vegetables for me and my family.

5. Some vegetables are especially good for me because they contain the highest amounts of nutrients. Vegetables like carrots, winter squash, broccoli, kale, garlic, watercress, sweet potatoes, peas, Brussels sprouts, and tomatoes are very important in my diet to keep me healthy from head to toe. Raw vegetables are also good for me because they are the highest in enzymes which can help to reverse aging, prevent cancer, and improve my digestion.
6. Many diseases might be prevented by eating a diet high in vegetables. The most common diseases that respond to better nutrition are: hypertension, diabetes, heart disease, cancers, constipation, diverticulitis, and cataracts.
7. Children love to eat vegetables when they have had some part in growing, shopping for, or preparing them. They also, often prefer to eat raw vegetables as snacks—things like carrot sticks, baby carrots, peas in the pod, red and green pepper strips, and even baby lettuce.
8. Cucumbers, garlic, leeks, and onions were the vegetables that the Israelites longed for in the desert. Cucumbers are a good source of water. Garlic, onions, and leeks are useful in reducing high blood pressure and cholesterol, aiding digestion, and reducing allergies. This made them very important health foods.

CHAPTER FIVE

1. Nuts! Specifically walnuts and almonds, and fruits. Nuts contain fat—the good kind of fat called essential fatty acids. This is very important for healthy skin, hair, and eyes, as well as healthy mucous membranes in all parts of the body. They also contain some forms of protein that are also essential for health.
2. I have tried to follow a low-fat diet for several years, and I am having trouble with dry skin and fly-away, dry hair, so I'm going to start adding some walnuts, almonds, and pistachio nuts and nut butters into my diet. I will also experiment with adding flaxseeds to cereals and breads. I realize that my cholesterol might be creeping up, and I want to work toward lowering it so the nuts and seeds will help.
3. Fruit is high in fiber which is good for digestion. Raisins and grapes contain two nutrients that will help prevent cancer, ellagic acid and resveratrol. Many fruits are known to prevent cerebrovascular disease and atherosclerosis because of the fiber and other phytonutrients they contain.
4. Fruits can help to reverse or prevent central nervous system problems, bladder infections, and incontinence. Eating a wide variety of fruit every day will provide these heath benefits. I especially try to have cranberries in some form every few days to prevent bladder problems.
5. Tomatoes, olives, and avocados are really fruits even though we usually eat them as if they were vegetables. I am going to begin having ripe olives in fruit salads along with avocados. I think I'll experiment with making homemade tomato jam and jelly this summer just like my grandmother used to do. I understand that small pear tomatoes make great jam. I'm also going to incorporate more of these three fruits into salads, pasta salads especially, and sandwiches. I even think I'll make scrambled egg sandwiches for breakfast with whole-wheat bread and sliced tomatoes. My mother gave me a really great recipe for mayonnaise, I'm going to try it with extra virgin olive oil.
6. The bitter principle of olive leaves is called oleuropein and it is very useful in warding off E. coli and salmonella. This might be why there is more trouble with bacteria in North America than there is in places where olives and olive oil are used more liberally.

CHAPTER SIX

1. Having dairy products daily is a good way to ensure that I am giving myself and my family enough calcium. My children do not want to drink milk but they will eat cheese, so we try to have some of the really natural cheeses for them, especially in their lunches each day so that they have enough calcium to keep relaxed at school and after they come home so they can concentrate on their school work.
2. There has been a controversy over cow's milk for thousands of years. Sometimes I think it is foolish because cow's milk is so readily available. But then again, there is a child in our Sunday School class who is really allergic to milk and suffers even when she drinks just a little.

3. God gave mothers the ability to produce milk for their newborn children. This is a really natural way to keep infants healthy. I'm not surprised that the ingredients in mother's milk protect babies from a lot of diseases and bacteria; it's part of God's plan!
4. Yogurt was eaten in Bible times and it has many health-giving properties.
5. Fermented milk products are very helpful when taking antibiotics because they reintroduce the good bacteria that is essential for health that the antibiotics kill off. I really feel that eating yogurt and kefir on a daily basis keeps digestion and intestines functioning better than without it. Fermented dairy products help to build up immunity to all sorts of bacteria. I would never travel without yogurt tablets or some form of probiotic to keep from getting sick because of the higher bacteria count in places like Mexico, India, South America, and China.
6. In New Testament times milk was primarily for children.

CHAPTER SEVEN

1. Many of Jesus' disciples were fishermen. Fishing was a big industry in the Mediterranean region. This is often cited as the reason for why one of the symbols of Christianity is the fish. Common people ate fish, fishermen were common people, and Jesus walked among common people.
2. Fish has been a mainstay in the Mediterranean Diet for thousands of years. Since this is considered to be one of the healthiest diets, it stands to reason that eating fish is also healthy. Fish have a lot of important nutrients in them like DHA and EPA.
3. The best fish to eat for health are the fatty and very fatty fish like sardines, salmon, tuna, cat fish and orange roughy, to name a few. I often eat fish sandwiches for lunch. Sometimes I serve my family some really old fashioned fish meals like tuna and noodle casserole or salmon patties from a recipe book that my grandmother gave me.
4. Medical research has shown that eating fish and fish oil help the following conditions: heart disease, high triglycerides, pain and inflammation, asthma, and rheumatoid arthritis. These are the diseases that are now considered to be the most troubling for a large percentage of the population. We seem to hear more about these diseases nowadays I think, because fewer people are eating right and even fewer people are eating fish. When people do eat fish, they eat processed or deep-fried fish and that is not as good for them.
5. Broiled, poached, or baked fish are the best ways to cook and eat fish. They can often be dressed up with herbs and low-fat sauces. It's really easy to bake fish in a foil or parchment-paper packet with herbs. You can even do it outdoors on the barbecue.
6. Anytime is a good time to eat fish. Jesus ate fish for breakfast. I'm not sure that I can do that myself, but I'm sure going to give it a try! I know that when I have broiled or poached fish, I always feel good afterwards. When I have deep-fried fish, I often feel too full afterwards, and all that grease makes me feel really groggy.

CHAPTER EIGHT

1. Passover includes bitter herbs as a remembrance of the bitter tears the Israelites shed while they were slaves in Egypt. This is also a meal where fat is eaten and the bitter herbs help my body digest the fat and use it effectively. They are also important because they contain minerals and vitamin A or beta-carotene and can also help to remove toxins from my body like lead and mercury.
2. Dandelions grow almost everywhere. I think I'll get some from the baseball diamond in the park. It is fenced in and dogs are not allowed. We have planned a special Seder at my church this spring and we will have parsley and dandelion greens then. I'm even going to do a special project in Sunday School with the bitter herbs and let the kids try them. There are farm-grown dandelions in my local supermarket so I can include them in my salads.
3. Including dark green, leafy vegetables in my diet or taking dark green algae can help reduce cancer, birth defects, macular degeneration, and vascular diseases. I'm going to start having only dark green, leafy salads. I'm going to make sure that all sandwiches have dark green lettuce on them. I'm going to use fresh parsley in foods and as a garnish on cooked foods. I think I'll even start growing parsley on my window sill, so I'll have some available at all times.
4. Parsley and cilantro are so plentiful in the supermarket that they can be

added to everything. This might even help my family have fewer colds next winter. People just ate more of the foods that were inexpensive and readily available in Bible times, like greens, fish, and olive oil. I'm going to start doing that too.

CHAPTER NINE

1. In Leviticus the Bible talks about all the fat belonging to the Lord. They were also told to burn that same fat as an offering to God. God was pleased by the scent of the fat burning as an offering.
2. The prohibited fats are the ones found around the organs in most animals. In pigs this fat is called lard; in beef, suet or tallow; in chickens, chicken fat, although many Europeans call it Chicken Schmaltz.
3. Fat is not really bad if we eat the right kind of fat like olive oil, nut and seed oils, and flaxseeds. These fats contain the essential fatty acids that help keep nerves, skin, hair, and brain healthy. We really need these fats, that's why they are called essential!
4. The Bible Diet says we should eat eggs and poultry a few times a week. That seems sensible to me because there are so many different proteins to choose from.
5. The following foods are to be eaten a few times per week: sweets, eggs, and poultry. I'm very careful about what I eat so I don't eat more of the foods than the amounts recommended in the Mediterranean/Bible Diet.
6. Even though I try to stay away from pork and pork products, I often end up eating bacon in salads or breakfast burritos. I don't make a really big deal about it though because I know that the New Testament says all foods are clean. I don't like to eat food with chemicals and preservatives so I stay away from bacon, ham, and lard for health reasons, not because they are unclean. It is more important for me to have a nice meal with great fellowship than to make a scene about eating bacon.

CHAPTER TEN

1. Honey was made from fruits like dates, from carob pods, and honey was made by bees too. Milk and honey were always mentioned together because they always ate them together and because they were symbols of wealth and privilege. They generally ate milk products with honey and other sweets so that the protein in the milk balanced the sweetness of the honey.
2. We should not eat sweets every day, they can be eaten a few times a week if I'm watching my health and following the Bible Diet. The really best forms of sweets are natural fruits. However, if I want to have a muffin, cake, or cookies, I will make them myself out of natural sweeteners and whole-wheat flour so they will be healthier.
3. Heart disease and high blood pressure are generally related to high-salt consumption. Cutting down on salt or cutting it out completely can help people who have these problems, but they should talk to their doctor first. People ate more salt as preservatives in foods during Bible times. I think it didn't affect them as much as us today in our many processed foods.
4. Water. I drink it frequently during the day and even have a glass as soon as I get up in the morning. I think there is more emphasis on drinking water lately because we keep our houses hotter, therefore dryer, and we need more water.
5. There is never an important time to drink wine as far as I'm concerned! If I drink wine I have the kind with no alcohol in it. My church never talks against drinking wine specifically, but they don't encourage it either. I'm glad there is a place that doesn't encourage drinking that I can go to for fun and fellowship.
6. The healthful properties in wine can be obtained by drinking grape or other fruit juices and eating grapes whole, including the seeds and skins. This can help prevent many kinds of cancers and prevent aging, which I'm all for preventing.

CHAPTER ELEVEN

1. Clean animals were beef, chickens, fish with scales, and lambs. Unclean animals were pigs, horses, shrimp, and lobster. Many people have gotten into the habit of eating a lot of pork products, and the pork producers say they are cleaner because they aren't fed garbage as much, but I still read that parasites are being found in many of the unclean foods mentioned in the Bible. That keeps me from eating them.

2. Peter was told in a vision to eat a lot of different foods and some of them were considered unclean. He was shocked because he had never eaten any of them and couldn't imagine God telling him to eat them. He later learned that Jesus had been preaching that people were not made unclean by the foods they ate but by the things they said.
3. God instituted the cleanliness rules of washing hands and feet and burying excrement, and they are still being done today.
4. Food should always be fresh and free of mold and bruises. Before preparing any food the surface of the preparation area should be clean. If meat will be cut, the cutting board should be cleaned with chlorine bleach before and after. Everything should be clean including your hands, knives, other utensils, board, and anything that is going to touch the food being prepared. All fruits and vegetables should be washed with soap and water before cooking or eating them.
5. Foods grown without pesticides or chemicals are called "organically grown." I think it is becoming more important because so many foods are being contaminated with harmful chemicals that many people have become chemically sensitive. There are so many chemicals that we can't keep away from in the air that I want to be included in keeping chemicals out of my body by using organically grown foods. This will also help the environment to become cleaner too.
6. God said to get rid of any mold in my house, and if I can't get rid of it, to tear the house down and throw away the materials. This seems radical, but in light of the many health problems due to mold and mildew, I'm going to get serious about mold and mildew.

CHAPTER TWELVE

1. I think Elijah had depression, major depression. He is important to this chapter because I realize that many people suffer from depression, both average and great like Elijah. I'm not so critical of people with depression now.
2. The angel told Elijah to eat several times a day. This is really important to bring good health to anybody even if they don't have depression. Eating frequently can keep my blood sugar levels stabilized and this will give me constant energy.
3. Depression symptoms include poor self-image or self-esteem, lack of self-confidence, withdrawal from social activities, changes in appetite, loss of energy or fatigue, and difficulty in concentrating.
4. The most important things I can do if I think I have depression is to see my doctor; eat small frequent meals; avoid sugar, caffeine, and alcohol; and get enough sleep.
5. David helped Saul by playing music for him. I really find some classical music uplifting, especially Vivaldi's *Four Seasons*. I like a lot of the old hymns, and many of the chant records; they make me feel close to God and this comfort prevents me from feeling down. Then again I don't have depression. I had a friend in college who was diagnosed with depression and she used to sit in her dorm room and listen to really loud acid rock music. It was very irritating. Her counselors made her stop playing the music, and she began to feel better, so I have been aware of this for many years.

CHAPTER THIRTEEN

1. Eve was tempted by the devil to eat the forbidden fruit and she got Adam involved. Jesus was also tempted by the devil to turn stones into bread when he was fasting in the desert. The devil figured that Jesus would be so hungry that he would go for it and turn stones into bread. Jesus resisted. Adam and Eve did not. It is important to know about them so that we can pattern our lives on Jesus—ask God for help when we are tempted and not give in to the temptations of other humans. They might be doing the work of the devil, as Eve was.
2. Hypoglycemia is low blood sugar and it happens when the body doesn't get enough food. Hyperglycemia is high blood sugar, which happens to people who have trouble handling sugar for one reason or another. These two conditions can be avoided by eating small, frequent meals of whole foods, and avoiding large amounts of sugar, caffeine, and nicotine.
3. Jesus gave the disciples fish for breakfast mainly because they were fishermen. It was also the custom to eat fish for breakfast.
4. White flour pretzels and crackers have been my snacks for a long time and I always feel tired later. Now I am going to start eating whole-grain pretzels and crackers. Even though God created all things, he did not create junk food.

5. Hannah was barren and also had an eating disorder. She refused to eat for a long time because her rival, Peninnah, was picking on her for her barrenness.

6. Compulsive overeating, Anorexia nervosa, and bulimia nervosa. Compulsive overeating is a common eating disorder that affects men and women. Anorexia nervosa and bulimia nervosa are two common eating disorders that mainly affect women, although more and more young men are exhibiting these disorders. Eating disorders can come from poor body image or self image or from being teased or put down by peers or parents. There are also indications that these disorders are often displays of power or control. There are a lot of new ideas being published now that show that often these disorders are the result of mineral deficiencies, food allergies, or brain chemical imbalances.

CHAPTER FOURTEEN

1. God cursed the Israelites with wasting diseases, blight, mold and mildew, among other things, because they had been disobedient.

2. People around the world are refusing to follow the laws of God. Even Jews and Christians are not following God's laws. This is causing a lot of problems with health, sanitation, and diseases. Candida seems like a real plague since so many people that I know seem to have it in varying degrees. Many people are too busy to pay attention to their children. The children feel this lack of love, and this suppresses their immune systems and allows candida to take hold. Eating processed foods can also be part of the problem since processed food also suppresses the immune system and allows candida to take hold.

3. They could not have bread, fermented foods, and wine, which encourage various yeasts to grow. The common element is disobedience to God, disregard for God's laws especially honoring your father and mother and not forgiving one another. They sound very similar to the kinds of things that were going on in Bible times to the Hebrews.

4. Eat whole foods, no yeast or fermented food, and eat lots of parsley, garlic, yogurt, olive oil, and perhaps take some of the nutritional supplements that can either kill yeast or prevent it from living. Also, find a sympathetic doctor or nutritionist who can help to rid my body of this plague.

CHAPTER FIFTEEN

1. Paul taught that Christians were to be serious at all times about following Jesus and loving God and that our bodies were the church, a holy temple. Our bodies are the way God gets to be known on this earth. We must talk about him to others, after carrying him in our hearts, so that we are the church or temple.

2. God often chooses to heal people who ask for healing through prayer and/or crying out. God has also inspired men to develop medicines that can also heal diseases. Many of the current medicines are designed from the herbs and other organic materials that God created.

3. We don't really know why Jesus was so adamant about forgiving, but he preached about forgiving all the time. From his words in the Bible we can deduce that forgiveness and forgiving were very important for healing to take place.

4. Many of the emotions that belong to what New Testament Christians called 'earthly way' can cause damage to various organs in our bodies. Such emotions as anger and rage have been shown to actually cause heart problems, encourage high blood pressure, and even bring on a stroke. Negative emotions, stress, rage, and tension can shut off the blood circulation causing lack of oxygen to many parts of the body. They can also use up the minerals that are necessary for relaxation thereby causing contractions of the heart and blood vessel muscles.

CHAPTER SIXTEEN

1. Jesus and his disciples walked everywhere because they had no other transportation besides donkeys! Even donkey carts took the same amount of time as walking, so people generally walked beside their donkeys.

2. The best way to start exercising is to start with walking, move onto power walking, and escalate to speed walking. There are a lot of things that I do in the normal course of my day that could be made into better exercise. Instead of using the dryer, I could hang the clothes outside, that would be more exercise.

3. Actually, I am more active than when I was a child. Now I ride a mountain bike, hike, and play several games at the gym plus lift weights. I try to walk everywhere possible. . Recently we got a dog and that creates more exercise just chasing after her and taking her for walks. I do a lot more activities now than when I was a child because I didn't like competitive sports. I did take tap dancing lessons for a while, that was a lot of exercise.

4. Often when I am at the gym on the treadmill or bike, I listen to Christian praise audio tapes specifically for exercising. I have often gotten a lot of comments when I lost track of what I was doing and began to sing, loudly I might add, while listening to a tape and jogging on the treadmill.

CHAPTER SEVENTEEN

1. The seven feasts are Passover, the Feast of Unleavened Bread, First Fruits, Pentecost, Trumpets, Atonement, and Tabernacles. There were given as times to remember God, read from scriptures, and attend services.

2. They didn't feast at all! Yom Kippur was also called Day of Atonement when people were to deny themselves pleasures including eating.

3. There was always the danger of eating too much food, eating over a long period time, and eating a lot of fatty foods. I work at eating a small amount when I am at a feast or pot luck dinner. I take small amounts and never go back for seconds.

4. Overweight has always been associated with overindulgence in food. We can develop digestive problems from eating too much food, and Syndrome X is often associated with too much food at one time. Eating a little before going to a feast can help us from becoming so hungry that we lose control and eat too much.

5. God appointed feasts for the Israelites to set aside time to remember him. God should be the center of all feasts.

CHAPTER EIGHTEEN

1. The Bible assigned fasts for the Israelites to follow including the fasts of the fourth, fifth, seventh, and tenth months. Fasts were generally done to commemorate historical occurrences.

2. There are the major and minor fasts. The major fast was to take no food or drink from sundown to sundown. The minor fast was to take no food or drink from sunup to sundown. Many cultures still practice one day of major fasting for the purpose of seeking God.

3. Christians often fast from one food for a period of time, generally over Lent. Many Christians are renewing the practice of fasting for one full 24-hour period, often every week. This kind of fast, when approached correctly, can be of spiritual and physical benefit.

4. Ease into a fast by reducing foods in a slow and methodical way and ending up on just juice, broth, or water for a period of time. No one should just stop eating food and go immediately to liquids, particularly one like coffee.

5. Fasting to seek God is between each person and God and is not to be discussed with anyone. In Jesus' day, many religious sects bragged about how they were fasting and even did things to themselves so everyone could see that they were fasting. This is not seeking God, but making a public show of fasting.

APPENDIX C — THE EXPERTS

Rita Bennet—Founder of The Emotionally Free® Course for Prayer Counselors. She is the author of *How To Pray For Inner Healing*, *Making Peace With Your Inner Child*, and *Emotionally Free*. Her ministry, Christian Renewal Association, which she began with her late husband Dennis, is located in Edmonds, Washington.

Reginald Cherry, M.D.—Practices diagnostic and preventive medicine in Houston, Texas and can be seen on the television show *The Doctor and the Word*. He is the author of *The Doctor and the Word* and *The Bible Cure*.

Francisco Contreras, M.D.—Specializes in improving the physical, mental, and spiritual lives of people with cancer using conventional and alternative therapies. He is the general director of the Oasis of Hope Hospital in Baja California, Mexico. He is the author of *Health in the 21st Century: Will Doctors Survive?* He is a frequent contributor to the *Eternally Fit* television show.

Kenneth H. Cooper, M.D., M.P.H.—Often called the Father of Modern aerobics since he was the person who coined the term "aerobics." He is the author of, *Aerobics*, *Controlling Cholesterol*, *Dr. Kenneth H. Cooper's Antioxidant Revolution*, *Dr. Kenneth H. Cooper's Advanced Nutritional therapies*, *Faith-Based Fitness*, and *It's Better To Believe*. He is also the founder of the Cooper Institute for Aerobics Research in Dallas, Texas.

Neva Coyle—Well-known speaker, writer, and prayer warrior. She is the author of more than twenty books including several novels. Her newest two: *A Woman of Strength* and *Loved on a Grander Scale*, show her concern for modern women of faith. She lives and has her prayer ministry in Ahwahnee, California.

William G. Crook, M.D.—Practicing physician, medical writer, and lecturer. He has written *The Yeast Connection*, *The Yeast Connection Cookbook*, *Chronic Fatigue Syndrome and The Yeast Connection*, and *The Yeast Connection and the Woman*. Dr. Crook lives in Jackson, Tennessee.

Anne and David Frähm—Founders of HealthQuarters, a nonprofit educational organization aimed at helping people with cancer. The late Anne spent much of her time helping others recover from cancer. They are the authors of *A Cancer Battle Plan* and *Healthy Habits*.

David W. Hager, M.D., and Linda Carruth Hager—Authors of *Stress and the Woman's Body*. Dr. Hager was named by Good Housekeeping as one of America's top doctors for women.

Jack and Judy Hartman—Authors of more than ten books on Bible study and faith as well as *Increased Energy And Vitality*. Through Lamplight Ministries in Dunedin, Florida they encourage people to have faith and to eat the foods God provided for us to eat.

T. D. Jakes—Founder and senior pastor of The Potter's House church in Dallas, Texas. He is the author of several books and has a weekly television show. Bishop Jakes is best known for his massive crusades and conferences across the country.

Florence Littauer—Internationally known speaker and author with over twenty books to her credit. She is the founder of CLASS (Christian Leaders, Authors, and Speakers Services) and encourages Christians to become the best speakers and presenters they can be. She lives with her husband Fred in San Marcos, California.

Joe S. McIlhaney, M.D.—OB/GYN and the author of *1001 Health-Care Questions Women Ask*. He is often heard on Focus On The Family radio show.

S. I. McMillan, M.D.—Author of the Christian classic: *None of the Diseases* , *Discern These Times,* and is currently working on another book, *You Can Be Sure.*

Mark Pearson—Author of *Christian Healing* and the President of the Institute for Christian Renewal in Plaistow, New Hampshire.

Rex Russell, M.D.—Radiologist in practice in Fort Smith, Arkansas and the author of *What The Bible Says About Healthy Living.*

Maureen Kennedy Salaman—Speaker and health writer. She is the author of *Nutrition: The Cancer Answer, Foods That Heal, Foods That Heal Companion Cookbook, The Diet Bible: The Bible For Dieters,* and *All YourHealth Questions Answered, Naturally.*

Jim Shriner—Fitness expert, the host of his own national television show, *Eternally Fit,* and the author of a fitness book also called *Eternally Fit.* He lives in Ormond Beach, Florida.

Pamela Smith, R.D.—Author of *Eat Well-Live Well* and *Healthy Expectations.* She is frequently heard on the Focus of the Family radio show.

Mary Ruth Swope, Ph.D.—Nutritionist, author, speaker, and seminar leader. She is the author of *Nutrition For Christians, Are You Sick and Tired of Feeling Sick and Tired?, The Spiritual Roots of Barley, Listening Prayer, Green Leaves of Barley,* and *Of These Ye May Freely Eat.* She also is involved with Nutrition With A Mission in Melbourne, Florida.

Cheryl Townsley—Author of *Food Smart!,* a seminar leader, cooking instructor, and the owner of Lifestyles for Health.

Herbert Wagemaker, M.D.—Christian psychiatrist in Jacksonville, Florida. He is the author of *How Can I Understand My Kids?, Parents and Discipline,* and *The Surprising Truth About Depression.*

Julian Whitaker, M.D.—Medical director of the Whitaker Wellness Institute. He is the author of many books, including *Shed Ten Years In Ten Weeks,* and *The Pain Relief Breakthrough,* co-authored by Brenda Adderly, M.H.A.

NOTE: To the best of our knowledge, all of the above information is accurate and up to date. In some cases we were unable to obtain biographical information.

—THE STARBURST EDITORS

APPENDIX D — RECIPES

HOW TO COOK WITH SUCCESS

1. Read over the recipe before you start.
2. Allow enough time to get ready, make the recipe, cook it, and clean up.
3. Check your supplies to see if you have all the necessary ingredients.
4. Make a list and purchase what you need.
5. Clean off the surface you are going to use with a damp cloth and dry it.
6. Get out all the utensils you will be using.
7. Get out all the ingredients you will be using (all ingredients should be room temperature unless otherwise specified).
8. Make the recipe as it is written the first time to see how it comes out. Then make substitutions if you want to.
9. Set a timer that will ring when the time is up so that you won't forget it.
10. Clean up as soon as you have finished cooking, baking, or making food.

Abbreviations and Conversions

tsp .... teaspoon
Tbsp .... tablespoon .... tsp
oz .... ounce
lb .... pound .... 16 oz
½ C .... 4 oz .... 8 Tbsp
1 C .... 16 Tbsp
¼ C .... 2 oz .... 4 Tbsp
⅓ C .... 5 Tbsp
g .... gram .... 1,000 milligrams
mg .... milligram .... one 1,000th gram
mcg .... microgram .... one 1,000,000th gram

Simple Grain Breakfast

Cook desired quantity of oatmeal, millet, buckwheat, or commercial hot cereal. While cooking, add one or more of the following:

- lima beans
- corn
- carrots, chopped or grated
- peas
- green beans
- precooked beans (like kidney or pinto)

Ladle cooked mixture into bowls and top with butter or olive oil or a mixture of both, flaxseeds, chopped fresh parsley, and soy sauce.

Simple Vegetable Breakfast

Using a steamer or steamer basket inside a large pot, bring water to full steam. Cut up and steam vegetables, starting with those that take the longest to cook—potatoes, brussel sprouts, broccoli stems, onions, beet and other roots, and sweet potato. Veggies that are cut into cubes about one-half inch should take 10 to 12 minutes to fully cook.

Add other veggies to the pot as the first ones continue to cook.

Peas, green or yellow beans, mushrooms, zucchini, summer squash, broccoli flowerets, peppers, or precooked veggies will take less time to cook. These can be added after the first vegetables have cooked for 6 or 7 minutes. Chopped spinach and other greens only take a minute or two.

Serve with butter or olive oil, chopped fresh parsley, cumin seeds, sunflower seeds, or even natural or homemade catsup. Salt and pepper, if desired.

You may add an egg or two for each person. Bring the egg to room temperature by covering it with hot water for 3 or 4 minutes. When the chopped greens have been added to the steaming veggies, carefully lower the eggs into the steamer and leave them for the last 4 minutes of cooking time. When the meal is finished, remove the eggs to cold water to stop the cooking. Break the egg shell by hitting it with a table knife so it opens into two halves. Scoop out the egg from each half into the veggies and serve with a little olive oil, chopped parsley and freshly squeezed raw garlic. Small cubes of cheese may be added instead of the eggs, or cream cheese, or even tuna fish or leftover meats. Fresh herbs can be added to the meal at serving time.

This recipe provides variety for breakfast because it can be made from any seasonally available vegetables.

Scrambled Tofu And Veggies

FOR EACH SERVING:

1 tsp olive oil
¼ cooking onion, chopped
½ stalk of broccoli, chopped and separated
2 mushrooms, chopped
⅛ red pepper, chopped
½ piece tofu in water
soy sauce to taste

Drain tofu in several layers of towels. Heat oil over medium heat. Sauté onion, broccoli stalk, and mushrooms until soft. Mash the tofu. Add broccoli flowerets to onion, broccoli, and mushrooms, and stir; then add red pepper and stir. Add the mashed tofu and soy sauce to taste; heat through.

Any combination of veggies can be used in this. Cumin, basil, oregano, tomatoes, curry powder, or salsa can be added to change the flavor. Tofu has no taste so you will want to add seasoning. Keep away from salt, though.

High-Fiber Breakfast Muffins

MIX TOGETHER:

1 C grated carrots
1 C zucchini
1 egg, beaten
1 C milk, low-fat or whole
¼ C evaporated sugar cane juice or Sucanat®
2 Tbsp canola oil
1 15-oz can or jar of beans*, pinto, great northern, white, etc., slightly mashed
½ C quick cooking oats

SIFT TOGETHER:

1½ C whole wheat pastry flour
¼ tsp baking soda
1 Tbsp baking powder

Preheat oven to 400° F. Grease or paper 16-18 muffin tins. Sift dry ingredients into wet and stir until it is just barely mixed together. Spoon into muffin tins. Fill to within ¼ inch of the tops. Bake for 25 to 30 minutes.

*Look for beans with no chemicals, spices, or preservatives. I like to use Haines or Eden Foods brands.

CHEESE MUFFINS: add a teaspoon of grated cheddar cheese to the top of each muffin before baking.

Basic Winter Stock

> 1½ Tbsp butter
> 3 medium carrots, coarsely chopped
> 2 medium onions, not peeled, coarsely chopped
> 1 medium turnip, coarsely chopped
> 1 medium parsnip, coarsely chopped
> 2 stalks celery, chopped
> 3 qt. water
> 2 cloves garlic, pressed or chopped
> ½ C fresh parsley, chopped
> ½ tsp each of dried thyme, ground cumin, black pepper

In a large soup pot, heat butter and sauté vegetables for 15 minutes or until lightly golden. Add water, herbs, and pepper. Turn to medium/high until soup begins to give off steam. Turn to simmer and cook for 1–2 hours. Strain. Discard vegetables.

This stock is very flavorful and can be used as a broth by itself. It can be made into a different soup by adding pre-cooked beans or pre-cooked grains while simmering.

Black Bean Soup

> 3 Tbsp extra virgin olive oil
> 1 large onion, chopped
> 2 ribs celery, chopped
> 2 cloves garlic, pressed or chopped
> 1 Tbsp whole wheat bread flour
> 6 C cold water or stock
> 3 C cooked black beans (2 15 oz cans, washed)
> ¼ C parsley, chopped
> 2 tsp natural liquid smoke
> 2 bay leaves
> 1 tsp ground cumin
> ½ C dry sherry (look for a nonalcoholic one)
> 2 Tbsp white wine vinegar (optional)
> salt & freshly ground pepper to taste
> 1 C sour cream, low fat is best, for garnish
> Jalapeño peppers for garnish

Heat soup pot over medium heat and add oil. Sauté onion, celery, and garlic until onion is translucent. Sprinkle flour over mixture and stir to coat. Cook 1 minute or more, until it gives off a nutty fragrance. Add water and stir. Add beans, parsley, smoke, bay leaves, cumin, sherry, vinegar, and salt and pepper, stir. Allow to come to just barely simmering, reduce heat to keep it simmering and cook, covered for 1 hour or more. Serve with a dollop of sour cream and chopped Jalapeño on top. Serves 6–10

Mushroom And Barley Soup

¾ lb mushrooms
1 Tbsp olive oil
2 Tbsp butter
⅓ C pearl barley
6 C boiling water or stock
1 stalk celery
2 sprigs parsley
1 tsp salt

Clean mushrooms, remove stems from caps and separate. Slice mushroom caps. Heat oil and butter in soup pot over medium heat. Sauté caps for 2 minutes or until they change color; remove from pan and set aside.

Add barley to oil and sauté until it just starts to turn golden. Chop mushroom stems and add. Stir. Cook until barley is very golden and mushrooms are cooked. Add water, celery, and salt and turn heat to high. Boil for 3 minutes. Turn heat to low, add parsley, cover and cook for 20 to 45 minutes or until barley is soft. Remove celery and parsley and discard. Add mushroom caps and simmer for 4 minutes to heat caps. Serves 4.

French Style Onion Soup

2 Tbsp virgin olive oil
1 Tbsp butter
3 cooking onions, peeled, quartered and sliced thin
2 Spanish onions, peeled, halved and sliced thin
1 clove garlic, chopped or pressed
½ C nonalcoholic sherry
2 qt cold water or stock
1 tsp thyme
1 Tbsp miso paste diluted in 2 Tbsp water

Heat oil and butter in soup pan until mixture foams up. Add cooking onions, stirring until very golden brown. Add Spanish onions and garlic, stir and cook until they are transparent. Add water and turn heat to medium/high. Bring just to the boiling point. Turn to simmer and add sherry while soup is cooling off. When it is simmering, add thyme and miso paste. Simmer 5 minutes. Serves 6.

Quick Vegetable Soup

2 Tbsp butter
1 Tbsp olive oil
1 cooking onion, peeled, quartered, and sliced thin
1–3 cloves garlic, chopped
2 C mixed vegetables, chopped (no leaves or flowers*)
2 ripe tomatoes, peeled and seeded

OR

2 slices lemon with peel
4 C cold water
1 tsp salt, optional
2 tsp dried savory

Heat oil and butter in soup pot over medium heat until butter melts. Add onion and garlic and stir. Sauté until golden, but not burnt. Add vegetables, starting with the ones that take the longest to cook, like potatoes, broccoli stems, parsnips, and carrots. Continue to add another type when each changes color. Add tomatoes last. Add water, turn heat to medium/high and bring just to the boil. Add lemon slices. Turn heat to low and simmer for 6-15 minutes, depending on the vegetables used. Add savory and simmer for an additional 5 minutes.

This soup can be made with any combination of veggies. Carrots, potatoes, celery, peas, green and yellow beans, and tomatoes are the most common. Okra, broccoli, mushrooms, corn, pea pods, zucchini, turnips, etc. can all be used in combinations.

*Add broccoli flowerets and chopped leaves of veggies or spinach at the very end.

CREAM SOUP

Make the *Quick Vegetable Soup* and add an additional potato or white turnip. After simmering enough to cook the veggies through, purée some of the veggies along with most of the potato. To make it a dairy cream soup, milk may be added. Soft tofu can be blended with some of the veggies to make a dairy-less cream soup. Add parsley or fresh herbs to taste.

Festive Risotto

1 Tbsp olive oil, extra virgin
1 onion medium-sized, peeled, and finely chopped
1 C arborio rice*
1 C fresh mushrooms, chopped
2 Tbsp fresh red pepper, minced
¼ C dry white nonalcoholic wine
¼ C chopped Just TomatoesÔ (dried tomatoes) soaked in ½ C water
2 C chicken or vegetable broth
1 tsp whole dried rosemary
¼ C grated Parmesan cheese
¼ C Italian parsley, finely chopped

In a 2-quart Duromatic Pressure Frypan or larger pressure cooker, heat olive oil over medium/high heat. Add onion and sauté until translucent . Add the rice and sauté until golden, stirring often. Add mushrooms and peppers and stir to coat with oil. Add the wine and stir to mix. Drain tomatoes and add, stirring into mix. Add the broth and increase heat to high until mixture comes to a boil. Stir. Add rosemary.

Close the lid and bring pressure to the first red ring over high heat. Reduce heat to stabilize the pressure at the first red ring. If using another brand of pressure cooker, bring it to the stage where the rocker is lightly rocking and keep it at that pressure. Cook seven minutes.

Remove the Pressure Frypan from the heat and release the pressure by running cool water over the rim of the pan, avoiding the steam valves. Remove the lid and stir. Stir in the Parmesan and parsley.

Serves 4 to 6.

*Never wash or rinse arborio rice before cooking. This may keep it from getting creamy during cooking.

Magic Meal

CLARIFIED BUTTER

Melt 1 lb unsalted butter over low heat or in microwave. Separate milk solids from clear oil, either by chilling or by using a skimmer or separator. In India clarified butter is called ghee and is made by heating butter over medium heat until the solids have separated out. The solid matter becomes firm and can then be strained away from the golden liquid. Be very careful not to burn the solids or the ghee will taste burnt.

ROUX

Start with equal parts of oil or clarified butter and flour. There is no precise measurement for the flour and fat. It depends on the type of flour used and the amount of bran and gluten. Use whole wheat, spelt, or other bread flour. Traditionally, clarified butter is used for this, but you could also use olive or Canola oil.

In a heavy pan over medium heat begin to mash the flour and fat together. All the flour should be coated with fat and all the fat should be saturated with flour. No visible oil or flour should be remaining in the pan. Adjust the mixture by adding more fat or flour.

Cook and mash with a fork until it begins to bubble up and give off a smell of toasted nuts. Reduce heat. If you want to use it for light sauces remove it from the heat. You can continue to heat and brown it until it is darker if you want a deep-colored sauce. This is very traditional in French cooking. Keep the finished roux in a glass container with a tight lid in the refrigerator. This will prevent rancidity.

To use roux, add 1 heaping spoonful to 1 C near boiling liquid. Stir until thickened. For a thicker sauce add more roux.

Roux can be used to thicken soup and stews or to give sauces body. The darker roux will add a richer taste to "flat" soups.

French Style Tempeh And Veggies

> 2 Tbsp clarified butter or oil, or a mixture (more as needed)
> 1 medium onion, chopped
> 2 garlic cloves
> 1 pkg tempeh or tempeh burgers
> 1 bunch broccoli (or 1 small head cauliflower)
> ½ lb mushrooms
> ½ red or yellow pepper
> 1–3 Tbsp flour (whole wheat is best)
> ¾ C cold water
> 1–3 C hot water as needed
> 1 tsp salt
> 1 tsp ground cumin
> 2 tsp basil
>
> OR
>
> 1 tsp tarragon
> Chopped fresh parsley as garnish

Heat oil in large heavy pan over medium or medium/high heat. Add chopped onion. Chop tempeh and garlic stir in, coating with oil. Cut stems from broccoli into small pieces. Add and stir. Slice mushrooms, if small or chop, if larger and stir in. Chop peppers. Cut florets into bite sized pieces. When broccoli stems are nearly cooked, add enough flour to coat all the veggies and tempeh. Sprinkle the flour on and stir. Cook and stir until the flour is toasted. Add cold water while stirring. It should foam up. Keep stirring and add hot water as needed to make the desired consistency of sauce. Add salt, cumin, flowerets, peppers and stir. Turn the heat down to simmer. When the mixture is simmering, add basil. Let simmer for 3–5 minutes and serve over rice or pasta.

East Indian Magic Meal

Ingredients from the French Veggies, except for the cumin and basil or tarragon.

> ¼ tsp ground cloves
> 1 tsp each of ground cinnamon, cardamom, turmeric, coriander, ginger fenugreek (optional)
> Chopped fresh cilantro as garnish

Sauté veggies as above. Pull veggies away from the center after stirring the mushrooms. Add 1 tsp additional oil or ghee. When ghee has melted add the spices. Let them cook until the fragrance is strong. Stir in the veggies and cook 1 minute. Add the flour and continue on as above. Serve over rice or pasta. Garnish with chopped cilantro.

Chopped cilantro could be added in with the dried spices if desired.

Chinese Magic Meal

Ingredients for French Veggies except for the flour, basil or tarragon, and cumin

> 1–2 inch piece fresh ginger
> 2 garlic cloves
> 1 Tbsp tamari
> 1 heaping Tbsp corn starch
> Cold water to dilute
> Hot water, as needed

Follow directions for French Veggies. After mushrooms have started to soften, pull veggies away from the side of the pan. Blend seasonings and cornstarch with enough water to make a runny paste. Pour into the center of the wok or pan and let it cook until it begins to get clear around the edges, stir into veggies. Add hot water to dilute to desired consistency. Add Florets and cook to the crisp stage. Serve over rice or mix with rice noodles.

Tofu 'Mayo'

8 oz soft tofu, Chinese style, or firm Japanese style
¼ C olive, canola oil, or a mixture
¼ tsp salt
¼ tsp dry mustard

OR

½ tsp Dijon mustard
¼ tsp paprika
1 Tbsp each, lemon juice and vinegar

Wrap tofu in several layers of towel to drain well. Place all ingredients except tofu in blender and blend. Remove feeder tube and add tofu in 3 pieces. Blend or process until desired consistency is obtained. Store covered in the refrigerator for 2 weeks. If water separates out, drain it off or stir it back in.

Tempeh Sloppy Joe

1 pkg Italian or regular tempeh

OR

1 pkg tempeh burgers, crumbled
2 tsp olive oil
1 small onion, chopped
½ green pepper, chopped
6 oz tomato sauce or catsup
1 tsp soy sauce
1 tsp veggie or regular Worcestershire sauce
½ tsp chile powder

Heat oil in heavy pan, add onion and green pepper and sauté until brown. Add tempeh. Continue to cook until tempeh is browned. Add remaining ingredients and simmer 5 minutes or to desired consistency. Serve over whole wheat buns.

Tofu And Winter Veggie Pot Pie

FILLING:

1 pkg firm tofu, drained or smoked
1 potato, yellow fin is great
1 small turnip
1 small carrot
1 small onion
2 garlic cloves
2 Tbsp oil or butter
2–3 Tbsp whole wheat bread flour
½ tsp salt
½ tsp ground cumin
2 tsp dried thyme
1 Tbsp red or brown miso paste or marmite

      OR

1 Tbsp veggie bouillon, chicken or beef*

Dice potato, turnip, and carrot into ½" cubes and steam for 3–4 minutes to precook. Slice tofu into ½" slabs and wrap in towels to drain, if using the white tofu. Chop onion and garlic. Heat oil or butter and sauté the onion and garlic until slightly brown. Stir in flour. All the fat should be absorbed in the flour. There should be no flour that is not coated with oil in the pan. Stir and cook over medium/high heat until flour is toasted. Add about ½ C of cold water and stir. As mixture begins to thicken, add more water, or bouillon to make a gravy (the veggies will give off liquid while cooking). Add the miso paste, diluted with a small amount of water. Stir in the veggies and herbs. Dice tofu into the same size pieces as the veggies and add.

*not essential if using smoked tofu.

CRUST:

2 C whole wheat pastry flour
⅔ C butter or soy margarine
1 tsp salt
5–6 Tbsp cold water or other liquid like milk, soy milk or broth

Preheat oven to 425° F. Sift flour and salt into food processor. Add butter, cut into small pieces. Process until a coarse meal forms. Add 5 Tbsp liquid and pulse until ball forms. Add remaining Tbsp as needed. Roll out into 2 round crusts.

    Place larger crust in 9 or 10" pie pan being careful not to stretch the bottom or sides. Put in filling. Dampen edges of crust and place top crust over it. Seal edges and flute. Prick the top with fork to allow steam to escape. Bake for 12 minutes and reduce heat to 375° F and bake 40–50 minutes or until crust browns. Serve warm with a green salad.

Tofu Dinner Loaf

2 Tbsp cooking oil (optional, see note)
2 onions
2 carrots
2 stalks celery
2 cloves garlic
1½ C cooked whole grains such as rice, buckwheat, millet (the grains are optional)
¾ C dry bread crumbs
1 lb tofu
1–2 Tbsp miso paste
5 sprigs fresh dill

   OR

2–3 Tbsp dried herbs such as thyme, marjoram, tarragon, basil

Grate or finely chop first 4 ingredients. Heat oil over medium heat and sauté the vegetables, stirring constantly, until deep brown, but not burnt.

Drain tofu in colander. Using a potato masher, mash tofu and all ingredients together. Or blend half the tofu until smooth and mash in remaining ingredients. Or using the plastic blade in a food processor, processed tofu and add remaining ingredients until mixed. Spoon into oiled loaf pan and bake at 350° F for one hour or until lightly browned. Serves 4–6 as a main protein serving.

Note: You can eliminate the oil by braising the chopped veggies in water with 2 Tbsp low sodium soy sauce added. Eliminate the miso paste.

The sautéing of the vegetables gives body to the loaf. The vegetables can be varied depending on how much body you want. This is one of those recipes that can be changed according to your mood or stock of food in the house.

Variations: substitute rolled oats for the grains and dried bread crumbs. Use a small can of tomato paste, and substitute 2 tsp basil and 1 tsp oregano for the dill. This is just like the meat loaf that mother used to make except that it isn't meat. You could also add chopped green peppers.

A favorite is made from tofu, tarragon, onions, garlic, carrots, celery, cashew or hazelnut pieces lightly dry toasted, and miso paste. Serve it topped with fresh mushroom and a baked potato with tofu sour cream and a green salad.

NOT MEAT LOAF

Make the tofu dinner loaf and use 2 pkgs of Gimme Lean™ in place of the tofu. You may use bread crumbs, tomato paste, basil, oregano, and green peppers as described above.

Macaroni, Veggies, And Cheese

1½ C boiling water
1 tsp salt
1 C whole grain elbow macaroni
2 C chopped mixed veggies (onion, garlic, mushrooms, carrot, celery, broccoli, green
    beans, red peppers, etc.)
¼ C milk powder (optional)
½ C milk, cow or soya
1½ C shredded or cubed cheese

Bring water to the boil in a 2-quart pan, add salt (optional). Add macaroni slowly so that the water continues to boil. Stir. Cook for 10 minutes. Stir in veggies, starting with the ones that take the longest to cook first.. Preheat oven to 325°F. Cook for another 10 minutes. Remove from heat and stir in milk, milk powder, and 1 C of the cheese. Put in baking dish and top with remaining cheese. Bake for 20 minutes.

Dried herbs, chopped tomatoes, or fresh parsley may also be added.

Tempeh And Sweet Potato Stew

4 Tbsp oil, butter, or a mixture of the two
1 pkg tempeh
2 small onions
2 cloves garlic
1 pkg tempeh burgers (or all regular tempeh)
3 tsp ground coriander
3–4 Tbsp whole wheat bread flour
About 2 C water, more or less as needed
3 sweet potatoes, cleaned
1 bunch fresh cilantro

In a large soup pot, melt butter over medium heat. Chop onions and tempeh into 1 inch pieces. Sauté until golden. Press the garlic into the pot, add the tempeh burgers in smaller pieces than the regular tempeh, stir. Add the flour, stir. When it begins to toast, add the ground coriander. Turn heat to medium/high and stir in 1 C of cold water. Add enough water to make a good consistency. Add sweet potatoes diced into ½" pieces. Stir. Add more water as needed. Reduce heat to medium. Cook until potatoes are done. Chop the cilantro and add half to the stew after it has cooked for 6 minutes. Use the rest as a garnish on the top of each serving. Stir frequently while the sweet potatoes are cooking.

Mushroom Paté

1 Tbsp each olive oil and butter OR all olive oil
2 cooking onions, chopped (8 oz)
3 garlic cloves, chopped
2 celery stalks, finely chopped, no leaves
1 lb white mushrooms, divided in 2
½ C white grape juice OR wine
1 C hazelnuts or almonds, chopped and toasted
⅓ C fresh parsley, chopped
1½ C dry whole wheat bread crumbs
1 pkg tofu (14 oz.)
¼ tsp ground sage
1 tsp marjoram
1 tsp thyme
¼ tsp dry mustard powder
¾ tsp sea salt, optional
Cooking spray, parchment paper

Preheat oven to 375° F. Heat olive oil and sauté onions, garlic, celery, and ½ of the mushrooms, very finely chopped. Cook and stir until it makes a paste. Add grape juice and remaining mushrooms, coarsely chopped. Stir and cook until soft. Process parsley, bread crumbs, tofu, herbs, and salt until smooth. Replace blade with plastic blade and blend in veggies and nuts. Spray pans with cooking spray and spoon in paté. Bake 45 minutes to an hour or until it is firm and starts to brown around edges. Run knife around edges to loosen. Release from mold onto plate and garnish with parsley. Serve with whole grain crackers.

Tofu Bean Paté

2 C firm tofu (500 mL)
1 C cooked black beans
1 Tbsp miso paste or tamari
1½ Tbsp dried thyme
1 Tbsp olive oil
1 large cooking onion, finely chopped
1–2 cloves garlic, finely chopped
Grinding of black pepper to taste

Wrap tofu in several layers of paper towel to drain. If using canned beans, rinse them. Heat oil over medium heat and sauté onions and garlic until brown. Mash or process beans and tofu together, add remaining ingredients. Spray pan with cooking spray and spoon in mixture. Bake in 375° F oven for 45 minutes to an hour or until firm and browned.

These can be made in small foil pans. It makes 3 Baby loaves. Or a larger bread pan can be used.

Easy Whole Grain Crackers

3½ C whole wheat pastry flour
½ C sesame seeds, optional
1 ¼ tsp salt or less
½ C natural oil, include 1 Tbsp toasted sesame
1 C + 2 Tbsp cool water

Using plastic blade in food processor, mix flour, seeds, and salt. Blend oil and water together and add to flour, process until blended. Roll out very thin on lightly floured surface or cloth. Prick all over with a fork and cut into shapes. Bake on ungreased baking sheet at 350° F oven for 15–20 minutes or until lightly brown.

You may save the salt to sprinkle on the tops before pricking and cutting instead of putting in the crackers. Dill, curry, caraway seeds, cumin seeds, poppy seeds, etc can be used on top.

Chickpea And Roasted Red Pepper Spread

2 C cooked chickpeas
1 red pepper, seeded, roasted and peeled
3–4 Tbsp lemon juice
2 tsp ground cumin seeds
⅛ tsp cayenne pepper
1 tsp vegetarian or regular Worcestershire sauce
1 Tbsp roasted sesame tahini
5 garlic cloves, roasted

Wash off chickpeas and drain. Put everything in food processor and process until almost smooth. Add more of anything to taste. Some like a lot more cayenne than this, but it is an acquired taste.

Green Olive Tapenade

1 ¼ C pitted manzanilla olives, rinsed and drained
1 tsp vegetarian or regular Worcestershire sauce
1 large garlic clove, pressed
1 tsp lemon juice
¼ C extra virgin olive oil
1 Tbsp cilantro or parsley, finely chopped

Chop olives in food processor. With motor running, add remaining ingredients except greens. Process to blend. Stir in parsley or cilantro.

Use Your Recipes For Bread

Most bread recipes can be made of all whole wheat flour, even if the recipe calls for all white flour or just part whole wheat. Always use bread flour for bread. If the flour has a lot of bran, you will want to sift it out to prevent the end product from drying out. Once you find a brand of flour that you can use, adjust your recipes to deal with using this brand of flour. If there is more bran, you will need to add less water, or more flour to make up for the space the bran takes up in the measuring cup.

How To Recover Dry Bread

Preheat oven to 250° F. Crumple up a paper bag. Wet it under the tap. If the bread is very hard, wet the bag fully being careful not to let it rip. If the bread is just stale, wet the bag lightly. Put the bread into the bag and put it in the oven for 20 minutes.

Olive/Egg Bread

2 pkgs dry, non-instant yeast
2¾ C warm water
5 Tbsp Sucanat, or other dehydrated cane juice or natural sugar
2 tsp sea salt
¼ tsp cardamom
⅓ C olive oil
4 eggs
3 C whole wheat bread flour, high protein if available
1 C kalamata olives, pitted and chopped
2 C whole durham flour
2¾ C unbleached white or all-purpose flour (or use all whole wheat)
1 egg yolk, blended with 1 tsp cold water
4 tsp sesame or poppy seeds

Warm a large mixing bowl with hot water. Dissolve yeast in the water with half of the Sucanat by stirring it in. Leave it to foam up for 10 minutes. (If yeast does not foam up, in may be inactive. Start over with fresh yeast. Put the re-maining Sucanat, salt, cardamom, eggs, oil and foamed yeast mixture into the warmed bowl. Beat for 2 minutes with a whisk or electric mixer.

Add the whole wheat flour and beat until all is mixed in. Add olives and stir with a wooden spoon. Add the durham flour and mix. Add the remaining flour in small amounts and stir in. When the mixture begins to leave the sides of the bowl, stop adding flour. Sprinkle a generous amount of the remaining flour onto a clean, dry surface—a bread board or cloth is easier to clean up than a counter top, but not necessary. Dump bread onto floured surface.

Knead the bread using the heels of your hands, turning it to ensure even kneading of each section. Add flour as needed. Knead until dough is smooth and elastic; it should have the same texture and feel as your ear lobe.

Rinse the bowl with hot water and dry it, then oil it well the olive oil. Oil the dough with a small amount of olive oil and place in bowl, smooth side up. Cover bowl with a clean, dry cloth and put it in a draft-free warm place. Allow to rise for 1½ hours or until it is triple in bulk.

Punch dough in the center with your fist and make a dent to the bottom, to release the dough. Then turn it onto a clean, dry surface. Gently knead dough again for about 1 minute. Divide it into 12 equal portions.

Roll each of the 12 into equal-sized rolls and set aside. Cover with a dry cloth. Remove three and braid together, turning the ends under to seal. Do this with the remaining rolls. Place in well-oiled bread pans, or on a baking sheet for a free-form loaf.

Cover with a dry cloth and let rise in a warm place 45 minutes, or until about triple in bulk.

Mix egg yolk and water and carefully brush the tops of the risen loaves. Sprinkle each with some of the seeds. Bake in a pre-heated 375° F oven for 25 to 30 minutes or until golden.

Makes 4 loaves. You can also make smaller loaves in small tins, free formed rolls on baking sheets, or dinner rolls by placing little braids in muffin tins.

Whole-Wheat Bagels In The Food Processor

1 pkg dry yeast
½ C luke warm water
½ Tbsp salt
1 Tbsp olive oil
3 ¼ C whole-wheat bread flour
¾ C lukewarm water
1 ½ Tbsp natural sugar, evaporated cane juice, or Sucanat®

Put the lukewarm yeast and half of the sugar into a warm cup and sprinkle the yeast over it. Stir the yeast. Let it stand for 8 to 10 minutes until it foams up. Sift the dry ingredients into the bowl of the food processor, add the oil. Process for 6 to 8 seconds. Add the dissolved yeast mixture and process for 10 seconds. Add water through the feeder tube while the machine is still running. Process until the dough forms a ball on the blades. Let the machine knead the dough for about 30–40 seconds from the time the ball stage is reached.

Turn out onto a lightly floured board and knead for 1–2 minutes until the dough is smooth and elastic. Lightly oil or butter a bowl and put the dough in it. Cover with a clean towel, leave it in a warm place and let it rise for 20 minutes.

Turn the dough out onto a lightly floured board and divide it into 12 equal pieces. Roll each piece into an 8-inch rope, join the ends to form a circle. Cover with a cloth and let rise for another 20–30 minutes. (Push your finger into the dough. If it leaves a dent, it is ready. If the hole springs back, it has to rise longer.)

In a large soup pan put 4 C water, 1 tsp salt, and 1 Tbsp honey. Bring to a boil. Gently put 2 or 3 bagels in the boiling water and cook 30 seconds on each side. Remove from the water, place on a baking sheet that has been greased or covered with corn meal. Bake in a preheated 400° F oven for 25 minutes.

Note: This recipe takes about and hour and a half or more to do. Please allow enough time when you are making this recipe. Keep the dough away from any drafts, especially cold ones.

Use Your Recipes For Quick Breads And Pastries

When you use your regular recipes, you can substitute whole wheat pastry flour equally for the white flour. If there is a lot of bran, sift it out with a coarse sifter to remove the bulk of it so that your cookies or cakes do not dry out. Save the bran and add it to cereal. Experiment with different brands of whole wheat pastry flour. There are many different varieties available. Some brands have more bran than others and some brands are organically grown. Start with a recognized quality brand such as ArrowHead Mills, Bob's Red Mill, Purity Foods, Eden Organic, or ask your health food store owner for a recommended brand.

Biscuits

> 2 C whole wheat pastry flour
> 2 tsp baking powder
> ½ tsp salt
> 5 Tbsp cool butter
> ½ C milk

Sift dry ingredients together into a bowl or the bowl of a food processor. Cut in the butter* or pulse in the food processor until the butter is in small pieces like tiny peas. Add the milk and fluff with a fork or pulse with the food processor. When the dough comes together, put it on a floured surface and knead it two or three times. Using a floured rolling pin, roll it until it is about ¼ inch thick. Spread it with butter and fold it over, or just fold it over. Roll lightly to press together. Cut biscuits with a floured biscuit cutter or the top of a glass. They can be any size you want from 2 inches to 4 inches. Place them on an ungreased pan so that the edges just touch and bake in a preheated 450° F oven for 12 minutes or until evenly browned. Makes 9 to 12 biscuits depending on the size of the cutter.

*Cut in the butter. Use 2 knives held next to each and chop the butter until it is all in very tiny pieces. A pastry blender can be used for this. Kitchenware stores or supermarkets often have this. It is a D shaped implement with many blades on the rounded part and a handle on the straight edge. Use this to cut into the butter to break it up into small pieces.

HERBED BISCUITS

Add in 2 Tbsp chopped fresh herbs during the brief kneading stage and bake as directed.

SHORTBREAD BISCUITS

Make as above and add 2–3 Tbsp of natural sugar or evaporated cane juice. This makes a great base for strawberry short cake. Or can be used as a topping for cobbler.

Corn Bread

> 1 C yellow or blue corn meal
> 1 C whole wheat pastry flour
> ½ tsp sea salt
> 4 tsp baking powder
> ¼ C natural sugar
> 1 egg, slightly beaten
> 1 C milk
> ¼ C melted butter or olive oil

Sift dry ingredients together into a large bowl. Mix remaining ingredients together and stir into dry ingredients. Stir until well mixed. Bake in a greased 8-inch pan at 400° F for 30 minutes or until lightly browned.

SWEET CORN BREAD COBBLER

Slice fresh fruit, or use berries, into a 9-inch cake pan. Make a layer of fruit about ½ inch deep. Spoon the corn bread over the top and bake as directed.

SAVORY CORN BREAD COBBLER

Lightly brown sausages, meat or vegetarian, and place them in the bottom of a lightly oiled pan in a sunburst or wagon wheel pattern. Spoon the corn bread over and bake as directed.

I often add chopped fresh parsley to the corn bread for this recipe. You can also make a gravy from the sausages or make tempeh gravy and put that on top of the sausages and then the corn bread. This is a Sunday morning favorite at our house.

Quick Onion Cheese Bread

1 Tbsp butter
½ C finely chopped onion, I like to use a 'sweet' variety
1 ½ C whole wheat pastry flour
3 tsp baking powder
½ tsp salt
2 Tbsp cold butter
1 C sharp cheddar cheese, grated
3 Tbsp fresh parsley, chopped
1 large egg
½ C milk

Preheat oven to 400° F. Grease an 8-inch round or square pan. In 1 Tbsp of butter, gently sauté onion until golden brown and set aside. In a large mixing bowl or the bowl of a food processor, sift the flour, baking powder, and salt. Add the butter and cut in* or pulse until the mixture is crumbly. Stir in ½ C of the cheese. (In food processor switch to the plastic blade for this.) Mix the onion, egg, and milk together and add to the cheese mixture. Press into the pan and sprinkle the remaining cheese over the top. Bake for 25 minutes or until golden.

This makes a great base for a vegetarian evening meal. Add a dark green leafy salad that includes ripe olives, red peppers, carrots, cucumbers, tomatoes, and other raw vegetables. Top with a light dressing of olive oil and lemon juice.

*See the instructions for this under Biscuits.

Scones

2 C whole wheat pastry flour (or half wheat and half spelt)
2 tsp baking powder
½ tsp baking soda
½ tsp ground nutmeg
½ tsp salt
4 oz cold, unsalted butter (½ C)
1 C raisins or currants
2 Tbsp natural sugar
1 egg yolk
¾ C buttermilk

Sift first 5 ingredients together. Cut in the butter or work it in with your fingers until it is the size of peas. (I generally use the food processor.) Stir in the raisins or currants and the sugar. Beat the egg yolk with the buttermilk and stir it into the mixture. Mix until blended. Turn it out onto a floured surface and knead 10–12 times. Cut it in half and pat into two 6 inch circles. Slice each into 6 wedges and transfer them to an ungreased baking sheet. Bake in a preheated oven for 18–20 minutes.

Spelt Scones

    2 C spelt flour
    2 tsp baking powder
    ½ tsp baking soda
    ½ tsp salt
    ⅓ C non-instant milk powder
    ⅛ tsp garlic powder
    1 Tbsp each dill weed and chives
    1 egg
    ⅔ C water
    ⅓ C canola or olive oil

Mix dry ingredients together in bowl. Mix wet ingredients together until egg is beaten and oil is blended in. Pour wet mixture over dry and mix. Dust the working surface with spelt flour. (You might even need to use up to ⅓ C) Knead it 12–15 times and pat it flat. Divide into 12 even pieces by cutting strips to form diamonds or use a large biscuit cutter. Transfer to an ungreased baking sheet and bake in a preheated 375° F oven for 18–22 minutes.

Banana Loaf

Mix together with a potato masher, electric mixer, or food processor.

    2 Tbsp soft butter
    2 Tbsp canola oil
    2 Tbsp honey
    2 ripe bananas
    2 eggs
    ¼ C milk
    1 tsp pure vanilla extract

SIFT TOGETHER INTO THE WET MIXTURE:

    2½ C whole wheat pastry flour*
    1 tsp baking powder
    1 tsp ground cinnamon
    ½ tsp salt (if using unsalted butter)

Preheat oven to 375° F. Grease an 8 inch loaf pan. Spoon mixture into pan and bake for 50 to 60 minutes or until a tooth pick comes out clean when inserted in the thickest part.

*Substitute 1 C spelt flour for 1 C of the whole wheat pastry flour.

"Eggless" Salad

> 1 pkg firm or extra firm tofu
> ½ pkg soft tofu
> 1 Tbsp fresh parsley, finely chopped
> 4 green onions, chopped
> 1/8 C green olives, chopped (optional)
> 1 stalk green celery, finely chopped
> ½–¾ tsp turmeric powder, for color
> ½–¾ tsp celery seeds, finely ground
> 2 tsp Dijon mustard
> Tofu 'Mayo' to taste

Drain tofu and wrap in towels to absorb extra water. Mash the soft tofu and add turmeric. Chop the firm tofu. Add to bowl with remaining ingredients and stir. Let stand for 1 hour or more, for best flavor.

Note: If you are planning to make sandwiches, don't. Pack the bread and lettuce in plastic wrap. Put the tofu "eggless" salad in a jar. Put the sandwich together just before eating. The water might soak into the bread and make it soggy.

Rice Salad

> 2 C cooked brown rice, chilled
> ½ green pepper, chopped
> ½ red pepper, chopped
> 4 sprigs parsley, finely chopped

Toss together and add Green Dressing. Chill and serve. This is nice to take to pot lucks and parties, especially at holiday time.

CHICK PEAS:

Add cooked chickpeas to this for extra protein.

GREEN DRESSING

> 2 green onions
> 1 bunch fresh parsley, cilantro, basil, or dill
> 1–2 cloves garlic
> ½ C olive oil
> 1–2 tsp lemon juice

Chop onions and parsley and put into a blender or food processor and blend.

Dinner Salad

FOR EACH PERSON USE:

1 leaf green leaf lettuce
1 leaf red leaf lettuce
1 leaf Romaine lettuce
2 leaves butter lettuce
4 leaves curly endive or escarole
2 leaves spinach
⅛ red pepper
⅛ green pepper
1/16 English cucumber
6 ripe olives
1 green onion
½ carrot, grated

OR

6 baby carrots

Wash and dry leaves and slice or tear into bite sized pieces. Put into the bottom of a large soup bowl. Chop the other vegetables and add arranged in roups or spread evenly over the top. Then add some protein source.

PROTEIN SOURCES FOR EACH PERSON:

1 firm cooked egg, sliced or chopped
2 slices real cheddar cheese
3 slices smoked tofu or natural tofu sandwich slices*
2 slices jack, colby, or other cheese
¼ can drained tuna fish

Arrange in pleasing design or toss with greens and vegetables. Add dressing of your choice and serve. This is a meal in itself. Or you may add some fresh whole grain rolls or bread.

*You might cut julienne slices of any naturally cured meats. Just make sure that it doesn't have nitrates, nitrites, and sulfitic agents in it.

SALAD NIÇOISE

Use the green lettuce base in Dinner Salad and add precooked green beans and cubed potatoes, tuna fish, and niçoise olives. The traditional dressing for this is made of 3 parts olive oil to 1 part lemon juice, tarragon, pepper, and garlic.

MY RECIPES

Use pages 286–290 to create your own recipe file. Write in your favorite recipes or paste recipes in from magazines or the Internet. Below is a convenient chart for recording the names of the recipes and the pages on which you can find them. Have fun!

MY RECIPE FILE

Recipe Title	Page Number

Add Your Own Recipes Here

Add Your Own Recipes Here

Add Your Own Recipes Here

Add Your Own Recipes Here

Add Your Own Recipes Here

APPENDIX E — SOURCES OF NUTRIENTS

Where Did This Information Come From?

There are many different sources for nutritional information. I have chosen to use information furnished by the USDA (United States Department of Agriculture) in handbooks and on the official web site. The USDA does not publish the full range of known nutrients in any of their nutrient guides. For this reason there is a limited amount of listings in this book. If you wish to find a complete nutritional breakdown for any specific food, please utilize their web site called the USDA Nutrient Database:

http//www.nal.usda.gov/fnic/cgi-bin/nut_search.pl

In this database you can search for specific foods by name. It will give you breakdowns of amino acids, fatty acids, vitamins, minerals, protein, carbohydrates, calories, and other nutrients.

Recommended Dietary Allowance

The Recommended Dietary Allowances (RDA) are a set of nutritional standards established by the Committee on Dietary Allowances in the United States. These recommendations have been published since the early 1940s and are continually changed to meet changing needs and information levels of consumers. The RDA are the average daily intakes of energy and nutrients considered the minimum to meet the needs of most healthy people under usual environmental stresses. If you have greater needs, you will want to seek professional help from your doctor, nutritionist, or other health care practitioner who is knowledgeable about health and nutrition. The foods and RDAs listed are suggested for an average adult.

It's As Easy As 1, 2, 3!

To get the most out of this information, use the following three-step process:

1. Look at what your RDA is for a certain nutrient.
2. Look at how much of that nutrient the listed foods contain.
3. Consume as much as you need to reach your RDA.

Abbreviations and Conversions

tsp=teaspoon	½ C=4 oz=8 Tbsp	g=gram=1,000 milligrams
Tbsp=tablespoon=3 tsp	1 C=16 Tbsp	mg=milligram=1/1,000 gram
oz=ounce	¼ C=2 oz=4 Tbsp	mcg=microgram=1/1,000,000 gram
lb=pound=16 oz	⅓ C=5 Tbsp	

Vitamin A

RDA for women: 8,000 IU (if obtained from fruits and vegetables), 2,640 IU (if obtained from animal sources)

RDA for men: 10,000 IU (if obtained from fruits and vegetables; 3,300 IU (if obtained from animal sources)

The foods listed here have about the equivalent of approximately 500 IU of vitamin A.

½ C tempeh
1½ Tbsp butter
½ C diced cheddar cheese
½ C diced colby cheese
2½ Tbsp cream cheese
¼ C Edam cheese
⅓ C diced gruyere cheese
½ C diced monterey jack cheese
½ C muenster cheese
½ C whole milk ricotta
1½ large eggs
1½ C whole milk yogurt
1 dried apricot
½ half avocado
2 C sweet cherries
⅔ C raw elderberries
one-sixteenth mango
1 ¼ C papaya cubes
½ raw peach
1 C watermelon
¼ C cooked oatmeal
⅓ tsp ground paprika
1½ oz simmered beef kidney

one-seventeenth oz chicken liver
4 oz bluefish
2 oz pickled Atlantic herring
½ C cooked chinook salmon
2 medium globe artichokes
⅔ C green beans
½ C raw broccoli flowerets
½ C cooked Brussels sprouts
½ C cooked savoy cabbage
2 Tbsp cooked Chinese cabbage (bok-choi)
3 medium baby carrots
1½ Tbsp cooked chopped Swiss chard
1½ Tbsp cooked collard greens
1½ Tbs garden cress
½ C raw endive
3 tsp cooked kale
1 C butterhead lettuce
⅓ C shredded romaine lettuce
½ C shredded leaf lettuce
8 pods cooked okra
2½ Tbsp parsley
½ C green peas
½ C chopped green bell pepper
3 Tbsp cooked pumpkin
2 tsp cooked spinach
½ C cooked zucchini
½ C baked acorn squash
1½ tsp baked butternut squash
1½ tsp baked hubbard squash
½ half medium cooked tomato
5 Tbsp watercress
3 oz of pan fried beef liver=30,689 IU
½ C chopped chicken liver=1,146 IU
1 medium baked sweet potato=25,752 IU
1 egg=260 IU

Vitamin B$_1$–thiamin

RDA for women: 1.1 mg
RDA for men: 1.5 mg

The foods listed here have approximately the equivalent of 0.25 mg of thiamin.

WOMEN: 4 SERVINGS

MEN: 6 SERVINGS

½ tsp brewer's yeast
½ C cooked black beans
⅔ C great Northern (white) beans
½ C kidney beans
1 Tbsp wheat germ
½ C raw pistachio nuts
¼ C brazil nuts
1½ Tbsp tahini (sesame seed butter)
1 C cooked lentils
⅔ C cooked navy beans
¼ C peanuts
⅔ C soy milk
1 C tempeh
1 C tofu cubes
1 whole wheat English muffin
1 piece whole wheat pita bread
¾ C cooked couscous
1 C cooked millet
⅓ C cooked oat bran
1 C cooked oatmeal
1 C cooked brown rice
1½ C cooked whole wheat spaghetti
½ C kidneys
½ C liver
¼ C filberts
6 Tbsp Atlantic salmon
6 Tbsp bluefin tuna
½ avocado
1 C orange juice
2 C plain yogurt

Vitamin B$_2$–riboflavin

RDA for women: 1.3 mg
RDA for men: 1.7 mg

The foods listed here have approximately the equivalent of 0.25 mg of riboflavin.

WOMEN: 5+ SERVINGS

MEN: 6+ SERVINGS

1¾ tsp brewer's yeast
2 Tbsp wheat germ
½ C cooked soybeans
1½ C soy milk
½ C cheddar cheese
1 C uncreamed cottage cheese
⅔ C creamed cottage cheese
2 Tbsp feta cheese
1½ Tbsp semisoft goat cheese
1 avocado
2 mangos
2 slices rye bread
⅔ C oatmeal
6 Tbsp beef tenderloin
6 Tbsp broiled lean ground beef
1 tsp kidney meat
⅔ tsp liver
3 oz (6 Tbsp) lamb
⅔ C roasted dark meat chicken
1½ Tbsp chicken liver
⅓ C whole almonds
4 Tbsp cooked mackerel
½ C orange roughy
4 Tbsp Atlantic salmon
½ C chum salmon
1 C raw mushrooms
1 C green peas
1¼ C cooked pumpkin
⅓ C spinach
1 sweet potato
2 soft or hard boiled eggs
2 bananas

Vitamin B₃–niacin

RDA for women: 15 mg
RDA for men: 19 mg

The foods listed here have approximately the equivalent of 5 mg of niacin.

WOMEN: 3 SERVINGS

MEN: 4 SERVINGS

1½ Tbsp brewer's yeast
6 Tbsp dry roasted peanuts
5 Tbsp peanut butter
1½ C tempeh
2 avocados (California) or 1 avocado
   (Florida)
2 C cooked pearl barley,
1 C cooked couscous
1½ C cooked millet
1¼ C cooked oatmeal
2 C brown rice
4 oz (½ C) beef eye of round
4 oz lean beef tenderloin
3½ oz broiled lean ground beef
6 Tbsp beef kidney
1½ oz (3 Tbsp) beef liver
3 oz roasted leg of lamb
2 oz broiled or roasted veal
⅓ C roasted and diced light meat chicken,
½ C roasted and diced dark meat chicken
½ C sunflower seed
3 oz bluefish
6 oz Atlantic or Pacific cod
4 oz haddock
3 oz Atlantic and Pacific halibut
3 oz mackerel
4 oz orange roughy
2 oz Atlantic or chinook salmon
4 oz sardines
1½ oz swordfish
3 oz rainbow trou
1½ oz fresh tuna
1½ C green peas
2 baked potatoes

Vitamin B₆–pyridoxine

RDA for women: 1.6 mg
RDA for men: 2.0 mg

The foods listed here have approximately the equivalent of .25 mg of pyridoxine

WOMEN: 6+ SERVINGS

MEN: 8 SERVINGS

¼ C cooked chickpea
1 C cooked great northern beans
1 C cooked kidney beans
¾ C cooked lentils
¾ C cooked lima beans
¾ C cooked navy beans
3 Tbsp natural peanut butter
½ C soybeans
½ C tempeh
2 C tofu
1 C white beans
2 C plain yogurt
½ avocado
⅓ C sliced bananas or ½ large
¾ C dates
¾ C elderberries
1½ C grapes
1 mango
1¼ C melon balls
2½ C orange juice
1 C pineapple juice
½ C prune juice
⅔ C seedless raisins
1 C watermelon balls
1½ pieces whole wheat pita bread
¼ C brown rice flour
½ C dark rye flour
2 C cooked buckwheat
1 C cooked couscous
¼ C cooked oatmeal
1 C cooked brown rice
¼ C toasted wheat germ
1 C cooked wild rice

6 Tbsp braised beef brisket
6 Tbsp roasted chuck
7 Tbsp braised beef short ribs
3 Tbsp beef eye of round
3 oz (6 Tbsp) broiled lean ground beef
¼ C beef kidney
1 Tbsp liver
⅓ C chicken liver
4 oz tongue
3 oz roasted veal leg
⅓ C roasted diced light meat chicken
½ C roasted dark meat chicken
1½ oz (3 Tbsp) filberts
⅔ C pistachio nuts
¼ C sunflower seeds
⅔ C unroasted Brazil nuts
⅓ C black walnuts
⅔ C unroasted cashew nuts
3 oz striped bass
2 oz bluefish
3 oz Atlantic and Pacific cod fish
3 oz flounder or sole
2½ oz grouper
3 oz haddock
3 oz Atlantic and Pacific halibut
7 Tbsp canned mackerel
3 oz monkfish
3 oz orange roughy
5 Tbsp chinook salmon
3 oz pink salmon
5 Tbsp sea bass
5 Tbsp snapper
3 oz rainbow trout
1½ oz bluefin tuna
1 oz yellowfin tuna
3 oz turbot
1 globe artichokes
1 C shredded savoy cabbage
1 C shredded Chinese cabbage (bok-choi)
1¼ C grated raw carrots
1 C cooked cauliflower
1 C kohlrabi
1 C onions

⅔ C green peas
⅔ C chopped green bell peppers
½ baked potato
⅔ C cooked spinach
1 C cubed cooked butternut squash
⅔ C cubed cooked hubbard squash
1 medium sweet potato
1 medium ripe tomato

Folate, folic acid, or folacin
(used to be called Vitamin B₉)

RDA for women: 180 mcg
RDA for men: 200 mcg

The foods listed here have approximately the equivalent of 30 mcg of folate

WOMEN: 6 SERVINGS
(14 IF PREGNANT OR PREPARING TO BE)

MEN: 7 SERVINGS

2 Tbsp cooked black beans
3 Tbsp cooked broad beans
3 Tbsp cooked chickpeas
2 Tbsp cooked kidney beans
1½ Tbsp cooked lentils
3 Tbsp cooked lima beans
2 Tbsp cooked navy beans
4 Tbsp cooked split peas, 1
½ Tbsp natural peanut butter
5½ Tbsp cooked soybeans
5½ Tbsp tempeh
1 cup cubed tofu
1½ C whole milk cottage cheese
1 C nonfat cottage cheese
1 C ricotta cheese
1 extra large egg
1 C plain yogurt
⅓ avocada
1 C sliced banana
⅔ C blackberries
1¼ C unsweetened grapefruit juice

1 kiwi fruit
1 mango
1 C cantaloupe balls
⅔ orange
⅓ C orange juice
⅔ C cubed papaya
⅔ C pineapple juice
1 C raspberries
1 C cubed strawberries
1 heaping C cooked pearl barley
1¼ C cooked buckwheat
1 C cooked bulgar
⅔ C cooked millet
2½ Tbsp cooked oatmeal
2 tsp wheat germ
1 oz cooked kidney
1 Tbsp beef liver
1½ tsp chicken liver
8 Tbsp almonds
1½ oz (3 Tbsp) filberts
⅓ C pistachio nuts
1½ Tbsp sunflower seeds
2 Tbsp sesame seed butter or tahini
4 oz chinook salmon
½ globe artichoke
2 spears asparagus
⅔ C green beans
¼ C beet slices
⅔ C raw broccoli florets
⅓ C Brussels sprouts
1 C shredded cabbage
½ C shredded cooked savoy cabbage
½ C raw cauliflower
1 C diced raw celery
⅓ C raw endive
⅔ C shredded butterhead lettuce
⅓ C shredded romaine lettuce
1 C shredded looseleaf lettuce
1 C shiitake mushrooms
7 pods cooked okra
1 C chopped raw onion
⅓ C raw parsley
⅓ C parsnips
5 Tbsp green peas

1 C chopped green peppers
⅔ C cooked mashed rutabaga
2 Tbsp cooked spinach
¾ C cooked acorn squash
¾ C cooked mashed butternut squash
1 C cooked hubbard squash
⅔ large cooked sweet potato
2 medium ripe tomatoes
1 C chicken liver=1080 mcg
1 C cooked spinach=263 mcg
1 C green peas=100 mcg

Vitamin B₁₂–cobalamin

RDA for women and men: 2 mcg

The foods listed here have approximately the equivalent of 1 mcg vitamin B₁₂.

¾ C tempeh
1 C cheddar cheese
⅔ C cottage cheese
½ C gruyere cheese
½ C muenster cheese
1¼ C milk
⅔ C plain yogurt
1½ oz beef brisket
1½ oz beef tenderloin
1½ oz lean ground beef,
  ½ oz roasted leg of lamb
3 oz roasted veal
2 C light meat chicken
½ oz sea bass
3 oz carp
1½ oz flounder or sole
3 oz haddock
3 oz halibut
1½ oz orange roughy
1½ oz salmon
1 oz red snapper
1½ oz turbot
3 oz liver=95 mcg
¼ C chicken livers=6.7 mcg
3 oz rainbow trout=5.36 mcg

Vitamin C

RDA for women and men: 60 mg

The foods listed here have approximately the equivalent of 30 mg vitamin C.

⅓ C apple juice+ C
½ C apricot nectar+ C
2 C raw apricot halves
1 C blackberries
¾ pint blueberries
2 ½ Tbsp dried black currants
¾ C elderberries
1 heaping C fresh gooseberries
⅓ C grapefruit sections including their juice
⅓ C unsweetened grapefruit juice
⅓ large kiwi fruit
½ mango
⅓ C cantaloupe balls
½ orange
¼ C orange juice
1 large tangerine
¼ papaya
1 C raspberries
5 ½ Tbsp sliced strawberries
3 Tbsp canned pimento
½ C liver
¾ C chicken livers
½ raw broccoli florets
⅓ C Brussels sprouts
1½ C shredded raw cabbage
¾ C shredded raw red cabbage
⅔ C raw cauliflower
1 C cooked Swiss chard
1¼ C cooked collards
⅔ C cooked kale
⅓ C cooked kohlrabi
3½ Tbsp chopped green bell peppers
3½ strips yellow bell peppers
1½ baked potato
⅔ C cooked rutabaga
½ C cooked spinach

1 C cubed cooked mashed butternut squash
¾ C fresh chopped tomatoes
1 medium tomato

Vitamin D

RDA for women and men: 5 mcg
(5 mcg = 200 IU)

The foods listed here have approximately the equivalent of 50 IU.

4 SERVINGS

1¼ C Kellog's corn flakes
¾ C Nutri-Grain wheat cereal
1¾ oz (4 Tbsp) Swiss cheese
2 boiled chicken eggs
4 Tbsp chicken liver
1½ oz canned salmon
2 oz canned tuna fish
½ C milk fortified with vitamin D*

*Most dairy products and even some baked goods are fortified with vitamin D; please read the labels of prepared foods.

Please Note: Vitamin D is made on your skin from the sun shining on it. If you are a person who goes in the sun even for 10 minutes a day, you are probably getting enough vitamin D that way. If you live in an area where the sun doesn't come out for days or months on end, you will want to make sure that you consume the necessary amount of vitamin D. When you do go in the sun, it takes very little exposure for this to happen, do not eliminate the use of sun screen. If you feel you are low in vitamin D, see your doctor for a test before you begin to consume large amounts of it in the form of supplements. Perhaps your basic daily vitamin and mineral tablets have the RDA in them. Please look before you begin to take supplements.

(References for Vitamin D from *Food Values of Portions Commonly Used*, Jean A.T. Pennington and Helen Nichols Church, Harper and Row, New York, 1985.)

Vitamin E

RDA for women: 8 mg
RDA for men: 10 mg

The foods listed here have approximately the equivalent of 1 mg.

WOMEN: 8 SERVINGS

MEN: 10 SERVINGS

7 Tbsp edam cheese
7 Tbsp parmesan cheese
7 Tbsp Swiss cheese
4½ Tbsp butter
1½ tsp corn oil
2 tsp olive oil
2 tsp peanut oil
2 tsp soybean oil
½ tsp sunflower seed oil
1½ tsp Atlantic salmon
½ mango
14 Tbsp (¾ C = 2 Tbsp) whole barley
1½ tsp wheat bran
7 Tbsp dry whole wheat cereal
½ small avocado
3½ Tbsp raw asparagus
3½ Tbsp beet greens
3½ Tbsp raw green cabbage
3½ Tbsp raw chard
3 Tbsp raw dandelion greens
1 heaping Tbsp raw kale
3½ Tbsp raw mustard greens
4 Tbsp raw parsley
7 Tbsp parsnip
6 Tbsp raw green bell pepper
4 Tbsp raw spinach
1½ Tbsp raw sweet potato
3 Tbsp raw turnip greens
1½ tsp almonds
1 Tbsp brazil nuts
1 tsp filbert
1 Tbsp natural peanut butter
5 tsp pistachio nuts

4½ Tbsp walnuts
7 Tbsp almonds=15 mg
7 Tbsp filberts=21 mg
7 Tbsp sunflower seeds=44 mg
7 Tbsp wheat germ=14 mg
7 Tbsp raw sweet potato=4.56 mg

(References for Vitamin D from *Food Values of Portions Commonly Used*, Jean A.T. Pennington and Helen Nichols Church, Harper and Row, New York, 1985)

Calcium

RDA for women: 1500 mg (Old recommendations were 800 mg)
RDA for men: 1000 mg

The foods listed here have approximately the equivalent of 100 mg.

WOMEN: 15 SERVINGS

MEN: 10 SERVINGS

2 C cooked black beans
1½ C cooked broadbeans
1¼ C cooked chickpeas
¾ C cooked great northern beans
2 C cooked kidney beans
¾ C cooked navy beans
½ C cooked soybeans
⅔ C tempeh
⅓ C tofu
⅔ C cooked white beans
2 Tbsp cheddar cheese
¾ C creamed cottage cheese
½ oz Edam cheese
1½ Tbsp Feta cheese
½ oz Gouda cheese
2 Tbsp Monterey jack cheese
1 oz whole milk mozzarella cheese
2 Tbsp Muenster cheese
½ C Neufchatel cheese
2½ Tbsp part skim ricotta
1 Tbsp Swiss cheese

3½ eggs
⅓ C low-fat milk
⅓ C goat milk
⅓ C sour cream
⅓ C plain yogurt
⅔ C dried black currants
4 dried figs
2 oranges
4 dried pear halves
4 slices whole wheat bread
½ C cooked oatmeal
2½ tsp poppy seeds
⅓ C almonds
⅓ C Brazil nuts
4 Tbsp hazelnuts or filberts
2 Tbsp Atlantic sardines with bone
2 C green beans
¾ C shredded raw Chinese cabbage (bok-choi)
1 C Swiss chard
1 C cooked kale
1¼ C raw parsley
¾ C mashed cooked rutabaga
⅓ C cooked spinach
1 heaping C cooked cubes acorn squash
2 sweet potatoes

Copper

RDA for women and men: 1.5–3 mg (This is actually called estimated safe and adequate daily intake.)

The foods listed here have approximately the equivalent of 1 mg of copper.

1–3 SERVINGS

1 C tempeh
½ C almonds
½ C Brazil nuts
⅓ C cashews
8 Tbsp hazelnut or filberts
¾ C pistachio nuts

3 Tbsp unsalted sesame seeds
4 Tbsp lobster.

Most foods contain trace amounts of copper.

Iron

RDA for women: 15 mg
RDA for men: 10 mg

The foods listed here have approximately the equivalent of 1 mg of iron.

WOMEN: 15 SERVINGS

MEN: 10 SERVINGS

¼ C cooked black beans
¼ C cooked broadbeans
⅓ C cooked chickpeas
⅓ C cooked great northern beans
3 Tbsp cooked kidney beans
2 Tbsp cooked lentils
¼ C cooked lima beans
3½ Tbsp cooked navy beans
⅓ C cooked split peas
4 Tbsp natural peanut butter
1/8 C cooked soybeans
⅔ C soy milk
⅓ C cooked tempeh
2 Tbsp tofu
1 C part skim ricotta cheese
1¼ C raw apricot halves
1 C apple juice
1 C apricot nectar
½ avocado
3 Tbsp dried currants
½ C pitted dates
⅓ C raw elderberries
3 dried figs
2 halves dried peach
⅓ C prune juice
4 Tbsp raisins
1 slice whole grain bread

½ piece whole wheat pita bread
½ C cooked barley
½ C cooked buckwheat
⅔ C cooked bulgar
⅔ C cooked millet
½ C cooked oat bran
2 Tbsp cooked oatmeal
1 C cooked brown rice
1 ½ Tbsp wheat germ
1 tsp cumin seeds
1 tsp fenugreek seeds
3 oz of most cuts of beef or lamb
⅓ C chicken
3 Tbsp almonds
4 Tbsp Brazil nuts
⅓ C cashews
½ shredded unsweetened fresh coconut
1 oz dried unsweetened coconut
1 oz filberts
10 pecan halves
1½ tsp sesame tahini
⅓ C sunflower seeds
2 oz bass
6 Tbsp grouper
3 oz haddock
3 oz halibut
4 oz all fresh salmon
3 oz fresh tuna
⅓ globe artichoke
⅔ C green beans
¾ C sliced beets
½ C Brussels sprouts
¼ C cooked Swiss chard
¾ C cooked kale
1 C raw mushrooms
¼ C raw parsley
⅔ C peas
½ baked potato
¾ C cooked pumpkin
⅔ C cooked rutabaga
2½ Tbsp cooked spinach
1 C cooked zucchini
½ C cooked acorn squash

¾ C cooked butternut squash
1 large cooked sweet potato
1 large tomato
1 C cooked oatmeal=8 mg

Magnesium

RDA for women: 280 mg
RDA for men: 350 mg

The foods listed here have approximately the equivalent of 100 mg magnesium.

WOMEN: 2 3/4 SERVINGS

MEN: 3 1/2 SERVINGS

¾ C cooked black beans
1¼ C cooked great northern beans
1½ C chickpeas
1¼ C cooked kidney beans
1¼ C cooked lentils
1¼ C cooked lima beans
1 C cooked navy beans
1 ⅓ C split peas
4 Tbsp dry roasted peanuts
4 Tbsp natural peanut butter
½ C +2 Tbsp cooked soybeans
¾ C tempeh
⅓ C tofu
¾ C cooked white beans
1 Florida avocado
2½ pieces whole wheat pita bread
1¼ C cooked buckwheat
1 C cooked millet
1¼ C cooked oat bran
2 C cooked oatmeal
1¼ C cooked brown rice
¼ C wheat germ
4 Tbsp almonds
⅓ C Brazil nuts
4 Tbsp unroasted cashews
1¼ oz filberts
¾ C pistachio nuts

¾ C sunflower seeds
⅓ C walnuts
3 oz chinook salmon
⅔ C cooked Swiss chard
⅔ C cooked spinach

Potassium

RDA for women and men: 2,000 mg

The foods listed here have approximately the equivalent of 250 mg of potassium.

8 SERVINGS A DAY

⅓ C cooked black beans
½ C cooked broadbeans
½ C cooked chickpeas
⅓ C cooked great northern beans
⅓ C cooked kidney beans
⅓ C cooked lentils
¼ C cooked lima beans
⅓ C cooked navy beans
2 Tbsp natural peanut butter
⅔ C soy milk
½ C tofu
⅔ C milk
¾ C whole milk yogurt
⅔ C low-fat yogurt
1 C apple juice
½ C raw apricot halves
1 C apricot nectar
¼ avocado
½ C sliced bananas
1 C blackberries
1 C sweet cherries
3 Tbsp dried currants
3 Tbsp dates
2 dried figs
¾ C grape juice
1 kiwi
¾ mango
½ C cantaloupe balls

1 nectarine
1 large orange
½ C orange juice
⅔ C cubed papaya
1 medium peach
1 large pear
1 ½ plums
½ C prune juice
3 Tbsp raisins
1 C strawberry halves

Sodium

RDA for women and men: 500 mg (This is actually called estimated safe and adequate daily intake.)

The foods listed here have approximately the equivalent of 100 mg of sodium.

TRY TO KEEP SODIUM UNDER 500 MG A DAY, 2–4 SERVINGS.

1 oz. canned chickpeas
1½ Tbsp salted peanut butter
⅓ tsp soy sauce (tamari)
2 Tbsp grated cheddar cheese
2 Tbsp colby cheese
2 Tbsp cottage cheese
½ oz gouda cheese
2 Tbsp mozzarella cheese
2 Tbsp neufchatel cheese
½ C whole milk ricotta
1 C whole milk
½ C 2% or nonfat milk
¾ C sour cream
1 C whole milk yogurt
¾ C low-fat or nonfat yogurt
2 tsp margarine
2 medium ripe olives
⅓ bagel
1 whole wheat dinner roll
¼ whole wheat English muffin

½ white hamburger or hotdog roll
4 triscuits or woven wheats
⅓ C cooked oats prepared with salt
1 tsp catsup
¾ C most meats
1 slice cooked bacon
1½ tsp ham
1 C roasted or stewed chicken
½ slice bologna
¼ hot dog
6 Tbsp baked carp
6 Tbsp cod
4 Tbsp canned sardines
1 C cooked fresh tuna
2 C shredded Chinese cabbage
2½ C grated carrots
3 C cooked cauliflower
1 C raw diced celery
¾ C cooked spinach.

Zinc

RDA for women: 12 mg
RDA for men: 15 mg

The foods listed here have approximately the equivalent of 1 mg of zinc.

WOMEN: 12 SERVINGS

MEN: 15 SERVINGS

½ C cooked black beans
⅓ C cooked chickpeas
⅔ C cooked great northern beans,

⅓ C cooked lentils
½ C cooked navy beans
½ C cooked split peas
2 Tbsp peanuts or peanut butter
½ C cooked soybeans
⅓ C tempeh
½ C tofu
¼ C diced cheddar or colby cheese
¾ C cottage cheese
1 C most milks
½ C yogurt
1 piece whole wheat pita bread
2 slices whole grain bread
⅔ C cooked barley
1 C cooked buckwheat groats
1 C cooked bulgur
½ C cooked millet
1 C cooked oats
⅔ C cooked brown rice
1 C cooked whole wheat cereal
1 C cooked whole wheat macaroni
1 C cooked whole wheat spaghetti
2 Tbsp most meats
⅔ C cooked chicken
2 Tbsp almonds
2 Tbsp Brazil nuts
2 Tbsp cashew nuts
3 Tbsp filberts or hazelnuts
⅔ C pistachio nuts
2 Tbsp sunflower seeds
½ C shiitake mushrooms
½ C green peas
⅔ C cooked spinach

ENDNOTES

Chapter 1

1. Graham, Billy, *ANGELS*, p. 149.
2. Jakes, T. D., *LAY ASIDE THE WEIGHT*, p. 68.
3. Cherry, Reginald, M.D., *THE BIBLE CURE*, p. 69.
4. Baldinger, Kathleen, *THE WORLD'S OLDEST HEALTH PLAN*, p. 44.
5. Whitaker, Julian, M.D., *MEDICAL MEMORY BOOSTERS AND BRAIN ENHANCERS*, p.
6. Cooper, Kenneth, M.D., *ADVANCED NUTRITIONAL THERAPIES*, p. 292.
7. Whitaker, Julian, M.D., *MEDICAL MEMORY BOOSTERS AND BRAIN ENHANCERS*, p.3.
8. U.S. Department of Agriculture Human Nutrition Service, *HOME AND GARDEN BULLETIN*, #252. Note: This and other government information can be obtained by calling the Consumer Information Department (toll free) at 1-888-878-3256. Or contact them through their internet site, www.pueblo.csa.gov.
9. Cooper, Kenneth H., M.D., *ADVANCED NUTRITIONAL THERAPIES*, p. 294.
10. Smith, Pamela, *HEALTHY EXPECTATIONS*, p. 18.
11. Hartman, Jack and Judy, *INCREASED ENERGY AND VITALITY*, p. 132.
12. Salaman, Maureen, *THE DIET BIBLE: THE BIBLE FOR DIETERS*, p. 59.
13. Swope, Dr. Mary Ruth, *ARE YOU SICK AND TIRED OF FEELING SICK AND TIRED?*, p. 116.
14. Frähm, Anne E. and David J., *HEALTHY HABITS*, p. 42.
15. Ibid., p. 43.
16. Swope, Dr. Mary Ruth, *ARE YOU SICK AND TIRED OF FEELING SICK AND TIRED?*, p. 116.

Chapter 2

1. Jacobs, D.R., Jr., Meyer, K.A., Kushi, L.H., Folsom, A.R., "Whole-Grain Intake May Reduce The Risk Of Ischemic Heart Disease Death In Postmenopausal Women: The Iowa Women's Health Study," *AMERICAN JOURNAL OF CLINICAL NUTRITION*, August 1998, pp. 248–257.
2. Chatenoud, L., Tavani, A., La Vecchia, C., Jacobs, D.R., Jr., Negri, E., Levi, F., Franceschi, S., "Whole Grain Food Intake And Cancer Risk," *INTERNATIONAL JOURNAL OF CANCER*, July 1998, pp. 24–28.
3. Jacobs, D.R. Jr., Marquart, L., Slavin, J., Kushi, L.H., "Whole-Grain Intake And Cancer: An Expanded Review And Meta-Analysis," *NUTRITION AND CANCER*, 1998, pp. 85–96.
4. Smith, Pam, *HEALTHY EXPECTATIONS*, p. 104.
5. Townsley, Cheryl, *FOOD SMART*, p. 116.
6. Thompson, L.U., *Antioxidants And Hormone-Mediated Health Benefits Of Whole Grains*, *CRITICAL REVIEWS IN FOOD SCIENCE AND NUTRITION*, 1994, pp. 473–497.
7. Slavin, J., Jacobs, D., Marquart, L., "Whole-Grain Consumption And Chronic Disease: Protective Mechanisms," *NUTRITION AND CANCER*, 1997, pp. 14–21.
8. Cherry, Reginald, M.D., *THE BIBLE CURE*, p. 89.
9. Purity Foods Internet Home Page (http://www.purityfoods.com)
10. Swope, Dr. Mary Ruth, *THE SPIRITUAL ROOTS OF BARLEY*, p. 87.
11. Cherry, Reginald, M.D., *THE BIBLE CURE*, p. 89.
12. Ibid., p. 89.
13. Salaman, Maureen, *THE DIET BIBLE: THE BIBLE FOR DIETERS*, p. 227.
14. Townsley, Cheryl, *FOOD SMART*, p. 116.

Chapter 3

1. Russell, Rex, M.D., *WHAT THE BIBLE SAYS ABOUT HEALTHY LIVING*, p. 104.
2. Salaman, Maureen, *THE DIET BIBLE: THE BIBLE FOR DIETERS*, p. 226.
3. Cherry, Reginald, M.D., *THE BIBLE CURE*, p. 88.
4. Townsley, Cheryl, *FOOD SMART*, p. 120.
5. Jones, L.A., Gonzalez, R., Pillow, P.C., Gomez-Garza, S.A., Foreman, C.J., Chilton, J.A., Linares, A., Yick, J., Badrei, M., Hajek, R.A., "Dietary Fiber, Hispanics, And Breast Cancer Risk?," *ANNALS OF THE NEW YORK ACADEMY OF SCIENCES*, December 1997, pp. 524-536.
6. Russell, Rex, M.D., *WHAT THE BIBLE SAYS ABOUT HEALTHY LIVING*, p. 104.
7. Cherry, Reginald, M.D., *THE BIBLE CURE*, p. 106.
8. Ibid., p. 89.
9. Townsley, Cheryl, *FOOD SMART*, p. 120.
10. Haak, V.S., Chesters, J.G., Vollendorf, N.W., Story, J.A., Marlett, J.A., "Increasing Amounts Of Dietary Fiber Provided By Foods Normalizes Physiologic Response Of Large Bowel Without Altering Calcium Balance Or Fecal Steroid Excretion," *AMERICAN JOURNAL OF CLINICAL NUTRITION*, September 1998, pp. 615–622.
11. Williams, C.L., "Importance Of Dietary Fiber In Childhood," *JOURNAL OF THE AMERICAN DIETETIC ASSOCIATION*, October 1995, pp. 1140-1146.
12. Anderson, J.W., Riddell–Lawrence, S., Floor, T.L., Dillon, D.W., Oeltgen, P.R., "Bakery Products Lower Serum Cholesterol Concentrations In Hypercholesterolemic Men," *AMERICAN JOURNAL OF CLINICAL NUTRITION*, November 1991, pp. 836–840.

13. *"Soy Protein In Adult Human Nutrition: A Review With New Data,"* in *SOY PROTEIN AND HUMAN NUTRITION,* edited by H. Wilcke, D. Hopkins, D. Waggle, Academic Press, 1979.
14. Jakes, T.D., *LAY ASIDE THE WEIGHT,* p. 125.
15. Contreras, Francisco, M.D., *HEALTH IN THE 21ST CENTURY,* p. 278.
16. Dalu, A., Haskell, J.F., Coward, L., Lamartiniere, C.A., *"Genistein, A Component Of Soy, Inhibits The Expression Of The Egf And Erbb2/Neu Receptors In The Rat Dorsolateral Prostate,"* PROSTATE, September 1998 pp. 36–43.
17. Contreras, Francisco, M.D., *HEALTH IN THE 21ST CENTURY,* p. 278.
18. Bingham, S.A., Atkinson, C., Liggins, J., Bluck, L., Coward, A., *"Phytoestrogens: Where Are We Now?"* BRITISH JOURNAL OF NUTRITION, May 1998, pp. 393–406.
19. Cherry, Reginald, M.D., *THE BIBLE CURE,* p. 117.
20. Blotman, F., Maheu, E., Wulwik, A., Caspard, H., Lopez, A., *"Efficacy And Safety Of Avocado/Soybean Unsaponifiables In The Treatment Of Symptomatic Osteoarthritis Of The Knee And Hip. A Prospective, Multicenter, Three-Month, Randomized, Double-Blind, Placebo-Controlled Trial,"* REVUE DU RHUMATISME, ENGLISH EDITION, December 1997, pp. 825–34.

Chapter 4

1. Russell, Rex, M.D.,*WHAT THE BIBLE SAYS ABOUT HEALTHY LIVING,* p. 183.
2. Hartman, Jack and Judy, *INCREASED ENERGY AND VITALITY,* p. 132.
3. Pearson, Mark A., *CHRISTIAN HEALING,* p.288.
4. Frähm, Anne E. and David J., *A CANCER BATTLE PLAN,* p.71.
5. Hartman, Jack and Judy, *INCREASED ENERGY AND VITALITY,* p. 131.
6. Favero, A., Parpinel, M., Franceschi, S., *"Diet And Risk Of Breast Cancer: Major Findings From An Italian Case-Control Study,"* BIOMEDICINE AND PHARMACOTHERAPY, 1998, pp. 109–115.
7. Frähm, Anne E. and David J., *HEALTHY HABITS,* p. 104.
8. Dennison, B.A., Rockwell, H.L., Baker, S.L., *"Fruit And Vegetable Intake In Young Children,"* JOURNAL OF THE AMERICAN COLLEGE OF NUTRITION, August 17, 1998, pp. 371–378.
9. Wolever, T.M., Jenkins, D.J., *"What Is A High Fiber Diet?"* ADVANCES IN EXPERIMENTAL MEDICINE AND BIOLOGY, 1997, pp. 35–42.
10. Hill, M.J., *"Nutrition And Human Cancer,"* ANNALS OF THE NEW YORK ACADEMY OF SCIENCES, December 29, 1997, pp. 68-78.
11. Cooper, Kenneth H., M.D., *ADVANCED NUTRITIONAL THERAPIES,* p.43.
12. Craig, W.J., *"Phytochemicals: Guardians Of Our Health,"* JOURNAL OF THE AMERICAN DIETETIC ASSOCIATION," October 1997, pp. S199–S204.
13. Cooper, Kenneth H., M.D., *ADVANCED NUTRITIONAL THERAPIES,* p. 191.
14. O'Keefe, J.H., Jr., Lavie, C.J., Jr., McCallister, B.D., *"Insights Into The Pathogenesis And Prevention Of Coronary Artery Disease,"* MAYO CLINIC PROCEEDINGS, January 1995, pp. 69–79.
15. Whitaker, Julian, M.D., *DR. WHITAKER'S GUIDE TO NATURAL HEALING,* p. 38.

16. Frähm, Anne E. and David J., *HEALTHY HABITS,* pp. 67-68.
17. Gonzaez de Mejia, E., Quintanar-Hernandez, A., Loarca-Pina, G., *"Antimutagenic Activity Of Carotenoids In Green Peppers Against Some Nitroarenes,"* MUTATION RESEARCH, August 7, 1998, pp. 11–19.
18. Cooper, Kenneth H., M.D., *ADVANCED NUTRITIONAL THERAPIES,* p. 68.
19. Whitaker, Julian, M.D., *DR. WHITAKER'S GUIDE TO NATURAL HEALING,* 1995, p. 41.
20. Townsley,Cheryl, *FOOD SMART,* p. 103.
21. Cherry, Reginald, M.D., *THE BIBLE CURE,* p. 101.
22. Contreras, Francisco, M.D., *HEALTH IN THE 21ST CENTURY,* p. 303.
23. Russell, Rex, M.D., *WHAT THE BIBLE SAYS ABOUT HEALTHY LIVING,* p. 196.
24. Kumar, M., Berwal, J.S., *"Sensitivity Of Food Pathogens To Garlic,"* JOURNAL OF APPLIED MICROBIOLOGY, February 1998, pp. 213–215.
25. Berthold, H.K., Sudhop, T., von Bergmann, K., *"Effect Of A Garlic Oil Preparation On Serum Lipoproteins And Cholesterol Metabolism: A Randomized Controlled Trial,"* JOURNAL OF THE AMERICAN MEDICAL ASSOCIATION, June 17, 1998, pp. 1900–1902.
26. Bordia, A., Verma, S.K., Srivastava, K.C., *"Effect Of Garlic On Blood Lipids, Blood Sugar, Fibrinogen And Fibrinolytic Activity In Patients With Coronary Artery Disease,"* PROSTAGLAN-DINS, LEUKOTRIENES, AND ESSENTIAL FATTY ACIDS, April 1998, pp. 257–263.
27. Steiner, M., Lin, R.S., *"Changes To Platelet Function And Susceptibility Of Lipoproteins To Oxidation Associated With Administration Of Aged Garlic Extract,"* JOURNAL OF CARDIOVASCULAR PHARMACOLOGY, June 1998, pp. 904–908.
28. Efendy, J.L., Simmons, D.L., Campbell, G.R., Campbell, J.H., *"The Effect Of Aged Gralic Extract, 'Kyolic', On The Development Of Experimental Atherosclerosis,"* ATHEROSCLE-ROSIS, July 1997, pp. 37-42.

Chapter 5

1. Russell, Rex, M.D., *WHAT THE BIBLE SAYS ABOUT HEALTHY LIVING,* p.122.
2. Chisholm, A., et al., *"A Diet Rich In Walnuts Favourably Influences Plasma Fatty Acid Profile In Moderately Hyperlipidaemic Subjects,"* EUROPEAN JOURNAL OF CLINICAL NUTRITION, January 1998, pp.12-16.
3. Frähm, Anne E. and David J., *HEALTHY HABITS,* p. 104.
4. Abbey, M., Noakes, M., Belling, G.B., Nestel, P.J., *"Partial Replacement Of Saturated Fatty Acids With Almonds Or Walnuts Lowers Total Plasma Cholesterol And Low-Density-Lipoprotein Cholesterol,"* AMERICAN JOURNAL OF CLINICAL NUTRITION, May 1994, pp. 995-999; Spiller, G.A., et al., *"Nuts And Plasma Lipids: An Almond-Based Diet Lowers Ldl-C While Preserving Hdl-C,"* JOURNAL OF THE AMERICAN COLLEGE OF NUTRITION, June 1998, pp. 285–290.
5. Reginald Cherry, M.D., *THE BIBLE CURE,* p. 73.
6. Gray, J.B., Martinovic, A.M., *"Eicosanoids And Essential Fatty Acid Modulation In Chronic Disease And The Chronic Fatigue Syndrome,"* MEDICAL HYPOTHESIS, July 1994, pp. 31–42.
7. Hornstra, G., et al., *"Essential Fatty Acids In Pregnancy And Early Human Development,"* EUROPEAN JOURNAL OF

OBSTETRICS, GYNECOLOGY, AND REPRODUCTIVE
BIOLOGY, July 1995, pp. 57–62.

8. Siguel, E.N., Lerman, R.H., "Prevalence Of Essential Fatty
    Acid Deficiency In Patients With Chronic Gastrointestinal
    Disorders," METABOLISM: CLINICAL AND EXPERIMENTAL,
    January 1996, pp. 12–23.

9. Kruger, M.C., Horrobin, D.F., "Calcium Metabolism,
    Osteoporosis And Essential Fatty Acids: A Review," PROGRESS
    IN LIPID RESEARCH, September 1997, pp. 131–151.

10. Russell, Rex, M.D., WHAT THE BIBLE SAYS ABOUT
    HEALTHY LIVING, p.122.

11. Cherry, Reginald, M.D., THE BIBLE CURE, p. 98.

12. Sieja, K., "Selenium Deficiency In Women With Ovarian Cancer
    Undergoing Chemotherapy And The Influence Of Supplementa-
    tion With This Micro-Element On Biochemical Parameters,"
    PHARMAZIE, July 1998, pp. 473–476.

13. Townsley, Cheryl , FOOD SMART, p.119.

14. Ibid., p. 119.

15. Ibid., p. 119.

16. Russell, Rex, M.D., WHAT THE BIBLE SAYS ABOUT
    HEALTHY LIVING, p.112.

17. Smith, Pamela, HEALTHY EXPECTATIONS, p. 233.

18. hriner, Jim, ETERNALLY FIT, p. 39.

19. Rodriguez, Artalejo F., et al., "Consumption Of Fruit And Wine
    And The Decline In Cerebrovascular Disease Mortality In Spain,
    Stroke," STROKE, August 29, 1998, pp. 1556–1561.

20. Cherry, Reginald, M.D., THE BIBLE CURE, p. 112.

21. Clement, M.V., et al., "Chemopreventive Agent Resveratrol,"
    BLOOD, August 1, 1998, pp. 996–1002.

22. Levi, F., et al., "Food Groups And Risk Of Oral And Pharyngeal
    Cancer," INTERNATIONAL JOURNAL OF CANCER, August
    31, 1998, pp. 705–709.

23. de Whalley, C.V., et al., "Flavonoids Inhibit The Oxidative
    Modification Of Low Density Lipoproteins By Macrophages,"
    BIOCHEMICAL PHARMACOLOGY, June 1, 1990, pp. 1743–
    1750.

24. Joseph, J.A., et al., "Long Term Dietary Strawberry, Spinach,
    Or Vitamin E Supplementation Retards The Onset Of
    Age-Related Neuronal Signal-Transduction And Cognitive
    Behavioral Deficits," JOURNAL OF NEUROSCIENCE,
    October 1, 1998, pp. 8047–8055.

25. Contreras, Francisco, M.D., HEALTH IN THE 21ST
    CENTURY, p. 279.

26. Smith, Pamela, HEALTHY EXPECTATIONS, p.174.

27. Contreras, Francisco, M.D., HEALTH IN THE 21ST
    CENTURY, p. 279.

28. Jakes, T.D., LAY ASIDE THE WEIGHT, p. 124.

29. Russell, Rex, M.D., WHAT THE BIBLE SAYS ABOUT
    HEALTHY LIVING, p.189.

30. Visioli, F., and Galli, C., "Oleuropein Protects Low Density
    Lipoprotein From Oxidation," LIFE SCIENCES, 1994, pp.
    1965–1971.

31. Russell, Rex, M.D., WHAT THE BIBLE SAYS ABOUT
    HEALTHY LIVING, p.134.

32. Aziz, N.H., et al., "Comparative Antibacterial And Antifungal
    Effects Of Some Phenolic Compounds," MICROBIOS, 1998, pp.
    43-54. BIOLOGY, June 1998, pp. 981–987; Tranter, H.S.,
    Tassou, S.C., Nychas, G33. Koutsoumanis, K., et al.,
    "Modelling The Effectiveness Of A Natural Antimicrobial On
    Salmonella Enteritidis," JOURNAL OF APPLIED MICRO.J.,
    "The Effect Of The Olive Phenolic Compound, Oleuropein, On
    The Growth Of Enterotoxin B Production By Staphyloccus

Aureus," JOURNAL OF APPLIED MICROBIOLOGY, March
1993, pp. 253-259; Austin, J.W., et al., "Growth And Toxin
Production By Clostridium Botulinum," JOURNAL OF FOOD
PROTECTION, March 1998, pp. 324–328.

34. Cherry, Reginald, M.D., THE BIBLE CURE, p. 82.

35. Baldinger, Kathleen O'Bannon, "Olive Leaf Extract: Ancient
    Solution To Modern Ailments," NATURE'S IMPACT, December/
    January 1999.

Chapter 6

1. Baldinger, Kathleen O'Bannon, THE WORLD'S OLDEST
    HEALTH PLAN, p. 166.

2. Kushi, L.H., Lenart, E.B., Willett. W.C., "Health Implications
    Of Mediterranean Diets In Light Of Contemporary Knowledge,"
    AMERICAN JOURNAL OF CLINICAL NUTRITION, June
    1995, pp.1407S–1415S.

3. Smith, Pamela, HEALTHY EXPECTATIONS, p. 87.

4. Schwartz, George, FOOD POWER, p. 96.

5. Strehlow, Wighard, HILDEGARD OF BINGEN'S MEDICINE,
    p. 32.

6. Smith, Pamela, HEALTHY EXPECTATIONS, p. 104.

7. Carper, Jean, FOOD YOUR MIRACLE MEDICINE, p. 18.

8. Albertson, A.M., Tobelmann, R.C., Marquart, L., "Estimated
    Dietary Calcium Intake And Food Sources," JOURNAL OF
    ADOLESCENT HEALTH, January 1997, pp. 20–26

9. Frähm, Anne E. and David J., HEALTHY HABITS, p. 63.

10. Cherry, Reginald, M.D., THE BIBLE CURE, p. 116.

11. Shriner, Jim, ETERNALLY FIT, p. 28.

12. Massey, L.K., Kynast-Gales, S.A., "Substituting Milk For Apple
    Juice Does Not Increase Kidney Stone Risk," JOURNAL OF THE
    AMERICAN DIETETIC ASSOCIATION, March 1998, pp.
    303–308.

13. McIlhaney, Joe S., M.D., 1001 HEALTH-CARE QUESTIONS
    WOMEN ASK, pp. 310.

14. Rubaltelli, F.F., et al., "Intestinal Flora In Breast- And
    Bottle-Fed Infants", JOURNAL OF PERINATAL MEDICINE,
    1998, pp. 186–191.

15. Murray, Michael, ENCYCLOPEDIA OF NATURAL MEDI-
    CINE, p. 157.

16. Erasmus, Udo, THE COMPLETE GUIDE TO FATS AND OILS
    IN HEALTH AND NUTRITION, p. 218.

17. Russell, Rex, M.D., WHAT THE BIBLE SAYS ABOUT
    HEALTHY LIVING, p. 216.

18. Ber, Leonid, Gazella, Karolyn, ACTIVATE YOUR IMMUNE
    SYSTEM, p. 41.

19. Rona, Zoltan, THE COLOSTRUM OPTION: ALL THE
    NATURAL ANTI-AGING GROWTH HORMONES AND
    IMMUNE ENHANCERS PROVIDED BY MOTHER NATURE!,
    p. 3.

20. Yamada, Y., Saito, S., Morikawa, H., "Hepatocyte Growth
    Factor In Human Breast Milk," AMERICAN JOURNAL OF
    REPRODUCTIVE IMMUNOLOGY, August 1998, pp. 112–
    120.

21. Li, Y.M., "Glycation Ligand Binding Motif In Lactoferrin,"
    ADVANCES IN EXPERIMENTAL MEDICINE AND BIOLOGY,
    1998, pp. 57–63.

22. Swart, P.J., et al., "Lactoferrin. Antiviral Activity Of
    Lactoferrin," ADVANCES IN EXPERIMENTAL MEDICINE
    AND BIOLOGY, 1998, pp. 205–213.

23. McIlhaney, Joe, 1001 HEALTH-CARE QUESTIONS WOMEN
    ASK, p. 311.

24. Salaman, Maureen, *THE DIET BIBLE:THE BIBLE FOR DIETERS*, p. 228.
25. Schaafsma, G., et al., *"Effects Of Milk Products, Fermented By Lactobacillus Acidophilus,"* EUROPEAN JOURNAL OF CLINICAL NUTRITION, June 1998, pp. 436–440.
26. Shalev, E., et al., *"Ingestion Of Yogurt Containing Lactobacillus Acidophilus,"* ARCHIVES OF FAMILY MEDICINE, November/December 1996, pp. 593–596.
27. Smith, Pamela, *HEALTHY EXPECTATIONS*, p. 87.
28. Salaman, Maureen, *THE DIET BIBLE:THE BIBLE FOR DIETERS*, p. 140.
29. Shriner, Jim, *ETERNALLY FIT*, p. 39.
30. Swope, Dr. Mary Ruth, *ARE YOU SICK AND TIRED OF FEELING SICK AND TIRED?* p. 86.

Chapter 7

1. Baldinger, Kathleen O'Bannon, *THE WORLD'S OLDEST HEALTH PLAN*, p. 281.
2. Barker, Kenneth, Ed., *THE NIV STUDY BIBLE*, p. 1602.
3. Shriner, Jim, *ETERNALLY FIT*, p. 30.
4. Cooper, Kenneth H., M.D., *ADVANCED NUTRITIONAL THERAPIES*, p. 167.
5. Maurage, C., et al., *"Effect Of Two Types Of Fish Oil Supplementation On Plasma And Erythrocyte Phospholipids In Formula-Fed Term Infants,"* BIOLOGY OF THE NEONATE, December 1998, pp. 416–429.
6. Petridou, E., et al., *"Diet During Pregnancy And The Risk Of Cerebral Palsy,"* BRITISH JOURNAL OF NUTRITION, May 1998, pp. 407–412.
7. Whitaker, Julian, M.D., *THE PAIN RELIEF BREAK-THROUGH*, pp. 153.
8. Dry, J., Vincent, D., *"EFFECT OF FISH OIL DIET ON ASTHMA,"* INTERNATIONAL ARCHIVES OF ALLERGY AND APPLIED IMMUNOLOGY, 1991, pp. 156-157; Hansen, G., et al., *"Nutritional Status Of Danish Patients With Rheumatoid Arthritis And Effects Of A Diet Adjusted In Energy Intake, Fish Content, And Antioxidants,"* UGESKRIFT FOR LAEGER, May 18, 1998, pp. 3074–3078.
9. Calder, P.C., *"Immunoregulatory And Inti-Inflammatory Effects Of N-3 Polyunsaturated Fatty Acids,"* BRAZILIAN JOURNAL OF MEDICAL AND BIOLOGICAL RESEARCH, April 1998, pp. 467–490.
10. Whitaker, Julian, M.D., *THE PAIN RELIEF BREAK-THROUGH*, p. 174.
11. Cherry, Reginald, M.D., *THE BIBLE CURE*, p. 82.
12. Gerster, H., *"Can Adults Adequately Convert Alpha-Linolenic Acid To Eicosapentaenoic Acid And Docosahexaenoic Acid?",* INTERNATIONAL JOURNAL FOR VITAMIN AND NUTRI-TION RESEARCH, 1998, pp. 159–173.
13. Cooper, Kenneth H., M.D., *ADVANCED NUTRITIONAL THERAPIES*, p. 220.
14. Sheard, N.F., *"Fish Consumption And Risk Of Sudden Cardiac Death,"* NUTRITION REVIEWS, June 1998, pp. 177-179; Landmark, K., *"Fish, Fish Oils, Arrhythmias And Sudden Death,"* TIDSSKRIFT FOR DEN NORSKE LAEGEFORENING, June 1998, pp. 2328–2381.
15. Bao, D.Q., et al., *"Effects Of Dietary Fish And Weight Reduction On Ambulatory Blood Pressure In Overweight Hypertensives,"* HYPERTENSION, pp. 710–717.
16. Jakes, T.D., *LAY ASIDE THE WEIGHT*, p. 95.

Chapter 8

1. Townsley, Cheryl, *FOOD SMART*, p. 246.
2. Negishi, T., Rai, H., Hayatsu, H., *"Antigenotoxic Activity Of Natural Chlorophylls,"* MUTATION RESEARCH, May 1997, pp. 97–100.
3. Harttig, U., Bailey, G.S., *"Chemoprotection By Natural Chlorophylls In Vivo,"* CARCINOGENESIS, July 1998, pp. 1323–1326.
4. Cherry, Reginald, M.D.,*THE BIBLE CURE*, p. 119.
5. Balch, James F. and Phyllis A., *PRESCRIPTION FOR NUTRITIONAL HEALING*, p. 75.
6. Townsley, Cheryl, *FOOD SMART*, p. 248.
7. Balch, James F. and Phyllis A., *PRESCRIPTION FOR NUTRITIONAL HEALING*, p. 69.
8. Omura, Y., et al., *"Significant Mercury Deposits In Internal Organs Following The Removal Of Dental Amalgam,"* ACUPUNCTURE AND ELECTRO-THERAPEUTICS RESEARCH, April 1996, pp. 133–160.
9. Contreras, Francisco, M.D., *HEALTH IN THE 21ST CENTURY*, p. 273.
10. Townsley, Cheryl, *FOOD SMART*, p. 250.
11. Tanaka, K., et al., *"Oral Administration Of A Unicellular Green Algae, Chlorella Vulgaris, Prevents Stress-Induced Ulcer,"* PLANTA MEDICA, October 1997, pp. 465–466.
12. Noda, K., et al., *"A Water-Soluble Antitumor Glycoprotein From Chlorella Vulgaris,"* PLANTA MEDICA, October 1996, pp. 423–426.
13. Kim, H.M., et al., *"Inhibitory Effect Of Mast Cell-Mediated Immediate-Type Allergic Reactions In Rats By Spirulina,"* BIOCHEMICAL PHARMACOLOGY, April 1998, pp. 1071–1076.
14. Buletsa, B.A., et al., *"The Prevalence, Structure And Clinical Problems Of Multiple Sclerosis,"* LIKARSKA SPRAVA, October/December 1996, pp. 163–165.
15. Cherry, Reginald, M.D., *THE BIBLE CURE*, p. 119.
16. Baldinger, Kathleen O'Bannon, *THE WORLD'S OLDEST HEALTH PLAN*, Starburst Publishers, 1994, p. 160.
17. Vehling, Joseph Dommers, editor and translator, *Apicius, Cookery and Dining in Imperial Rome*, Dover Publications, New York, 1977.
18. Smith, Pamela, *HEALTHY EXPECTATIONS*, p. 87.
19. Townsley, Cheryl, *FOOD SMART*, p. 249.
20. Seddon, J.M., et al., *"Dietary Carotenoids, Vitamins A, C, E, And Advanced Age-Related Macular Degeneration,"* JOURNAL OF THE AMERICAN MEDICAL ASSOCIATION, November 9, 1994, pp. 1413–1420.
21. Seddon, J.M., et al., *A Prospective Study Of Cigarette Smoking And Age-Related Macular Degeneration In Women*, JOURNAL OF THE AMERICAN MEDICAL ASSOCIATION, October 9, 1996, pp. 1141–1146.
22. Cooper, Kenneth H., M.D., *ADVANCED NUTRITIONAL THERAPIES*, p. 219.
23. Jennings, E., *"Folic Acid As A Cancer-Preventing Agent,"* MEDICAL HYPOTHESES, September 1995, pp. 297–303.
24. Contreras, Francisco, M.D., *HEALTH IN THE 21ST CENTURY*, p. 278.
25. Eskes, T.K., *"Open Or Closed? A World Of Difference: A History Of Homocysteine Research,"* NUTRITION REVIEWS, August 1998, pp. 236–244.

Chapter 9

1. Townsley, Cheryl, *FOOD SMART*, pp. 114–115.
2. Contreras, Francisco, M.D., *HEALTH IN THE 21ST CENTURY*, p. 293.
3. Kushi, L.H., Lenart, E.B., Willett, W.C., *"Health Implications Of Mediterranean Diets In Light Of Contemporary Knowledge,"* AMERICAN JOURNAL OF CLINICAL NUTRITION, June 1995, pp. 1416s–1427s.
4. Whitaker, Julian, M.D., *THE PAIN RELIEF BREAKTHROUGH*, p. 153.
5. Salaman, Maureen, *THE DIET BIBLE: THE BIBLE FOR DIETERS*, p. 57.
6. Shriner, Jim, *ETERNALLY FIT*, p. 29.
7. DeMarini, D.M., *"Dietary Interventions Of Human Carcinogenesis,"* MUTATION RESEARCH, May 1998, p. 457–465.
8. Shriner, Jim, *ETERNALLY FIT*, p. 29.
9. Cherry, Reginald, M.D., *THE BIBLE CURE*, p. 78.
10. Salaman, Maureen, *THE DIET BIBLE: THE BIBLE FOR DIETERS*, p. 59.
11. Ibid., p. 63.

Chapter 10

1. Hepper, Nigel F., *BAKER ENCYCLOPEDIA OF BIBLE PLANTS*, p. 118.
2. Townsley, Cheryl, *FOOD SMART*, p. 113.
3. Ibid., p. 113.
4. Ibid., p. 112.
5. Swope, Dr. Mary Ruth, *ARE YOU SICK AND TIRED OF FEELING SICK AND TIRED?* p. 165.
6. Chisholm, D.J., Campbell, L.V., Kraegen, E.W., *"Pathogenesis Of The Insulin Resistance Syndrome (Syndrome X),"* CLINICAL AND EXPERIMENTAL PHARMACOLOGY AND PHYSIOLOGY, September 1997, pp. 782–784.
7. Barnard, R.J., et al., *"Diet-Induced Insulin Resistance Precedes Other Aspects Of The Metabolic Syndrome,"* JOURNAL OF APPLIED PHYSIOLOGY, April 1998, pp. 1311–1315.
8. Yip, J., Facchini, F.S., Reaven, G.M., *"Resistance To Insulin-Mediated Glucose Disposal As A Predictor Of Cardiovascular Disease.,"* JOURNAL OF CLINICAL ENDOCRINOLOGY AND METABOLISM, August 1998, pp. 2773–2776.
9. Baillie, G.M., et al, *"Insulin And Coronary Artery Disease,"* ANNALS OF PHARMACOTHERAPY, February 1998, pp. 233–247.
10. Hardin, D.S., et al., *"Treatment Of Childhood Syndrome X,"* PEDIATRICS, August 1997, p. E5.
11. Cherry, Reginald, M.D., *THE BIBLE CURE*, p. 106.
12. Russell, Rex, M.D., *WHAT THE BIBLE SAYS ABOUT HEALTHY LIVING*, p. 204.
13. Cappuccio, F.P., et al., *"Double-Blind Randomised Trial Of Modest Salt Restriction In Older People,"* LANCET, September 1997, pp. 850–854.
14. Smith, Pamela, *HEALTHY EXPECTATIONS*, p. 191.
15. Cooper, Kenneth H., M.D., *ADVANCED NUTRITIONAL THERAPIES*, p. 324.
16. Fuenmayor, N., et al., *"Salt Sensitivity is Associated with Insulin Resistance in Essential Hypertension,"* AMERICAN JOURNAL OF HYPERTENSION, April 1998, pp. 397–402.
17. Cooper, Kenneth H., M.D., *ADVANCED NUTRITIONAL THERAPIES*, p. 337.
18. Salaman, Maureen, *THE DIET BIBLE: THE BIBLE FOR DIETERS*, p. 163.
19. Russell, Rex, M.D. *WHAT THE BIBLE SAYS ABOUT HEALTHY LIVING*, p. 235.
20. Cook, C.C., *"B Vitamin Deficiency And Neuropsychiatric Syndromes In Alcohol Misuse,"* ALCOHOL AND ALCOHOLISM, July 1998, pp. 317–336.

Chapter 11

1. Russell, Rex, M.D., *WHAT THE BIBLE SAYS ABOUT HEALTHY LIVING*, p. 153.
2. Swope, Dr.Mary Ruth, *ARE YOU SICK AND TIRED OF FEELING SICK AND TIRED?* p. 77.
3. Frähm, Anne E. and David J., *HEALTHY HABITS*, p. 46.
4. Townsley, Cheryl, *FOOD SMART*, p. 121.
5. Russell, Rex, M.D., *WHAT THE BIBLE SAYS ABOUT HEALTHY LIVING*, p. 155.
6. McMillen, S.I., M.D., *NONE OF THESE DISEASES*, p. 25.
7. *FOOD SAFETY IN THE KITCHEN: A "HACCP" APPROACH*, Food Safety and Inspection Service, United States Department of Agriculture, Consumer Education And Information Booklet.
8. McMillen, S.I., M.D., *NONE OF THESE DISEASES*, p. 23.
9. Ibid., p. 15.
10. Huang, S.W., Kimborough, J.W., *"Mold Allergy Is A Risk Factor For Persistent Cold-Like Symptoms In Children,"* CLINICAL PEDIATRICS, December 1997, pp. 695-699.
11. Halonen, M., et al., *"Alternaria As A Major Allergen For Asthma In Children Raised In A Desert Environment,"* AMERICAN JOURNAL OF RESPIRATORY AND CRITICAL CARE MEDICINE, April 1997, pp. 1356–1361.
12. Li, C.S., Hsu, C.W., Tai, M.L., *"Indoor Pollution And Sick Building Syndrome Symptoms Among Workers In Day-Care Centers,"* ARCHIVES OF ENVIRONMENTAL HEALTH, May-June 1997, pp. 200–207.
13. Contreras, Francisco, M.D., *HEALTH IN THE 21ST CENTURY*, pp. 86.
14. Fung, F., Clark, R., Williams, S., *"Stachybotrys, A Mycotoxin-Producing Fungus Of Increasing Toxicologic Importance,"* JOURNAL OF TOXICOLOGY. CLINICAL TOXICOLOGY, 1998, pp. 79–86.
15. Yin, M.C., Cheung, W.S., *"Inhibition Of Aspergillus Niger And Aspergillus Flavus By Some Herbs And Spices,"* JOURNAL OF FOOD PROTECTION, January 1998, pp. 123–125.

Chapter 12

1. Townsley, Cheryl, *FOOD SMART*, p. 16.
2. Wagemaker, Herbert, M.D., *THE SURPRISING TRUTH ABOUT DEPRESSION*, p. 161.
3. Ibid., p. 161.
4. Blumenthal, D.R., Neeman J., Murphy, C.M., *"Lifetime Exposure To Interparental Physical And Verbal Aggression And Symptom Expression In College Students,"* VIOLENCE AND VICTIMS, 1998, pp. 175–196.
5. Beardslee, W.R., Versage, E.M., Gladstone, T.R., *"Children Of Affectively Ill Parents: A Review Of The Past 10 Years,"* JOURNAL OF THE AMERICAN ACADEMY OF CHILD AND ADOLESCENT PSYCHIATRY, November 1998, pp. 1134–1141.
6. Townsley, Cheryl, *FOOD SMART*, p. 16.
7. Russell, Rex, M.D., *WHAT THE BIBLE SAYS ABOUT HEALTHY LIVING*, p. 98.

8. Markus, C.R., et al., *"Does Carbohydrate-Rich, Protein-Poor Food Prevent A Deterioration Of Mood And Cognitive Performance Of Stress-Prone Subjects When Subjected To A Stressful Task?,"* APPETITE, August 1998, pp. 49-65.
9. Edwards, R., Peet, M., Shay, J., Horrobin, D., *"Omega-3 Polyunsaturated Fatty Acid Levels In The Diet And In Red Blood Cell Membranes Of Depressed Patients,"* JOURNAL OF AFFECTIVE DISORDERS, March 1998, pp. 149–155.
10. Shriner, Jim, ETERNALLY FIT, pp. 25–26.
11. Hager, W. David, M.D., and Hager, Linda Carruth, STRESS AND THE WOMAN'S BODY, p. 207.
12. Wells, A.S., et al., *"Alterations In Mood After Changing To A Low-Fat Diet,"* BRITISH JOURNAL OF NUTRITION, January 1998, pp. 23–30.
13. Townsley, Cheryl, FOOD SMART, pp. 16, 21.
14. Smith, Pamela, HEALTHY EXPECTATIONS, p. 224.
15. Townsley, Cheryl, FOOD SMART, p. 90.
16. Bennett, Rita, HOW TO PRAY FOR INNER HEALING, p. 77.
17. Alpert, J.E., Fava, M., *"Nutrition And Depression: The Role Of Folate,"* NUTRITION REVIEWS, May 1997, pp. 145-149.
18. Birdsall, T.C., *"5-Hydroxytryptophan: A Clinically-Effective Serotonin Precursor,"* ALTERNATIVE MEDICINE REVIEW, August 1998, pp. 271–280.
19. Bloomfield, Harold, M.D., Nordfors, Mikael, M.D., McWilliams, Peter, HYPERICUM AND DEPRESSION, p. 54.
20. Whitaker, Julian, M.D., THE PAIN RELIEF BREAK-THROUGH, p. 168.
21. Grisaru, N., et al., *"Transcranial Magnetic Stimulation In Mania,"* AMERICAN JOURNAL OF PSYCHIATRY, November 1998, pp. 1608–1610.
22. Whitaker, Julian, M.D., THE PAIN RELIEF BREAK-THROUGH, p. 68.

Chapter 13

1. Jakes, T.D., LAY ASIDE THE WEIGHT, p. 68.
2. Littauer, Florence, YOUR PERSONALITY TREE, p. 203.
3. Swope, Dr.Mary Ruth, ARE YOU SICK AND TIRED OF BEING SICK AND TIRED? p. 118.
4. Jakes, T.D., LAY ASIDE THE WEIGHT, p. 49.
5. Shriner, Jim, ETERNALLY FIT, pp. 38–39.
6. Jakes, T.D., LAY ASIDE THE WEIGHT, p. 49.
7. Smith, Pamela, HEALTHY EXPECTATIONS, p. 11.
8. Jakes, T.D., LAY ASIDE THE WEIGHT, p. 125.
9. Wagemaker, Herbert, M.D., THE SURPRISING TRUTH ABOUT DEPRESSION, p. 42..
10. Cooper, Kenneth H, M.D., IT'S BETTER TO BELIEVE, p. 7.
11. Steward, H. Leighton, Morrison, C. Bethea, Samuel, S. Andrew, Balart, Luis, SUGAR BUSTERS! p. 35.
12. Coyle, Neva, LOVED ON A GRANDER SCALE, p. 74.
13. Siegel, A.J., *"The Biblical Diagnostician And The Anorexic Bride,"* FERTILITY AND STERILITY, January 1998, pp. 8-10.
14. McIlhaney, Joe, M.D., 1001 HEALTH-CARE QUESTIONS WOMEN ASK, p. 80.
15. Littauer, Florence, YOUR PERSONALITY TREE, p. 195.
16. Coyle, Neva, LOVED ON A GRANDER SCALE, p. 76.
17. Bennett, Rita, THE EMOTIONALLY FREE® COURSE PRAYER COUNSELOR'S STUDY GUIDE, p. 33.
18. Jimerson, D.C., et al., *"Decreased Serotonin Function In Bulimia Nervosa,"* ARCHIVES OF GENERAL PSYCHIATRY, June 1997, pp. 529–534.
19. Littauer, Florence, YOUR PERSONALITY TREE, p. 203.
20. Fråhm, Anne E. and David J., HEALTHY HABITS, p. 180.

ALSO OF INTEREST:

Pipher, Mary , Ph.D. REVIVING OPHELIA, G.P. Putnam's Sons, 1994.
O'Neill, Cheryl Boone, STARVING FOR ATTENTION, Continuum, 1982.
Minirth, Frank, M.D., Meier, Paul, M.D., Hemfelt, Robert, M.D., Sneed, Sharon, M.D., LOVE HUNGER, Thomas Nelson, 1990.
Littauer, Fred and Florence, FREEING YOUR MIND FROM MEMORIES THAT BIND, Thomas Nelson.

Chapter 14

1. Crook, William, M.D., THE YEAST CONNECTION, preface, p. i.
2. Huang, S.W., Kimbrough, J.W., *"Mold Allergy Is A Risk Factor For Persistent Cold-Like Symptoms In Children,"* CLINICAL PEDIATRICS, December 1997, pp. 695–699.
3. Crook, William, M.D., THE YEAST CONNECTION AND THE WOMAN, p. 56.
4. Ibid., pp. 42–43.
5. Cherry, Reginald, M.D., THE BIBLE CURE, p. 38.
6. Salaman, Maureen, THE DIET BIBLE: THE BIBLE FOR DIETERS, p. 131.
7. Ramsey, K.H., Poulsen, C.E., Motiu, P.P., *"The In Vitro Antimicrobial Capacity Of Human Colostrum Against Chlamydia Trachomatis,"* JOURNAL OF REPRODUCTIVE IMMUNOLOGY, July 1998, pp. 155-167; Wakabayashi, H., et al., *"Enhanced Anti-Candida Activity Of Neutrophils And Azole Antifungal Agents In Th Presence Of Lactoferrin-Related Compounds,"* ADVANCES IN EXPERIMENTAL MEDICINE AND BIOLOGY, 1998, pp. 229–237.
8. Concha, J.M., Moore, L.S., Holloway, W.J., *"Antifungal Activity Of Melaleuca Alternifolia (Tea-Tree) Oil Against Various Pathogenic Organisms,"* JOURNAL OF THE AMERICAN PODIATRIC MEDICAL ASSOCIATION, October 1998, pp. 489–492.
9. Cherry, Reginald, M.D., THE BIBLE CURE, p. 38.
10. Littauer, Florence, YOUR PERSONALITY TREE, p. 204
11. Cherry, Reginald, M.D., THE BIBLE CURE, p. 38

Chapter 15

1. Townsley, Cheryl, FOOD SMART, p. 20.
2. Salaman, Maureen, THE DIET BIBLE: THE BIBLE FOR DIETERS, p. 6.
3. Russell, Rex, M.D., WHAT THE BIBLE SAYS ABOUT HEALTHY LIVING, p. 235.
4. Nurminen, M.L., Korpela, R., Vapaatola, H., *"Dietary Factors In The Pathogenesis And Treatment Of Hypertension,"* ANNALS OF MEDICINE, April 1998, pp. 143–150.
5. Breithaupt-Grogler, K., et al., *"Protective Effect Of Chronic Garlic Intake On Elastic Properties Of Aorta In The Elderly,"* CIRCULATION, October 1997, pp. 2649–2655.
6. Lau, E.M., Woo, J., *"Nutrition And Osteoporosis,"* CURRENT OPINION IN RHEUMATOLOGY, July 1998, pp. 368–372.
7. Townsley, Cheryl, FOOD SMART, p. 21.
8. Pearson, Mark, CHRISTIAN HEALING, pp. 120-121.
9. Townsley, Cheryl, FOOD SMART, p. 22.
10. Cooper, Kenneth H., M.D., IT'S BETTER TO BELIEVE, p. 183.
11. Pearson, Mark, CHRISTIAN HEALING, p. 58.
12. Hager, W. David, M.D., and Hager, Linda Carruth, STRESS AND THE WOMAN'S BODY, p. 209.

Chapter 16

1. Gosselink, R., Decramer, M., *"Peripheral Skeletal Muscles And Exercise Performance In Patients With COPD,"* MONALDI ARCHIVES FOR CHEST DISEASE, August 1998, pp. 419–423.
2. Platz, E.A., et al., *"Physical Activity And Benign Prostatic Hyperplasia,"* ARCHIVES OF INTERNAL MEDICINE, November 1998, pp. 2349–2356.
3. Zerahn, B., et al., *"Bone Loss After Hip Fracture Is Correlated To The Postoperative Degree Of Mobilisation,"* ARCHIVES OF ORTHOPAEDIC AND TRAUMA SURGERY, 1998, pp. 453–456.
4. Shriner, Jim, *ETERNALLY FIT*, p. 94.
5. Smith, W.A., *"Fibromyalgia Syndrome,"* NURSING CLINICS OF NORTH AMERICA, December 1998, pp. 653–669.
6. Tanaka, H., Reiling, M.J., Seals, D.R., *"Regular Walking Increases Peak Limb Vasodilatory Capacity Of Older Hypertensive Humans,"* JOURNAL OF HYPERTENSION, April 1998, pp. 423–428.
7. Iwamoto, J., et al., *"Effect Of Increased Physical Activity On Bone Mineral Density In Postmenopausal Osteoporotic Women,"* KEIO JOURNAL OF MEDICINE, September 1998, pp. 157–161.
8. Contreras, Francisco, M.D., *HEALTH IN THE 21ST CENTURY*, p. 291.
9. Jakes, T.D., *LAY ASIDE THE WEIGHT*, p. 53.
10. Whitaker, Julian, M.D., *DR. WHITAKER'S GUIDE TO NATURAL HEALING*, p. 32.
11. Whitaker, Juilan, M.D. and Adderly, Brenda, M.H.A., *THE PAIN RELIEF BREAKTHROUGH*, p. 39.

Chapter 17

1. Whitaker, Julian, M.D., *DR. WHITAKER'S GUIDE TO NATURAL HEALING*, p. 27.
2. Jakes, T.D., *LAY ASIDE THE WEIGHT*, p. 52.
3. Townsley, Cheryl, *FOOD SMART*, p. 33.
4. Petrie, J.R., Cleland, S.J., Small, M., *"The Metabolic Syndrome: Overeating, Inactivity, Poor Compliance Or 'Dud' Advice?"*, DIABETIC MEDICINE, November 1998, pp. S29–S31.
5. Cherry, Reginald, M.D., *THE BIBLE CURE*, p. 110.
6. Christen, A.G., Christen, J.A., *"Horace Fletcher (1849–1919): "The Great Masticator,"* JOURNAL OF THE HISTORY OF DENTISTRY, November 1997, pp. 95–100.
7. Jakes, T.D., *LAY ASIDE THE WEIGHT*, p. 109.

Chapter 18

1. Strassfeld, Michael, *THE JEWISH HOLIDAYS*, p. 85.
2. Jakes, T.D., *LAY ASIDE THE WEIGHT*, p. 93.
3. Townsley, Cheryl, *FOOD SMART*, pp. 182-183.
4. Russell, Rex, M.D., *WHAT THE BIBLE SAYS ABOUT HEALTHY LIVING*, p. 89.
5. Ibid., p. 93.

The following excerpts are used by permission with all rights reserved:

Cherry, Reginald, *THE BIBLE CURE*; Creation House, Orlando, FL

Cooper, Kenneth, *ADVANCED NUTRITIONAL THERAPIES*; *IT'S BETTER TO BELIEVE*; Thomas Nelson, Nashville, TN

Russell, Rex, *WHAT THE BIBLE SAYS ABOUT HEALTHY LIVING*; Regal, A Division of Gospel Light, Ventura, CA

Smith, Pamela, *HEALTHY EXPECTATIONS*; Creation House, Orlando, FL

Townsley, Cheryl, *FOODSMART*; Jeremy P. Tarcher/Putnam, NewYork, NY. For additional information about Cheryl Townsley's book, contact LIFESTYLE FOR HEALTH, P.O. Box 3871, Littleton, CO 80161.

INDEX

A

Abbess, **24**
Abimelech, 78
Abraham, 81
Acid, **43**
Acidophilus culture, **198**
Acquired Immune Deficiency
    Syndrome (AIDS), **88–89**
Acute, **103**
Acute psychotic state, **186**
Adam, 4, 180
ADD, **239**
Additives in meat, 152–153
Aerobic, **221**
Age-related macular degeneration,
    118
AIDS, **88**
Alcohol, 146–147
    dangers of, 147
Algae, virtues of, 116–117 (*See also*
    individual types of algae)
Alginates, **61**
Allergens, **89**
Allergies, mechanism of, 85
Almonds, 66, 67
    virtues of, 67
Alpha-linolenic acid, **102**
Alternaria, **161**
Amaranth, **20**
Amino acids, **36,** 45, 83
    essential, 36
information resources on, 37
Amy's, 39
Anger, deleterious effects of, 212
Anointing, **11**
Anorexia nervosa, **188**
    characteristics of typical patient,
        192

Anti-aggregate, **45**
Anti-atherosclerotic, **74**
Antibiotics:
    cautions about, 198
    in meat, 152–153
Antibiotic resistant, **153**
Anti-inflammatory agents, **103**
Antimicrobial, **77**
Antioxidants, **12**
    sources of, 56, 75, 147
    types of, 65
Aorta, **208**
Ark, **5**
Arrogance, **155**
Arrowhead Mills, 39
Arteriosclerosis, **56,** 61
Artificial sweeteners, 16
Asafoetida, **41**
Ashpenaz, 50
Atherogenetic, **76**
Atherosclerosis, **12, 56**
Autism, **197**
Autoimmune, **88**
Avocados, 6
    virtues of, 47

B

Babylon, 35
Baked, **106**
Baker Encyclopedia of Bible Plants,
    66
Baking soda, 43
Barbara's Bakery, 39
Barley, 8, 20, **25–27,** 36
    in Bible times, 25–26
    as home remedy, 26
    roasted, 23
    soup, 27

used by Jesus, 25, 26
uses of, 26–27
Barley Green, 116
Barley water, 26
B complex vitamins, **9,** 59
    depletion by alcohol, 147
    depletion by white flour
        products, 42
    functions of, 24, 42
    in grains, 21
    replacing, in white flour
        products, 28
    sources of, 38, 66
Beano™, 41
Beans, 6, 35, 36, 37, 38–39, 40–47,
    49, 65, 115
    canned, 40, 43
    cooking, 42, 43–44
    and diabetes, 41
    freezing, 43
    and gas, 41
    healthiest ways to prepare, 43,
        44
    as medicine, 39–40
    nutritional properties of, 38
    pressure cooking, 43
    production of, 9
    recommended allowance of, 39
    slow cooking, 43
    soaking, 42, 43
    sugar content of canned, 40
    types of, 9
    virtues of, 38, 40
    (*See also* individual types of
        beans)
Bedsores, **111**
Beef tallow, **90**
Benign prostatic hyperplasia, **216**

Bennett, Rita:
  on anorexia/bulimia, 192
  on depression, 176
Beta-carotene, 54
  functions of, 57
  sources of, 52, 75
Beta-1,3-D-glucan, **89**, 90,
  202
Bible Diet:
  cheese in, 82
  dairy foods in, 81–96
  derivation of, 7
  fish in, 97–107
  fruit in, 71–79
  grains in, 19–33
  legumes in, 35–48
  nuts in, 65–69
  olives in, 75
  salt in, 141–145
  scriptural basis of, 3, 7
  sweeteners in, 135–140
  vegetables in, 49–63
  weight loss and, 186
  yogurt in, 82
  (*See also* Mediterranean
    Diet)
Bible times, **7**
  barley in, 25–26
  bread in, 8, 29, 30
  diet in, 55, 58
  eating customs during,
    226
  fasting in, 233–234
  feasts in, 225
  fishing in, 98
  milk in, 95
  pasta in, 32
  salt in, 142
Bilberry, **118**
Bile, **114**
Bingen, Hildegard von:
  on goat's milk, 84
  on spelt, 24
Bioavailable, **86**
Biotin, **202**
Birth Order Book, 192
Bitter herbs, **109**
  nutritional properties
    of, 111
  in Seder, 109–110, 224
  virtues of, 119
  ways to use in cooking,
    110, 111–112
  when to eat, 111
Black cherry juice, virtues
  of, 74

Blight, **195**, 196
Blood sugar:
  causes of fluctuations
    in, 182
  and depression, 171
  function of, 181
  symptoms of wrong
    levels of, 181, 184
  (*See also* Hyperglyce-
    mia; Hypoglycemia)
Blue-green algaes, **116**
Bob's Red Mill, 39
Body fat, **40**
Bok choy, **119**
Boron, **86**, 87
Bovine, **90**
Bran, **22**, 23
  functions of, 24
Brazil nuts, nutritional
  properties of, 68
Bread:
  in Bible times, 8, 29, 30
  breaking, commanded
    by Jesus, 31
  Ezekiel, 36, 37, 38, 47
  importance in ancient
    diets, 8–9, 30
  in prayers of Jesus, 8–9
  unleavened, 109
  use of as wages, 9
Breakfast, importance of,
  183, 184
Breakfast food, 57–58, 94,
  105, 128–129, 183,
  185
Breast-feeding, benefits of,
  88–89
Brine, **76**, **142**
Broiled, **106**
Buckwheat, **20**
Bulgar wheat, **39**
Bulimia nervosa, 189
  characteristics of
    typical patient, 191,
    192
Bulk fiber, **71**
Butter:
  production of, 13
Buttermilk, 91

C
Calcium, **13**, 44, 58
  depleted by soft drinks,
    86
  recommended
    allowance of, 86, 87

sources of, 82, 86, 87,
  209
  virtues of, 52
Camembert cheese, **196**
Candida albicans, **196**
  effects of, 196–197
  (*See also* Yeast
    Syndrome)
Capillaries, **45**
Carbohydrates, **9**
  complex, 40
  sources of, 38
  and Syndrome X, 140
  types of, 139
Carcinogenic, **56**
Carcinogenic hormones,
  75
Carcinogens, **22**, **74**
Cardiac, **77**
Cardiac arrhythmia, **104**
Cardiovascular, **22**
Cardiovascular disease,
  140
Carob pods, **135**
Carotenoids, **56**, **118**
Carrots, 49, 56
Cascadian Farm, 39
Cataracts, **56**
Cattle:
  domestication of, 81
  modern husbandry
    practices, 83, 152–
    153
Cellulose, 70
Cerebral palsy (CP), **103**
Cerebrovascular, **72**
Chard, 209
Cheddar cheese, 13, 94
  nutritional properties
    of, 44
Cheese, 91
  in Bible Diet, 82
  discovery of, 93
  goat's milk, 84
  mold in, 196
  nutritional properties
    of, 13, 95
  production of, 13, 93,
    94–95
  recommended
    allowance of, 95
  sheep's milk, 84
  as source of protein, 12,
    13
  types of, 13, 94
  virtues of, 13

Cherry, Reginald:
  on barley, 25
  on beans, 41
  on Brazil nuts, 68
  on calcium, 86
  on causes of poor
    health, 200
  on chlorophyll, 111
  on Ezekiel bread, 38
  on fiber and blood
    sugar, 140
  on fiber and diabetes,
    41
  on fish, 104
  on garlic, 59
  on Mediterranean Diet,
    8
  on millet, 28
  on nuts, 67
  on olive oil, 78
  on protein, 127
  on soybeans, 46
  on spelt, 23, 28
  on spiritual causes of
    disease, 202, 204
  on spirulina, 116
  on wheat, 23
Chewing, importance of,
  40, 58, 229
Chinese parsley (*See*
  Cilantro)
Chlorella, 116
Chlorophyll, **111**
  uses of, 112
Cholesterol, **11**, 17
  HDL, 61, 66, 67
  LDL, 12, 66, 67, 76
  serum, 45, 114
Choline, **130**
Chronic, **103**
Chronic fatigue syndrome,
  67
Chronic gastrointestinal
  disorders, **67**
Chronic obstructive
  pulmonary disease
  (COPD), **216**
Cilantro:
  as aid in removing lead,
    115
  as aid in removing
    mercury, 114
Clean, **42**
Clear liquids, **236**
Cognitive behavioral
  deficits, **74**

Collard greens, **86**
Colon, **70**
Colostrum:
    benefits of, 89–90
    composition of, 89–90
Commands, **195**
Complete protein, **36**, 44, 45
Complex carbohydrates, **40**
Condiments, **128**
Coney, **132**, **151**
Confess, **176**, 203
Contreras, Francisco:
    on amount of exercise needed, 218
    on fat, 122
    on fruits, 74, 75
    on garlic, 59
    on herbs, 114, 119
    on indoor contaminants, 162
    on soybeans, 45, 46
    on vegetables, 74, 114, 119
Cooper, Kenneth:
    on beta-carotene, 56
    on fish, 102, 104
    on greens and eye disease, 118
    on importance of emotional health, 212
    on olive oil, 12
    on Mediterranean Diet, 10
    on need for a healthy diet, 186
    on salt, 144
    on vegetables, 55
    on water, 145
Copper, 59, 83
Coriander (*See* Cilantro)
Coyle, Neva:
    on bulimia, 191
    on healthy diet, 188
Cranberries, virtues of, 74
Crave, **181**
Cravings, 180–181, 182
Created, **3**
Creation, story of, 3–4
Crohn's disease, **67**
Crook, William, on *Candida* syndrome, 196, 197
Cruciferous, **115**

Cucumbers, 51, 58
    nutritional properties of, 59
    virtues of, 59
Cud, **151**
Curdle, **91**
Curds, 13, 14, **91**. 93
    formation of, 91
Curses, **195–205**
    in the Bible, 195–196
Cystic fibrosis, **67–68**

D
Dairy foods, 36
    in Bible Diet, 81–96
    in Mediterranean diet, 13–14
    necessary in vegetarian diets, 83
    nutritional properties of, 83
    recommended allowance of, 82, 83
    recommended types of, 14
    (*See also* Cheese; Curds; Milk; Yogurt)
Dandelion greens, 109
    uses of, 113
    virtues of, 114
Daniel, 49–50
Davis, Adelle, 86, 106
Day of Atonement (Yom Kippur), **225**
    observance of, 225
Deceit, **155**
Decrees, **195**
Dehydrated, **145**
Dehydrated cane juice, **138**
Dementia, **128**
Dental amalgams, **114**
Depression, 165–178
    advice for dealing with, 168
    in the Bible, 165–166, 171
    blood sugar and, 171
    causes of, 168
    levels of, 166, 167
    methods of treating, 170–177
    music and, 174–175
    nutrition and, 170, 171–173, 176–177
    prayer and, 176

symptoms of, 166–167
    use of medication in treatment, 175
Despondent, **174**
Detoxify, **111**, **145**
DHA, **102**
Diabetes:
    and fiber, 40–41
    and overeating, 229
Diet, **7**
    of Adam and Eve, 4
    addition of meat to, after Flood, 6
    in Bible times, 55, 58
    composition of ideal, 10, 55
    decision making regarding, 62
    in depression, 170
    development in human infants, 6
    high-fiber, 54
    importance to health, 6, 50
    importance of proper, 17–18
    importance of variety in, 6
    individual choices about, 156
    of Israelites, 15
    of Jesus, 8–9, 14, 154, 185
    keeping log of, 141
    Mediterranean, *see* Mediterranean Diet
    of Noah, 5
    precautions before changing, 40
    in pregnancy and lactation, 90, 103, 126
    of Romans, 15
    for weight loss, 185, 186
    for Yeast Syndrome, 199–202
Diet for a Small Planet, 37
Diseases, **3**
Diverticulitis, **39**
DNA, **118**
Drosophila, **111**
Dulse, **61**
Durum wheat, **20**
Dysthymia, **167**
    symptoms of, 167

E
Eating disorders, 179–194
    advice for coping with, 189, 192–193
    in the Bible, 188–193
    causes of, 189–190, 191
    as form of rebellion, 191–192
    means of treating, 192
    (*See also* Anorexia nervosa; Bulimia nervosa)
Edema, **142**
Eden Foods, 39
EDTA, **43**
Eggs, 36, 129–131
    as hidden ingredient, 132
    nutritional properties of, 130
    recommended allowance of, 15, 129–130, 131–132
    in Seder, 224
    virtues of, 130
    ways of preparing, 131
Elijah, depression of, 165–166, 167, 168, 169–170, 181
Elisha, 25, 26, 98
Elkanah, 188
Emmer wheat, 8, 23
Emotions, effect on health, 207–213
Empty calories, 124
Endocrine glands, **114**
Enzymes, **52**, **110**
EPA, **102**
Ephah, **22**
Esau, 44
Essential amino acids, **36**
Essential fatty acids (EFAs), virtues of, 67
Estrogen, synthetic versus natural, 46
Euphrates river, 5
Eutychus, 31
Eve, 4, 180
Exercise, 215–221
    amount needed, 218, 221
    checking pulse during, 219
    importance of, 187

incorporating into daily
    life, 218–219
and osteoporosis, 217
types of, 215, 220
    (*See also* Walking)
Ezekiel, punishment of, 35
Ezekiel bread, 36, 47
    nutritional properties
      of, 37
    virtues of, 38
Ezra, 16

F
Fable, **78**
Fall of man, **14**
Family dynamics, **189**
Farming:
    development of, after
      Flood, 6
    role in civilization, 6
Fasting, 233–241
    in Bible times, 233–234
    benefits of, 239–240
    cautions before
      attempting, 235,
      237
    coming off, 238
    how to do, 236–239
    Jesus' view of, 240
    in other cultures, 233,
      237
    possible health
      problems associated
      with, 233, 234–235
    practices of Jesus, 234
    reasons for, 235–236
    types of, 233, 234
Fat, **11**, 121–133
    biblical rules about,
      121–122
    dangers of, 18, 122–
      123, 125
    functions of, 123, 124
    healthiest types of, 125,
      173
    hydrogenated, 122
    necessity for health,
      123–124
    nutritional properties
      of, 124
    polyunsaturated, 11
    recommended
      allowance of, 124
    types of, 11, 121–122
Fat-soluble vitamins, **68**
Fatty acids:

types of, 67
unsaturated, 124
Feast of Atonement, 223,
    225
Feast of First Fruits, 223
Feast of Tabernacles, 223
Feast of Trumpets (Rosh
    Hashanah), **16**, 223
Feast of Unleavened Bread,
    223, 224
Feasts, 223–231
    in Bible times, 225
    definition of, 223
    of Jews, 223–225
Fermented, **14**
Fertility and Sterility, 188
Feta cheese, 13, 84
Fiber, **9**, 54
    bulk, 71
    and diabetes, 40–41
    in grains, 21
    recommended
      allowance of, 44–45,
      54
    soluble versus
      insoluble, 70
    sources of, 38, 39
    virtues of, 23–24, 39,
      41, 54
Fibromyalgia, **197, 217**
Figs, 73, 86
    cakes of, 74
Fish:
    advice on buying, 106
    benefits to heart, 104–
      105, 208
    in the Bible, 97, 98
    in Bible diet, 97–107
    as "brain food," 104
    as breakfast food, 105
    cautions about, 98
    fat in, 101
    in Jesus' diet, 14
    in Mediterranean diet,
      14–15, 98, 99, 100
    nutritional properties
      of, 14, 100, 105
    recommended
      allowance of, 100,
      103, 104
    recommended ways of
      preparing, 15, 100,
      106
    shellfish, 102
    smell of, 106
    as a snack, 105

as symbol of Jesus, 97
tuna, 100
types of, 100–102
virtues of, 52, 102, 103
Fishing:
    in Bible times, 98
    occupation of Jesus'
      disciples, 97, 98
Fish oil, 104
    anti-inflammatory
      properties of, 103
    and cerebral palsy, 103
5-HTP, **177,** 192
Flash frozen, **53**
Flavonoids, **74**
Flax:
    benefits of, 208
    uses of, 70
Flaxseed, **65,** 70–71, 170
    in the Bible, 70
    nutritional properties
      of, 71
    ways of preparing, 70–
      71
Fletcher, Horace, 229
Folate, 59, 83, 172, 176
    sources of, 177
Folic acid, **73**
    and birth defects, 119
    sources of, 118
    virtues of, 118–119
Foods:
    allergenic, 85
    best places to purchase,
      36
    clean versus unclean,
      132–133, 151–157
    cravings for, 180–181,
      182
    created by God, 3–4
    how often to eat, 172,
      182, 185
    Jesus' view on clean
      versus unclean,
      154–155
    Jewish law regarding,
      151
    parasites in, 155–156
    Peter's vision about,
      151
    proper amounts to eat,
      171, 181
    safe handling of, 155,
      158–159, 196
    sensitivities to, 228,
      229

(*See also* Diet; names of
    individual foods)
Forbidden fruit, 4
Forgiveness, importance to
    health, 210–211
Forsaking, **195**
Fröhm, David and Anne:
    on calcium, 86
    on carrots, 56
    on healthy diet, 193
    on healthy snacks, 53
    on live foods, 52
    on meat, 17, 153
    on nuts, 66
    on osteoporosis, 86
Fresh, **52**
Fruit, 45, 65
    in Bible Diet, 71–79
    and cerebrovascular
      disease, 72
    dried, 75
    forbidden, 4
    importance of, 10–11
    nutritional properties
      of, 10
    recommended
      allowance of, 10, 71
    as a snack, 75
    types of, 6, 71, 73
    virtues of, 73–74
Fungi, **196**
Futurebiotics Superfood
    Powders, 116

G
Garbanzo bean, **39**
Garden of Eatin', 39
Garden of Eden, 4
    map of, 5
Garlic, 49, 55, 58, 59, 115
    aged extract of, 61
    antibacterial qualities
      of, 60
    odor of, 60, 112
    raw versus processed,
      61
    recommended
      allowance of, 59
    uses of, 60
    virtues of, 59, 70, 208
Gastrointestinal, **85**
Genistein, **45**
Georgics, 81
Gills, **106**
Glean, **21**
Glucose, **41, 139,** 170

Glucose Tolerance Test (GTT), 41, 182
Gluten, **27,** 45
  as allergen, 28
Goat's milk, benefits of, 84
Graham, Billy, on Eden, 4
Grain offerings, **11**
  use of oil in, 11–12
Grains, **6,** 8–9, 37, 65
  ancient versus modern, 20
  in Bible Diet, 19–33
  in dream of Pharaoh, 19–20
  dried versus fresh, 21
  Jesus and, 21
  nutritional properties of, 8, 21–22
  as part of Mediterranean Diet, 8–9
  recommended allowance of, 8, 22
  roasting, 22–23
  types of, 8, 20
  whole versus refined, 9, 21–22
  (*See also* Bread; individual types of grains)
Grapes, 65
  nutritional properties of, 73
Grape seeds, virtues of, 65, 147
Great Flood, 5
Greece:
  as olive oil producer, 12
Green, **21**
Green Magma, 116
Greens, 109–120
  dandelion (*See* Dandelion greens)
  and eye problems, 118
Gregarious, **189**
Groats, **23**
Gross toxins, **198**
Growth deterrent, **111**
GTT, **41,** 182

H
Hager, W. David and Linda Carruth:
  on importance of trusting God, 213
  on serotonin, 172
Hain's, 39

Hand washing:
  importance of, 157–158, 159
  when to do, 158, 159
Hannah, 188, 189
Haroset, **109**
Harris, Searle, 41
Hartman, Jack:
  on fruit, 52
  on Jesus' diet, 14
  on vegetables, 50, 52
Harvard School of Public Health, **7**
HDL-cholesterol, **61, 66,** 67
Health food stores, 36, 43
Hepatocyte, **90**
Hepper, F. Nigel, 66
Herbs, 109–120
  bitter (*See* bitter herbs)
  ways to use in cooking, 120
  (*See also* individual herbs)
Hezekiah, 209
High blood pressure, **104**
Hippocrates, 237
Histamines, **85**
Honey, 16
  healthiest ways to eat, 136
  as symbol of abundance, 82, 83, 91, 136
  types of, 135
Howler Rainforest Sorbet, 138
Hull, **24**
Husbandists, **6**
Husk, **24**
Hybridized, **20**
Hydrogenated fat, **122**
Hyperglycemia, **181**
Hyperinsulinism, **41**
Hyperlipidemia, **140**
Hypersomnia, **166**
Hypertension, **55, 140, 208**
  aggravating factors, 208
Hypertensives, **104, 217**
Hypoglycemia, **41, 181**
  symptoms of, 186

I
Immune system, **88**
Immunity, **88**

Immunoreactive, **89**
Impotence, **197**
Incontinence, **74**
Indecisiveness, **181**
Infants, **88**
Inflammation, **84**
Inhalant, **198**
Iniquities, **191**
Inositol, **130**
Insoluble fiber, **70**
Insomnia, **166**
Instant foods, 42
Insulin, **40,** 182
Insulin resistance, **140**
Intractable, **114**
Iron, 59
Ischemic heart disease, **21**
Ishmael, 12
Isoflavones, **46**
Israelites:
  diet of, 15, 17, 19
  importance of bread to, 9

J
Jacob, 44, 67
Jael, 84
Jakes, T. D.:
  on breakfast foods, 183
  on eating healthy at festivities, 230
  on fasting, 234
  on fish, 105
  on food temptation, 180
  on the importance of breakfast, 184
  on incorporating exercise into daily life, 219
  on overeating, 228
  on proper diet, 4
  on separating food from fellowship, 225
  on snacks, 75
  on soybeans, 45
JAMA, **104**
Jenkins, David, 54
Jesse, 22
Jesus:
  and barley, 25, 26
  and bread, 31
  diet of, 8–9, 14, 154, 185

disciples of, 97, 98, 99, 185
  fasting practices of, 234
  fish as symbol of, 97
  and grains, 21
  multiplying fish, 99
  multiplying loaves, 26, 99
  temptation by Satan, 180
  view on clean and unclean foods, 154–155
  view on drunkenness, 211, 223
  view on fasting, 240
Joseph (Israelite ruler of Egypt), 19–20, 67, 226
Jotham, 78
Juice, **236**

K
Kale, **86**
Kamut, **8, 20,** 23
Kava Kava, 177
Kcal, **54**
Kefir, **14**
Kegel exercise, **74–75**
  how to do, 75
Kelp, **116** (*See also* Kombu)
Kernels, **21**
Kidney stones, 87
Kombu, **41,** 43, 61–62
Kyo-dophilus®, 93
Kyo-Green, 116
Kyolic®, 60, 61, 90

L
Labels, importance of reading, 31, 42, 43
Lactating, **126**
Lactic acid, **217**
Lactoferrin, **90**
Lacto-ovo vegetarians, 15
Lactose intolerance, 85
Lacto vegetarians, 15
Langerhans cells, **89**
Lappé, Frances Moore, 37
Lard, **90**
Law, **16**
LDL-cholesterol, **12, 66,** 67, 76
Leavening, **224**
Lecithin, **130**

Leeks, 59
Legumes, **9–10, 35**
  in Bible Diet, 35–48
  recommended
    allowance of, 9, 39
  terminology, 39
  uses of, 36
Leman, Kevin, 192
Lentils, 36, 43, 44, 47
  in the Bible, 44
  nutritional properties
    of, 44
  recommended
    allowance of, 39
  soaking not required, 44
Lewdness, **155**
Lewis, C. S., 210
Lignan, 70
Linen, 70
Lipids, 40, **61**
Littauer, Florence:
  on emotional causes of
    eating disorders,
    190
  on heritability of
    physical disorders,
    181
  on negative family
    patterns, 192
  on spiritual causes of
    disease, 203
Liver, function of, 17
Lord's Prayer, 8
Lord's Supper, 31
Lozenges, **69**
Lundberg Family Farms,
  39
Lutein, **118**
Lymphatic system, **117**
Lysine, 37

M
Macroforce™, 90
Macrophages, 88
Magnesium, 59, 83
Magnets, healing proper-
  ties of, 177
Major fasts, **234**
Malice, **155, 211**
Mammals, **83**
Manna, **179–180**
  double portion on
    Sabbath, 180
MAO inhibitor, **177**
Maror, **109**
Massachusetts Institute of

Technology (M.I.T.),
  45
Matzah, **224**
mcg, **73**
McIlhaney, Joe:
  on breast-feeding, 88,
    90
  on eating disorders,
    189
Meat, 36
  addition to human diet,
    6
  additives in, 152–153
  advice on buying, 152,
    153, 154
  dangers of, 152
  in Mediterranean Diet,
    16–17
  proper use of, 18
  recommended
    allowance of, 17
  red, 122–123
  role in biblical
    celebrations, 16–17
  types of, 17
Mediterranean Diet, 7–11,
  13–17, 39, 120
  benefits of, 82, 140
  composition of, 7–11,
    171
  dairy foods in, 13–16
  eggs in, 15
  fish in, 14–15, 97
  grains in, 8–9
  legumes in, 8–9
  meat in, 16–17, 123
  olive oil in, 11
  poultry in, 15
  pyramid model of, 7–8,
    127–128
  sweets in, 16
  vegetables in, 50
Mediterranean region, **7,**
  97
Melaleuca, **202**
Melanoma, **56**
Menopause, **48**
Metabolism, **184**
Metaphor, **15**
Metastasize, **45**
mg, **73**
Microflora, **88**
Middle East, **11,** 29, 81,
  91, 98
Mildew, 160–162, **195,** 196
  biblical rules about,

160–161, 196
  precautions against,
    162–163
Milk:
  allergic reactions to, 85
  in Bible times, 95
  breast, 88–89
  goat's, 84
  greens cooked in, 86
  and kidney stones, 87
  mixing with meat, 81
  nutritional properties
    of, 82
  sheep's, 84
  as symbol of abun-
    dance, 82, 83, 91,
    136
  as symbol of spiritual
    immaturity, 95
  types of, 81, 83
Millet, **8,** 20, **27–28,** 36
  uses of, 27
Minerals, **10**
  (*See also* individual
    minerals)
Minor fasts, **234**
M.I.T., **45**
Mold:
  in cheeses, 196
  dangers of, 161–162
  precautions against,
    162–163
  types of, 161, 162
Molested, **210**
Monounsaturated fatty
  acids, **11**
  sources of, 65, 76, 83
Mortality, **72**
Mouth breathing, **143**
MSG, **90, 186**
Mucilage, **70**
Mucous membranes, **57**
Multiple sclerosis (MS),
  116, 197
Mung beans, 43
Mushroom and barley
  soup, 27
Music, emotional effects
  of, 174–175
Mutagenic, **56**

N
National Cancer Institute,
  70
Natural Choice Organic
  Sorbet, 138

Natural practicing doctors,
  142
Nehemiah, 15, 16
Neural, **119**
New Testament, 97, 98
NIDDM, **140**
Nikken Emerald Harvest,
  116
Nitrates, **186**
Nitrites, **186**
NIV, **196**
Noah, 5
Not totally healthy, **237**
NSAIDS, **47, 103**
Nut butters, 69
Nutrients, **9**
  (*See also* individual
    nutrients)
Nuts, 6, 37
  in Bible Diet, 65–69
  cautions when buying,
    68–69
  nutritional properties
    of, 66, 67
  recommended
    allowance of, 39, 68
  as snacks, 69
  storing, 68–69
  (*See also* individual
    types of nuts)

O
Oats, 20
Obesity, **140**
Oils, healthy, 77
Old Testament, 97
Oldways Preservation and
  Exchange Trust, 7
Oleuropein, 77, **79**
Olive leaf extract, healing
  properties of, 79
Olive oil, 11–12, 173
  antibacterial properties
    of, 77
  benefits of, 12, 77–78
  in grain offerings, 11–12
  importance in Mediter-
    ranean diet, 11
  nutritional properties
    of, 11
  production of, 12
  uses of, 11, 12
Olives, 6, 75–79
  antibacterial properties
    of, 77
  in Bible Diet, 75

green versus black, 76
nutritional properties
   of, 65, 76, 77
recommended
   allowance of, 75
Omega-3 essential fatty
   acids, **14,** 170, 173
sources of, 65, 70, 101
Onions, 49, 58, 59
odor of, 60, 112
Organic, **138**
Organically grown, **153**
Osteoporosis, **68**
benefits of exercise, 217
nutrients that help, 208
Overeating:
causes of, 228
and diabetes, 229
harmful effects of, 223,
   227, 228–229
methods for avoiding,
   229–230
Ovo vegetarians, 15
Oxalic acid, **117**
Oxidation, **12**

P
Parasites, 155–156
Parsley, 109
nutritional properties of,
   112, 113
recommended
   allowance of, 113
virtues of, 112
Passover, **17, 224**
feast (Seder), 109–110,
   224
Haggadah, **110**
observance of, 224
Pasta:
in Bible times, 32
instant, 42
rice, 28
whole-grain, 31
Pathogenic, **196**
Paul, 31
Pearson, Mark:
on importance of
   emotional health,
   212
on importance of
   forgiveness, 210
Pearson, Mary Grace, on
   vegetables, 51
Peas, 49, 51
as a snack, 54

Penninah, 188
Pentecost (Shavuot), 223
Peppers, 49, 51, 58
cancer-fighting
   properties of, 56
Perimenopause, **48**
Pesach, 110, 224 (*See also*
   Passover)
Peter, 98
vision of clean and
   unclean foods, 151
Petrochemicals, 154
Pharyngeal cancer, **74**
Phenolic, **77**
Phosphorus, 59, 82
Phytochemicals, **45, 55**
sources of, 52, 55, 57
virtues of, 55
Phytoestrogens, **22, 46**
Phytohormones, **46**
Phytonutrient, **45**
Pigging out, **229**
Pilaf, **28**
Pistachios, 66, 67
Plasters, **209**
Platelet adhesion, **61**
PMS, **48, 197**
Poached, **106**
Polyunsaturated fats, **11**
Polyunsaturated fatty
   acids, **67**
Pork:
absence from diet of
   Israelites, 17
dangers of, 152
Postnasal drip, **197**
Potassium, **13,** 59, 82
Potatoes, 49, 52
best ways of preparing,
   51
sweet, 49, 56
Potent, **59**
Poultices, **209**
Poultry, 129–131
recommended
   allowance of, 15,
   129–130, 131
skin on, 131
Prayer:
and depression, 176
healing powers of, 203
Prayer warriors, **176**
Premenstrual Syndrome
   (PMS), **47**
Pressure ulcers, **67–68**
Proanthocyanidin, **65**

Probiotic, **92**
ProGreens, 116
Prostaglandins, **103**
Prostate, **75**
Protein efficiency ratio
   (PER), 130
Proteins, **6**
as allergens, 85
complementary, 37
complete, 36, 44, 45, 65
incomplete, 37
recommended
   allowance of, 126
sources of, 12, 14,
   36–37, 38, 44, 45,
   82, 127, 130
types of, 36–37
Psoriasis, **197**
Pulmonary Hemosiderosis,
   162
Pulses, **36**
Pumpkin seeds, 69
Pure water, **236**
Purine, **125**
Purity Foods, 24, 31

Q
Quiche, **117**
Quinoa, **8, 20**

R
Rabbits, 152
Raffinose, 41
Raisins:
cakes of, 74
nutritional properties
   of, 73
Ramadan, **233,** 234
Raw, **52**
Real food, **51**
Really hungry, **238**
Rebekah, 17
Rebuke, **195**
Red meat, 122–123
Reduced, **135**
Refined, **9**
Rehydrated, **42**
Rendered, **122**
Rennet, 93
Repent, **225**
Restaurants, finding
   healthy food in, 28
Resveratrol, **73**
Retina, **104**
Rheumatoid arthritis, **103,**
   239

Rhinorrhea, **197**
Rice, 20, 28–29
brown versus white, 28,
   31
pasta, 28
roasted, 22, 23, 29
Righteous man, **176**
Risotto, **28**
Roasted grain, **22**
Romans, diet of, 15
Rosh Hashanah, **16**
Russell, Rex:
on alcohol, 147, 208
on benefits of fasting,
   237
on breast-feeding, 89
on clean versus unclean
   foods, 152
on coping with illness,
   170
on dried fruit, 75
on Ezekiel bread, 36
on fasting, 239
on flaxseed, 70
on garlic, 60
on nuts, 66, 68
on olive oil, 77
on required amounts of
   fiber, 40
on salt, 142
on unclean food, 155
on vegetables, 50
Rutabagas, **113**
Rye, 20

S
Sabbath, **21**
double portion of
   manna on, 180
St. John's wort, **177,** 192
Salaman, Maureen:
on beans, 38
on bread, 30
on butter, 91
on eggs, 15, 129, 130
on fat, 124
on healthy diet, 208
on water, 145
on Yeast Syndrome, 201
on yogurt, 92
Saliva, digestive properties
   of, 40
Salmonella, **111**
Salt:
in Bible diet, 141–145
in Bible times, 142

dangers of, 142–143
functions of, 142
ways to lessen intake
of, 144
Scavengers, **152**
Schiff, Isaac, 188
Schiff, Morty, 188
Schizophrenia, **67–68,
239**
Scleroderma, **67**
Scourge, **162**
Scrimshaw, Nevin, 45
Sea vegetables, **115**
Seaweed:
cautions about use of,
61–62
nutritional properties
of, 61
virtues of, 61–62, 115
ways of preparing, 62
Sebaceous cyst, **209**
Seder, **109**
Seeds, 6, 37, 65, 69–71
Selenium, **56, 102,**
as aid to chemotherapy
patients, 68
as mood elevator, 68,
177
sources of, 102
Serotonin, **42,** 192
sources of, 172
Serum cholesterol, **45, 114**
Sheep's milk, 84
Shellfish, 102
Shriner, Jim:
on boron, 87
on fat, 125
on fish, 102
on fruit, 72
on glucose, 170
on healthy breakfast
foods, 94
on the importance of
breakfast, 184
on walking, 216
Shurtleff, Bill, 45
Sick building syndrome,
161
symptoms of, 161
Sinned, **176**
Sisera, 84
Slander, **155**
Slow simmer, **42**
Smith, Pamela:
on dairy products, 82,
85, 92

on flaxseed, 71
on healthy snacks, 13
on the importance of
breakfast, 184
on sodium, 143
on spinach, 117
on stress relief, 174
on whole grains, 22
Smoking, adverse effects
of, 56–57, 143
Snacks:
changing nature of, 137
fat in, 122
healthy, 53–54, 69, 73,
75
for weight loss, 185
when to eat, 187
Soba, **42**
Sodium, **143**
Soft drinks:
adverse effects of, 86,
183, 190
consumption levels of,
137–138, 190
Solomon, 55
garden of, 65, 66
Soluble fiber, **70**
Soup, instant, 42
Soybeans, 36, 43, 45–47,
55
hormones in, 46
nutritional properties
of, 44, 86
recommended
allowance of, 45
uses of, 46, 47
virtues of, 45, 46, 47
ways of preparing, 47
Soy Deli, 39
Spelt, **8,** 23, **24,** 36
history of, 24
as medicine, 24
in pasta, 31
virtues of, 24
Spermatozoa, **104**
Spinach, 56
cautions about, 117
nutritional properties
of, 117
uses in cooking, 117
virtues of, 52, 74
Spiritual causes of disease,
202–204
Spiritual food, 95
Spirulina, 116
Spleen, **88**

Spring tonic, **113**
Sprouted, **36**
Squash, ways of preparing,
57
Stachybotrys, 162
Stachyose, 41
Staff of life, **20**
Starch, **9**
Strawberries, virtues of, 74
Subconsciously, **228**
Sudden cardiac death, **104**
Suet, **90, 122**
Sugar:
amounts consumed by
Americans, 16
in canned beans, 40
dangers of, 155–156,
182, 190
natural versus refined,
138
nutritional properties of,
16
other names of, 138
recommended
allowance of, 173
role in a healthy diet,
139–140
Sullenness, **165,** 171
Summons, **82**
Sun exposure, dangers of,
89
Sunflower seeds:
nutritional properties
of, 69–70
uses of, 68
Suppressed, **69**
Sweet, **16**
Sweet potatoes, 49, 56
Sweets/sweeteners:
in Bible diet, 135–140
proper use of, 17
recommended
allowance of, 16,
173
role in biblical feasts,
16
(*See also* individual
sweetening agents)
Swiss chard, **115**
Swope, Mary Ruth:
on barley, 25
on importance of
proper diet, 17
on Jesus' diet, 152
on sugar, 182
on sweets, 16

Syndrome X, 140
symptoms of, 228
Synoptic gospels, **99**

T
Tempeh, **47,** 117, 128
Thrush, **196**
Thymus gland, **88**
Thyroid, **83**
Tigris river, 5
Tofu, **39,** 45, 86
Tomatoes, 49, 51
nutritional properties of,
75
Toronto's *Globe and Mail,*
57
Totally healthy, **236**
Townsley, Cheryl:
on benefits of fasting,
236
on dealing with
emotions, 212
on depression, 166, 169
on emotional habits,
209
on endive, 110
on food allergies, 228
on healing effects of
good nutrition, 173
on honey, 139
on humor and
emotional health,
175
on hydrogenated fats,
122
on kombu, 41
on legumes, 39
on maintaining good
health, 208
on meat, 153
on nut butters, 69
on nuts, 69
on parsley, 112
on pasta, 32
on seeds, 69, 70
on spinach, 117
on sugar, 140
on sweeteners, 139
on Swiss chard, 115
on vegetables, 57
on white flour, 22
Toxic substances, 238
Toxins, **23**
Trace, **59**
Tree of Knowledge of
Good and Evil, **4**

Triglycerides, **61**
Triticale, **8**, 20
Troas, 31
Truss, C. Orian, 196
Tumors, **45**
Tuna, 100
Tourista, **93**, 160
Turtle Island Foods, 39
Type A behavior, **212**
Tyrosine, **83**, 177

U
United States Department
    of Agriculture
    (USDA), 10
    food safety advice from,
        159
    website, 159
Unsaturated fatty acids,
    67, 69, 124
Uric acid, **114**

V
Vascular disease, **77**, **119**
Vegans:
    lifestyle choices of, 15
    vitamin deficiencies of,
        117
Vegetables, 45, 49–63
    in Bible Diet, 49–63
    as breakfast food, 57–
        58
    Daniel and, 49–50
    fresh versus processed,
        52–53
    importance of, 10–11
    in Mediterranean Diet,
        50
    in North American diet,
        51
    nutritional properties
        of, 10, 54
    recommended
        allowance of, 10,
        50–51, 54
    repeating, 58
    from the sea, 61–62
    as snacks, 53–54
    types of, 49

virtues of, 50
    ways of preparing, 58
Vegetarian, **15**
Vegetarianism:
    lack of Scriptural basis
        for, 4, 156
    role of dairy products
        in, 83
    types of, 15
Vietnam War, 22
Virgil, 81
Vitamin A, 54, 57, 59, 83
    sources of, 113
Vitamin B$_6$ (*See* Folate)
Vitamin B$_{12}$, 176
    importance of, 128
    sources of, 128, 177
Vitamin C, 54, 69
    depleted by smoking,
        56
    sources of, 52
Vitamin D, sources of, 102
Vitamin E, virtues of, 52,
    69, 74
Vitamin F (*See* Essential
    fatty acids)
Vitamins, **10**
    fat-soluble, 68
    (*See also* individual
        vitamins)
VitaSpelt, 31

W
Wagemaker, Herbert:
    on depression, 167
    on self-esteem, 168
    on symptoms of
        hypoglycemia, 186
Walking, 216–221
    benefits of, 216–217
    correct method of,
        220–221
    in Jesus' time, 215, 217
    spiritual benefits of,
        218, 220
Walnuts, 66
    virtues of, 65, 66, 67
Wanda's, 39
Wasting disease, **195**

Water:
    importance of, 145–
        146
    pure, 236
    recommended
        allowance of, 145,
        146
Weight loss, 125, 183–188
    and Bible Diet, 186
    correct meals for, 185
    snacks for, 185
Westbrae, 39
Wheat, **23–24**, 36
    bulgar, 39
    types of, 20, 23
    uses of, 20
Whey, **13**, **92**, 93–94
    uses of, 13
Whitaker, Julian:
    on amount of exercise
        needed, 221
    on antioxidants, 56
    on EPA, 103
    on exercise, 220
    on fat, 123
    on importance of fruits,
        10
    on importance of
        healthy choices, 226
    on magnets and
        healing, 177
    on omega-3 oils, 103
    on smoking, 57
    on vitamins B$_6$ and B$_{12}$,
        177
    on whole grains, 9
White flour, 22
    dangers of, 42, 155–
        156
White Wave, 39
Whole, **182**
Whole food stores, 36
Whole grains, 45, 47, 49
    introducing into your
        diet, 28, 31–32
    sources of, 29
    virtues of, 9, 21–22, 25,
        26, 29
Whole-wheat, nutritional

properties of, 24
Whole-wheat udon, **42**
Wine:
    nonalcoholic, 147
    in Seder, 224
Winter squash, ways of
    preparing, 57
World Health Organiza-
    tion, **7**
Wrath, **211**
WWJD?, 211

X
Xanthophylls, **56**

Y
Yeast, **12**
Yeast connection, **197**
Yeast Syndrome, 196–202
    causes of, 197–199
    foods that help, 199–
        201
    nutrients used to treat,
        202
    symptoms of, 196–197
Yogurt, 91
    antibacterial properties
        of, 92–93
    in Bible Diet, 82
    natural versus
        pasteurized, 92
    nutritional properties
        of, 13
    recommended
        allowance of, 95
    as source of protein, 12,
        13
    virtues of, 13, 92
Yogurt cheese, **13**
Young, Vernon, 45

Z
Zechariah, 234
Zeaxanthin, **118**
Zinc, 59, 69, 83, 143
    sources of, 102

Books by Starburst Publishers®
(Partial listing—full list available on request)

God's Word for the Biblically-Inept™ Series:

☞ **Health and Nutrition** *Kathleen O'Bannon Baldinger*
☞ **Revelation** *Daymond R. Duck*
☞ **Daniel** *Larry Richards*
☞ **The Bible** *Daymond R. Duck*
☞ **Women of the Bible** *Kathy Collard Miller*
☞ **Men of the Bible** *Larry Miller*
(see pages iii to v for ordering information)

Announcing Our New Series:
What's in the Bible for...™?

What's In the Bible for . . . ™ Teens?
Mark R. Littleton
The first release of the *What's in the Bible for...*™ series is a book that teens will love! *What's In the Bible for™ Teens* contains topical Bible themes that parallel the challenges and pressures of today's adolescents. Learn about Bible Prophecy, God and Relationships, and Peer Pressure in a conversational and fun tone. Helpful and eye-catching "WWJD?" icons, illustrations, and sidebars included.
(trade paper)   ISBN 1-892016-05-2 $16.95

The World's Oldest Health Plan
Kathleen O'Bannon Baldinger
Subtitled: *Health, Nutrition and Healing from the Bible.* Offers a complete health plan for body, mind and spirit, just as Jesus did. It includes programs for diet, exercise, and mental health. Contains foods and recipes to lower cholesterol and blood pressure, improve the immune system and other bodily functions, reduce stress, reduce or cure constipation, eliminate insomnia, increase circulation and thinking ability, eliminate "yeast" problems, improve digestion, and much more.
(trade paper)   ISBN 0914984578 $14.95

More of Him, Less of Me
Jan Christensen
Subtitled: *A Daybook of My Personal Insights, Inspirations & Meditations on the Weigh Down™ Diet.* The insight shared in this year-long daybook of inspiration will encourage you on your weight-loss journey and bring you to a deeper relationship with God. Each page includes an essay, Scripture, and a tip-of-the-day. Perfect companion guide for anyone on the Weigh Down™ diet!
(cloth)   ISBN 1892016001 $17.95

God's Abundance
Edited by Kathy Collard Miller
Subtitled: *365 Days to a More Meaningful Life.* This day-by-day inspirational is a collection of thoughts by lead-ing Christian writers like, Patsy Clairmont, Jill Briscoe, Liz Curtis Higgs, and Naomi Rhode. *God's Abundance* is based on God's Word for a simpler, yet more abundant life. Learn to make all aspects of your life—personal, business, financial, relationships, even housework—a "spiritual abundance of simplicity."
(hardcover)   ISBN 0914984977 $19.95

Promises of God's Abundance
Kathy Collard Miller
Subtitled: *For a More Meaningful Life.* The second addition to our best-selling *God's Abundance* series. This perfect gift book filled with Scripture, questions for growth and a Simple Thought for the Day will guide you to an abundant and more meaningful life.
(trade paper)   ISBN 0914984098 $9.95

Stories of God's Abundance—for a More Joyful Life
Compiled by Kathy Collard Miller
Like its successful predecessor, *God's Abundance* (100,000 sold), this book is filled with beautiful, inspirational, real life stories. Those telling their stories of God share scriptures and insights that readers can apply to their daily lives. Renew your faith in life's small miracles and challenge yourself to allow God to lead the way as you find the source of abundant living for all your relationships.
(trade paper)   ISBN 1892016060 $12.95

God's Unexpected Blessings
Edited by Kathy Collard Miller
Witness God at work and learn to see the *unexpected blessings* in life through essays by such Christians writers as Billy Graham and Barbara Johnson.
(hardcover)   ISBN 0914984071 $18.95

Seasons of a Woman's Heart—
A Daybook of Stories and Inspiration
Compiled by Lynn D. Morrissey
A woman's heart is complex. This daybook of stories, quotes, scriptures, and daily reflections will inspire and refresh. Christian women share their heart-felt thoughts on Seasons of Faith, Growth, Guidance, Nurturing, and Victory. Including Christian women's writers such as Kay Arthur, Emilie Barnes, Luci Swindoll, Jill Briscoe, Florence Littauer, and Gigi Graham Tchividjian.
(cloth)   ISBN 1892016036 $18.95

Beanie Babies® Stories
Susan Titus Osborn and Sandra Jensen
The FIRST and ONLY Beanie Baby® Book that is NOT just a price catalog! Adults and children share their

stories and trivia knowledge of those collectable, lovable, squeezable Beanie Babies® with the world. This book includes wonderful, inspiring Beanie Baby® stories from collectors of all ages and quotable quotes as only kids can give them. A book which surely will touch your heart, just as Beanie Babies® have!
(trade paper)   ISBN 1892016044 $10.95

Why Fret That God Stuff?
Edited by Kathy Collard Miller
Subtitled: *Stories of Encouragement to Help You Let Go and Let God Take Control of All Things in Your Life.* Occasionally, we all become overwhelmed by the everyday challenges of our lives: hectic schedules, our loved ones' needs, unexpected expenses, a sagging devotional life. *Why Fret That God Stuff* is the perfect beginning to finding joy and peace for the real world!
(trade paper)   ISBN 0914984500 $12.95

God's Vitamin "C" for the Spirit™
Kathy Collard Miller & D. Larry Miller
Subtitled: *"Tug-at-the-Heart" Stories to Fortify and Enrich Your Life.* Includes inspiring stories and anecdotes that emphasize Christian ideals and values by Barbara Johnson, Billy Graham, Nancy L. Dorner, and many other well-known Christian speakers and writers. Topics include: Love, Family Life, Faith and Trust, Prayer, and God's Guidance.
(trade paper)   ISBN 0914984837 $12.95

God's Vitamin "C" for the Spirit™ of WOMEN
Kathy Collard Miller
Subtitled: *"Tug-at-the-Heart" stories to Inspire and Delight Your Spirit.* A beautiful treasury of timeless stories, quotes, and poetry designed by and for women. Well-known Christian women like Liz Curtis Higgs, Patsy Clairmont, Naomi Rhode, and Elisabeth Elliott share from their hearts on subjects like Marriage, Motherhood, Christian Living, Faith, and Friendship.
(trade paper)   ISBN 0914984934 $12.95

God's Vitamin "C" for the Hurting Spirit™
Kathy Collard Miller & D. Larry Miller
The latest in the best-selling *God's Vitamin "C" for the Spirit* series, this collection of real-life stories expresses the breadth and depth of God's love for us in our times of need. Rejuvenating and inspiring thoughts from some of the most-loved Christian writers such as Lucado, Cynthia Heald, Charles Swindoll, and Barbara Johnson. Topics include: Death, Divorce/Separation, Financial Loss, and Physical Illness
(trade paper)   ISBN 0914984691 $12.95

Purchasing Information:

Books are available from your favorite bookstore, either from current stock or special order. To assist bookstores in locating your selection be sure to give title, author, and ISBN. If unable to purchase from the bookstore you may order direct from **STARBURST PUBLISHERS®** by mail, phone, fax, or through our secure website at **www.starburstpublishers.com**.

When ordering enclose full payment plus $3.00 for shipping and handling ($4.00 if Canada or Overseas). Payment in US Funds only. Please allow two to three weeks minimum (longer overseas) for delivery.

Make checks payable to and mail to:

STARBURST PUBLISHERS®
P.O. Box 4123
Lancaster, PA 17604

Credit card orders may also be placed by calling **1-800-441-1456** (credit card orders only), Mon-Fri, 8:30 a.m.–5:30 p.m. Eastern Standard Time. Prices subject to change without notice. Catalog available for a 9 x 12 self-addressed envelope with 4 first-class stamps.